THE EDITING OF OLD ENGLISH

The papers in this book, from a distinguished team, offer a wide spectrum of views on the editing of Old English, frequently taking contrasting positions, to the benefit of general discussion. The texts covered include items of literary and historical prose and poetry, for the most part those within the traditional canon, but there is also some discussion of the constitution of that canon. There are detailed instructions on how to present editorial information concisely and clearly, informed discussion of what types of material are appropriate alongside an edited text, and consideration of the requirements of a variety of specialist readers, from students and those from other disciplines to scholars with particular and limited interests such as lexicographers. There are new ideas on the presentation of texts which have proved notoriously difficult to edit in the past, such as the Charms and King Alfred's translation of *Boethius*, there are studies of the problems offered by manuscript context, and there are studies of the history of the editing of Old English.

THE
EDITING OF
OLD ENGLISH

PAPERS FROM THE
1990 MANCHESTER CONFERENCE

sponsored by the
Manchester Centre for Anglo-Saxon Studies
and the
Center for Medieval and Early Renaissance Studies,
State University of New York at Binghamton

edited by
D. G. Scragg
and
Paul E. Szarmach

with the assistance of
Helene Scheck
and
Holly Holbrook

D. S. BREWER

First published 1994
D. S. Brewer, Cambridge

ISBN 0 85991 413 5

D. S. Brewer is an imprint of Boydell & Brewer Ltd
PO Box 9, Woodbridge, Suffolk IP12 3DF, UK
and of Boydell & Brewer Inc.
PO Box 41026, Rochester, NY 14604–4126, USA

British Library Cataloguing-in-Publication Data
Editing of Old English:Papers from the 1990
Manchester Conference
    I. Scragg, D. G.   II. Szarmach, Paul E.
    829.09
    ISBN 0–85991–413–5

Library of Congress Cataloging-in-Publication Data
Conference on the Editing of Old English Texts (1990 : University of
Manchester)
    The editing of Old English : papers from the 1990 Manchester
conference / edited by D.G. Scragg and Paul E. Szarmach.
        p.   cm.
    Includes bibliographical references.
    ISBN 0–85991–413–5
    1. English literature – Old English, ca. 450–1100 – Criticism,
Textual – Congresses.   2. Manuscripts, English (Old) – Editing –
Congresses.   3. Paleography, English – Congresses.   I. Scragg, D.G.
II. Szarmach, Paul E.   III. Title.
PR179.T48C65   1990
829'.09–dc20   94–26434

This publication is printed on acid-free paper

Printed in Great Britain by
St Edmundsbury Press Ltd, Bury St Edmunds, Suffolk

CONTENTS

ILLUSTRATIONS

ACKNOWLEDGEMENTS

Permission to publish facsimiles from books and manuscripts has been given by the British Library (figs 1–3 and 9); the Master and Fellows of Corpus Christi College, Cambridge (fig. 4); and the Fawcett Library, London Guildhall University (figs 5–8).

ABBREVIATIONS

ASSAH	*Anglo-Saxon Studies in Archaeology and History*
ASE	*Anglo-Saxon England*
ASPR	Anglo-Saxon Poetic Records
BAR	British Archaeological Reports
CSASE	Cambridge Studies in Anglo-Saxon England
EEMF	Early English Manuscripts in Facsimile
EETS	Early English Text Society
ES	*English Studies*
JEGP	*Journal of English and Germanic Philology*
MLR	*Modern Language Review*
N&Q	*Notes and Queries*
NM	*Neuphilologische Mitteilungen*
OEN	*Old English Newsletter*
PBA	*Proceedings of the British Academy*
PMLA	*Publications of the Modern Language Association of America*
RES	*Review of English Studies*

INTRODUCTION

Paul E. Szarmach

THE PAPERS IN THIS collection comprise nearly all those delivered at the May 25–27, 1990 conference on 'The Editing of Old English Texts' held at the University of Manchester, including the John Rylands Library. Jointly sponsored by the Manchester Centre for Anglo-Saxon Studies and the Center for Medieval and Early Renaissance Studies at the State University of New York at Binghamton, the conference sought to describe present attitudes and interests in editing as well as to consider practical and theoretical problems in the editing of a variety of Old English texts. The editors asked the contributors to this volume to revise their presentations in the light of the intellectual interchange with each other and with the more than seventy who attended, to amplify their papers so as to give full scope and context for their ideas, and, of course, to offer necessary scholarly documentation. On their part the editors re-arranged and re-ordered the papers from the original nine sessions so that this volume would be no mere record of the proceedings; and they have included Helmut Gneuss's classic statement on editing for the Dictionary of Old English, with appropriate updating, which was used, with the author's permission, as a starting point for the conference in the opening session.

The conference, and indeed this collection, are a specific and focussed response to a set of concerns in Anglo-Saxon studies. After some 150 years of an active and directed tradition of editing texts that has produced such estimable scholarship as Klaeber's edition of *Beowulf* and Pope's magisterial two-volume edition of the *Homilies of Ælfric: A Supplementary Collection,* not to mention such school texts as Sweet's *Anglo-Saxon Reader,* holding strong in many editions since 1882, and the Mitchell-Robinson *Guide,* holding sway in its fifth edition,[1] Anglo-Saxonists find themselves in a position much like Kafka's country doctor: beset by a blizzard of opinions and views, and almost paralyzed by the elements that have killed off the faithful horse and rendered the carriage useless in the attempt to save the maybe dying young patient. Some of the current swirl may owe its power to the introduction of 'theory' within the last decade – for some, perhaps, the lusty and demonic groom in Kafka's story who offers the doctor two remarkable replacement

---

[1] *Beowulf,* ed. F. Klaeber, 3rd ed. (Boston, 1950); *Homilies of Ælfric: A Supplementary Collection,* ed. J.C. Pope, EETS os 259–60 (London, 1967–68); originally *An Anglo-Saxon Reader in Prose and Verse,* ed. H. Sweet (Oxford, 1876), subsequently revised by D. Whitelock as *Sweet's Anglo-Saxon Reader in Prose and Verse* (Oxford, 1967) and then re-issued; *A Guide to Old English,* ed. B. Mitchell and F. C. Robinson, 5th ed. (Oxford and New York, 1992).

steeds who can do more than the doctor is ready for – but, truth be known, even before *adventus theoriae* there was a continual grumbling that a given introductory school text had not got it 'right', or that an editor had 'overedited'. But it is clear that theoretical challenges have given the old complaining a newer key. Accompanying all this unhappiness, there have been the bang, woof, and tweet of the computer, another nominee for Kafka's grinning groom.

Much of the current debate in editing Old English reflects the controversy between the Old Philology and the New Philology. In the broadest terms possible the dispute is between the devotees of Parmenides and the votaries of Heraclitus or between those who see the possibility for the stable, the fixed, and the unchanging and those who see only process, continuing change, and varying relations of connections. In more focussed terms the argument is about positivism and its methods or between those who believe that they can ascertain and fix a text once and for all and those who believe that such certitude is neither possible nor desirable (if possible). Often the charge against editing of the old style is specifically that editors display biases, or rather, less pyrotechnically, unexpressed and embedded orientations of thought that influence their editorial choices and colour their presentations.

The debates as debates, however, often show caricature and abstraction rather than balance or capacious judgment. Thus, it is not true that old philologists are tired members of the same old party. Textual criticism *ante theoriam* had – and in the current discussion still has – a deep division between those who chose either Optimism or Recensionism as their method to attain the fixed text. Simply put, in the 'optimist' tradition an editor presents the 'best' text of a given work. No doubt the best known 'best' text in Medieval Studies is the Ellesmere manuscript of the *Canterbury Tales*. Those very dissatisfied with the logical circularity involved in choosing the 'best' text sometimes argue that a genealogy of texts, or a *stemma codicum*, must be established to sort out the (family) relationships of various manuscript witnesses. When one can determine that B is a copy of A, for example, B loses 'authority' and its readings can only be something less than the *ipsissima verba auctoris*. Recensionists often produce eclectic texts, that is, they attempt to recreate the author's text by choosing readings from various witnesses. The Optimist-Recensionist argument generally becomes, as the classicist Edward J. Kenney suggests, a cautious empiricism in the application of recensionist principle – at least in Latin texts.[2] In this grand argument editors of Old English become *de facto* optimists because most Old English poetic texts are sole and unique survivors. Typically, there are no other manuscripts for comparison in poetry, Cædmon's *Hymn* being the most significant exception to this general rule. It is easier to become methodologically pure because there is no other evidence to cloud the

---

2 E.J. Kenney, 'Textual Criticism,' in *Encyclopedia Britannica, Macropedia* XVII (New York, 1974–5), 189–95, offers a concise treatment of the major issues. For a bibliography on editing see L.E. Boyle, *Medieval Latin Palaeography: A Bibliographical Introduction*, Toronto Medieval Bibliographies 8 (Toronto, Buffalo, London, 1984), 308–14.

picture of the text. In fact there is at the present a hyper-pure Optimist position holding that intervention in the text, however mangled the text might appear to be, is an intellectual profanation for, after all, the scribes knew their language better than twentieth-century readers do. The newly organized project to produce Anglo-Saxon Manuscripts in Microfiche Facsimile carries within its rationale the seeds of hyper-pure optimism.[3]

But if editors of Old English poetic texts avoid most of the burden of the optimist-recensionist controversy, they must take on other problems. Perhaps the most significant problem is the oral basis of Old English poetry. The two post-War generations of Old English scholars have established on a methodological basis and with relative clarity of description what earlier generations considered more impressionistically, viz. that the written records of Old English poetry imply, if not document, a special tradition of oral composition. The significance of this scholarly fact goes beyond mere style to suggest that an oral culture offers a different way to organize experience, implies radical characteristics of human memory, and gives a different cast to the idea of 'the author'. For the editor of Old English poetic texts the oral dimension of the literature forces a different view on the materiality of the text now extant, its physical reality, layout, and design. Katherine O'Brien O'Keeffe offers one of the first explorations of the problems of transitional literacy in her study *Visible Song*.[4] How to convey the oral nature of Old English poetic texts to scholar and beginning student alike remains a problem that technology may help solve. In oral literature, where there would appear to be no text that is *the* text, editors take snapshots when they should produce moving pictures.

The general tendency in Old English textual scholarhip, then, is a tendency towards non-intervention in the textual evidence and an attempt to preserve the text as received. Of course, such a tendency does not prevent textual notes from being written so as to emend and amend the text of *Beowulf,* most noticeably. Yet, the tendency to avoid intervention has gone so far that Michael Lapidge calls for a return to the standards of editing associated with Classical Studies, where conjectural emendation, or the process whereby an editor infers a reading beyond the mere accumulation of pieces of evidence, is an act of quasi-creation.[5] For Lapidge conjectural emendation is true editing. Though many theorists will be unhappy that Lapidge has seemed to resurrect the author from the happy dead, he issues a tough challenge to Old English editors to show what they know in a context of full understanding of literary and cultural forms what the text says and means. Non-intervention, Lapidge indicates, may very well be a smokescreen for ignorance.

When Old English textual scholars, uncertain about whether and how to intervene in a text that is part of a changing process over time, meet beginning students in the classroom, the chasm between scholarship and pedagogy seems insurmountable.

---

[3]   For a description of this project see *OEN* 25.3 (1992), 5.

[4]   K. O'Brien O'Keeffe, *Visible Song: Transitional Literacy in Old English Verse,* CSASE 4 (Cambridge, 1990).

[5]   See below, pp. 53–67.

Practical editing makes other demands on the scholar-turned-teacher. The pedagogical tools of the Old Philology seem thoroughly out-of-step and out-of-date, while the New Philology has not yet developed a set of tools that has met the present teaching situation. Where the tendency of scholars to avoid intervention may be still good and current doctrine among scholars, how can anyone not intervene in a school text in the name of love for one's students? As I have already hinted, the Old Philology shares a heritage with Classical Studies, and in the classroom this heritage appears as grammar texts in the old Greco-Roman mode with paradigms flaunting declensions and conjugations. However one might decide the finer points of theoretical textual criticism, the text remains inaccessible to vast numbers of students because the grammars can no longer reach them. Truth be known, Old Philology never did finish its job, for there is no winning consensus on the representation of major Old English language forms in matters large and small. And so even stodgy Old Philologists can join with trendy New Philologists to complain about the failure of Old Philology to deliver texts to students.

The computer has offered its potential to Old Philology[6] and may even find a more harmonious operating relationship with the New Philology. In *Hypertext: The Convergence of Contemporary Critical Theory and Technology* (1992) George P. Landow makes some very strong claims for the congruence of Derrida, Barthes, Foucault, Benjamin, among others, with the developments of hypertext packages. Manuscript and book culture will yield to electronic culture, while physical text (here meaning the book, not manuscript) will yield to virtual text, and by implication editions for students and researchers will never be the same. In one sense Landow offers (some) theoretical underpinnings to the development of the *Beowulf* workstation and 'Project Seafarer.'[7] In their contribution to this volume Marilyn Deegan and Peter Robinson suggest some of the potential for editing offered by the computer.

The contributors to this volume offer their own views and within the group offer contrasting and differing opinions and judgments on these and other issues. Rather than offer a summary of each contribution the editors offer this topical guide to the contents:

Editing classical texts:
  Gneuss, Lapidge, Howlett, Pheifer

Use of special letters:
  Gneuss, Deegan-Robinson, Rumble, Scragg

Modern capitalization and punctuation:
  Gneuss , Dumville, O'Keeffe, Dammery

---

[6] Constance B. Hieatt and O.D. Macrae-Gibson have, for example, created 'Beginning Old English', a computer-assisted text for teaching Old English, now *OEN Subsidia* 21 (1994).

[7] For information on 'The *Beowulf* Workstation' see the abstract of Patrick Conner's conference paper on the program, *OEN* 24.3 (1991), A-1 and A-2. "Project Seafarer", an activity associated with A.J. Frantzen, J. Ruffing, et al., is still in development.

4

Apparatus (esp. variants):
  Gneuss, Healey

Modern English translation:
  Dumville, Sutherland, Magennis, Scragg

Reconstruction of supposed original:
  Dumville, Lapidge, Howlett, Lees, Doane, O'Keeffe, Godden, Hill, Dammery

Defence of manuscript forms:
  Healey, Doane

Sources:
  Deegan-Robinson, Healey, Scragg

Emendation:
  Lapidge, Scragg

History of editing:
  Lapidge, Lees, O'Keeffe, Hall, Dammery, Pheifer

Canon:
  Lees, Magennis

Editing within the manuscript context:
  Lees, Caie, O'Keeffe, Hill, Leinbaugh, Dammery

Student editions:
  Lees, Magennis

Material text:
  Doane, O'Keeffe, Sutherland

Hypertext:
  Deegan-Robinson, Lees, Doane

Diplomatic editions:
  Rumble, Doane, O'Keeffe

The important point to note here is that virtually all the essayists writing directly on editing have either edited texts or are in the process of editing texts. They offer their opinions and views about editing from experience in *praxis*. The different voices one hears coming from the whole collection give testimony that texts vary, audiences for texts vary, and indeed the *mentalités* of editors vary. Perhaps the hardy empiricism that makes Anglo-Saxon Studies resistant to certain theoretical concerns finds its roots in the editing enterprise, where one, after all, responds to a reality outside the self and, as all the editor-essayists seem to agree, one has an obligation to render faithfully (however defined). The habit of empirical thinking, bred from engagement with manuscripts and producing a template adversive to theory *per se*, offers a book-length theme requiring another venue, however.

Both coordinator-editors would like to thank here the several individuals who assisted with the conference and the collection. At Manchester all went smoothly because of the hard work before, during and after it of Mrs Mary Syner, Secretary to the Manchester Centre for Anglo-Saxon Studies. At Binghamton Mrs Ann DiStefano, the CEMERS secretary, assisted conference administration with her usual efficency and good humour, while Ms Helene Scheck and Ms Holly Holbrook, two graduate students affiliated with the CEMERS, did almost all of the word-processing. We owe all these our appreciation.

GUIDE TO THE EDITING AND PREPARATION OF TEXTS
FOR THE *DICTIONARY OF OLD ENGLISH*

Helmut Gneuss

HEADNOTE (1993)

This 'Guide to the Editing and Preparation of Texts for the *Dictionary of Old English*' first appeared as a contribution to *A Plan for the Dictionary of Old English*, edited by Roberta Frank and Angus Cameron, and published by the University of Toronto Press in 1973; it has here been reprinted with only minor additions or alterations. The editors of *A Plan* had decided to call it a 'Guide', but I ought perhaps to mention that I had originally suggested to begin the title – more modestly and more appropriately – with 'Preliminary Notes', or simply 'Notes'.

The idea to provide such 'Notes' occurred to me at a meeting of the International Advisory Committee and the Editors of the *Dictionary of Old English* held in Toronto in March 1972. At this meeting it became clear that the preparatory work for the *Dictionary* project had reached a stage at which the availability and the quality of printed editions of Old English texts was becoming an issue of great importance. Like myself, the members of the Committee and the Editors saw the need to provide the future entry-writers with reliable text editions and, over and above this, with editions that do not leave it to the reader – or the lexicographer – to solve difficult problems of language and interpretation that should have been properly treated by the editor of the respective text. It was therefore hoped by the Committee and the Editors of the *Dictionary* that Anglo-Saxonists – university teachers and Ph.D. candidates – would be willing to assist the work on the *Dictionary* by concentrating on the preparation of new editions, and on the revision of existing ones. As it turned out, this hope was somewhat unrealistic; a number of important critical and annotated editions of Old English texts have been produced during the past twenty years, yet many more are needed. But one has to realize that not every Anglo-Saxonist is trained – or inclined – to become an editor. All those who have written entries for the *Dictionary of Old English* will confirm, however, that the lack of adequately annotated editions of texts is one of the worst obstacles that they have had to face in the course of their work.

For various reasons, this edition of the 'Guide' has not been updated. Anglo-Saxonists will have no difficulty in adjusting a few passages and references to the state of scholarship (and hardware) in 1991: there are hardly any Old English texts now that have never been edited before (section 2.1); there are recent and reliable editions of the *Old English Martyrology* and of the *Spelman Psalter* (2.2); Stanley Greenfield's and Fred Robinson's *Bibliography of Publications on Old English*

Literature to the End of 1972 has been available since 1980, now supplemented by Phillip Pulsiano, *An Annotated Bibliography of North American Doctoral Dissertations on Old English Language and Literature* (East Lansing, MI, 1988) (3.1); and not a few technical problems have disappeared since the 'standard typewriter' (section 3) has been largely replaced by the personal computer.

More important are a few points on which my views – and certainly those of other scholars – tend to be less certain than they were in 1972. I should still prefer Old English texts to be provided with modern capitalization and punctuation, but it has to be admitted that an edition of Old English homilies that preserves the manuscript punctuation has much to recommend it, as can be seen from Malcolm Godden's *Ælfric's Catholic Homilies: The Second Series*, EETS ss 5 (London, 1979).[1] Similarly, there is something to be said for reproducing manuscript accents; students of historical phonology and grammar would no doubt be grateful for their inclusion. Interlinear glosses that are not continuous (and marginal glosses) have been treated far too summarily in the 'Guide'; nobody who has to deal with them should miss the instructive article by R.I. Page, 'The Study of Latin Texts in late Anglo-Saxon England [2]: The Evidence of English Glosses', in *Latin and the Vernacular Languages in Early Medieval Britain*, ed. N. Brooks (Leicester, 1982), pp. 141–65.

In section 3.5 below, I suggested the division of the critical apparatus (in cases where there is more than one manuscript of a text) into four separate sections. The fourth section, 'Explanatory notes', which has turned out to be far more important for lexicographical work than I had assumed, should not really be considered part of the critical apparatus, but this is merely a question of terminology. The distinction made between 'lexical variants' and 'phonological and spelling variants', however, is a serious problem. It was meant to bring together – in the 'lexical variants' section – those variant readings that lexicographers would have to consider for their work, while they might then ignore (except for the 'attested spellings' section in the *DOE*) the other variants. This distinction between two different types of variant readings has been consistently made in very few editions of Old English texts so far; one of these is by Günter Kotzor: *Das altenglische Martyrologium*, Bayerische Akademie der Wissenschaften, Philos.-Histor. Klasse, Abhandlungen N.F. 88/1–2 (Munich, 1981); the editor explains his procedure and criteria in vol. I, pp. 460*–461*. In the course of his work, however, both he and I

---

[1] On the significance of manuscript punctuation and on arguments against the indiscriminate employment of modern punctuation, see the important essays by Malcolm Godden, 'Old English', in *Editing Medieval Texts English, French and Latin Written in England. Papers given at the twelfth annual Conference on Editorial Problems, University of Toronto, 5–6 November 1976*, ed. A.G. Rigg (New York, 1977), pp. 9–33, at 19, and by Bruce Mitchell, 'The Dangers of Disguise: Old English Texts in Modern Punctuation', *Review of English Studies*, ns 31 (1980), 385–413, as well as the same author's *Old English Syntax* (Oxford, 1985), I. 769–72. For punctuation and capitalization in the manuscripts of poetry, the reader may now consult *Exodus* ed. P.J. Lucas (London, 1977), pp. 17–24, and especially K. O'Brien O'Keeffe, *Visible Song: Transitional Literacy in Old English Verse*, CSASE 4 (Cambridge, 1990).

realized that in a considerable number of cases it was difficult if not impossible to decide where a variant reading should be placed, and as a consequence I should now hesitate to recommend a division of the critical apparatus according to the type of variant readings.[2]

As is pointed out below (section 3.3), editorial conventions and the use of special symbols vary a great deal. Editors or editorial boards of some serial publications have issued pertinent instructions, like the 'Notes for Editors' of the Early English Text Society. Editors of texts may also find it useful to acquaint themselves with one of the very detailed systems of symbols developed by palaeographers and epigraphers for the close transcription of texts and inscriptions. An interesting system of this kind, devised by the late Professor Julian Brown, has now been published (with modifications) by Michelle P. Brown, *A Guide to Western Historical Scripts from Antiquity to 1600* (London, 1990), pp. 6–7. Stählin's book on editorial technique (see footnote 5) has now found a successor: Martin L. West, *Textual Criticism and Editorial Technique, applicable to Greek and Latin texts* (Stuttgart, 1973).

Finally, attention must be drawn to two recently published standard and reference works that every text editor will want to consult:

B. Bischoff, *Latin Palaeography: Antiquity and the Middle Ages*, translated by D. Ó Cróinín and D. Ganz (Cambridge, 1990);

L.E. Boyle OP, *Medieval Latin Palaeography: A Bibliographical Introduction* (Toronto, 1984), with a comprehensive section covering textual criticism and editorial method on pp. 298–316; see also the useful historical review of theory and practice in these fields by H. Fuhrman, 'Réflexions d'un editeur', in *Les problèmes posés par l'édition critique des textes anciens et médiévaux*, ed. J. Hamesse (Louvain-la-Neuve, 1992), pp. 329–59, and – for Old English texts – the two recent and important treatments of the subject: E.G. Stanley, 'Unideal Principles of Editing Old English Verse', Sir Israel Gollancz Memorial Lecture 1984, *Proceedings of the British Academy*, LXX (1984), 231–73 [also published separately], and M. Lapidge, 'Textual Criticism and the Literature of Anglo-Saxon England', The T. Northcote Toller Memorial Lecture 1990, *Bulletin of the John Rylands University Library of Manchester* 73 (1991), 17–45 [also published separately].

---

[2] The distinction between lexical and non-lexical variants has also been made in *The Old English Finding of the True Cross*, ed. and translated by M-C. Bodden (Cambridge, 1987), pp. 61–101. For the difficult question whether spelling variants could or should be excluded from the critical apparatus, see Godden, 'Old English', pp. 24–5.

1 THE PROJECT

The new *Dictionary of Old English* (DOE) will be produced in three stages:

1 Editing, checking, and preparing the texts.
2 Assembling the lexicographical material in alphabetical order, i.e.,
   (a) concording each text
   (b) compiling an alphabetical slip-index from the concordances.
3 Editing the *Dictionary* entries from the material thus concorded and sorted.

Stages 1 and 2a are now in progress; they can be carried out concurrently. Stage 2b could start fairly soon, while stage 3 cannot begin before stages 2a and 2b have been completed. The following comments are exclusively concerned with stage 1.

Two principles govern work on the DOE:

A slip-index or concordance containing the complete vocabulary (i.e., all lexemes, with all their forms and occurrences or 'word-tokens')[3] of every literary or non-literary text, of every charter and inscription, must be available to the lexicographers as the basis of their work.

For each of these texts a completely reliable edition must be used in the concording process. Only editions based upon all extant manuscripts and including in their critical apparatus at least the lexical variants from these manuscripts (see section 3.5 below) are acceptable.

In order to satisfy the demands listed above, it will be necessary to check the existing editions of all Old English texts and to edit or re-edit those found wanting. These texts must then be specially prepared for the concording stage. The steady continuation of work in stage 2 depends on the editorial work in stage 1 being carried out on a large scale and as quickly and reliably as possible.

2 OLD ENGLISH TEXTS

For the present purpose, Old English texts[4] may be divided into three categories or groups:

Texts never edited before.
Texts published in unsatisfactory editions.
Texts edited according to the standards outlined in this chapter.

---

[3] For a small number of lexemes (forms of the personal and of the demonstrative pronouns, forms of 'beon' and 'wesan,' the words 'and ' and 'on') the index need not be complete, but this is not relevant to most of the work in stage 1. Cf. the figures given in J.F. Madden and F.P. Magoun, *A Grouped Frequency Word-List of Anglo-Saxon Poetry* (Cambridge, MA, 1967), 1; in J.B. Bessinger, Jr, and P.H. Smith, Jr, *A Concordance to Beowulf* (Ithaca, New York, 1969), p. 339, and those quoted by A.J. Aitken, 'Historical dictionaries and the computer,' *The Computer in Literary and Linguistic Research*, ed. R.A. Wisbey (Cambridge, 1971), p. 5 and n. 1.

[4] For a complete inventory of Old English texts in manuscripts, including charters, see A. Cameron, 'A List of Old English Texts' in *A Plan for the Dictionary of Old English*, ed. Roberta Frank and Angus Cameron (Toronto, 1973), pp. 25–306. For inscriptions see E. Okasha, *Handlist of Anglo-Saxon Non-runic Inscriptions* (Cambridge, 1971); a corpus of Anglo-Saxon runic inscriptions is being prepared by R.I. Page.

2.1 TEXTS NEVER EDITED BEFORE

There are very few Old English texts which have never been edited in any form, and editions of several such texts are now in progress (see section 5 below). Section 3 of this paper is an attempt to outline the methods and problems of editorial work on Old English texts, with special reference to the needs of the DOE editors. It is hoped that the hints provided in section 3 will as far as possible be taken into consideration by future editors of Old English texts. Such editors may have to deal with items not only from the first category listed above, but also from the second, since a number of the available editions cannot be turned into 'standard texts' by mere collating and checking, but must be re-edited. New editions of Old English texts can be published in the series to be edited in connection with the DOE, the Toronto Old English Series.

2.2 TEXTS PUBLISHED IN UNSATISFACTORY EDITIONS

This group comprises all texts in editions known to be unreliable (such as the glosses to the *Durham Hymnal*, C.18.2 in 'A List of Old English Texts', and the Old English *Martyrology*, ibid. B.19), in editions that do not satisfy present-day standards (such as the *Spelman Psalter*, edited in 1640, C.7.10), in editions that are not based on all the known manuscripts (such as Alfred's *Cura Pastoralis,* B.9.1), or which offer only a selection of the variant readings (such as the Old English *Orosius*, B.9.2). There are other kinds of editorial shortcomings: Schröer's edition of the Old English *Rule of St. Benedict*, B.10.3.1, gives us a reliable text and a satisfactory critical apparatus, but Schröer missed a complete manuscript. G. Caro's subsequent collation of the overlooked manuscript (B.10.3.2) is so full of errors and omissions that it is practically useless.

As was mentioned before, in some cases only a completely new edition will help. In others, a thorough collation must be carried out, based on all the manuscripts and covering both text and apparatus. The standards and principles of such a collation should correspond to those for new editions outlined below in section 3. Accordingly, if several manuscripts have to be collated, it is sufficient to record the lexical variants from the non-basic manuscripts. If the collator has to work with microfilms or photocopies, he should also have the manuscript or manuscripts checked for details that may not be visible on a photograph, such as erasures, etc.

The results of a collation should be recorded on an interleaved copy of the text, or on a xerox copy with wide margins; the collator must write very clearly, and must indicate clearly by means of traditional symbols what should stand and what should be added, altered, or deleted in the original printed edition. The collated copy thus produced (or a photocopy of it) should then be put at the disposal of the DOE editors who will xerox the edition and return it or the xerox to the collator. Ideally, the collated edition will have gone through the preparation stage (described in section 4 below) before it is sent to the DOE editors as an actual master-copy.

Collators are also reminded that, in addition to producing a master-copy, they may publish collations not exceeding a certain length in periodicals, thus making them accessible to Old English scholars everywhere long before a new edition can appear.

2.3 TEXTS IN SATISFACTORY EDITIONS

A large number of Old English printed texts appear to be ready for immediate lexicographical use, provided that they have been properly prepared (see section 4 below). However, not enough is known at present about the accuracy of most of our editions of Old English texts, particularly in the case of prose texts, glosses, and glossaries. Since the DOE editors cannot risk having to revise entries in their slip-index or in any other form at a later stage, random checking of nearly every text in the third group should be carried out before these texts reach the concording stage.

The principles underlying this process of checking will be the same as for the second group above. About one tenth of the edited text should be checked, including variant readings and passages taken from various parts of the text. If no misreadings or other serious editorial shortcomings are found, the text so checked should be considered suitable for use in the DOE. If doubts arise as to the reliability of an edition, it should be treated as a member of the second group, that is, the whole text and apparatus will have to be checked.

A great deal of time and labour could be saved if scholars who have information about the trustworthiness of any edition would contact the DOE editors; but such information must always be based on a comparison of the edition with the manuscript or manuscripts, or at least with photographs or microfilms.

In the three categories listed above no account has been taken of the fact that there are numerous printed Old English texts which are badly in need of comprehensive introductions and explanatory notes. For the time being, in order to give all possible support to the DOE project, all efforts should be concentrated on the textual side of editorial work.

3   EDITING OLD ENGLISH TEXTS

The following notes are not meant as a set of rules and do not hope to offer a solution to every problem. Each text has its individual history, and each demands its specific editorial procedure. What follows is intended:

to draw the prospective editor's attention to some problems he may have to face, and

to offer some suggestions which, on the whole, are based on editorial practice in standard editions of Old English texts printed during the last one hundred years.

A number of books and articles have been written, mainly by classical scholars, on the technique of critical editions, sometimes intended as instructions for editors of a particular text series.[5] So far, however, uniformity of methods and devices in

---

[5]   By far the best of these are O. Stählin, *Editionstechnik*, 2nd edn (Leipzig, 1914), and J. Bidez and A.B. Drachmann, *Emploi des signes critiques: Disposition de l'apparat dans les éditions savantes de textes grecs et latins: Conseils et recommandations*, 2nd edn by A. Delatte and A. Severyns (Brussels, 1938). Stählin's book in particular has a great deal of sensible and useful advice.

editions of classical, medieval, or modern texts has not been attained and perhaps is not desirable. There are, nevertheless, two aims which an editor should always have in mind: to be absolutely consistent in his methods, and to arrange his text and apparatus in as lucid a form as possible. An edition of an Old English text does not only have to satisfy the specialist, who may be spending hours, days, or even years in studying it; it also has to serve the occasional reader, who may just want to see a particular word in its context and who should not be expected to read through a lengthy introduction in order to be able to use the edition.

The editor should personally inspect all the manuscripts to be edited or collated. Photographs, microfilms, or a facsimile edition may be extremely useful in preparing an edition, but when it comes to erasures, certain types of alterations, and other details, it is only the manuscript itself that can bring ultimate certainty. The editor should, of course, utilize earlier editions of his text, if there are any, as well as the relevant literature. He should also try to ascertain if copies of such earlier editions with handwritten annotations by their editors or by other leading scholars are still in existence.[6] Finally, the editor must take into account the typographical devices at his disposal. If his edition is a Ph.D. thesis which will remain in manuscript form (and will be available as a xerox or microfilm copy), or if the printed edition will be a photomechanical reproduction of an edition prepared with a standard typewriter (lacking italics, small capitals, boldface type, etc.), the editor must be careful to use what devices he has (such as underlining, spacing) as clearly and economically as possible.

3.1 INTRODUCTORY MATTER

Ideally, every edition of an Old English text would be preceded by a comprehensive introduction, which should include a detailed description of the manuscript(s) (i.e., their contents, collation, script, decoration, etc.) and of all peculiarities of the Old English text (spelling, characteristic mistakes, punctuation, accents). It should also include a discussion of the date, provenance, and history of each manuscript, and should give information about the history and transmission of the text, post-medieval copies, and earlier editions. The literary and historical significance and influence of the work edited, its metre, style, sources and antecedents, authorship, date, dialectal provenance and language (including syntax and, in particular, vocabulary) should also be discussed. All this would be followed by a full bibliography, annotated if possible.

However, an introduction of this kind may take years to prepare. At a time when new or revised editions of many Old English texts are urgently needed, a brief introduction with full references to work already published on the particular text

---

[6] A list of such annotated copies of printed Old English texts and of other pertinent modern manuscript material is a desideratum. Discoveries in this field can still be made; see, e.g., T. Westphalen, *Beowulf 3150–55: Textkritik und Editionsgeschichte,* (Munich, 1967), 109–24, on Thorpe's collation of the *Beowulf* MS. See also E.G. Stanley in *Archiv für das Studium der neueren Sprachen und Literaturen,* 206 (1970), 459.

will suffice, and not only for the lexicographers working on the DOE. References to research tools which are now available everywhere and which will save the editor a great deal of time and labour – for example, N.R. Ker's *Catalogue of Manuscripts Containing Anglo-Saxon* – could sometimes take the place of lengthy descriptions and discussions. A complete bibliography will certainly be appreciated by all users of an edition, at least until a comprehensive bibliography of writings on Old English literature is in existence.[7] No edition, however, whether it has a full introduction or not, must be published without certain items which should be placed immediately before the text. I shall call these items the 'textual introduction', which should not be confused with what the editor has to say about the text in the introduction proper. The textual introduction, or introductory apparatus, should consist of:

An explanation of the editorial principles. Apart from an introduction to the arrangement of text and apparatus, this should include the editor's reasons for his choice of the basic manuscript (on grounds of date, reliability, linguistic interest, etc.), or a reference to the place in the introduction where this information has been given.

A list of all signs, conventions, and abbreviations employed in the text, in the apparatus, and in the explanatory notes, including abbreviated names of former editors of the text. If the editor has a list of abbreviations at the beginning of the book (i.e., preceding the introduction), then this should be complete for introduction and text, so that a reader does not have to look twice for an explanation.

Shortened titles of Old English poetical texts should be given according to F.P. Magoun, 'Abbreviated Titles for the Poems of the Anglo-Saxon Poetic Corpus', *Etudes anglaises*, 8 (1955), 138–46, or to the list of short titles of Old English texts being prepared by Dr Bruce Mitchell, St Edmund Hall, Oxford. Abbreviated titles of scholarly periodicals should always be those used in the annual *MLA Bibliography*. All bibliographical references here and elsewhere should, of course, be given in conformity with *The MLA Style Sheet* 2nd edn (New York, 1970).

A list of all manuscripts used in the edition, together with their sigla and, if possible, with a brief indication of the date and provenance of each manuscript. This list is not made superfluous by a detailed treatment of the manuscripts in the introduction. A reader of the text should not have to search through an introductory chapter to find out what A, B, etc., mean.

3.2 THE TEXT

Editors of Old English prose and poetry have hardly ever made an attempt to reconstruct a critical text from the variant readings of several manuscripts or by means of conjectural emendation, as is feasible and usual in classical texts. Editions of Old English texts have generally tended to be very conservative, and

---

7 See the bibliographical project announced by S.B. Greenfield and F.C. Robinson in *Neuphilologische Mitteilungen* 68 (1967), 196.

14

quite a number could actually be called diplomatic, that is, they reproduce the text exactly as it stands in the manuscript. For various reasons – because of the linguistic interest of the texts, because many texts have been transmitted in only one manuscript, etc – it seems desirable to continue this general policy in future editions and to produce editions of Old English texts in a conservative or even diplomatic form.

Consequently, where there is more than one manuscript for a text, the printed text should follow one manuscript, the 'base manuscript' or the basic manuscript, while the variant readings from the others will appear in the critical apparatus. The choice of the basic manuscript will often be a difficult task, and no hard and fast rules can be given for this. Usually, the oldest manuscript or the one with a text believed to be closest to the original will be chosen.

In some cases, the linguistic or textual value of two or more manuscripts of the same text may justify a different editorial procedure, that of printing two or more versions of a text synoptically (e.g., on facing pages). This seems advisable where there is a considerable number of additions, omissions, and lexical variants in one or more members of a group of manuscripts.[8] It will often be difficult to decide whether a text should be printed synoptically or from a basic manuscript together with variant readings. This question is also of utmost importance for the DOE lexicographers, and every editor who is faced with a decision of this kind should get in touch with the Dictionary editors before he starts his work.

This is not the place to discuss the pros and cons of emendation.[9] I would suggest, however, that editorial emendations to Old English texts be avoided unless there is an obvious mistake or omission in the manuscript, and then only if the emendation is based upon sufficient evidence from variant readings in other manuscripts or upon other reliable criteria. Scribal alterations in the basic manuscript are to be recorded in the apparatus; they should not normally appear in the text. In some cases, however, an alteration made by the original scribe may have produced alternative authoritative readings from which to choose. Here, the editor can either judge each case on its own merits, or come to a more general decision, printing the original readings only or the secondary readings only in the text.

3.3 SIGNS AND CONVENTIONS

There has never been a uniform system of signs, symbols, and conventions used in editing classical or medieval texts. This is particularly true of Old English texts. Among more than two dozen standard editions of Old English prose and poetry,

---

8 See, e.g., *Bischof Wærferths von Worcester Übersetzung der Dialoge Gregors des Grossen*, ed. H. Hecht, Bib. ags. Prosa 5 (Leipzig and Hamburg, 1900–7; repr. Darmstadt, 1965), I, 1–174.

9 See George Kane, 'Conjectural Emendation', *Medieval Literature and Civilization: Studies in Memory of G.N. Garmonsway*, ed. D.A. Pearsall and R.A. Waldron (London, 1969), pp. 155–69. It is not possible to deal with the subject of textual criticism here; there is now a great deal of specialized literature in this field, and every editor should be conversant with its methods and problems. For some important bibliographical references see G. Kane, *Piers Plowman: The A Version* (London, 1960), 53, n. 3.

published by scholars such as S.J. Crawford, E.V.K. Dobbie, B. Fehr, M. Förster, H. Hecht, K. Jost, F. Klaeber, G.P. Krapp, F. Liebermann, A.S. Napier, W.J. Sedgefield, W.W. Skeat, H. Sweet, R. Vleeskruyer, K. Wildhagen, C.L. Wrenn, R.P. Wülcker, and J. Zupitza, no two editions agree in the arrangement of text and apparatus and in the use of square brackets, italics, etc.

A system which has been widely used in editions of classical texts consists of the following four elements:[10]

< > enclose matter added by the editor (where he conjectures a gap in the manuscript).

[ ] enclose matter in the manuscript which, in the editor's opinion, has to be deleted.

†† enclose a *locus desperandus*.

*** stand for what the editor believes to be a gap in the text (which he cannot fill).

This system has never been adopted for Old English texts,[11] and it seems in fact doubtful if any satisfactory set of signs could be devised for the various cases of scribal or editorial interference in a text. A brief list of only the most significant of such cases may demonstrate this:

MS reading damaged or illegible
Words or letters erased in manuscript
Basic manuscript omits one or more words
Scribal alteration in manuscript by original scribe, or by a contemporary scribe, or later scribe
Scribal addition; superscript words
MS reading faulty, but not emended by editor
MS reading emended by editor
MS reading omitted by editor
Reading substituted by editor (from other manuscript)
Words or letters added by editor.

This list could easily be expanded. Providing symbols and conventions for all these cases would result in unsightly pages, confusing rather than assisting the reader.[12]

---

[10] See the literature referred to in footnote 5 above. A different system has been developed for editions of classical inscriptions. Similarly, there is a set of special signs for Old English inscriptions; see E. Okasha, *Hand-list of Anglo-Saxon Non-runic Inscriptions*, p. 45.

[11] But cf. the corresponding use of [ ] and < > in *Die altenglische Version des Halitgar'schen Bussbuches*, ed. J. Raith, Bib. ags. Prosa 13 (Hamburg, 1933; 2nd edn Darmstadt, 1964), vii and *passim*. In most editions of Old English texts, however, square brackets enclose what has been omitted in the manuscript and supplied by the editor.

[12] Cf. the typographical devices employed by K. Wildhagen, ed., *Der Cambridger Psalter*, Bib. ags. Prosa 7 (Hamburg, 1910; repr. Darmstadt 1964), which help us to understand the complex relations between the Old English psalter glosses, but which could hardly be employed for a normal prose text.

It is essential not to overload a page with critical signs or typographical devices such as boldface type or superscript numbers. The latter should never be used to refer the reader to the critical apparatus or to explanatory notes. Details about alterations, emendations, etc, can all be explained in the apparatus. One thing is of chief importance: whenever the editor departs from the text of the manuscript, he must draw the reader's attention to this fact, preferably by printing in italics all that is not in the manuscript. Similarly, editorial omissions (which should be rare) could be indicated by italics for the words immediately preceding and following the omitted matter. The editor should also mark words or passages which appear to be corrupt; this could be done by means of an asterisk following each word in question.

3.4   SOME TECHNICAL POINTS

The following technical points must be carefully considered when a text is being edited.

Spelling

This should always be that of the manuscript or basic manuscript; it should never be normalized or standardized. Normalization may be useful and perfectly legitimate in texts printed for classroom use, but has no place in a standard edition.[13] For corrections of obvious misspellings see above (section 3.2).

Special letter-forms

The printer's type-fount (and, as far as possible, the editor's typewriter) should include þ, ð, æ (and for some texts œ) and their equivalents in capitals. But ȝ instead of g is unnecessary, since we no longer employ the special letter-forms for insular d, f, r, s, t, w, as the early editions and dictionaries do. The use of the runic symbol ƿ for w should be particularly avoided, since even the competent reader may occasionally confuse it with þ.[14]

Capitalization

This should be modernized, so that all sentences and all proper names begin with a capital letter. The editor may choose whether he wants to capitalize words for the deity or not. To indicate in the text each case in which a capital letter was

---

[13] See G.L. Brook, 'The Relation between the Textual and the Linguistic Study of Old English', *The Anglo-Saxons: Studies in some Aspects of their History and Culture presented to Bruce Dickins*, ed. P. Clemoes (London, 1959), pp. 280–91; F.P. Magoun, 'A Brief Plea for a Normalization of Old-English Texts', *Les Langues Modernes* 45 (1951), 63–9; F.P. Magoun, *The Anglo-Saxon Poems in Bright's Anglo-Saxon Reader Done in a Normalized Orthography* (Cambridge, MA, 1956), pp. iii–iv.

[14] This symbol now seems to have disappeared from editions of Old English texts, with the exception of some volumes in Methuen's Old English Library. The situation is different, however, in editions of Middle English texts.

introduced, or in which a manuscript capital letter was replaced by one in lower case (as is done by Fehr),[15] seems unnecessary.

Vowel quantity

The marking of long vowels is characteristic of readers used in introductory courses. Standard editions, however, with the exception of a few such as Klaeber's *Beowulf*, do not normally mark vowel quantity, and this seems a satisfactory practice; nor do they mark palatalized c and g by means of diacritics.

Abbreviations and contractions

These should be silently expanded; there is no need to print letters supplied by the editor in italics, unless there is doubt about the interpretation of the abbreviation. In this case, the most probable solution could be printed in the text (using italics), while an explanation should be given in the first section of the critical apparatus (see below, 3.5). Similar cases in manuscripts utilized for section two of the critical apparatus must be treated there accordingly. Except for 7 (=and) and ꝥ (=oþþe), signs of abbreviation should not be retained in the text; and 7 and ꝥ may be expanded as well.[16] A difficult problem is presented by abbreviated words without abbreviation marks, particularly among glosses; these words ought to be dealt with in the explanatory notes.[17]

MS accents

These are 'generally irregular, and representative of more than one system,' as C. and K. Sisam have noted.[18] Their value for the reader of an Old English text and for the lexicographer is doubtful, and there seems to be no need to reproduce them in a printed edition. But the editor would do well to discuss in his introduction the use and frequency of accents in each of the manuscripts. It should not be forgotten that accent marks, as well as punctuation marks, have often been added or altered by a later scribe, and that it is not always easy to detect this, even in the manuscript itself.

---

[15] *Die Hirtenbriefe Ælfrics*, ed. B. Fehr, Bib. ags. Prosa 9 (Hamburg, 1914; repr. with a supplement to the introduction by P. Clemoes, Darmstadt, 1966), p. vii.

[16] Cf. A. Campbell, *Old English Grammar* (Oxford, 1959), § 24, and the list given by H. Wanley, *Librorum Vett. Septentrionalium Catalogus* Vol. 2 of Hickes's *Thesaurus* (1705; repr. Hildesheim, 1970), Praefatio, sig. a2.

[17] For examples, see A.S. Napier, *Old English Glosses* (Oxford, 1900), p. vi; *Ælfric's First Series of Catholic Homilies*, ed. N. Eliason and P. Clemoes, EEMF 13 (Copenhagen, 1966), p. 29; *Ælfrics Grammatik und Glossar* , ed. J. Zupitza, Sammlung englischer Denkmäler 1 (Berlin, 1880); repr. with intro. by H. Gneuss (Berlin, 1966), p. 148: critical apparatus; H. Gneuss, *Hymnar und Hymnen im englischen Mittelalter*, Buchreihe der Anglia 12 (Tübingen, 1968), p. 166.

[18] *The Salisbury Psalter*, ed. C. and K. Sisam, EETS 242 (London, 1959), p. 9. See also K. Sisam, *Studies in the History of Old English Literature* (Oxford, 1953), pp. 186–8; N.R. Ker, *Catalogue of Manuscripts Containing Anglo-Saxon* (Oxford, 1957), p. xxxv; A. Campbell, *Old English Grammar*, § 26; E. Sievers, K. Brunner, Altenglische Grammatik, 3rd edn Tübingen 1965, § 8; T. Westphalen, *Beowulf 3150–55*, 137 n. 211, and the literature quoted by these authors.

Word-division

This is a notoriously tricky problem for the editor. Although it is now clear that word-division in Old English manuscripts is less erratic than it may formerly have seemed,[19] the editor will always have to divide according to the parts of speech and not according to the rhythmic units or accentual groups in the manuscript. A nominal compound, for instance, should be written as one word. Even so, some difficult categories of words or word-groups remain, in particular verbs with separable prefixes,[20] and a number of pronouns, adverbs, and conjunctions: for example, 'aweggewitan': 'aweg gewitan'; 'for ðon ðe': 'forðon ðe': 'for-ðon-ðe'; 'swa swa': 'swaswa.' Editorial practice differs widely in these cases, and it seems highly desirable that a set of rules for the regulation of word-division in Old English printed texts should be developed. For the time being, four general hints may be useful:

MS word-division (or lack of such division) should *not* be considered as authoritative.

Consistency within a text edition should be the guiding principle.

Hyphens should not be used, so that differences and difficulties are minimized.[21]

In all doubtful cases, editors are advised to follow the form of entries in J.R. Clark Hall and H.D. Meritt, *A Concise Anglo-Saxon Dictionary*. The few hyphenated forms in this dictionary should, however, be written as one word.

Punctuation

This should normally be modern and not that of the manuscript. However, the editor should be familiar with the principles of medieval punctuation and take the manuscript into account when preparing and punctuating his edition. The system and peculiarities of punctuation employed in the manuscript (or manuscripts) should be briefly discussed in the introduction.[22] As with classical texts, there are as yet no rules as to how far the system of punctuation of the editor's native

---

[19] More work needs to be done on word-division in Old English manuscripts. The first scholar to note the problem seems to have been F. Kluge, in *Englische Studien* 7 (1884), 480–1; see also A. Schröer, *Englische Studien* 9 (1886), 292–4. The only detailed treatment, based on a few facsimile editions, is M. Rademacher, *Die Worttrennung in angelsächsischen Handschriften*, Münster Ph.D. thesis, 1921, (Münster, 1926). There are brief but useful notes by W. Keller, *Angelsächsische Paläographie*, Palaestra 48 (Berlin, 1906), I, 51–2, and 'Zur Worttrennung in den angelsächsischen Handschriften', *Britannica: Max Förster zum 60. Geburtstag* (Leipzig, 1929), pp. 89–90. See also A. Campbell, *Old English Grammar*, § 29.

[20] See Campbell, *Old English Grammar*, §§ 78–80; K.D. Bülbring, *Altenglisches Elementarbuch* (Heidelberg, 1902), pp. 24–30; T. Perrin Harrison, *The Separable Prefixes in Anglo-Saxon* (Baltimore, 1892).

[21] For hyphens in Old English manuscripts, see Ker, *Catalogue*, pp. xxxv–xxxvi.

[22] For punctuation in Old English manuscripts, see Ker, *Catalogue*, p. xxxiii–xxxv; Campbell, *Old English Grammar*, § 28; P. Clemoes, *Liturgical Influence on Punctuation in Late Old English and Early Middle English Manuscripts* (Cambridge, 1952); C.G. Harlow, 'Punctuation in some Manuscripts of Ælfric,' *Review of English Studies*, ns 10 (1959), 1–19.

language (usually Modern English) should be adopted for an Old English text.[23] It is the editor's task to help the reader understand the text, and, for this reason, consistency is perhaps less important than clarity.

References

Throughout the text, references to the beginning of the recto and verso of each manuscript folio should be given (f. 81^r, *not* f. 81a), either in the text (preferably in square brackets), or in the margin (with a vertical stroke in the text preceding the first word of the manuscript page). Line numbering should normally be provided for all texts in prose and verse. Where an edition consists of a number of separate prose texts (e.g., a collection of homilies), the lines within each piece may be numbered through; otherwise, lines should be numbered separately for each page. Numbering by fives in the margin is the normal procedure, but fewer errors in references to texts would occur if all editors could be persuaded to number by threes. No line numbers are needed in prose texts which have been divided into small numbered sections (e.g., the *Disticha Catonis* or interlinear versions of psalms). The lineation of the manuscript should not be preserved, nor is it desirable to indicate the line endings of a manuscript.

Running titles at the head of each page are often helpful; they should not give the title of the whole book where a psalm number, the number and title of a homily, etc, would be more useful. Whenever an earlier edition of the Old English text exists, the editor should make every effort to facilitate reference and to avoid confusion. Line numbers of verse texts, and the numbering for chapters, sections, or paragraphs of prose texts, as found in the earlier edition or editions, should be retained under all circumstances, even if they seem impractical. It is also essential to indicate the beginning of each page of a previous edition, either in the text or in the margin. Such a notation may, for example, help somebody who is looking for the context of a quotation in a dictionary (such as Bosworth-Toller) which used the older edition. A substitute for page-references to earlier editions may be offered in the form of a table of correspondences between the two editions at the beginning or the end of the text,[24] but running references are always preferable.

Glossaries and interlinear glosses

These demand their own editorial methods. Continuous interlinear glosses must always be printed together with the Latin text with each Old English gloss word normally printed above its Latin lemma.[25] Gloss-spacing should be regularized and, in order to avoid costly and time-consuming typing and printing, the first letter of the gloss should always stand exactly above the first letter of the lemma.

---

23 See S. Harrison Thomson, 'Editing of Medieval Latin Texts in America,' *Progress of Medieval and Renaissance Studies in the United States and Canada Bulletin* 16 (1941), p. 48.

24 See, e.g., *Ælfrics Grammatik und Glossar* (1966 reprint), pp. xv–xvi.

25 For a different arrangement, which may be practical in some cases, see H. Gneuss, *Hymnar und Hymnen im englischen Mittelalter*, pp. 266–407.

No punctuation should be introduced into the gloss, while that of the lemma should be normalized. The spelling of the lemmata should remain unchanged, and abbreviations of Latin words should be silently expanded. An Old English gloss which translates a word or form other than its lemma may be marked with an asterisk and explained in section four of the apparatus.

If a number of Old English glosses are found scattered in a Latin text, it seems best to print them in the form of a glossary, but only if each Latin lemma is accompanied by a reference to page, line, or verse in a standard edition of the Latin text.[26]

3.5 THE CRITICAL APPARATUS
It is advisable to divide the apparatus into four separate sections:

Textual notes on the manuscript or basic manuscript.
Lexical variants from other manuscripts.
Phonological and spelling variants from other manuscripts.
Explanatory notes.

Dividing the apparatus like this may at first sight seem awkward and pedantic, yet it will greatly increase the usefulness of the edition for readers and lexicographers. The first section is, of course, indispensable. Sections two and three are only needed for a limited number of Old English texts which have been transmitted in more than one manuscript. Separating the lexical variants from those variants which do not imply any change of wording and meaning has obvious advantages. Section four is not an absolute necessity at a time when reliable editions are needed within a short period, and a great deal of the information usually found in explanatory notes could be published in separate monographs or articles.

Sections one to three should be printed below the corresponding text on the same page (or, in exceptional cases, on the facing page); section four, if it is not too elaborate, should also be placed there. In all sections, references must be to lines or verses of the text, not to superscript numbers, which may spoil the text typographically and which are often difficult to find. All Old English readings in the apparatus should be in Roman Type; all the rest, including the manuscript sigla, in italics. Some further details about the individual sections follow.

Section 1: Textual notes on the basic manuscript
All the peculiarities of the manuscript text (damaged portions, scribal corrections, alterations, etc) and all changes made by the editor should be recorded here, unless their nature has been made explicit in the printed text. However, lengthy discussions (on why a particular emendation was chosen, etc) belong not here, but in

---

[26] A more elaborate version of this type of gloss edition has been devised by H.D. Meritt, *The Old English Prudentius Glosses at Boulogne-sur-Mer* (Stanford, 1959), esp. p. xii. Here, in addition to gloss and lemma, the Latin context for each lemma has been supplied.

section four. Emendations suggested by previous editors or other scholars, whether the present editor has adopted them or not, may also be recorded in section one.

Line or verse numbers should be typographically prominent (for instance, in bold type) so that reference is facilitated. Signs and symbols such as + (=added), ~(=transposed), etc, should be avoided, and abbreviations used instead, but *all* abbreviations so used must have been previously explained. The language of the apparatus should be English, not Latin.[27] If the text is accompanied by a considerable number of glosses (Old English, Middle English, or Latin), these may be recorded in an additional section of the apparatus.

As far as possible, scribal alterations and corrections should be identified and dated. The following use of sigla is recommended:

A written by original scribe
A^1 altered, added by original scribe
A^2, A^3. . . altered, added by other scribes, contemporary or later.

Do not use A^1 for matter clearly not by the original scribe.

If different individual scribes who have made additions or alterations can be identified, the approximate date of their work should be given in the introduction. The editor may use A^x if it is uncertain whether an alteration is by scribe A or by somebody else; again A^2 may be used for several hands other than those of A, if the hands cannot be clearly distinguished. But this procedure must be explained in the textual introduction.

Section 2: Lexical variants
In this section the editor is to record all lexical variants from all manuscripts other than the basic manuscript; this includes all variants affecting sense or grammar, words or passages not in the basic manuscript, words or passages in the basic manuscript but missing in one or more of the other manuscripts, words or sequences of words differing from those of the basic manuscript, and differences in case, number, person, tense, and mood. All variants which are merely orthographic or phonological (including dialectal) belong in section three of the apparatus.

The sigla used for the manuscripts should be single capital letters; in view of the limited transmission of Old English texts, there is no need for the use of other letters or combinations of letters (like Ca, C^a, etc). If Greek or other letters are employed, they should be reserved for lost exemplars, archetypes, etc, referred to when discussing the history of a text. Whenever single capital letters have been used as sigla in a previous edition of the text, they should be retained in order to avoid confusion.

It is essential that individual 'critical units' be carefully constructed and clearly separated from each other. Each critical unit consists of the lemma (i.e., a word or sequence of words as found in the text printed from the basic manuscript),

---

27 Nor should Latin abbreviations, such as those listed in *Emploi des signes critiques*, pp. 45–6, be employed even though they may seem time-honoured and internationally recognized.

followed by the variant or variants and their manuscript sigla. The editor will have to choose between two types of apparatus, positive or negative, and the critical units have to be arranged accordingly. In the *positive apparatus*, whenever there is a variant reading differing from that of the basic manuscript (or from the reading adopted by the editor), all the readings from all the manuscripts are recorded. In the *negative apparatus* only the readings differing from the basic manuscript are recorded. The latter method may save a great deal of space, but has to be employed very carefully. Consider the following example:

MS readings
A (basic manuscript)   wiðcwedennysse
B and C   wiðcwedennysse
D and F and J   wiðersæce
P   leahtrunge

Positive apparatus
wiðcwedennysse ABC, wiðersæce DFJ, leahtrunge P

Negative apparatus
wiðcwedennysse] wiðersæce DFJ, leahtrunge P

In a negative apparatus, the variant reading should normally be preceded by the lemma, to prevent errors and to facilitate reference. The lemma is to be separated from the variant readings by a square bracket open on the left. Each variant reading should be followed by the manuscript siglum or sigla. The order of the sigla need not be alphabetical; it will usually be determined by the relations of the manuscripts. But the order should always be the same, and under no circumstances must expressions like '*cett.*' or 'the rest' be used instead of the sigla. Punctuation, preferably a comma, is required between the variant readings (i.e., after the sigla) within each critical unit. The critical units must be clearly separated from each other. This should not be done simply by spacing (which is of no use if a new critical unit begins a new line), unless each unit begins with a line or verse number. Some editors employ a vertical stroke or a colon to separate critical units, but the use of a full stop or a semicolon seems to be the most practical solution.

4   PREPARING OLD ENGLISH TEXTS FOR CONCORDING

Texts edited, collated, or checked according to the principles outlined in sections 2 and 3 of this paper need further preparation before they can be fed into a data-processing system which will then produce the concordances and the slip index.[28] Part of this preparatory work will have to be left to the DOE editors.

---

[28] For a description of the data-processing system, see Richard L. Venezky in *A Plan for the Dictionary of Old English* (cf. footnote 4, above), 307–27.

Beyond this, there are two major tasks which must be completed before keypunching occurs or before the text can be retyped in a special fount and then transferred to magnetic tape. One is to indicate in the text certain points about which the lexicographer working with his slips must be informed. The other is to enable the DOE editors to utilize the lexical variants in the critical apparatus of texts extant in more than one manuscript. This may be done by editors or collators as the final step in the preparation of their mastercopies (see above, section 2) according to the following suggestions.

4.1 PREPARING THE TEXT

The lexicographer working from his slips will often be able to determine the exact meaning of a word and its place in the DOE entry from the context printed on the slip. There will then be no need for him to go back to the edition of the complete text for each occurrence of a word. But this is only practicable if the lexicographer is warned of every case where a quotation departs in any way from the manuscript reading, or where, in the editor's opinion, the text of the quotation (although taken from the manuscript) is at any point faulty or corrupt. It is therefore suggested that in all these cases one and the same symbol, a slash, /, should *follow* the relevant words. This symbol would then be recorded by the data-processing system, together with the text, and it would signal to the lexicographer working in stage 3 that, in addition to his slip, he must consult the edition of the text and its critical apparatus.

The slash should follow:

Words altered or emended by the editor.

Words supplied by the editor (whether from other manuscripts or not).

Words affected by scribal alterations, where both alternative readings (before and after the alteration) make sense.

Words or passages that seem meaningless, doubtful, or corrupt.

Where more than one word is involved, each word must be marked by a slash following it. Where long passages requiring frequent marking are involved, the DOE editors should be asked for advice. It will not be sufficient merely to point out such passages by means of symbols at the beginning and end, since on a quotation slip of limited length one or both of these symbols may not appear. Use fine pens for marking.

4.2 MARKING LEXICAL VARIANTS

Concording each manuscript of every Old English text for the DOE would be wasteful and would in no way increase the usefulness of the Dictionary. Such concording will not be done unless two or more manuscript versions of an Old English text differ considerably from each other. On the other hand, nothing that could in any way contribute to our knowledge of the vocabulary and usage of Old English should be omitted from the concordances. For this reason, all lexical variants recorded in critical apparatuses or collations (whether they are alterations in the basic manuscript, or variants in the other manuscripts) will have to be concorded, along with the text of the basic manuscript itself. However, all phonological or spelling variants will not be concorded; consequently, those elements in each critical apparatus or collation which ought to be included in the concording process have to be marked before this stage of the work. This should be done by means of a single underline; if the edition is in typescript, the underlining must be in red. The following parts of an apparatus or collation will have to be marked:

All Old English words or sequences of words added to the basic manuscript and only recorded in the apparatus.

All Old English words, phrases, or sentences in other manuscripts differing from the basic manuscript or not found in the basic manuscript in any form at all.

All Old English words differing from those of the basic manuscript by their inflexional category (e.g., dative instead of accusative), or by belonging to a different inflexional class (e.g., the same verb is shown to belong to two different conjugations).

The following parts must not be underlined:

Words or sentences of the basic text that have been omitted in other manuscripts.
Phonological or spelling variants.
Dialectal or other variants of inflexional forms.

A printed edition of an Old English text which has been checked or collated according to the suggestions in section 2 of this paper (or which has been newly edited), and which has been prepared for concording in conformity with sections 4.1 and 4.2 , will then constitute a true master-copy for all future work on the DOE.

5 CO-ORDINATION OF WORK

In order to prepare for the concording stage of the DOE project, numerous Old English texts will have to be treated in accordance with the plan and requirements outlined above. This should be done within the next few years, if the *Dictionary* is to be completed within the coming twenty or thirty years. Competent scholars who can help are urgently needed. Individuals willing to edit, re-edit, collate, check, or prepare for concording any Old English text are advised to get in touch with the DOE editors before beginning the task, to avoid duplication or overlapping of work.

Work in progress on new editions of Old English texts has been listed and published for several years now by F.C. Robinson.[29] However, scholars should keep in mind that listed projects may have been dropped or new projects may have been started since the last 'Old English Research in Progress' was compiled. The DOE

---

[29] 'Old English Research in Progress', first published for 1964–5 in *Neuphilologische Mitteilungen* 66 (1965), 235–50, and since then annually in the same periodical.

editors should be informed immediately of any new project in this field. They will then be able to tell the prospective editor if any specific lexicographical considerations (e.g., the need for a synoptical edition) must be taken into account for his particular text.

Please direct all enquiries to:

The Editors
Dictionary of Old English
Centre for Medieval Studies
University of Toronto
Toronto M5S 1A1
Canada

THE ELECTRONIC EDITION

Marilyn Deegan and Peter Robinson

THE SCHOLARLY EDITION is an essential resource for textual studies; its purpose is to make available to readers a work which for some reason is difficult to obtain or to use in the form in which it was originally produced. Scholarly editing has, of course, a long and distinguished history, and there are certain rules and conventions which editors follow in order to work towards a uniformity of practice. These rules, however, are only guidelines, for each text has its own individual characteristics and will demand a degree of individuality in its treatment and presentation by the editor.[1] Many of the tasks involved in the preparation of a complex edition are laborious and time-consuming, as well as demanding of the most precise accuracy on the part of the editor. The performance of such tasks is prone to such human failings as tiredness or boredom, and many of them could be as well or better carried out by computer under the control of the editor as by the editor alone. We propose to examine here the different elements which go to make up the editorial process and suggest ways in which some degree of automation could be used. We also wish to suggest some new means of presenting editions in electronic form. We should like to stress that computers themselves cannot edit texts, being incapable of taking the kinds of decisions which human editors take daily. The goal of artificial intelligence is as illusory as it was twenty years ago.

THE EDITORIAL PROCESS

The traditional scholarly edition of an Old English work will consist of a text prepared by the editor and supported by a (generally) large amount of editorial apparatus to help the reader of the text understand or interpret it. Mostly editions are read by other scholars, but often the non-expert may need access to the works and this should always be kept in mind when editing texts. In general, the process of scholarly editing has the following stages:

Transcription of text(s).

---

[1] See Helmut Gneuss, 'Guide to the Editing and Preparation of Texts for the Dictionary of Old English', which appears as the first essay in this book (updated from its original appearance in *A Plan for the Dictionary of Old English*, ed. Roberta Frank and Angus Cameron, Toronto, 1973), *passim*, for some rules on the preparation and editing of Old English texts; see also the 'Notes for Editors' produced by the Early English Text Society.

Preparation and editing of text(s); this involves certain editorial decisions/problems:

is there one manuscript or more?

which should be the base manuscript?

how to represent special characters?

how to represent punctuation?

how to resolve difficult readings/cruces?

how to deal with damaged manuscripts? can any readings be recovered?

Presentation of the apparatus, which may consist of:

variants;

sources and parallels;

textual notes;

glossary;

index;

bibliography;

introduction;

list of abbreviations;

translation;

illustrations: these are not often presented in a scholarly edition, even if they are crucial to an understanding of the text as, for instance, in a herbal.

Specialized appendices may also be necessary, depending on the kind of text being presented. These could be

linguistic;

philosophical;

historical;

medical or herbal;

legal;

other topics dictated by the subject matter or particular difficulties presented by the text(s) being studied.

As well as considering the use of computers in the preparation of a scholarly edition, we also need to think about the final presentation of the edited material for publication. Increasingly, authors are being encouraged to take a larger part in producing the final text, either by supplying their word processor disks or by producing actual camera-ready copy. There are many reasons the individual author should resist pressure upon him or her to play a large role in final book production, but some may feel that with a complex edition it is easier to allow typesetting from disks prepared by the editor, even if this means extra work, than to proof-read the edition as set up from typescript. Indeed, current economic realities often dictate that complex editions will not be produced if the publishers have to incur the high costs of expert typesetting.[2]

---

[2] EETS has now produced its first volume printed entirely from camera-ready copy supplied by the author-editor, D. G. Scragg: *The Vercelli Homilies and Related Texts*, EETS os 300 (Oxford, 1992).

COMPUTERS IN EDITING

Transcription and preparation of the text

Most editors have, in the last ten years, discovered some of the ways in which computers can be of assistance in their work. The greatest revolution has been in the production of cheap desktop microcomputers supplied with user-friendly word-processing software and attached to laser printers. This has made the production of high quality typescript no more difficult than using a typewriter, with the advantage that the work never need be typed more than once. The latest revolution in microcomputer hardware is the production of the cheap, fast, light, laptop machine, which is now being followed by what is known as the 'palmtop', a hand-held computer which has a full QWERTY keyboard. Most libraries allow laptop computers to be used provided they are silent and do not need to be plugged into the library's own power supply.[3] With these computers the scholar can transcribe the text(s) directly in machine-readable form. The text therefore never need be reprocessed. The electronic text as transcribed can then be converted to most other text editors or word processors and manipulated as the scholar wishes. It is possible that some of the material needed by the scholar may be available already in machine-readable form. The Dictionary of Old English project, for instance, has produced a machine-readable version of every extant Old English text; generally an edited version of the text has been used rather than the manuscript, but dubious readings have usually been checked against the manuscript(s). This is a wonderful resource and is available at no cost from major text archives like the Oxford Text Archive.[4] Some universities also provide on-line access to the Old English Corpus with searching software attached to it, thus allowing scholars to search for individual words and collocates.[5]

Text encoding

One important consideration when preparing machine-readable versions of texts is how to encode certain features of the text so that information which is contained in the manuscript is preserved. In the past scholars have generally used their own system of encoding features. This has resulted in the proliferation of incompatible systems with the consequence that a text prepared by a scholar for one purpose may be useless for any other purpose. This problem is now being addressed by the

---

[3] There are numerous such computers now available: details given here would be out of date by the time of publication, but one machine which is popular is the Cambridge Z88 which weighs only two pounds and fits into a briefcase.

[4] Oxford Text Archive, Oxford University Computing Services, 13 Banbury Road, Oxford OX2 6NN; e-mail: ARCHIVE@VAX.OX.AC.UK.

[5] The Oxford Text Archive makes the Corpus available throughout the Oxford campus with the BASIS free-text retrieval system providing the search engine. At the University of Michigan, the Corpus (and many other texts) is provided on a network of UNIX workstations and accessed through the PAT/LECTOR text retrieval software developed at the University of Waterloo for the New Oxford English Dictionary Project.

Text Encoding Initiative (TEI), an international research project which aims to provide a set of Guidelines for the encoding of electronic texts. The first draft of the Guidelines is now available.[6] The task of the TEI is three-fold: to define those features of texts which need to be represented; to provide tags for their representation; to recommend a metalanguage in which to encode the tags. The metalanguage which has been chosen by the TEI to encode textual features is the Standard Generalized Markup Language (SGML).[7] The features which need to be encoded by the editor of an Old English text may include: special characters (ȝ ð þ etc.); scribal abbreviations; glosses; in fact, all of the notable characteristics of manuscripts that editors of Old English texts need to mark as in some way distinctive. The version of the Toronto Corpus of Old English now available from the Oxford Text Archive has many special characters and other features encoded in SGML.[8] The following example, of the first few lines of *Beowulf* from the Oxford Text Archive SGML encoding, gives some indication of the flexibility of TEI dialect of SGML markup:[9]

```
<text>
<body>
<lb n='1'><s id=s1>Hw&a;t.</s>
<s id=s2>We Gardena in geardagum,
<lb n='2'> &t;eodcyninga, &t;rym gefrunon,
<lb n='3'> hu &d;a &a;&t;elingas ellen fremedon.<s/>
</body>
</text>
```

Firstly, the statement <text> indicates that what follows is the encoded text itself, thus marking it off from any preparatory matter (statements of the source of the edition, who encoded it, etc.) which might precede. Then the statement <body> indicates that this is the main portion of the text itself and not 'front matter' such as title page, table of contents, etc. The next statement <lb n='1'> is used to indicate that this is a new line, numbered '1'. The next statement <s id=s1> indicates that what follows immediately is a segment of text (in this case, a logical sentence unit) identified as 's1'.

---

6 *Guidelines for the Encoding and Interchange of Machine-Readable Texts*, ed. C.M. Sperberg McQueen and Lou Burnard, Version 1.1, 1990. This document is available from the editors; to obtain a free copy (one per institutional address) contact (US) C.M. Sperberg McQueen, Computer Center (MC 135), Box 6998, University of Illinois at Chicago, Chicago, IL 60680, USA; e-mail: U35395@UICVM, or (Europe) Lou Burnard, Oxford University Computing Services, 13, Banbury Road, Oxford OX2 6NN, UK; e-mail: LOU@VAX.OXFORD.AC.UK.
7 A much revised and expanded version is now available from the editors. For an introduction to SGML, see Charles F. Goldfarb, *The SGML Handbook* (Oxford, 1990).
8 The best introduction to the TEI as it relates to the needs of medievalists is C.M. Sperberg McQueen, 'Texts in the Electronic Age: Textual Studies and Text Encoding with Examples from Medieval Texts', *Literary and Linguistic Computing* 6 (1991), 34–46.
9 The OTA markup has been slightly modified for the clarity of the example. We thank Lou Burnard for permission to use this example.

This segment contains just the one word, 'Hw&a;t'. The string '&a;' is an example of what SGML calls an 'entity reference', where the string '&xxx;' can be used to stand for whatever 'entity' the encoder chooses to define as 'xxx': a character, or string of characters, or a whole file, or an image. In this case, the entity reference '&a;' stands for the æ character. Other entity references in this example, &t; and &d;. stand for thorn and eth respectively. This 'entity reference' feature provides a useful mechanism for encoding characters outside the standard computer character sets. Especially, it adds greatly to the portability of SGML encoded texts from computer system to system, across networks and different displays.

The segment of text containing 'Hw&a;t.' is closed by a <s/> marker, indicating the end of this first segment identified as 's1'. Notice that the 's' element differs from the 'lb' element: the 's' element contains text (in this case, 'Hw&a;t.' while the 'lb' element is empty, containing no text but analogous to a marker laid in the text indicating (in this case) a line-break. The '<s id=s2>' statement opens the second segment, concluding with 'fremedon.' The fragment finishes with a '</body>' statement, indicating that we are at the end of this main portion of text, and the '</text>' closes off all the encoded text.

This example gives an idea of the power of this markup. With a suitable application one could search for words within a particular named segment, or range of segments, or named lines or range of lines, or a combination of segments or lines. One could search for collocations within the same segments or lines or both, or in adjoining segment or lines. SGML markup is often criticized for verbosity: this example shows that valuable effects can be achieved with quite brief SGML markup.

There are many advantages in encoding texts according to the guidelines established by the TEI. Texts so encoded can be transmitted electronically anywhere in the world with all their significant features preserved. The texts are independent of any particular hardware or software, so they can be used on any computer with any text processing or analysis software. When the text comes to be typeset by the publisher the markup can be translated to typesetting codes, avoiding rekeying and therefore the introduction of error. The text will survive beyond the life of current hardware and software and can be used in years to come with whatever systems are then in use.

Damaged manuscripts: enhancement of some readings

Many of the manuscripts used by editors of Old English texts have been severely damaged, some in the Ashburnham House fire in 1731 where so many were lost, others by the ravages of time. High quality colour photography and the use of ultra-violet light has revealed some readings hitherto invisible to the naked eye. Recently, using techniques borrowed from space technology, digital image processing has provided information for scholars which allows them to pronounce with authority on some previously disputed readings.[10]

---

[10] For a fascinating account of digital image processing in the enhancement of some readings in the

Collation of variants and management of large manuscript traditions

In Peter Shillingsburg's words, manual collation of variant texts is 'long, tedious, expensive and time-consuming'.[11] Moreover, collation requires minute accuracy and precise consistency over the longest task, and collation can be a very long task indeed. It is just the sort of mechanical and repetitive work at which computers excel: they do not nod.

Yet, computers have been very little used in collation.[12] Given the wide use now made of computers in (for example) concordancing and index-making, beside routine text-preparation with wordprocessors, this is somewhat surprising. There are two reasons for this. Firstly, computer collation may require far more input of text than does (for example) concordancing. To make a concordance, you need only have one copy of the text you are concording. To do a collation, you will need a copy of each text you are collating. If you are collating the eighty-three manuscripts of the *Canterbury Tales*, then you will need to input copies of all eighty-three manuscripts. Until very recently, the clumsiness of computer input devices made input of even one text problem enough. The advent of cheap, powerful and 'user-friendly' personal computers has made input of texts so much easier that the prospect of typing in copies of each text one wishes to collate need no longer appall. Indeed, one may not have to type in the texts at all. Optical character reading technology is no longer an expensive exoticism: well-printed texts, in many different languages, can now be read from the page into the computer with exceptional speed and reliability. The increasing success in teaching computers to decipher hand-writing suggests that even manuscripts may, in time, be read by computer.[13]

The second reason is that previous collation programs did not address the particular problems of manuscript traditions. Typically, the programs were designed to cope with collation of modern printed texts.[14] They did not take into account the enormous difficulties caused by widely varying orthographies and great range and density of variation. Collation of modern novels, for instance,

---

Beowulf manuscript, see Kevin Kiernan, 'Digital Image Processing and the *Beowulf* Manuscript', *Literary and Linguistic Computing* 6 (1991), 20–27.

[11] P.L. Shillingsburg, *Scholarly Editing in the Computer Age: Theory and Practice* (Athens and London, 1986), pp. 132–3.

[12] There are useful surveys of collation programs in S. Hockey, *A Guide to Computer Applications in the Humanities* (London, 1980), pp. 144–6, and in I. Lancashire and W. McCarty, *Humanities Computing Yearbook* (Oxford, 1988), pp. 108–10, 205. No collation program has achieved the general use of the Oxford Concordance Program or WordCruncher. Indeed, many of the collation programs listed in Hockey and Lancashire appear to have been used only by those who wrote them.

[13] See, for example, D.P. Wright and C.L. Scofield, 'Divide and Conquer', *Byte* 16 Number 4 (1991), 207–16, on the use of neural networks in handwriting recognition.

[14] For example, Shillingsburg's CASE system, *Scholarly Editing in the Computer Age*, and Dearing's programs for collation of Dryden, in V. Dearing, 'Computers Aids in Editing the Text of Dryden', in *Art and Error: Modern Textual Editing*, ed. R. Gottsmann and S. Bennett (London, 1970).

might yield one variant a page: collation of medieval vernacular manuscripts might yield variants on almost every word.

Collation of medieval texts needs special strategies, even its own program. The newly released collation program *Collate*, running on the Apple Macintosh and written by one of the authors of this article, aims to meet this need. As this program is now generally available, and has been fully discussed elsewhere, we will not here describe it in detail.[15] Briefly, it can collate up to a hundred variant texts at once; it includes special facilities for regularization of spelling and orthography during collation; it enables the master text to be switched or altered at any point; it permits the scholar to tailor the collation as desired; it allows the collation to be output in many different formats, including ready for direct submission to a typesetting system.

Computer collation is now possible, as it has not been formerly. However, the obstacle of input of every text requiring collation remains. Until optical character reading comes to our aid, we are replacing one tedium (manual collation) by another (input of all the variant texts). It might be objected that the traditional method, choosing a base text and then manually registering the variants in each manuscript against it, still has merit: at least, it might be quicker. It is certainly quicker if one is interested only in collating a selection of variants. But if one wants to do a complete word-for-word collation, like those of Kane's edition of *Piers Plowman* or the Manly and Rickert *Canterbury Tales*, then it is very likely that computer transcription of a single manuscript will be just as fast – perhaps even faster – than manual collation of that manuscript against the master.[16] Once you have transcribed one text into the computer, transcription of the next text will be just a matter of altering that first text after the manuscript. Further, it is much easier to check a transcription against a manuscript than to check a manual collation. In the first case, you are comparing just two things (the transcript and the manuscript); in the second you have to compare three things (the manuscript, the master, and the collation). In this respect at least, manual collation is rather more prone to error than computer collation.[17]

In our opinion, the advantages of computer collation are so considerable as to make the tedium of transcribing manuscript after manuscript (a task with its own fascinations) well worthwhile. Firstly, it provides complete transcriptions of all the manuscripts. This will permit concordancing, indexing and other exploration of

---

[15] P.M.W. Robinson, '*Collate*: A Program for Interactive Collation of Large Textual Traditions', in *Research in Humanities Computing 3*, ed. S. Hockey and M. Ide (Oxford, forthcoming).

[16] G. Kane, *Piers Plowman: The A Version* (London, 1960); also G. Kane and E.T. Donaldson, *Piers Plowman: The B Version* (London, 1975). J.M. Manly and E. Rickert, *The Text of the Canterbury Tales*, 8 vols (Chicago, 1940). Two groups of scholars, associated respectively with Professor Hoyt N. Duggan and Dr Robinson are currently (March 1993) seeking funding for transcription and collation of the manuscripts of *Piers Plowman* and the *Canterbury Tales*.

[17] Compare Charles Moorman's statement that 'approximately 5 per cent' of the collations in Manly and Rickert are in error. 'Computing Housman's Fleas', *Journal of the Association for Literary and Linguistic Computing* 3 (1982), 15.

these, and the transcriptions might be worthy of distribution in their own right. Secondly, if the texts have to be regularized before collation (as will be usual with medieval vernacular texts) *Collate* can provide a complete record of all the regularizations, a facility not available with manual collation where regularization is necessarily piece-meal and ad hoc. This will allow the regularization to be precisely controlled and consistent throughout. It will also generate potentially immense amounts of information about the spelling habits of different scribes, at different periods in different manuscripts, information itself of great possible value. Thirdly, all the information in the collation itself about just what manuscripts agree or disagree with what on what variants can be output to a database or other programs for further analysis. This might form the basis for detailed and far-reaching conclusions about how the manuscripts relate to one another.[18] Fourthly, one can change the master text and recollate against it with great ease. Editors whose final text is identical with the text with which they began and against which they manually registered all the variants are rare indeed. Electronic collation removes the pain from the recollation consequent on every alteration of the master. Fifthly, computer collation vastly reduces the possibility of error. Beside the likelihood that the collation itself will be more accurate, typesetting direct from the collation output eliminates all the stages of rekeying of variant apparatus and proof-reading, with all the attendant opportunities for error.

Preparation of glossaries and linguistic studies

After the use of wordprocessors, the availability of text analysis and concordancing software is probably the area of computing that has had the most impact on the working lives of editors in recent years. Once a text is available in machine-readable form it is now possible to produce a complete concordance to it in a matter of minutes instead of years. This is enormously helpful in the preparation of glossaries and in the kinds of linguistic studies traditionally carried out as part of the editing process. One can, for instance, retrieve all occurrences of a given word with a particular spelling, or all instances of a phonological alternation, /io/ versus /eo/ or /a/ plus nasal versus /o/ plus nasal, for example. Having rendered the text he or she is editing machine-readable, the editor can have on his or her own microcomputer a text analysis program which can perform such tasks with ease. If comparisons are required with other texts or with the entire corpus of Old English, more powerful hardware and software is currently needed. Such facilities are, however, available through the mainframe computer facilities provided on all university and college campuses. The use of concordancing software to produce indexes of all words in a given text can also save the editor time in rekeying the

---

[18] See P.M.W. Robinson, 'The Collation and Textual Criticism of Icelandic Manuscripts (2): Textual Criticism', *Literary and Linguistic Computing* 4 (1989), 174–81, for an example of such an analysis, based on a computer collation of a whole manuscript tradition.

glossary: having produced the index it can be imported into a wordprocessor and the extra information (part of speech, meaning, etc.) added.[19]

Sources and parallels

The finding of sources and parallels to the text being edited can be something of a haphazard affair. With textual corpora which have been the subject of considerable scholarly effort (homiletic and liturgical writings, for instance) there is a wealth of information available on sources and parallels to the Old English texts. This information is being collected formally by the *Fontes Anglo-Saxonici* and SASLC (Sources of Anglo-Saxon Literary Culture) projects. The *Fontes Anglo-Saxonici* project has set up a database of sources of texts in Old English at the University of Manchester, and a bibliography and database of sources of Anglo-Latin texts are being established at Cambridge University. In theory, such databases could be made available electronically for individual scholarly use; in practice such availability is not yet planned, publication in traditional book form being currently envisaged. Scholarly publishers are now realizing the size of the market for electronic versions of standard scholarly works and are therefore producing some of these with celerity.[20] Many texts useful to editors are already available in machine-readable form; for instance the *Thesaurus Linguae Graecae* (TLG) corpus of Greek texts available on CD-ROM is an invaluable resource, as is the Centre for the Computational Analysis of Texts (CCAT) CD-ROM of Greek, Latin, and Hebrew biblical materials.[21]

A POSSIBLE ALTERNATIVE TO THE TRADITIONAL SCHOLARLY EDITION

The decisions an editor makes at all stages in the process of preparing a scholarly edition are mostly concerned with how to select and present the information he or she is amassing. We use and produce much more information than we can ever present and so selection of the material involves experience and judgement. But viewed in the light of certain reasonable reading expectations, the legitimate exercise of editorial selectivity imposes arbitrary and subjective limits on the interpretation of texts, and what is a justifiable and intelligent limitation from one

[19] The Oxford Concordance Program (OCP) is one of the earliest and most popular concordance packages in England; it has been available for mainframe use since 1980 and is now used throughout the world. There is a microcomputer version of this program, MicroOCP. There are now numerous other such programs available for a variety of hardware platforms and operating systems.

[20] Chadwyck-Healey have recently announced the electronic publication of the complete 221 volumes of the *Patrologia Latina*. Publication will be in four CD-ROMs, and will include powerful search facilities. BREPOLS have announced electronic publication of the Corpus Christianorum, Series Latina. The first CD-ROM contains 945 texts from 211 authors, with further CD-ROMs to follow.

[21] The TLG disk is available from the TLG Project, University of California at Irvine, Irvine, CA 92717, USA; for CCAT collection of texts, contact the Packard Humanities Institute, 300 Second Street, Suite 201, Los Altos, CA 94022, USA.

scholarly angle may appear, from another, an unnecessary restriction of possibilities. Prospective readers of Old English texts may represent a variety of disciplines and a range of special interests (archaeological, philological, historical, literary, philosophical, medical, etc.) which the editor may not have envisaged, but which the text itself may, sited in another context, amply justify. The reader of the edition, too, has to trust that the editor made the 'right' decision about a reading or a variant or a gloss; the materials upon which that decision was made reside in his or her filing cabinet and are not presented as part of the edition. Sometimes, indeed, there is no 'right' or single decision, but presentation of a homogenous text demands that a decision be made.

We would like to suggest here an alternative to the traditional scholarly edition: the 'electronic hypertext edition'. This would not be a substitute for the traditional edition, rather it would be a supplement to it, allowing the editor to present not only the edited text but also all the materials which were used in the preparation of the edition and upon which editorial decisions were based. This is a revolutionary notion and we offer here a brief explanation of the principles upon which such an edition would be based and what might be included in it.

The term 'hypertext' was coined some twenty years ago by Theodore Nelson.[22] A hypertext is a document which is essentially a database with active cross-references allowing non-sequential reading and writing. A reader follows 'links' in the text, links being pointers to pieces of information which the creator of the hypertext has deemed relevant to the text. A scholarly edition functions already as a non-electronic hypertext, the 'links' here being footnote signals, lemmata, headwords, etc. In using the non-electronic hypertext, however, the reader is constrained by the linear page structure; in the electronic hypertext these constraints are removed, allowing more flexible access to the information. In the electronic hypertext, too, much larger amounts of information can be stored and organized because of the current capacities of electronic storage media, capacities which are increasing exponentially every year. Hypermedia (sometimes known as multimedia) is an extension to the notion of hypertext; the term is used when other kinds of media are linked to the text: graphics, sounds, video, for instance.

What would the electronic hypertext edition contain? First of all it would need to preserve the features of the traditional scholarly edition, so it would have all the elements of the edition described above. We propose that it should also contain transcripts of all the manuscripts prepared as described above for collation, as well as possibly digitized images of some or all manuscripts so that the transcriptions could be checked by other scholars if necessary. Hypertext links would be provided to take the reader from, for instance, the collation to an individual manuscript or from a manuscript to a transcription.

The hypertext authoring software currently available allows management of the

---

[22] T.H. Nelson, *Congress of the International Federation for Documentation (FID) Abstracts 10–15 October 1965*. Nelson expanded his ideas on hypertext in *Literary Machines* (Swarthmore, PA, 1981).

large volumes of text and images that would need to be stored and manipulated in systems as proposed here. Such software is also constructed for maximum ease-of-use both for the author of the hypertext system as well as for the end user. This is of paramount importance in the construction of large-scale scholarly reference tools. Also of great importance is the preparation of the materials in standard encoding formats as described on pp. 29–31, for we need our texts to be interchangeable, to be understandable by other scholars or software systems, and to allow us the possibility of linking other texts in with them.[23] We could, for instance, have available the entire Toronto Corpus of Old English, as well as perhaps the *Patrologia Latina*, the *Fontes Anglo-Saxonici* database, and the entire resource of SASLC. With the right software also available to us, *Collate* and a concordance program, for example, it would then be possible to check the collation of a text, recollate against a different manuscript, search for sources and parallels, retrieve linguistic examples, look up words in a lexicon, all interactively and virtually instantaneously on a personal workstation. Such systems already exist and more are in preparation. The CDWord package developed by the CDWord Project, Dallas Theological Seminary, is one such system. It offers several translations of the Bible in Greek and English, biblical commentaries, a lexicon, a parser which offers a grammatical analysis of every word in the Greek versions of the Bible, a sophisticated search and concordance program, maps, plans, tables and graphics. This package is so organized that all the information required for biblical scholarship is available at the touch of a button to the least sophisticated user of computers. It is possible, for instance, to have a text window open on a Greek translation, with an English translation and a commentary also open at the same point. When any one of these windows is scrolled, all three will scroll synchronously. To aid study, while there are three (or even more) windows open, it is also possible to search the lexicon, access the parser, and use the concordance program.[24] CDWord offers us, perhaps, a model for the Old English edition of the future.[25]

---

[23] See Steven J. DeRose, 'Biblical Studies and Hypertext', in *Hypermedia and Literary Studies*, ed. Paul Delaney and George P. Landow (Cambridge, MA, and London, 1991), pp. 185–204.

[24] For further details of CDWord, contact CDWord Project, 3909 Swiss Avenue, Dallas, TX 75204, USA.

[25] This paper is based on our presentation at the Manchester conference, and has been updated to the end of 1993. Readers will appreciate that advances in this area are constantly being made.

PALAEOGRAPHY AND THE EDITING OF OLD ENGLISH TEXTS

Alexander R. Rumble

A SOUND KNOWLEDGE and appreciation of palaeography may be taken to be essential to the accurate editing of Old English texts. The process of editing, a conversion process in which the editor intervenes to modify the form of a text into one more acceptable to a particular audience, always has a strong graphic component. Once past the initial change from an oral/mental composition to a written draft, the production of a fair copy, of secondary copies, and of printed editions each usually entail the making of the text visually more formal and consistent, both by modifying the character of the letter-forms and by the rationalization of punctuation, word-division, capitals, page-layout, etc. In this, the modern editor often stands at the end of a long line of earlier editors – from the Anglo-Saxon, medieval and early modern periods – each formulating and using their own set of conventions for the benefit of their contemporaries. In the early modern and modern periods the range of forms that an edition may take, and the size of its readership, have increased with the use of imitative type-founts and various forms of facsimile reproduction, and visual aspects of editions have stayed very much to the fore.

The first editors of Old English were the Anglo-Saxons themselves. Changes of an editorial nature were imposed on texts each time that they were copied. Makers of collections in particular tended to modify the form of individual items to make them more consistent with each other. Thus King Alfred declared that he had selected from the laws of, amongst others, his predecessor King Ine those laws which seemed to him most just, and had incorporated them into his own code.[1] In Alfred's code, the law-code of Ine almost loses its identity, individual chapters being numbered as part of the Alfredian capitular sequence with their separate origin only being discernible from Alfred's retention of Ine's Prologue.[2] Elsewhere, the makers of legal, glossarial and poetical collections imposed a 'batch order' on

---

[1] Laws of Alfred, Prologue, 49.9; see *English Historical Documents*, i, *c.500–1042*, ed. D. Whitelock, 2nd edn (London, 1979), no. 33, and *The Parker Chronicle and Laws (Corpus Christi College, Cambridge, MS. 173)*, ed. R. Flower and [A.]H. Smith, EETS os 208 (London, 1941 for 1937, repr. 1973).

[2] *The Parker Chronicle and Laws*, ed. Flower and Smith, fols. 47a–52b. Ine, Prologue and 1–76 are numbered in Corpus 173 as Alfred, 44–120. King Alfred's further reference (Prologue, 49.9) to laws of Offa of Mercia is less clearly to a law-code, however, and may refer instead to capitular injunctions issued during the visit to England in 786 of a papal legation, see P. Wormald, 'In search of "Offa's law-code"', *People and Places in Northern Europe, 500–1600: Essays in Honour of Peter Hayes Sawyer*, ed. I. Wood, N. Lund (Woodbridge, 1991), pp. 25–45.

originally separate items; this batch order may be retained in part or in whole by later copyists, leading to similarities in the sequence of individual texts within different manuscripts. When it comes to documentary texts, we have the sole surviving pre-Conquest cartulary, *Tib. I* from Worcester cathedral priory, whose maker converted a collection of separate documents on single sheets of parchment into the form of a book, imposing uniformity of script and layout on originally diverse items.[3] In the original diplomas themselves we have represented a 'fair copy' or edition, usually by a single scribe, of three separate texts – the Latin text recording the terms of the grant, the vernacular boundary description, and the list of witnesses – each of which almost certainly had its own draftsman and its own draft text.[4]

In the post-Conquest period too, the making of cartularies constituted the editing of text. The varied scripts of the original documents were converted in the cartulary into one formal bookscript of the type in fashion at the date at which the cartulary was made, usually a protogothic or gothic *textura*. This may be seen as a process comparable with the conversion of manuscript text to type by modern editors. Also involved in the making of such books of documents was the modernization of the spelling of vernacular texts to a norm imposed by the copyist. Thus in the twelfth-century parts of the *Codex Wintoniensis* this meant a standardization to a southern type of early Middle English.[5] Such imposed editorial conventions also deserve study in their own right; they should not be dismissed by students of Old English as simply 'bad copies' of older material. The translation of vernacular texts into Latin in the post-Conquest period is also an area that deserves attention from those interested in the editing of Old English, e.g. the documents included respectively in the twelfth-century *Liber Eliensis* and Ramsey Chronicle.[6] This practice was one which made the content of such texts more acceptable to the reader, Latin being the official language of administration in medieval England. It also provides evidence for us of the quality of knowledge of Old English in the post-Conquest period.

Another type of edition that comes to the attention of a palaeographer is that represented by catalogues of manuscripts. If done thoroughly, as produced by

---

3 G.R.C. Davis, *Medieval Cartularies of Great Britain: A Short Catalogue* (London, 1958), no. 1068(i); N.R. Ker, 'Hemming's cartulary: a description of the two Worcester cartularies in Cotton Tiberius A. xiii', *Studies in Medieval History Presented to Frederick Maurice Powicke*, ed. R.W. Hunt, W.A. Pantin, R.W. Southern (Oxford, 1942), pp. 49–75.

4 Draft lists of witnesses are attached to the original diplomas now London, BL, Cotton Augustus ii. 98 and Stowe Charter 17; P.H. Sawyer, *Anglo-Saxon Charters: An Annotated List and Bibliography*, Royal Historical Society (London, 1968), nos. 163 and 293; see M.P. Parsons, 'Some scribal memoranda for Anglo-Saxon charters of the 8th and 9th centuries', *Mitteilungen des Österreichischen Instituts für geschichtsforschung*, Erg-Band 14 (1939), 13–32, at pp. 15–19, 21–2.

5 Davis, *Medieval Cartularies*, no. 1042: A.R. Rumble, 'The structure and reliability of the *Codex Wintoniensis* (British Museum, Additional MS. 15350; the cartulary of Winchester cathedral priory)', University of London Ph.D thesis 1980, 2 vols, i. 247–54 and ii. appendix 3, *passim*.

6 *Liber Eliensis*, ed. E.O. Blake, Camden Society, 3rd series 92 (London, 1962): *Chronicon Abbatiae Ramesiensis*, ed. W.D. Macray, Rolls Series 83 (London, 1886).

scholars such as Humfrey Wanley and Neil Ker, such catalogues include portions of edited text in the form of transcriptions of incipits, explicits, colophons, marginalia, etc.[7] In the case of Wanley, some of these catalogue descriptions now constitute the primary authority for the text of items from manuscripts since lost or damaged.[8] The very act of producing a catalogue description of the contents of a manuscript should be recognized as a form of editing, allowing the reader of the catalogue to obtain a swift overview of the make-up of a collection in its present codicological context. Such an overview can be significant in breaking down the artificial separation by modern editors of items which have a manuscript association. It follows that the editorial conventions used in the production of such catalogues and in the quotation of parts of the text should be both clear and consistent.

The publication of facsimiles of manuscripts is also of great importance in the process of learning how to read and edit Anglo-Saxon and medieval texts. Such published facsimiles themselves constitute a form of edition. From the seventeenth century onwards engravings of insular scripts, based on manuscript text, were included as illustrations in printed books.[9] Modern facsimile editions usually consist of more than just a photograph, and include editorial additions such as foliation, quire signatures, and a running identification of texts at the minimum;[10] and diplomatic transliteration with full notes on the manuscript at the other extreme.[11] Their contents can also most usefully be indexed.[12]

There is a great need for the publication of more affordable facsimiles of whole texts or of whole codices. These are useful and important in the teaching of how to read manuscript text within its codicological context. While it is now possible to reproduce pages of manuscript text on a computer screen this will never be a satisfactory substitute for a facsimile produced in book form. In this respect the Early English Text Society has done good service in the past, issuing reasonably priced reproductions of important Old and Middle English texts, including Beowulf, the Parker Chronicle and Laws, The Owl and the Nightingale, Sir Gawayn and related poems, the Harley Lyrics, and the Winchester Malory.[13] There

---

[7] H. Wanley, *Librorum Vett. Septentrionalium . . . Catalogus Historico-Criticus . . .*, the second volume of G. Hickes, *Linguarum Vett. Septentrionalium Thesaurus . . .* (Oxford, 1705); N.R. Ker, *Catalogue of Manuscripts Containing Anglo-Saxon* (Oxford 1957, repr. 1991).

[8] See Ker, *Catalogue*, nos. 156–7, 168–73, 175–81, 183, 195, 222, 224.

[9] J. Mabillon, *De Re Diplomatica Libri VI . . .* (Paris, 1681), book V, contained facsimile script engravings by P. Giffart.

[10] Thus *Parker Chronicle and Laws*, ed. Flower and Smith. It should be noted, however, that this was first published during the Second World War and therefore lacks the full introduction which had been intended by its editors, see *ibid.*, Preface.

[11] Thus *Beowulf: Reproduced in Facsimile from the Unique Manuscript British Museum MS. Cotton Vitellius A. xv*, with transliteration and notes by J. Zupitza, EETS os 245 (with introductory note by N. Davis; London, 1959 for 1958, repr. 1967, 1981).

[12] For example, *Textus Roffensis: Rochester Cathedral Library MS. A.3.5*, ed. P.H. Sawyer, 2 vols, EEMF 7, 11 (Copenhagen, 1957, 1962), ii. 23–42 (index of persons and places).

[13] *The Parker Chronicle and Laws* and *Beowulf*, see above, nn. 1 and 11; *The Owl and the Nightingale: Reproduced in Facsimile from the Surviving Manuscripts Jesus College Oxford 29*

is still a need for further cheap but serviceable facsimiles of this sort to be published though. In contrast the Early English Manuscripts in Facsimile volumes are now so expensive that they are out of the reach of some libraries, let alone of most individuals.[14]

Students should be constantly informed/reminded of what texts look like in the original manuscript. Many, if not most, undergraduate students today do not even realize that the texts they study even exist outside of the printed edition. How can they therefore fully appreciate the difference in textual provenance and character between a piece of Old English prose and a chapter in a modern novel? The use of relevant facsimiles can be a great help to the teacher in demonstrating to a class the reasons for gaps in a surviving text, the genesis of copying errors, as well as the raw immediacy of a hand-written piece of literature. A greater familiarity on the part of students and other readers with the external appearance of the actual manuscripts would obviate the need for some editorial interventions in printed editions. Thus, consistent systems of original punctuation could be retained, and the (from a palaeographer's point of view) unsustainable modern convention that the Anglo-Saxon letter *wynn* be replaced in print by a quite different letter (w) would be unnecessary. This latter convention is the imposition of an anachronism – since the letter 'w' is not an Anglo-Saxon one, and use of it in an edition alters both the appearance and the character of the text. Modern printers have often claimed not to be able to distinguish between the Anglo-Saxon letters thorn and wynn and have therefore persuaded editors to drop one of them. With the now-widespread use of word processing by authors and editors there can be no problem in this respect though. Readers of printed editions who are unfamiliar with manuscript text have also claimed to have difficulty in distinguishing wynn from thorn but this has mostly been due to the use by printers of a thorn of later medieval shape, lacking an ascender: there is a case here for the redesign of the printers' version of thorn, to a more conservative shape, rather than for the exclusion of wynn. If students can be taught to accept *ab initio* the Anglo-Saxon letters ash, thorn, and eth, as well as the tironian abbreviation for *and*, there is no reason why they should not be introduced to wynn at the same time, thus obviating future unfamiliarity with it. In the interests of editorial accuracy it should be returned to its rightful place in the alphabet used for Old English texts.[15]

---

and British Museum Cotton Caligula A. ix, with introduction by N.R. Ker, EETS os 251 (London, 1963 for 1962); *Pearl, Cleanness, Patience and Sir Gawayn: Reproduced in Facsimile from the Unique MS. Cotton Nero A. x*, ed. I. Gollancz, EETS os 162 (London, 1923 for 1922, repr. 1931, 1955, 1971); *Facsimile of British Museum MS. Harley 2253*, with introduction by N.R. Ker, EETS os 255 (London, 1965 for 1964); *The Winchester Malory: A Facsimile*, with introduction by N.R. Ker, EETS ss 4 (London, 1976).

[14] To date 25 volumes have been published (Copenhagen 1951–93).

[15] The new edition of *Anglo-Saxon Charters*, British Academy (London, 1973–) uses wynn in the edited text of documents wherever it occurs in the manuscripts concerned, but does not use it in the indices. This would appear to be a sensible compromise on grounds of economy.

Essentially, it is highly desirable that all editors of Old English and medieval texts should have an opportunity for some formal training in palaeography, not only to ensure the accuracy of their own transcription of texts from manuscripts or microfilm, but also to enable them to imagine what might have gone wrong in the earlier transmission process through inaccuracy of copying by a medieval editor or copyist.[16] Here again the modern editor may be part of a continuum, but should take the opportunity of gaining from an acquired knowledge of palaeography to ensure that he or she does not repeat or even add to the errors of past copyists.

[16] For those without the opportunity for formal training, a start may be made by studying the Introduction to Ker, *Catalogue*; the Introduction to A.G. Petti, *English Literary Hands from Chaucer to Dryden* (London, 1977), which is much wider than the title of the book suggests; and the earlier plates in C.E. Wright, *English Vernacular Hands from the Twelfth to the Fifteenth Centuries* (London, 1960).

EDITING OLD ENGLISH TEXTS FOR HISTORIANS
AND OTHER TROUBLEMAKERS

David N. Dumville

REVIEWING HANS SAUER'S EDITION of the Old English *Capitula Theodulfi* a decade ago, Malcolm Godden regretted the lack of a modern-language translation, observing that this was the sort of text (a guide for parochial clergy) which various kinds of historian would need to consult and suspecting (no doubt rightly) that many would continue to use the mid-nineteenth-century (1840) English translation of the A-text in the absence of a new version.[1] Discussing the same book, I noted the further absence, from its 550 pages, of any consideration of the content of the text or of the reason for and context of the acts of translation.[2]

Here, then, we have one literary and linguistic scholar making certain assumptions about historians' needs, attitudes, and methods of working, and one historian drawing attention to a way in which an editor (of what one would be hard pressed to describe as a literary text) has restricted himself to essentially philological concerns. Who are these historians whose concerns may be thus addressed or ignored? It is all too often the case that, given the rigidity of the departmental and disciplinary boundaries within which many scholars both received and offer education, students in – say – English language and literature have in their minds a cardboard cut-out image of a historian (and vice versa). The further implication is that quite commonly students of Old English know all too little of Anglo-Saxon history while historians of early England know little or no Old English. 'The historian' may then be a professional with or without appropriate linguistic equipment. But equally he may be a student (at whatever level) or part of a very much wider reading public with a more or less amateur interest in the Middle Ages.

What kinds of text do these 'historians' want to read? Again, it is easier to have in mind the cardboard cut-out: everyone knows that historians like documents – inscriptions, charters, wills, lists (for example, of property, or of succession in Church or State), genealogies, or legal texts (whether royal lawcodes or ecclesiastical texts such as penitentials or synodal proceedings) – and perhaps only secondarily the potentially literary and decidedly non-documentary text such as the chronicle. But only a moment's thought should suffice to establish that there is much in Old English literature at large which has fascinated historians. One may

---

[1] *Theodulfi Capitula in England*, ed. H. Sauer (Munich, 1978), reviewed by M.R. Godden, *Medium Aevum* 48 (1979), 262–5 (see especially p. 265).

[2] *Archiv für das Studium der neueren Sprachen und Literaturen* 223 (1986), 389–92.

remember H.M. Chadwick's books,[3] or Dorothy Whitelock's paper on 'Anglo-Saxon poetry and the historian'.[4] There is almost no division of Old English literature which has not at one time or another provided raw material for the historian of Anglo-Saxon England, and that is as it should be. For example, glossary-evidence has loomed large – perhaps too largely – in discussion of the Anglo-Saxon chancery;[5] practical, quasi-literary texts such as homilies have been mined by historians of late Anglo-Saxon England;[6] and heroic literature, its origins and transmission, have engaged generations of historians wishing to comprehend the nature of heroic society and the interaction of Christianity with the Germanic warrior-ethos.[7] In principle, historians may seek to understand and/or to use any class of Old English text. It goes without saying, I imagine, that their concerns are, nonetheless, more likely to be admitted by editors of texts in some genres than in others. Imagine telling an editor of *The Wanderer* that he should have the historian's interests clearly in mind when preparing his work – and shudder at the thought of the response which one would get!

In what form, then, might historians want an Old English text presented? *Quot historici, tot sententiae* is a likely summary of the responses to such a question. Nevertheless, we might expect certain concerns generally to make themselves felt. The first concern of most readers who are not professional philologists will be to have a text which (inherent difficulties of comprehension aside) is presented in such a way as to offer easy readability – in other words, modern punctuation, preferably heavy, and modern capitalisation. Necessary emendations – necessary, that is, to make unforced sense, to say nothing of good grammar – will need to be incorporated into the texts, but *visibly* so, and any hopelessly faulty passages obelised. In other words the tendency so apparent in Old English studies – towards editions which are ever more diplomatic and in which less and less editorial activity is visible – runs directly contrary to the needs of almost every user other than those professionals working in certain corners of philology and palaeography.[8] What I have elsewhere called 'the compulsive nervousness of editors of Old English texts' may be understandable but it does not help most would-be

---

3   *Studies in Anglo-Saxon Institutions* (Cambridge, 1905); *The Origin of the English Nation* (Cambridge, 1907; 2nd edn, 1924); *The Heroic Age* (Cambridge, 1912).
4   *Transactions of the Royal Historical Society*, 4th series, 31 (1949), 75–94.
5   S. Keynes, *The Diplomas of King Æthelred 'the Unready' 978–1016* (Cambridge, 1980), pp. 145–7; P. Chaplais, 'The Royal Anglo-Saxon "Chancery" of the Tenth Century Revisited', *Studies in Medieval History presented to R.H.C. Davis*, ed. H. Mayr-Harting and R.I. Moore (London, 1985), pp. 41–51.
6   See, for example, F.M. Stenton, *Anglo-Saxon England*, 3rd edn (Oxford, 1971); D. Whitelock, *The Beginnings of English Society* (Harmondsworth, 1952), and *English Historical Documents c.500–1042*, 2nd edn (London, 1979); D.P. Kirby, *The Making of Early England* (London, 1967).
7   The classic statement remains that of H.M. Chadwick and N.K. Chadwick, *The Growth of Literature*, 3 vols (Cambridge, 1932–40), I.
8   On 'pseudo-diplomatic' editions, see E.G. Stanley, 'Unideal principles of editing Old English verse', *Proceedings of the British Academy* 70 (1984), 231–73, at pp. 240–1 in particular.

readers of the literature.[9] In this context the question which the historian must put to the editor is, 'How much can one expect a historian to be a professional philologist?' The question will recur. But if the answer will admit that a lesser competence in Old English may decently be expected from a historian than from a professional student of the language, then the foregoing suggestions should be applied to the editing of historical texts.

A more troublesome question must also be faced. In the cases of various texts with which the historian may most naturally be concerned, the pristine form of the text may not be available. This is, of course, no uncommon problem in Anglo-Saxon studies. What is more, however, intermediate but still very interesting versions of the text may be deduced but not survive. The most obvious cases are presented on the one hand by the Anglo-Saxon Chronicle and on the other by individual members of the corpus of charters. To take the latter case first, let us consider Sawyer 566, from the Peterborough Abbey archive: this is what appears to be a post-Conquest English translation of a mid-tenth-century royal diploma of the so-called 'alliterative' group, by which an estate in Huntingdonshire was conveyed to a thane called Ælfsige Hunlafing. Diplomatic criticism enables much of the original Latin text to be tentatively reconstructed. Aspects of this have been discussed by a succession of scholars since 1939: it would be possible to print a Latin version of the text to serve as a helpful basis for discussion and for further comparison with the remainder of the alliterative group.[10] The diplomatist or historian would be helped by the presentation of such a version. Yet one suspects that many students of Old English would recoil from such a suggestion. This is by no means the only document in the corpus defined by Sawyer whose criticism might be moved forward in this way.

On an altogether different scale is the question of the growth of chronicles, particularly annalistic chronicles. The criticism of such texts is by no means a problem unique to Anglo-Saxon studies. But one of the flagships of Anglo-Saxon textual and historical studies in the last century has been the critical investigation of the development of the texts which we call collectively 'The Anglo-Saxon Chronicle'.[11] To be sure, there is a long way to go; but what had already been achieved by, say, 1980 is the envy of historians of neighbouring societies and subsequent eras. What remains to be done is a very great deal of detailed refinement of the textual history of the whole corpus which constitutes the Anglo-Saxon Chronicle. This is a matter of considerable complexity: to participate in the study requires a good knowledge of the Old English texts and their Latin relatives and, perhaps above all, of the accumulated scholarship. Now text-historical studies are not to the taste of all historians – and I dare say that there are philologists too who

---

[9] See my review of Sauer's book (n. 2 above), p. 391.

[10] P.H. Sawyer, *Anglo-Saxon Charters* (London, 1968), p. 204, no. 566; cf. A.J. Robertson, *Anglo-Saxon Charters*, 2nd edn (Cambridge, 1956), pp. 56–9, 311–14 (no. 30).

[11] This work was most satisfactorily summed up by Dorothy Whitelock, *English Historical Documents*, pp. 109–25.

would rather leave such matters to someone else. But before the social historian, say, can use a particular part of the Chronicle, he needs to be reassured as to its age and the accuracy of the text available to him. He could be so, much more easily, if – or (should I say?) he will be so when – reconstructed texts of the several text-historically defined stages of development of the Chronicle are available for consultation.[12] Such reconstructions of the content of these lost Chronicle-versions will make hypothesized stages of textual development tangible and capable of being discussed. They will make the discussion of text-historical points less arcane. There is little doubt – on the evidence of the reception accorded to such exercises in other areas of study – that they will be welcome to historians. Some Old English philologists are prepared to produce such editions but others would perhaps rather let historian-editors hang themselves in the attempt. Yet here is an area where historians' needs can be rather well defined.

The question of reconstruction inevitably raises the question of language. Any process of reconstruction – one might indeed say any editorial act – requires one to work back, whether minimally or radically, from the existing manuscript-texts. If the job is going to be done comprehensively, then the language of the text should also be reconstructed to that of the time and place of the hypothesized text. However, when a text at most such definable stages of transmission is admittedly composite, the theoretical basis for such linguistic reconstruction is weak. Given that the act of reconstruction to an earlier and dialectally or scriptorially different stage of language is less likely to produce its own effective controls in a prose text than in a poem – and that, in the case of the Chronicle, it is the content which is at stake – all parties might be satisfied by retention of the mixed and perhaps anachronistic language of one of the principal surviving manuscript-witnesses. One would have to recognize that this method of editing would lead to the creation of a text which in certain respects never existed, but which will nonetheless be helpful to us. But in the case of a text where metrical controls might be applied or of a homogeneous text by a known author, one might reach a very different conclusion. On that, however, I had a say in print some years ago and for now I pass on.[13]

The level and nature of annotation which an editor might be expected to produce for a history-text should perhaps have a mention here. There is a good deal of evidence that many historians cannot stand to read an edition of a text which does not bear copious annotation on historical points, and that their tolerance of technical introductory discussions intended to establish the date and history of a text is often strikingly limited.[14] On the other hand – as witness Sauer's *Theodulfi*

---

[12] Such editions will comprise vols 1–2, 10–14, of *The Anglo-Saxon Chronicle: a Collaborative Edition*, gen. ed. D. Dumville and S. Keynes, 23 vols (Cambridge, 1983–).

[13] ' "Beowulf" and the Celtic world: the uses of evidence', *Traditio* 37 (1981), 109–60, especially pp. 121–32.

[14] This has been manifested in reviews of the early volumes of the editions of the Anglo-Saxon Chronicle – notably by N.P. Brooks and E.M.C. van Houts. I return to questions raised by these

Capitula in England – a philologist might happily pass by all such matters with his head in the air.

As regards both annotation and reconstruction the best solution may of course be collaboration, with philologist and historian productively arguing their way to an edition more or less acceptable to both. But is this pie in the sky? I remember from some years ago a plan to edit a short but difficult Old English documentary text, *Gerefa*, surviving in a single manuscript, a plan which involved collaborators from a number of disciplines and which would show historians and others how a text of historical interest should be edited. There are clearly difficulties attending such collaborative projects.

Since the Early English Text Society changed its policy of including Modern English translations in its editions, and retreated (for whatever reason) into its disciplinary bunker, those wishing to read Old and Middle English literature have been dependent on aged renderings or on sporadic publication of the odd translation by freebooters, or on the even more occasional bilingual edition. Certainly nowadays the general rule in English studies seems to be to offer no translation with an edition of an Old or Middle English text, but sometimes instead to provide a glossary. If the Editorial Secretary of the EETS could be persuaded to take up the spirit of his own very welcome remarks[15] and persuade his Society to start a series of translations of the texts whose editions it publishes, a signal service would be rendered to a wide public.

There is no doubt that historians of Anglo-Saxon England should gain a working knowledge of Old English and of its historical grammar. But, whatever one may say, not all will do so. Nor is it possible for many students of the history of the period to acquire such knowledge, and the same is true of a wider public, including colleagues in more distant disciplines whose primary source-material is not the written word – such as archaeology. In other words, there are weaker brethren and distracted collateral relatives who would all be glad of some help. But the historian – or anyone else who is not a professional philologist and editor of texts – is, I think, entitled to put a pair of searching questions to editors of Old English texts. Why would you not wish to purvey your chosen text to a wider audience? And how can you convey your detailed understanding of the text which you have edited, even to your immediate fellow professionals, without displaying that understanding (and perhaps its limits) in a translation? One could add that we have all heard a good many enthusiastic – even extravagant – claims made for Old English literature, no doubt in some cases with justice. Some of us may regard claims made for the literary qualities of some divisions of the prose literature as rather far-fetched. Is it then timidity which has prevented the communication of much of this prose to a wider readership?

At any rate, unless students of Old English language and literature expect

and other reviewers in a paper forthcoming in *Studi medievali* on the problems and principles involved in editing the Anglo-Saxon Chronicle.

[15] Malcolm Godden in his paper to the Manchester Conference.

colleagues in another discipline to be as proficient in Old English as they themselves are – therefore presumably as proficient in Old English as in their own discipline, and how many could meet reciprocal expectations? –, translations, and *not* glossaries, are the means by which Old English texts would be most satisfactorily conveyed to those colleagues. If a non-philological colleague is being made to plod very laboriously through an untranslated text which in the end may or may not be of interest to him, he will no doubt learn many things; but whether he will have much understanding of the text as a whole, rather than some of its many individual syntactical units, is a nice question. Have mercy on him!

Up to now I have talked about historians' needs and about the reasons why they have to make requests for editorial performances which many philologists would regard as embodying concessionary or charitable acts. Historians as, by definition, weaker brethren are likely to constitute a much-cherished image in a gathering of editors. However, there are historians who edit texts, whether texts in Latin or texts in a vernacular. Yet they risk life and limb by so doing. There are two principal hazards. The average historian regards the editing of texts as drudge-work, requiring an absence of critical imagination: I have heard the task described as 'work fit for a librarian, not someone concerned with ideas and issues'. One may therefore be considered by one's colleagues to be, at best, 'some sort of a historian'. If one's own side is Scylla, the Charybdis who might cause one's final destruction is the professional philologist who does not like outsiders or amateurs on his carrot-patch.

Is it not then better to remain as a feeble suppliant at the philologist's door? Why would a historian risk the trouble of getting involved in editing? In this case I had better reply for myself alone, rather than attempting to generalize on behalf of those of my historical colleagues who have taken the editorial plunge. At the outset, I should say that I enjoy the challenge. I have always been interested in the history of texts, because it has been my experience that therein lies much useful and important historical information: what it tells us about (for example) the circulation, availability, and use of texts can be crucial for our understanding of some texts and genres – the Old English lawcodes and the sermon-literature are cases in point. Secondly, in the Latin tradition it has always been quite common for historians to edit their own texts and in the cases of troublesome things like verse or particularly difficult *Kunstprosa* to associate with professional philologists – consider, for instance, a century and a half of the work of the Monumenta Germaniae Historica. But finally, in the case of certain Old English historical texts, one has to say that the philologists have made a lousy job of it. For example, I find myself involved in editing the Anglo-Saxon Chronicle because, about a decade ago, I got furious – or systemically irritated – about the way in which someone trying to find out which Chronicle-text said what (about a particular event) was frustrated at every turn. Yet this was something which I, as a practising historian, needed to know routinely almost every day.[16]

---

[16] For the edition, see n. 12 above. To achieve the end described one had (and still has) to gather

As I have explained, historians have therefore two principal needs in respect of the Chronicle: to be able straightforwardly to consult and read texts of the several versions of the Chronicle; and to be able to know what was said by a Chronicle-version whose former existence has been text-historically demonstrated but which has not survived in that guise. The editions (since Benjamin Thorpe's for the Rolls Series in 1861) failed in general to meet these requirements.[17]

Accuracy, clarity, and readability are what most readers will appreciate in editions of texts. But not everyone will measure these qualities in the same way. Donald Scragg has issued an appeal for conformity or standardization of conventions throughout the discipline.[18] But we would probably all agree that there is only one way in which this could be achieved – to await (with enthusiasm, of course) the publication of Scragg's *Corpus Palaeo-anglicum* or *Bibliothek der angelsächsischen Literatur*! For differences of temperament and training will ensure that editors of Old English will have various views on the subject – and diversity of approach may be a healthy sign of life in any discipline.

Temperament, with original sin, we can do nothing much about, but what of training? Anyone who has edited, or attempted to edit, a text will know that on-the-job learning is an essential part of the editor's experience and subsequent equipment. More, or more effective, training in the language and its history is undoubtedly a desideratum. Training, too, in editorial and text-historical theory and method would produce more flexible editorial activity, and that (to my mind) would be very welcome. For, at present, Anglo-Saxon editorial behaviour is very much constrained by recent practice within the discipline. Malcolm Godden has spoken with emotion of the thrills to be contemplated in producing a boldly reconstructed text of an Old English work: but he has expressed the fear that his punishment for flagellating his text would be to see his edition cast from the Garden of Eden.[19]

Yet there are kindred disciplines where extensive linguistic reconstruction of a text is regarded as a normal and desirable, indeed essential, aspect of the editorial process.[20] The academic tradition is the determinant: in Old English that tradition is timid, not bold, and thus restrictive: but it has not always and everywhere been so, and it does not have to be so now.[21]

---

around one editions of very varying age and quality, edited according to different principles; and, even then, the whole field was not covered. It remained necessary to consult the manuscripts to gain routine textual information.

17 *The Anglo-Saxon Chronicle*, ed. and tr. B. Thorpe, 2 vols (London, 1861): in it the Old English texts were disposed in six parallel columns in vol. 1, the translation in vol. 2. Because of its layout it remains one of the most useful of the older editions of the Chronicle.

18 See below, p. 308.

19 See below, pp. 171–2.

20 As, for example, in mediaeval Irish studies: see the remarks of D. Greene, 'Linguistic considerations in the dating of early Welsh verse', *Studia Celtica* 6 (1971), 1–11, and Dumville, ' "Beowulf" and the Celtic world', pp. 121–32.

21 On reconstruction, see *ibid.*, pp. 123–6, 131–2; Lapidge, below, pp. 53–67; Godden, below, pp. 168–72.

For the historian, however, the problem will always be the extent of his linguistic training when for him it is (and must be) a *Hilfswissenschaft*, however important. And however tempting it might be to say that the editing of historical source-material is (for the historian) too important to be left to the non-historians, collaborative endeavour is surely the way forward. Yet complex editorial projects are always at the mercy of their own complexity. And in the end someone must take the responsibility for the form of edition, if the editorial work is to have coherence, and for chivvying or bullying contributors. In Manchester, one is bound to remember the long-drawn-out project, *Councils and Synods* (whose Anglo-Saxon volume was one of Dorothy Whitelock's last works), which long looked set for failure but which was eventually brought to a successful conclusion by the vision, skill, tenacity, and (where necessary) bloody-mindedness of Professor Christopher Cheney, as anyone who has heard his or Christopher Brooke's accounts of that project will know.[22] The historian as editor must therefore say that when he attempts to improve upon the efforts of his predecessors he may ultimately fail; but in the light of past experience and common sense he cannot reasonably expect others to edit with his concerns largely in mind or to take potentially unpopular decisions. With the aid of the right collaborators he may succeed at least in producing texts which are accurate, clear, and readable, even if in other respects they fail to satisfy all interested parties.

Historians are not the only troublemakers who may demand texts edited to their own specifications. Lawyers, diplomatists, latinists, students of neighbouring vernaculars – all of these will have legitimate interests within the Old English canon.[23] If editors are ignorant or oblivious of their colleagues' concerns and conventions, their editions will fail. The lesson to be learned in all this is no doubt that circles cannot be squared. If one is asked (as I have been during this conference) how Old English texts are usually edited for historians, the answer is that they are not. If it should sometimes seem to philologists that historians are troublesome and can never be satisfied, one can perhaps reflect that historians are by no means unique in that.[24]

---

[22] *Councils and Synods with Other Documents relating to the English Church, I: A.D. 871–1204*, ed. D. Whitelock *et al.*, 2 pts (Oxford, 1981), and later volumes.

[23] For the diplomatic edition and the edition of a diploma, see *British Academy-Royal Historical Society Committee on Anglo-Saxon Charters: Guidelines for Editors*, ed. S. Keynes (1990 ed., available from the editor).

[24] I should like to thank the organizers of the Manchester conference for the invitation to speak at what proved to be a stimulating gathering, for much kind and attentive hospitality, and now also for their editorial labours.

ON THE EMENDATION OF OLD ENGLISH TEXTS

Michael Lapidge

IT IS AN OBVIOUS FACT that Anglo-Saxon authors wrote both in Latin and Old English. Sometimes they used both languages in the course of the same work. Throughout his *Grammar* and *Glossary*, for example, Ælfric wanders between the two languages, supplying English equivalents of Latin words and phrases, and Byrhtferth in his *Enchiridion* alternates passages in Latin with passages in Old English. By the same token, these two languages were copied alongside each other in Anglo-Saxon scriptoria, very often by the same scribes. There are numerous manuscripts in which we can observe the one scribe copying alternate passages in Latin and Old English. Several unambiguous examples were signalled by Neil Ker: these include London, British Library, Cotton Cleopatra B. xiii (a mid-eleventh-century collection of homilies from Exeter); Oxford, Bodleian Library, Bodley 865 (an early eleventh-century copy of the bilingual version of the *Capitula* of Theodulf); Oxford, Bodleian Library, Junius 121 (a late eleventh-century collection of ecclesiastical institutes from Worcester); and Oxford, Corpus Christi College 197 (a late tenth-century copy of the bilingual *Regula S. Benedicti*).[1] Many more examples could be cited. Yet in spite of the fact that Latin and Old English were composed and copied side by side in the same scriptoria, prevailing editorial attitudes to texts in the two languages are strikingly different.[2] The difference may stem from the fact that there is a long and established tradition of Latin textual criticism, stretching back to the seventeenth century and beyond,[3] whereas the scholarly edition of Old English texts does not antedate the nineteenth century and textual criticism of Old English literature as a theoretical discipline may scarcely be said to exist.[4] Editors of Latin texts have long been aware that medieval scribes

---

[1] See N.R. Ker, *Catalogue of Manuscripts containing Anglo-Saxon* (Oxford, 1957), pls. II–V.

[2] I have treated this matter in some detail elsewhere: in the 1990 Toller Lecture, 'Textual Criticism and the Literature of Anglo-Saxon England', *Bulletin of the John Rylands Library* 73 (1991), 17–45, and in 'The Edition, Emendation and Reconstruction of Anglo-Saxon Texts', in *The Politics of Editing Medieval Texts*, ed. R. Frank (New York, 1993), pp. 131–57.

[3] This tradition is brilliantly elucidated by E.J. Kenney, *The Classical Text: Aspects of Editing in the Age of the Printed Book* (Berkeley, CA, 1974); see also U. von Wilamowitz-Moellendorff, *History of Classical Scholarship*, ed. and trans. A. Harris and H. Lloyd-Jones (London, 1982).

[4] Recent exceptions include: M. Godden, 'Old English', in *Editing Medieval Texts*, ed. A.G. Rigg (New York, 1977), pp. 9–33; W.G. Busse, 'Assumptions in the Establishment of Old English Poetic Texts: P.J. Lucas's Edition of "Exodus" ', *Arbeiten aus Anglistik und Amerikanistik* 6 (1981), 197–219; E.G. Stanley, 'Unideal Principles of Editing Old English Verse', *PBA* 70

were human, and therefore fallible,[5] and that the texts which they transmitted could, when in obvious error and probably on other occasions also, scarcely represent what the author had written. Now it is the editor's principal duty to establish what the author wrote; and therefore the manuscripts – in cases where they transmit nonsense, or even something deemed unworthy of the author – require to be emended. The process of *emendatio* or emendation is something which no conscientious editor can avoid. The matter is put incisively by E.J. Kenney, and it is worth quoting his discussion in full:

> *Recensio* may be shirked; *emendatio* cannot be. That is to say, the editor must print something, and what he prints is determined by the choices made at the stage of *emendatio*. His choice may of course be negative, a decision to do nothing by accepting the reading of the transmitted text, but a choice it is; and it is the quality of the choices made at this stage of the editorial process which determines the quality of the final product, the published text. If one sees *emendatio* as essentially consisting in the exercise of critical judgement, then *emendatio* is the activity by which the stature of a critic is apt to be measured, and the doctrinal position (so to call it) of any particular critic is liable to be assessed chiefly in relation to his attitude to *emendatio*. This is not improper, for criticism is, as its name suggests, concerned with judgement.[6]

The process of *emendatio* is an indispensable part of editing a text, and the excellence of Classical editors is indeed judged by their ability to detect error in the transmitted text and to emend it so as to restore what the author *may* originally have written. The boldest editors would say, 'what the author *did* write', and the boldest editors are very bold indeed. A.E. Housman once quoted a *dictum* of Moritz Haupt to the effect that, 'if the sense requires it, I am prepared to write *Constantinopolitanus* where the MSS. have the monosyllabic interjection *o*'.[7] Housman himself was a bold editor who could be utterly scathing about the incompetence (as he judged it) of other less adventurous editors who were content

---

(1984), 231–73; and J.R. Hall, 'Old English Editing', in *Scholarly Editing: an Introduction to Research*, ed. D.C. Greetham (New York, forthcoming).

5   Opinions among editors vary widely on the reliability and accuracy of medieval scribes, depending in particular (it would seem) on the extent of the individual editor's familiarity with medieval manuscripts. An extreme position is adopted by J. Willis (*Latin Textual Criticism*, Illinois Studies in Language and Literature 61 (Chicago, IL, 1972)), for whom all medieval scribes are simply 'monastic blockheads' (p. 12). The opposite view is taken by A. Dain (*Les manuscrits*, 3rd edn (Paris, 1975), pp. 17–18): 'Le copiste est en principe un honnête homme, zélé et appliqué à son travail. Il a d'ordinaire plus de soin et de patience que nous. Nous devrions au contraire admirer l'étonnante fidelité avec laquelle nos scribes ont reproduit telle graphie rare, telle forme désuète, tel vocable qu'ils ne connaissent plus' (p. 17). The truth lies somewhere between these two extremes, for there is no doubt that even the best scribes occasionally nodded. On scribal accuracy in the copying of Old English (prose) texts, there are some valuable remarks by A.C. Amos, *Linguistic Means of Determining the Dates of Old English Literary Texts* (Cambridge, MA, 1980), pp. 171–96, and cf. the discussion of Hall, 'Old English Editing'.

6   *The Classical Text*, pp. 112–13.

7   'The Application of Thought to Textual Criticism', in *The Classical Papers of A.E. Housman*, ed. J. Diggle and F.R.D. Goodyear, 3 vols (Cambridge, 1972) III, 1058–69, at 1065.

simply to print what the manuscripts transmitted.[8] In this respect Housman is not untypical of the tradition of classical editing from Bentley to the present day.

It was against the background of this tradition that, in the early nineteenth century, scholarly editions of Old English verse began to appear. The first edition of *Beowulf* was produced by the Icelander Grímur Jónsson Thorkelin (1752–1829)[9] and printed in 1815 at Copenhagen where Thorkelin was working in the Danish civil service.[10] The Old English poem was presented by Thorkelin exactly as a Classical text might have been: a Latin dedication to Thorkelin's patron, Johann von Bülow, a preface in Latin in which *Beowulf* is compared in various ways with the *Aeneid*,[11] six prefatory hexameters composed by Thorkelin himself, and a Latin translation accompanying the Old English text in an adjacent column. Most revealing is the fact that, in his preface, Thorkelin felt obliged to deliver some scathing remarks about the incompetence of the scribe of the Cottonian manuscript (which he cites erroneously as 'Vitell. A. IX'):

> Caeterum in textu edendo ita versatus sum, ut ab autographo, et vago scribae pro more sui seculi orthographiae mirum negligentis, et alia absurde, alia violenter detorquentis literarum usu ne ungvem latum recedere tutum duxerim.[12]

In spite of his scorn for the scribe, Thorkelin did not venture to emend the transmitted text; my point is simply that, in its presentation and in the attitude of its

---

8 Cf. the remarks in the preface to the first volume of Housman's edition of Manilius, published in 1903: 'An editor of no judgment, perpetually confronted with a couple of MSS to choose from, cannot but feel in every fibre of his being that he is a donkey between two bundles of hay. What shall he do now? Leave criticism to critics, you may say, and betake himself to any honest trade for which he is less unfit. But he prefers a more flattering solution: he confusedly imagines that if one bundle of hay is removed he will cease to be a donkey. So he removes it. Are the two MSS equal, and do they bewilder him with their rival merit and exact from him at every other moment the novel and distressing effort of using his brains? Then he pretends that they are not equal: he calls one of them 'the best MS', and to this he resigns the editorial functions which he is unable to discharge. He adopts its readings when they are better than its fellow's, adopts them when they are no better, adopts them when they are worse: only when they are impossible, or rather when he perceives their impossibility, is he dislodged from his refuge and driven by stress of weather to the other port. This method answers the purpose for which it was devised: it saves lazy editors from working and stupid editors from thinking. But someone has to pay for these luxuries, and that someone is the author . . .' (*M. Manilii Astronomica*, ed. A.E. Housman, 5 vols (London, 1903–30) I, xxxi–xxxii).

9 On whom see *Dansk Biografisk Leksikon* 14 (Copenhagen, 1983), 514–15. See also the essay by J.R. Hall, below, pp. 239–50.

10 *De Danorum Rebus Gestis secul. III & IV* (Copenhagen, 1815).

11 *Ibid.* p. xiii: 'Caetera de creatione mundi relata nihil aliud continent [*scil.* the poem of *Beowulf*] qvam qvae coram Didone et Ænea

cithara crinitus Jopas
Personat aurata, docuit qvae maximus Atlas.'

The quotation is from *Aen.* I. 740–1.

12 *Ibid.* p. xviii: 'Moreover, in editing the text I was so disposed that I did not consider it safe to depart even one jot from the autograph and from the aberrant practice of the scribe, who – in common with his age – is astonishingly ignorant of orthography, misrepresenting some things absurdly, others violently.'

editor, the *editio princeps* of *Beowulf* was produced in the manner then reserved for classical texts.

By any standard, Thorkelin's representation of the transmitted text is appallingly inaccurate. Thorkelin's knowledge of Old English was rudimentary (if that), and no-one with any proficiency in the language would need even to consult the manuscript to correct the text as he printed it. Thus the very nature of the *editio princeps* encouraged the practice of emendation from the outset. In the very year in which Thorkelin's edition appeared, the distinguished Danish scholar and man of letters, Nikolai Frederik Severin Grundtvig (1783–1872),[13] initiated a series of essays in the journal *Nyeste Skilderie af Kjobenhavn* in which he attacked Thorkelin's feeble understanding of the poem which he had just edited; he proposed a substantial number of emendations to Thorkelin's text.[14] Many of Grundtvig's emendations, especially his identification of proper names in the text, have stood the test of time;[15] and it was Grundtvig who first identified Hygelac of the poem with the Chochilaicus mentioned by Gregory of Tours, thereby providing scholars with a fixed terminus for dating the (legendary) events described in the poem.[16] In any event, it was the inadequate nature of Thorkelin's text, in combination with the prevailing spirit of Classical scholarship, which from the outset encouraged the use of *emendatio* to solve the difficulties presented by the transmitted text.

It is interesting to note in passing that, at the time Thorkelin and Grundtvig were conducting their vitriolic public debate on the nature of *Beowulf*, Copenhagen was the home of another Danish scholar who was to become one of the most influential textual critics of the nineteenth century, especially in the domain of conjectural emendation, namely Johan Nicolai Madvig (1804–86).[17] Already by the 1820s Madvig's distinction as a critic was clear from his Master's thesis (*Emendationes in Ciceronis libros de legibus et Academica*, 1826) and his doctoral dissertation (*De Q. Asconii Pediani in Ciceronis Orationes Commentariis*, 1828); but it was during the 1830s that he achieved an international reputation with his edition (1839) of Cicero's *De finibus bonorum et malorum*, one of the greatest of nineteenth-century editions and a classic demonstration of the genealogical or stemmatic method of classifying manuscripts which subsequently became associated with the name of Lachmann.[18] Indeed it was Madvig who first coined the term 'archetype' to

---

13 *Dansk Biografisk Leksikon* 5 (Copenhagen, 1980), 318–27.

14 See F. [D.] Cooley, 'Early Danish Criticism of *Beowulf*', *ELH* 7 (1940), 45–67, esp. 54–8.

15 See B. Kelly, 'The Formative Stages of *Beowulf* Textual Scholarship, part I', *ASE* 11 (1983), 247–74, esp. 253–4 and 259–60.

16 See F.D. Cooley, 'Contemporary Reaction to the Identification of Hygelac', in *Philologica: the Malone Anniversary Studies*, ed. T.A. Kirby and H.B. Woolf (Baltimore, MD, 1949), pp. 269–74.

17 *Dansk Biografisk Leksikon* 9 (1981), 344–8; and see also P.J. Jensen, *J.N. Madvig, avec une esquisse de l'histoire de la philologie classique au Danemark*, trans. A. Nicolet (Odense, 1981).

18 *Ciceronis De finibus*, ed. J.N. Madvig (Copenhagen, 1839), pp. xx–xxi. On the genealogical method of classifying manuscripts, usually referred to as the 'method of Lachmann' but in fact anticipated by Madvig and others, see S. Timpanaro, *La genesi del metodo del Lachmann*, 3rd edn (Padua, 1985), as well as the qualifications suggested by P.L. Schmidt, 'Lachmann's

describe the hypothetical ancestor from which a family of related manuscripts may be demonstrated to descend. Throughout his life, Madvig was interested in the theory as well as the practice of emendation: in what circumstances emendation was permissible or necessary, what controls governed the spirit of conjecture, and so on, and it was Madvig who wrote one of the earliest comprehensive treatises on the theory and practice of conjectural emendation, his 'Artis criticae coniecturalis adumbratio' of 1871.[19] The treatise is inspired throughout by penetrating intelligence, profound learning and common sense: a model of what a treatise on this subject should be.

I mention Madvig not because he has any direct relevance to the Old English work of Thorkelin and Grundtvig, but because he was their contemporary and like them lived and studied in Copenhagen. His work on Classical texts and the theory of textual emendation provides a useful index to the earliest phase of textual criticism of Old English. It was the first half of the nineteenth century which saw the elaboration of modern principles of textual criticism and their application to Classical texts, above all in the work of Madvig and his contemporaries – Jacob Bernays, Carl Gottlob Zumpt, Hermann Sauppe, Friedrich Ritschl, Karl Lachmann and Carolus Gabriel Cobet, to name only the most influential.[20] During this same half century the edition of Old English texts as a scholarly discipline first came into being, albeit with faltering steps in the initial stages. Given the tradition of scholarly edition of Classical texts, and the developments which were taking place in the earlier nineteenth century in the work of scholars such as Madvig, it is not surprising that the edition of Old English texts should have followed suit. We have seen how Thorkelin cloaked his *editio princeps* of *Beowulf* in Latin dress and, after the fashion of the time, prefaced it with some scathing remarks about the accuracy of medieval scribes. The inaccuracy of his text encouraged Grundtvig to set about restoring the original text by the process of emendation. Thus from the very outset contempt for the transmitted text and a corresponding awareness of the need for conjectural emendation were determinant factors in the textual criticism of *Beowulf*.

Textual criticism of *Beowulf* was soon taken up in England, and the same determinant factors were in operation there. Thus in his *Illustrations of Anglo-Saxon Poetry* (1826), the then Professor of Anglo-Saxon at Oxford, John Josiah Conybeare, printed many passages of *Beowulf* and, like Thorkelin before him, accompanied them with Latin translations;[21] like Thorkelin, too, Conybeare had

---

Method: On the History of a Misunderstanding', in *The Uses of Greek and Latin: Historical Essays*, ed. A.C. Dionisotti, A. Grafton and J. Kraye, Warburg Institute Surveys and Texts 16 (London, 1988), 227–36.

[19] J.N. Madvig, *Adversaria critica*, 3 vols (Copenhagen, 1871–84) I, 1–184.

[20] See Wilamowitz-Moellendorff, *History of Classical Scholarship*, trans. Harris and Lloyd-Jones, pp. 130–44.

[21] J.J. Conybeare, *Illustrations of Anglo-Saxon Poetry*, ed. W.D. Conybeare (London, 1826), pp. 82–136. Conybeare also collated the Cottonian manuscript with Thorkelin's printed text and supplied a long list of corrections (pp. 137–55); see K. Malone, 'Conybeare and Thorkelin', *ES*

formed the opinion that the transmitted text was corrupt in many places and concluded that, 'much must still be left to . . . conjectural skill'.[22] Unfortunately, Conybeare's own expertise in Old English was inadequate for the task of editing *Beowulf* – as the young Cambridge Anglo-Saxonist John Mitchell Kemble very quickly and very savagely pointed out[23] – but at least in his attitude to the transmitted text, Conybeare was in sympathy with the prevailing spirit of his times.

It was John Mitchell Kemble (1807–1857)[24] who made the next substantial contribution to the editing of Old English verse with his edition of *Beowulf* in 1833.[25] Although the edition was privately printed in only 100 copies, it marks a decisive watershed in the history of Anglo-Saxon scholarship, for Kemble was the first editor of *Beowulf* – or indeed of any Old English poem – who had sufficient philological expertise for the task. Kemble was a brilliantly gifted scholar who – uniquely at that time in England – was abreast of the best philological work being done in Germany, especially by Jacob Grimm in Göttingen. Kemble dedicated his *Beowulf* to Grimm and conducted a lengthy correspondence with him over many years.[26] This is not the place to review Kemble's impressive achievements in nearly every domain of Anglo-Saxon Studies – philological, historical, archaeological; it is sufficient to remark that, after nearly 150 years of scholarly endeavour in the field in which he was one of the great pioneers, much of his editorial work has yet to be superseded (I am thinking here especially of charters edited in his *Codex Diplomaticus Aevi Saxonici* of 1839–48). Our present concern is with textual criticism. Kemble's edition of *Beowulf*, though published while he was still in his twenties, bears the impress of a master. In his scathing remarks on earlier editors of Old English texts we hear the tone of a Bentley or a Housman.[27] Kemble had been

---

49 (1968), i–xi [ptd in fact in *ES* 50 (1969)], and W.F. Bolton, 'The Conybeare Copy of Thorkelin', *ES* 55 (1974), 97–107, who presented the additional evidence of an annotated copy of Thorkelin's edition formerly in the possession of Conybeare and owned subsequently by Bolton himself.

22 *Ibid*. p. 155.

23 J.M. Kemble, 'Oxford Professors of Anglo-Saxon', *Gentleman's Magazine* n.s. 2 (1834), 601–5, at 602, where he noted that, '. . . it [Conybeare's work on *Beowulf*] is a slovenly and most inaccurate performance . . . that in many cantos . . . plainly proves the Professor not to have understood the meaning of a single line'.

24 There is a learned and sympathetic account of Kemble by B. Dickins, 'John Mitchell Kemble and Old English Scholarship', *PBA* 25 (1939), 51–84, repr. in *British Academy Papers on Anglo-Saxon England*, ed. E.G. Stanley (Oxford, 1990), pp. 57–90; see also R.A. Wiley, 'Anglo-Saxon Kemble: the Life and Works of John Mitchell Kemble 1807–1857, Philologist, Historian, Archaeologist', *ASSAH* 1 (1979), 165–273; and also the essay by J.R. Hall, below, pp. 239–50.

25 J.M. Kemble, *The Anglo-Saxon Poems of Beowulf, the Traveller's Song and the Battle of Finnesburh* (London, 1833); a second edition, with corrigenda, appeared in 1835. See also J.M. Kemble, *A Translation of the Anglo-Saxon Poem of Beowulf* (London, 1837), which includes a glossary and much philological discussion.

26 See *John Mitchell Kemble and Jakob Grimm: a Correspondence, 1832–1852*, ed. R.A. Wiley (Leiden, 1971).

27 See, for example, his remarks in *The Anglo-Saxon Poems*, ed. Kemble, pp. xxix–xxx: 'Nothing but malevolence could cavil at the trivial errors which the very best scholars are daily found to commit, but the case is widely different when those errors are so numerous as totally to destroy

trained (at Trinity College, Cambridge) as a classicist, and his contemptuous attitude to the text as transmitted in medieval manuscripts is very much in keeping with that of early nineteenth-century editors:

> All persons who have had much experience of Anglo-Saxon MSS. know how hopelessly incorrect they in general are . . . which can perhaps only be accounted for by the supposition that professional copyists brought to their task (in itself confusing enough,) both lack of knowledge, and lack of care. A modern edition, made by a person really conversant with the language which he illustrates, will in all probability be much more like the original than the MS. copy, which, even in the earliest times, was made by an ignorant or indolent transcriber.[28]

In such circumstances, as also in places where the manuscript is physically damaged, the conscientious editor must resort to conjecture in order to restore what (in his opinion) might have constituted the original text. Kemble is explicit on the need for editorial intervention at such places. In the case of corruption, he states that, 'corrections, which for the most part either the laws of the grammar or of the versification suggest almost without possibility of error, are added at the foot of each page' [*scil.* of his edition];[29] and again,

> In cases where portions of the text have perished, which has happened unfortunately by the edge of every page, and which is a progressing evil, I have generally from conjecture (if conjecture it can be called, to restore letters to words whose form no scholar can doubt for a moment,) endeavoured to supply the deficiencies: such interpolations are all confined within brackets. Lastly where the MS. seemed to be hopelessly in fault I have marked the passage thus, <†>[30]

The quality of Kemble's work as a textual critic may be gauged from the fact that more of his conjectures on the text of *Beowulf* have been accepted by all modern editors than have those of any other early editor (that is to say, previous to 1857).[31]

---

the value of a work. I am therefore most reluctantly compelled to state that not five lines of Thorkelin's edition can be found in succession, in which some gross fault either in the transcript or the translation, does not betray the editor's utter ignorance of the Anglo-Saxon language. Even the works of Mr. Turner and Professor Conybeare, although in some respects immeasurably superior to Thorkelin's, are marked with mistranslations and false readings of no light kind.' The controversy which Kemble's vitriolic remarks (both here and elsewhere: see above, n. 23) on the incompetence of earlier editors sparked off, is discussed by A.G. Kennedy, 'Odium Philologicum, or, a Century of Progress in English Philology', in *Stanford Studies in Language and Literature 1941*, ed. H. Craig (Stanford, CA, 1941), pp. 11–27, esp. 13–17.

28 *Ibid.* pp. xxiii–xxiv.
29 *Ibid.* p. xxv.
30 *Ibid.* p. xxvi.
31 See Kelly, 'The Formative Stages', pp. 254–5, where eighteen of Kemble's accepted conjectures are listed. For Kemble's overall impact on the text of the poem, see *idem*, 'The Formative Stages of *Beowulf* Textual Scholarship, part II', *ASE* 12 (1984), 239–75, at 270, where it is shown that the total number of Kemble's conjectures (94) which have been either adopted or seriously

I wish merely to stress that the early nineteenth-century editors of *Beowulf* regarded it as part of their duty to identify error in the transmitted text and to correct it to the best of their abilities. It is characteristic of this attitude that when in 1850 the learned Anglo-Saxonist Ludwig Ettmüller published his *Engla and Seaxna Scopas and Boceras*, which contained substantial extracts from *Beowulf*, he announced on his title-page that he *collegit, correxit* and *edidit* the Old English texts contained in his volume.[32] For these nineteenth-century editors, the correction and emendation of the transmitted text was a necessary and indispensable part of their editorial activity.

The tradition of textual criticism initiated in the earlier nineteenth century by Grundtvig, Kemble and Ettmüller continued, and may be said to have reached its apogee in the edition of *Beowulf* produced in 1904 by Moritz Trautmann (1842–1920), then Professor of English at the University of Bonn.[33] Trautmann clearly saw himself as belonging to the tradition of Old English editorial work which I have been delineating: he identified with their assumptions about the corrupt manuscript transmission of the poem, and approved of their readiness to emend it where necessary.[34] He set out his own editorial attitude to the transmitted text with eminent good sense:

> Bei der vorliegenden ausgabe bin ich bestrebt gewesen, die überlieferung weder zu hoch noch zu niedrig anzuschlagen. Nicht zu hoch. Die handschrift wimmelt von groben schreibefehlern und erweist sich schon dadurch als unzuverlässig. Doch auch an sehr vielen stellen, an denen die fehler nicht sofort in die augen springen, ist der text ohne zweifel verderbt. Der Beowulf ist ein klassisches werk, ein gipfel der kunst seiner art; daher sind wir, wo wir auf schiefen ausdruck, unklarheit des gedankens, widersprüche, stilwidrige wendungen, unbelegbare satzfügungen stoßen, berechtigt und verpflichtet, fehlerhafte überlieferung zu vermuten und auf besserung zu denken.[35]

entertained by modern editors of the poem, is more than twice that of his nearest rival among the early editors, namely Ludwig Ettmüller (on whom see below, n. 32).

[32] L. Ettmüller, *Engla and Seaxna Scopas and Boceras* (Quedlinburg, 1850). Ettmüller's book was dedicated to Jacob Grimm, John Mitchell Kemble and Benjamin Thorpe – an interesting indication of the editorial tradition in which Ettmüller conceived himself to be working. On Ettmüller as textual critic, see briefly Lapidge, 'Textual Criticism', pp. 38–9.

[33] *Das Beowulflied*, ed. M. Trautmann, Bonner Beiträge zur Anglistik 16 (Bonn, 1904).

[34] *Ibid.* p. iv: 'Die älteren herausgeber, Kemble, Thorpe, Ettmüller, Grein, Grundtvig, waren sich voll bewusst, dass die überlieferung des Beowulf äußerst fehlerhaft ist. In diesem bewusstsein haben sie viele änderungen vorgenommen, und es ist anzuerkennen, dass besonders Kemble, Thorpe, Ettmüller und Grein den üblen text an zahlreichen stellen glücklich und überzeugend berichtigt haben.'

[35] *Ibid.* pp. iv–v: 'In the present edition I have been anxious to rate the transmitted text neither too highly nor too poorly. Certainly not too highly. The manuscript is crawling with gross scribal errors and thus shows itself to be unreliable. Yet even in many places in which such errors do not immediately strike the eye the text is undoubtedly corrupt. *Beowulf* is a classic work, a highpoint of its kind of art; accordingly, when we come upon awkward expressions, unclear thinking, contradictions, stylistically incongruous phrases, unattested constructions, we are justified – and indeed obliged – to assume corrupt transmission and to contemplate emendation.'

Given this attitude to the transmitted text of *Beowulf*, Trautmann undertook to emend it as he thought necessary. He has been accused of violent and wilful emendation; but he explains his own attitude to emendation with eminent good sense once again:

> Das aber kann ich sagen, dass ich nie ohne zwingenden grund, wenigstens für mich zwingenden grund, geändert habe, so dass ich viele meiner änderungen mit einiger zuversicht vorlege; eine nicht ganz kleine zahl freilich hab ich gewagt nicht sowol in der überzeugung das richtige geben zu können, als in dem wunsche recht nachdrücklich zu sagen 'hier kann das überlieferte nicht richtig sein', und so die mitstrebenden zur ergründung und beseitigung des fehlers aufzufordern.[36]

In the conviction that the transmitted text of *Beowulf* was corrupt, Trautmann emended it on more occasions than recent editors would dare or would think necessary.[37] In doing so he very frequently helped to probe and elucidate the meaning of passages in which the meaning is not entirely clear, and thereby rendered a valuable service to the study of the poem.[38] But in his readiness to emend the text, Trautmann provoked the indignation of even the boldest of editors, and reaction very quickly set in.

In fact by the time Trautmann's *Beowulf* appeared in 1904, the spirit of reaction against emendation had steadily been growing for many years. Already in 1857 Christian Grein had emphasized the need to 'salvage' (the verb which he used was *retten*) wherever possible the reading of the transmitted text,[39] and Grein's emphasis was reinforced two years later by his friend and colleague F.E.C. Dietrich, who in 1859 published an article entitled 'Rettungen', which might be rendered as 'salvage operations'.[40] In this article Dietrich demonstrated persuasively that many passages of Old English verse which had been emended by previous editors

---

[36] *Ibid*. p. v: 'I can, however, say this: that I have not altered anything without a compelling reason – at least compelling for me – so that I present many of my alterations with some confidence; I propose no small number of these not in the conviction that I am restoring the correct reading, but rather in the hope of being able to say that "at this point the transmitted text cannot be right", and thereby to help students of the text in the exploration and elimination of error.'

[37] It is not possible to form a clear impression of Trautmann's treatment of the poem without studying his text line by line; but note, for example, Trautmann's conjectures to passages in which all editors assume corruption, such as lines 149, 157, 166–7 (plus lacuna), 306, 389–90, 445, etc.

[38] Cf. the remarks of Kenneth Sisam, who – like Trautmann – was not too timid to challenge the authority of the transmitted text in places where its meaning was dubious: '. . . there would be a real gain if conjecture, instead of being reserved for the useful but disheartening task of dealing with obvious or desperate faults, were restored to its true functions, which include probing as well as healing' (*Studies in the History of Old English Literature* (Oxford, 1953), p. 44).

[39] *Bibliothek der angelsächsischen Poesie I*, ed C.M.W. Grein (Göttingen, 1857), p. iv: 'Bei der Behandlung des Textes galt als erste Pflicht, handschriftliche Lesarten, wo es nur immer möglich war, zu retten . . .'

[40] [F.E.C.] Dietrich, 'Rettungen', *Zeitschrift für deutsches Altertum und deutsche Literatur* 11 (1859), 409–48; see also discussion by Stanley, 'Unideal Principles', p. 241.

deserved to stand as transmitted. The lead given by Grein and Dietrich was soon followed by other editors of Old English. Thus in 1883 Richard Wülcker prefaced his edition of *Beowulf* by saying that he had followed Grein's precedent and concerned himself as far as possible to preserve the readings of the manuscript.[41] Wülcker was as good as his word: his edition of the poem is purely diplomatic, with the text set out not in lines of verse but exactly as it is copied in the manuscript, including its capitalization, punctuation and word-division. The same editorial attitude was adopted by A.J. Wyatt in his 1894 edition of *Beowulf*: although Wyatt did not follow Wülcker in presenting the text diplomatically, he went one better than Wülcker by asserting that he had 'indulged but sparingly in the luxury of personal emendations, because they are obviously the greatest disqualification for discharging duly the functions of an editor'.[42] Here we see in a nutshell the profound difference in attitude which now separates editors of Classical works from those who edit Old English texts: whereas (to repeat the words of E.J. Kenney quoted earlier) for classical editors '*emendatio* is the activity by which the stature of a critic is apt to be measured', and hence is the principal qualification for undertaking an edition, for Wyatt – and the majority of Old English editors after him – the willingness to emend a text is the principal disqualification.

In any case, it is clear from Wyatt's remarks that, by the 1890s, the conservative approach to the editing of Old English texts was growing in strength and confidence. Then, ten years later, came Trautmann's edition of *Beowulf*. The appearance of this edition threw conservative editors into a frenzy. Eduard Sievers accused Trautmann of substituting 'personal arbitrariness of judgement' for 'patient familiarization with . . . the text':

> Here, if I understand the situation correctly, it is not a question of a few conjectures or interpretations quickly dashed off . . . they are rather for me symptomatic of something deeper. They reveal to me at every step, even if perhaps unconsciously, a programmatic tendency: the tendency, in the treatment of our ancient poetry, to substitute personal arbitrariness of judgement for patient familiarization with the specific problems of the text. With sublime indifference Trautmann passes over delicate questions of usage, style, development of thought and similar matters: only personal taste and individual preference are taken as guidelines. Such procedure does not bring honour, but only disgrace, to our subject . . .[43]

---

[41] *Das Beowulfslied*, ed. R.P. Wülcker, Bibliothek der angelsächsischen Poesie, 3 vols (Kassel, 1883–98) I, viii: 'In bezug auf die textherstellung habe ich mich, nach Grein's vorgang, bemüht möglichst die lesungen der handschrift zu wahren.'

[42] *Beowulf*, ed. A.J. Wyatt (Cambridge, 1894), p. xii.

[43] E. Sievers, 'Zum Beowulf', *BGDSL* 29 (1904), 305–41, at 305: 'Hier handelt es sich, wenn ich die sachlage richtig verstehe, nicht um ein paar hingeworfene conjecturen oder deutungen . . . für mich haben sie vielmehr eine symptomatische bedeutung. Sie verraten mir auf schritt und tritt eine, wenn auch vielleicht unbewusst, programmatische tendenz: die tendenz, bei der behandlung unserer alten dichtungen persönliche willkür des urteils an die stelle geduldiger vertiefung in die zur rede stehenden probleme zu setzen. Ueber alle intimeren fragen des sprachgebrauchs, des stils, der gedankenführung und ähnliche dinge geht Trautmann souverän

Sievers created the impression that Trautmann's work on the poem was slapdash and ill-considered (which it manifestly was not, whatever one makes of his solutions to individual problems), and although Trautmann replied sharply to Sievers's remarks,[44] the impression remained (and yet remains). Thus Frederick Tupper Jr, in an article of 1910 entitled 'Textual Criticism as a Pseudo-Science',[45] reacted violently against Trautmann and his Bonn school of textual criticism. For Tupper, emendation was tantamount to 'arrant guesswork', and he went so far as to question whether emendation was ever in any circumstances justified: 'The proper attitude to this slaughter of transmitted forms is not to ask whether the critic is happy or unhappy in his emendation, but rather whether any emendation is necessary'.[46] The same conservative spirit animated R.W. Chambers, who in 1920 issued a revised version of Wyatt's edition of *Beowulf*. Chambers's attitude to the transmitted text is even more conservative than Wyatt's (if that is possible): 'I have therefore followed, and indeed bettered, Mr Wyatt's example: he made few personal emendations: I have made none.'[47] Then, like so many conservative critics,[48] Chambers went on to justify his conservative attitude by appeal to (what he conceived as) the excesses of Trautmann:

> For, indeed, conjectural emendation has been allowed to run riot. Advocates of a conservative text are often taunted with credulous belief in the letter of the manuscript . . . But, in fact, the charge of superstitious credulity might more justly be brought against those who believe that, with the miserably inadequate means at our disposal, we *can* exactly restore the original text. Prof. Trautmann assures us that the extant manuscript is grossly faulty, and on the strength of this belief puts forth an edition full of the most drastic and daring alterations. But, if we grant (for sake of argument) that the manuscript is as grossly

---

hinweg: nur der eigene geschmack und das individuelle belieben wird zur richtschnur genommen. Ein solches verfahren, das unserer wissenschaft nicht zur ehre, nur zum schaden gereicht.'

[44] M. Trautmann, 'Auch zum Beowulf, ein gruß an herren Eduard Sievers', *Bonner Beiträge zur Anglistik* 17 (1905), 143–74; see esp. 146: '. . . bin vielmehr der meinung geblieben dass ich stets mit allem ernst und mit ehrlichem bemühen die sich erhebenden fragen erwäge . . . Gewiss, ich verhaue mich trotz aller sorgfalt zuweilen ganz hübsch, wie es jedem, auch dem besten widerfährt; dem aber, der mich leichtfertiges urteilens beschuldigt, dem ruf ich entgegen: "das leugst du, Plump von Pommerland".'

[45] *PMLA* 25 (1910), 164–81.

[46] *Ibid.* p. 166.

[47] *Beowulf with the Finnsburg Fragment*, ed. A.J. Wyatt, rev. R.W. Chambers (Cambridge, 1920), p. xxvii.

[48] Cf., once again, Housman's remarks: 'The average man, if he meddles with criticism at all, is a conservative critic. His opinions are determined not by reason, – 'the bulk of mankind' says Swift 'is as well qualified for flying as for thinking,' – but by his passions; and the faintest of all human passions is the love of truth. He believes that the text of ancient authors is generally sound, not because he has acquainted himself with the elements of the problem, but because he would feel uncomfortable if he did not believe it; just as he believes, on the same cogent evidence, that he is a fine fellow, and that he will rise again from the dead' (*M. Manilii Astronomica*, ed. Housman I, xliii).

erroneous as Prof. Trautmann's emendations postulate, then it follows that it is too bad to afford a sound basis for conjectural emendation at all.[49]

And since we cannot be absolutely sure where the transmitted text is sound, so Chambers reasons, it is safer to do nothing and to reproduce the text as preserved in the manuscript.

By 1920 the main battle-lines in the debate were drawn: on the one hand were those like Kemble, Ettmüller and Trautmann who were prepared to emend the transmitted text where they judged it to be corrupt; and, on the other, those like Wülcker, Wyatt and Chambers who were determined to conserve the text as transmitted, on the grounds that we have insufficient knowledge to emend it. The next textual critic who entered this debate, Johannes Hoops, attempted to adjudicate the merits of both positions, and to steer a middle course between them. In an article on the textual criticism of *Beowulf*, published in 1932,[50] Hoops enunciated as a fundamental principle the fact that the critic 'should alter the transmitted text as little as possible' (*so wenig wie möglich ändern*); emendations should be attempted only in clear cases of scribal error, or where the transmitted text still yielded no sense after every attempt to elucidate it had been tried:

> Änderungen des überkommenen Textes sollten nur dann vorgenommen werden, wenn es sich um offensichtliche Schreibfehler handelt, oder wenn die Lesart des Textes nach Erwägung aller Erklärungsmöglichkeiten keinen Sinn gibt. Daß der Text der Handschrift, so wie er auf uns gekommen ist, zahlreiche Schreibfehler, Mißverständnisse, Entstellungen, Auslassungen enthält, kann nicht bestritten werden; eine lange Reihe solcher Fehler ist seit den Zeiten von Thorkelin, Kemble, Grundtvig, Thorpe und Grein durch unermüdliche kritische Arbeit zahlreicher Forscher richtig gestellt worden . . .[51]

Yet in spite of his opinion that the text was undoubtedly corrupt in places, and that the early editors had rightly corrected it in such places, Hoops was prepared to emend only in the most flagrant cases of corruption. In other words, he sided on the whole with the conservatives. And since Hoops's time, the conservatives have gained the ascendancy, with the result that they have now silenced the opposition of those critics who would in principle think that corruptly transmitted texts require to be emended. This much is clear from the most recent discussion of the principles

---

[49] *Beowulf with the Finnsburg Fragment*, ed. Wyatt, rev. Chambers, p. xxvii.

[50] 'Grundsätzliches zur Textkritik der *Beowulf*', in his *Beowulfstudien*, Anglistische Forschungen 74 (Heidelberg, 1932), 1–13.

[51] *Ibid.* p. 12: 'Alterations to the transmitted text should only be undertaken if there is a clear case of scribal corruption, or if the reading of the text yields no sense after every effort to explain it has been tried. That the text of the manuscript, as it has come down to us, contains numerous scribal errors, misunderstandings, interpolations and omissions, cannot be disputed; a long list of such errors has rightly been brought to light through the tireless critical labours of numerous scholars since the time of Thorkelin, Kemble, Grundtvig, Thorpe and Grein.'

of Old English textual criticism – that by E.G. Stanley – which concludes with the following statement:

> We should feel happiest as editors when we have demonstrated that a manuscript reading, spurned and excised by previous editors, deserves to stand in the text. A *Rettung* is worth more than a palmary emendation.[52]

These sentiments would have seemed very salutary in 1860, no doubt; but after a century and more of conservative criticism, one wonders whether there are any readings left to 'salvage'. Certainly the ghost of Trautmann has long since been laid, and there are very few, if any, editors of Old English literature who nowadays resort as a matter of course to emendation in cases where they are confronted by (what they judge to be) corrupt transmission.

On the contrary, the prevailing attitude of modern editors of Old English texts is conservative through and through.[53] In setting out guidelines for the preparation of texts to be used by the *Dictionary of Old English*, Helmut Gneuss in 1973 delineated this attitude precisely:

> Editors of OE prose and poetry have hardly ever made an attempt to reconstruct a critical text from the variant readings of several MSS or by means of conjectural emendation, as is feasible and usual in classical texts. Editors of OE texts have generally tended to be very conservative, and quite a number could actually be called diplomatic, that is, they reproduce the text exactly as it stands in the MS. For various reasons . . . it seems desirable to continue this general policy in future editions and to produce editions of OE texts in a conservative or even diplomatic form.[54]

The advice given here seems to have been followed universally by editors of Old English texts who have published editions since 1973: indeed, Gneuss's words served as the focal point for discussion in the opening address by Donald Scragg

---

[52] Stanley, 'Unideal Principles', p. 273. On Stanley's misunderstanding and misuse of the word 'palmary', see Lapidge, 'Textual Criticism', p. 44, n. 114. One might expect a basic understanding of the terminology of a discipline from those who would enunciate its principles.

[53] The saurian 'principles' advocated by Stanley and others bring some remarks of Housman forcibly to mind: 'It would not be true to say that all conservative scholars are stupid, but it is very near the truth to say that all stupid scholars are conservative. Defenders of corruptions are therefore assured beforehand of wide approval; and this is demoralizing. They need not seriously consider what they say, because they are addressing an audience whose intelligence is despicable and whose hearts are won already; and they use pretexts which nobody would venture to put forward in any other cause' (*M. Annaei Lucani Belli Civilis Libri Decem*, ed. A.E. Housman (Oxford, 1926), p. xxvii).

[54] *A Plan for the Dictionary of Old English*, ed. R. Frank and A. Cameron (Toronto, 1973), p. 15, repr. above, pp. 14–15. On the question of emendation, Gneuss (*ibid.*) has expressed – more or less – the views of Hoops: 'This is not the place to discuss the pros and cons of emendation. I would suggest, however, that editorial emendations to OE texts be avoided unless there is an obvious mistake or omission in the MS, and then only if the emendation is based upon sufficient evidence from variant readings in other MSS or upon other reliable criteria.'

delivered to the Manchester Conference, and have been reprinted here (above, pp. 7–26) by way of encouraging further discussion. Two examples will illustrate the point briefly. In her edition of the *Guthlac* poems, Jane Roberts stated unequivocally that her 'texts are presented in a conservative edition'.[55] And in his edition of *Genesis A*, A.N. Doane justified the conservative principles on which his text is based as follows:

> My editing principles have been more conservative than those of previous editors of *Genesis A* . . . even in cases where the text obviously seems to be disturbed, I have made every effort to construe the text as it stands, perhaps erring too far in this direction . . . I have regarded every emendation as, strictly speaking, a logical absurdity, and practically speaking, a small defeat, an abandonment of the text . . .[56]

We have heard this 'logic' before: it is the logic of Wyatt, and Chambers after him, reacting against the textual criticism of Trautmann. Doane's statements represent (in my view) the nadir of conservative criticism: for it can be no benefit to the text, and certainly none to the reader, if the editor on principle refuses to intervene in the text even where it 'obviously seems to be disturbed'. In erecting such principles, modern editors – and Doane is an extreme, but not an isolated, example – have lost sight of the cardinal tenet of textual criticism, that of establishing what the author wrote.

During the past 175 years the textual criticism of Old English literature has veered from one extreme pole to the other: from deep suspicion of the transmitted text, and a correspondingly ready (and sometimes reckless) impulse to emend it, to the comprehensive rejection of emendation as a text-critical tool advocated by modern conservative critics. Perhaps this polarity will not strike students of human nature as surprising.[57] The proper approach to the transmitted text lies somewhere between the two poles: the critic must exercise due suspicion about the transmitted text, but must not emend it for reasons of impatience or mere querulousness. The matter is put judiciously by Kenney:

> A good critic will try, if he knows his business, to cultivate both radical and conservative habits of thought as may be appropriate. On the one hand he will nurture what Bentley called the *animus suspicax*; on the other he will respect

---

[55] *The Guthlac Poems of the Exeter Book*, ed. J. Roberts (Oxford, 1979), p. 82.

[56] *Genesis A: a New Edition*, ed. A.N. Doane (Madison, WI, 1978), pp. x–xi.

[57] Cf. Kenney, *The Classical Text*, p. 113: 'Traditionally, and unfortunately, textual criticism has always been and no doubt always will be affected by two opposed attitudes, which spring from the personal temperament of the critic. As Gilbert nearly wrote, "Every boy and every girl who's born into this world alive, Is either a little radical or else a little conservative". The dichotomy, however firmly rooted in human nature, is scientifically false and misleading, as Leo insisted: "Criticism is neither conservative nor liberal; it distinguishes the false from the true". It is probably too deeply innate ever to be eradicated.'

the principle that the transmitted text . . . may be altered only when it is *demonstrably* faulty.[58]

It is in the light of these remarks that I am pleading, on behalf of Old English editors, for a more balanced attitude to the transmitted text than prevails in the present climate of conservatism.

I began these reflections by observing that Latin and English texts were often composed by the same Anglo-Saxon authors and copied by the same Anglo-Saxon scribes: the implication of this observation being that we should logically apply the same text-critical principles to Old English texts as are – and have been for centuries – applied to Latin texts. The Manchester Conference provided an appropriate opportunity to reassess the principles which are currently followed by editors. We have a responsibility as editors to conserve the transmitted text when it is sound, but – and here I dissent from prevailing opinion – to emend it when it is not. There is no need to shrink from emendation, and no justification for doing so. No doubt these remarks will provoke rage and fury in conservative editors: their conservative attitudes provoke me to rage and fury. But I hope that, when the rage and fury have passed, it will be seen that the editor's first duty is not to dictionary-makers, not to beginning students, not to historians, not to 'trouble-makers', nor to all the other constituencies whose requirements were canvassed at the Manchester Conference, but to someone far more important than any of these – the author.[59]

---

[58] *Ibid.* pp. 113–14.

[59] In discussion following this paper at Manchester an interesting point was raised by Professor J.D. Niles, who suggested that, given the reworkings which Old English poems underwent at the hands of scribes, it is inappropriate to think in terms of one 'author'. This question has recently been addressed in detail by Katherine O'Brien O'Keeffe, *Visible Song: Transitional Literacy in Old English Verse*, CSASE 4 (Cambridge, 1990), a book which – *pace* the foolish comments of the reviewer in *N & Q* n.s. 38 (1991), 199–200 – needs to be digested by anyone seriously interested in the transmission of Old English poetry.

NEW CRITERIA FOR EDITING *BEOWULF*

D. R. Howlett

'IN THE BEGINNING was the Word, and the Word was with God, and God was the Word. He was in the beginning with God. All things through Him came into being, and without Him came into being not one thing. What came into being in Him was life, and the life was the light of men. And the light in the darkness shines, and the darkness has not overcome it.'

We may safely infer that a Christian poet like the author of *Beowulf* knew this text, the Prologue to St John's Gospel, I.1–5, by heart. He would have heard these most famous words of the New Testament said or sung as the Gospel for the Eucharist on Christmas Day. He would have read them many times. What might he have seen in them? This?[1]

A1	Εν αρχηι	In principio
2	ην	erat
3	ο λογος	Verbum
4	και ο λογος	et Verbum
5	ην	erat
6	προς τον θεον	apud Deum
7	και	et
6'	θεος	Deus
5'	ην	erat
4'	ο λογος	Verbum
3'	ουτος	Hoc
2'	ην	erat
1'	εν αρχηι προς τον θεον.	in principio apud Deum .
B1	Παντα	Omnia
2	δια αυτου εγενετο	per ipsum facta sunt
3	και	et
2'	χωρις αυτου εγενετο	sine ipso factum est
1'	ουδε εν.	nihil .
C1	Ο γεγονεν εν αυτωι	Quod factum est in ipso
2	ζωη ην	vita erat
3	και	et

---

1 *The Greek New Testament*, ed. K. Aland *et al.*, 3rd edn corr. (Stuttgart, 1983); *Biblia Sacra Iuxta Vulgatam Versionem*, ed. B. Fischer *et al.* (Stuttgart, 1969).

2'	η ζωη ην	vita erat
1'	το φως των ανθρωπων.	lux hominum .
D1	Και το φως εν τηι σκοτιαι φαινει	Et lux in tenebris lucet
1'	και η σκοτια αυτο ου κατελαβεν.	et tenebrae eam non comprehenderunt .

The author's idea at the beginning of the first half of A, 'In the beginning', and the idea at the end of the first half of A, 'with God', are restated together at the end of the second half of A, 'in the beginning with God'. Everything else is chiastically disposed. Compare 'was' in 2 with 'was' in 2', 'the Word' in 3 with 'He, the same' in 3', 'the Word' in 4 with 'the Word' in 4', 'was' in 5 with 'was' in 5', 'with God' in 6 with 'God' in 6', around the central 'and' 7.

Again the author writes chiastically in B, balancing 'all things' in 1 with 'not one thing' in 1', 'through Him came into being' in 2 with 'without Him came into being' in 2', around the central 'and' in 3.

Yet again he writes chiastically in C, balancing 'what came into being in Him' in 1 with 'the light of men' in 1', 'life was' in 2 with 'life was' in 2', around the central 'and' in 3.

Finally he writes parallel in D, balancing 'And the light in the darkness shines' in 1 with 'and the darkness has not overcome it' in 1'.

Observe the incremental unfolding of ideas. First the author defines his subject as one with God twice. Second he combines 'Him' with 'came into being' twice. Third he puts 'Him' and 'came into being' together with 'life', mentioned twice, which he defines as 'light'. Fourth he contrasts 'light' with 'darkness' twice. His thought runs first 'in the beginning God', second 'He being or becoming or making', third 'He begetting life', 'life light', and fourth 'light shining triumphant'. Ten of the verbs are past or aorist or perfect, but this one verb 'shines' is present.

These chiastic and parallel structures, coinciding exactly with the statement and incremental restatement of ideas, are as clear as they could possibly be. There is not the slightest doubt about where they begin and where they end, nor about what they say. But there is more to them than this.

Counting the words in A one finds twenty-four, arranged twelve and twelve. In B there are ten, arranged five and five. In C there are fourteen, arranged seven and seven. In D there are thirteen, of which the seventh and central is the one present tense verb of the entire passage, 'shines'.

There is more. Counting the syllables in A one finds thirty-three, arranged sixteen – one – sixteen. In B there are twenty-two, arranged eleven – eleven. In C there are twenty-one, arranged eleven – ten. In D there are twenty-three syllables, eleven in the first clause and twelve in the second. These symmetries of word and syllable are apprehensible by ear. But there are more, apprehensible only by eye.

Counting the letters in A one finds seventy-seven, arranged thirty-seven – three – thirty-seven. In B there are forty-six, arranged twenty-three – twenty-three. In C there are forty-five, arranged twenty-three – twenty-two. In D there are twenty-six letters in the first clause and twenty-five in the second. But by following the variant reading αυτον, assuming that the antecedent was masculine λογος or ουτος or αυτος rather than neuter φως, there would be twenty-six letters in each clause.

All these symmetries are either perfect or within one of perfection. The author grabs and holds our attention with chiastic and parallel statement and incremental restatement, and whether we consider ideas or meanings of words or numbers of words or numbers of syllables or numbers of letters the centre is always in the same place. Symmetries for the ear and the eye. But there is more.

The number of words in the entire passage is 61, which divides by golden section or extreme and mean ratio[2] at 38 and 23. As the thirty-eighth word from the beginning and the twenty-third word from the end are αυτωι ζωη, the golden section of the Prologue falls at 'in Him life'. The number of syllables is 99, which divides by extreme and mean ratio at 61 and 38. (Note the sequence: 23+38=61, 38+61=99). The sixty-first syllable from the beginning and the thirty-eighth syllable from the end are in αυτωι. The number of letters is 219, which divides by extreme and mean ratio at 135 and 84. The 135th letter from the beginning and the eighty-fourth letter from the end are in the centre of αυτωι.[3]

This Prologue prefigures the structure of the entire Gospel. The passage which follows, chapter I verse 6, the beginning of the Gospel proper, reads, 'There was a man sent from God whose name was John. He came for testimony, to bear witness to the light'. The chiastic pair to this is chapter XXI verse 24, 'This is the disciple who is bearing witness to these things and who has written these things, and we know that his testimony is true.' The former passage alludes to St John the Baptist, testimony, and witness; the latter alludes to witness, testimony, and St John the Evangelist, whose name is thus built into the fabric of the work without being explicitly mentioned.

When one has begun to appreciate the literary competence of a man who can write like this it is hard to accept the scholarly judgement of a critic who thinks that the Prologue 'remains intolerably clumsy and opaque' and that 'it is more consistent with the Johannine repetitive style, as well as with Johannine doctrine, to say nothing concerning the sense of the passage, to punctuate with a full stop after ὃ γέγονεν.'[4]

---

[2] For discussion of division by golden section or extreme and mean ratio see the appendix.

[3] What might these numbers represent? Beginning with part A, one recalls from the number of words that there were 12 tribes, 12 apostles, and 24 elders in the Apocalypse; from the number of syllables that the age of Jesus was 16+1+16; from the number of letters that He was in the wilderness 37+3 days and that there were 3+37 days from the Resurrection to the Ascension. In the account of the perfection of Sabbath rest after Creation in Genesis II.1–4 there are 46 Hebrew words. In the Vulgate account of Creation in Job XXXVIII.4–7 there are 46 Latin words. The numerical value of the Greek letters of the name ΑΔΑΜ is 1+4+1+40=46. As the works of men should reflect the work of God in Creation it took, according to John II.20, 46 years to build the Temple. So in B the number of letters in the account of Christ's Creation of the universe is 46, a figure reproduced in the Vulgate account of the same passage.

[4] B.M. Metzger, *A Textual Commentary on the Greek New Testament*, corr. ed. (London and New York, 1975), p. 196.

To discover where St John learned to write like this one need look no further than his first two words, which are quoted from Genesis I.1. Although he wrote in Greek he could not have learned this mode of composition from the Septuagint, which does not exhibit these features in Genesis I.1–II.4. He must have learned them from the Hebrew Bible.[5]

In Jerome's Vulgate translation of the Prologue there are nineteen words in A, arranged nine – one – nine; thirty-seven syllables, arranged eighteen – one – eighteen; eighty-three letters, arranged forty-one – two – forty. In B there are eleven words, arranged five – one – five; nineteen syllables, arranged nine – one – nine; forty-six letters, arranged twenty-two – two – twenty-two. In C there are twelve words, arranged eight – four, the golden section of 12 falling at 7.4 and 4.6; twenty syllables, arranged twelve – eight, the golden section of 20 falling at 12 and 8; forty-seven letters, arranged twenty-nine – eighteen, the golden section of 47 falling at 29 and 18. In D there are ten words, five in the first clause and five in the second; twenty syllables, twelve in the first clause and eight in the second, the golden section of 20 falling at 12 and 8; fifty-one letters, twenty in the first clause and thirty-one in the second, the golden section of 51 falling at 31.5 and 19.5.

God is mentioned three times (3×1). The first example *Deum* is the ninth word (3×3). From the first *Deum* to the second *Deus* inclusive there are three words (3×1). From the second *Deus* to the third *Deum* inclusive there are nine words (3×3). After that there are thirty-three words (3×11) to the end of the Prologue. The verb *facere* appears three times, first as *facta*, the fourth word (4×1) of part B. Between the first *facta* and the second *factum* there are four words. After *factum* the fourth word is *factum*, after which there are twenty words (4×5) to the end of the Prologue. The fourth word after *factum* is *vita*. From *vita* to *vita* inclusive there are four words. From *lux* to *lux* inclusive there are four words. From *tenebris* to *tenebrae* inclusive there are four words, and *tenebrae* is the fourth word from the end of the Prologue.

The author of *Beowulf* understood these compositional rules, which he applied throughout the poem.[6]

> **HWÆT WE GARDE**na   in geardagum .
> þeodcyninga   þrym gefrunon
> hu ða æþelingas   ellen fremedon .
>
> **O**ft Scyld Scefing   sceaþena þreatum
> monegum mægþum   meodosetla ofteah   5
> egsode eorl   syððan ærest wearð
> feasceaft funden   he þæs frofre gebad

5 D. Howlett, 'The Story of Creation, Genesis 1.2–2.4', *Birthday Celebration for Naky Doniach O.B.E.*, ed. G. Cigman and D. Howlett (Oxford, 1991), pp. 1–13.

6 *Heyne-Schückings Beowulf*, ed. E. von Schaubert, 18th edn (Paderborn, 1963); *Beowulf Reproduced in Facsimile . . . With a Transliteration and Notes by Julius Zupitza*, 2nd edn (with an introductory note by N. Davis), EETS 245 (London, 1959; repr. 1967); *The Nowell Codex*, ed. K. Malone, EEMF XII (Copenhagen, 1963).

weox under wolcnum   weorðmyndum þah .
oðþæt him æghwylc   þara ymbsittendra
ofer hronrade   hyran scolde   10
gomban gyldan   þæt wæs god cyning .

ðæm eafera wæs   æfter cenned
geong in geardum   þonc God sende
folce to frofre   fyrenðearfe ongeat
þæt hie ær drugon   aldorlease .   15
lange hwile   him þæs Liffre[ge]a
Wuldres Wealdend   woruldare forgeaf .
Beow wæs breme   blæd wide sprang
Scyldes eafera   Scedelandum in .

Swa sceal geong guma   gode gewyrcean   20
fromum feohgiftum .   on fæder bearme
þæt hine on ylde   eft gewunigen
wilgesiþas   þonne wig cume .
leode gelæsten   lofdædum sceal
in mægþa gehwære   man geþeo[ha]n .   25

Him ða Scyld gewat   to gescæphwile
felahror feran   on Fre[ge]an wære
Hi hyne þa ætbæron   to brimes faroðe
swæse gesiþas   swa he selfa bæd
þenden wordum weold   wine Scyldinga   30
leof landfruma   lange ahte
Þær æt hyðe stod   hringedstefna
isig 7 utfus   æþelinges fær .
aledon þa   leofne þeoden
beaga bryttan   on bearm scipes   35
mærne be mæste   þær wæs madma fela
of feorwegum   frætwa gelæded .
Ne hyrde ic cymlicor   ceol gegyrwan
hildewæpnum   7 heaðowædum
billum 7 byrnum   him on bearme læg   40
madma mænigo   þa him mid scoldon
on flodes æht   feor gewitan .
Nalæs hi hine læssan   lacum teodan
þeodgestreonum   þon þa dydon
þe hine æt frumsceafte   forð onsendon   45
ænne ofer yðe   umborwesende
Þa gyt hie him asetton   segen gyldenne
heah ofer heafod   leton holm beran
geafon on garsecg   him wæs geomor sefa
murnende mod   Men ne cunnon .   50
secgan to soðe   selerædenne
hæleð under heofenum   hwa þæm hlæste onfeng .

The poet begins, as he means to go on, in Biblical style.[7]

A1	in geardagum	1'	ða
2	þeodcyninga	2'	æþelingas
3	þrym	3'	ellen

The poem consists of three parts centred around fights with three monsters. The Prologue begins with three lines containing a parallelism of three parts each. The poet speaks of 'days gone by', of 'kings', and their 'might'; 'then', of 'princes', and their 'strength'. There are two lines in the first part and one line in the second, together three, which divide by extreme and mean ratio at 2 and 1. There are eight words in the first part and five in the second, together thirteen, which divide by extreme and mean ratio at 8 and 5. There are seventeen syllables in the first part and eleven in the second, together twenty-eight, which divide by extreme and mean ratio at 17 and 11.

Two verse paragraphs follow in lines 4–11 and 12–19.

B1a	Oft Scyld Scefing
bi	monegum mægþum
ii	meodosetla
iii	egsode
iv	ærest wearð feasceaft funden
c	weox
d	under wolcnum
d'	weorðmyndum
c'	þah .
b'i	æghwylc
ii	ymbsittendra
iii	hyran scolde
iv	gomban gyldan
a'	þæt wæs god cyning .

---

7   For earlier discussions of this form of structure see A.C. Bartlett, *The Larger Rhetorical Patterns in Anglo-Saxon Poetry* (New York, 1935); D.R. Howlett, 'Form and Genre in *Beowulf*', *Studia Neophilologica* XLVI (1974), 309–25; C.B. Hieatt, 'Envelope Patterns and the Structure of *Beowulf*', *English Studies in Canada* I (1975), 249–65; T.E. Hart, 'Calculated Casualties in *Beowulf*: Geometrical Scaffolding and Verbal Symbol', *Studia Neophilologica* LIII (1981), 3–35; J.D. Niles, *Beowulf* (Cambridge, MA, 1983); D.R. Howlett, 'Biblical Style in Early Insular Latin', *Sources of Anglo-Saxon Culture*, ed. P.E. Szarmach and V.D. Oggins (Kalamazoo, 1986), 127–47; *Idem*, '*Ex Saliva Scripturae Meae*', *Sages, Saints and Storytellers*, ed. D. Ó Corráin *et al.* (Maynooth, 1989), 86–101; *Idem*, 'A Verse Critique of the Brendan Legend', *Bodleian Library Record* XIV (1992), 125–35; *Idem*, '*Orationes Moucani*: Early Cambro-Latin Prayers', *Cambridge Medieval Celtic Studies* XXIV (1992), 55–74; *Idem*, 'Inscriptions and Design of the Ruthwell Cross', *The Ruthwell Cross*, ed. B. Cassidy (Princeton, 1992), 71–93; *Idem*, 'Some Criteria for Editing Abaelard', *Bulletin du Cange, Archivum Latinitatis Medii Aevi* LI (1992–3), 195–202; *Idem*, 'Bodley's Librarian's Learned Nonsense', *Bodleian Library Record* XIV (1993), 446–8; *Liber Epistolarum Sancti Patricii Episcopi, The Book of Letters of Saint Patrick the Bishop*, ed. and transl. D.R. Howlett (Dublin, 1994).

```
1'ai      ðæm
   ii        eafera
   iii          in geardum
   bi            þone
   ii               God
   iii                 sende folce to frofre
   c                     hie ær drugon
   d                       aldorlease .
   c'                    lange hwile
   b'i           him
   ii              Liffre[ge]a Wuldres Wealdend
   iii                 woruldare forgeaf .
   a'i       Scyldes
   ii          eafera
   iii            Scedelandum in .
```

The poet refers in 1 to the founder of the Scylding dynasty in a and a', to the signs of his power in b and b', to retainers in i, to seats and sitting in ii, to terror and obedience in iii, to Scyld's destitution at first and his riches at last in iv, to thriving in c and c', and to the circumstances in d and d'. Similarly in 1' the poet refers to the founder in ai and a'i, to his son in aii and a'ii, to his kingdom in aiii and a'iii. He mentions what God sent in b and b', the long suffering of the Danes in c and c', and the plight of their lordlessness in d. A capital letter in line 4 introduces the passage. In both verse paragraphs punctuation points mark both the crux and the end. The first verse paragraph is eight lines long and contains forty words and seventy-seven syllables. The second is eight lines long and contains forty words and seventy-six or seventy-five syllables.[8] The central twenty-first word of the first is the beginning of the crux of the chiasmus, *weox*. The central twenty-first word of the second is the crux of the chiasmus, *aldorlease*. The golden section of 8, the number of lines in each paragraph, falls at 5 and 3. Five lines bring one to the end of the crux of the first chiasmus. In the second chiasmus the crux falls at the symmetrical centre, at the end of the fourth line. The golden section of 40, the number of words in each paragraph, falls at 25 and 15. The twenty-fifth word of the first paragraph is the end of the crux of the chiasmus, *þah*. In the second paragraph the crux falls at the symmetrical centre at *aldorlease*.

The poet linked the first verse paragraph to the second in a chiasmus.

```
1       Scyld Scefing
2         he þæs frofre gebad
3           þæt wæs god cyning .
3'          þæm eafera wæs æfter cenned
2'        folce to frofre
1'      Scyldes eafera
```

---

[8] Seventy-seven or seventy-six syllables if one reads *Beowulf* as in the manuscript.

The crux of the entire Prologue is a six-lined proverb, 20–25.

C 1 a	Swa sceal geong guma
b	gode gewyrcean
2 a	fromum feohgiftum .
b	on fæder bearme
3	þæt hine on ylde eft gewunigen wilgesiþas
4	þonne wig cume .
3'	leode gelæsten
2'a	lofdædum sceal
b	in mægþa gehwære
1'a	man
b	geþeo[ha]n .

The poet considers in 1 and 1' what a man must do to flourish, in 2 and 2' how one should accomplish this, in 3 and 3' the loyalty it should effect, and in 4 the state for which it prepares. The sentence begins with a capital letter in line 20. Punctuation points mark the crux and the end. There are six lines, which divide by extreme and mean ratio at 4 and 2. The crux ends at the fourth line. There are thirty words, which divide by extreme and mean ratio at 19 and 11. The nineteenth word is the first word of the crux, *þonne* in 4. There are fifty-nine syllables, which divide by extreme and mean ratio at 36 and 23. The thirty-sixth syllable is the first of *þonne*.

Another chiastic verse paragraph follows in lines 26–52.

B'1	Him ða Scyld gewat to gescæphwile
	felahror feran on Fre[ge]an wære
2	hi hyne þa ætbæron
3	to brimes faroðe
4 a	wine Scyldinga
b	leof landfruma
c	hringedstefna
d	isig
e	7
d'	utfus
c'	æþelinges fær .
b'	leofne þeoden
a'	beaga bryttan
4' ai	on bearm scipes
ii	madma fela
iii	of feorwegum
b	frætwa
c	gelæded .
d	Ne hyrde ic cymlicor ceol
c'	gegyrwan
b'	hildewæpnum 7 heaðowædum billum 7 byrnum
a'i	on bearme læg

ii	madma mænigo
iii	þa him mid scoldon feor gewitan .
3'	ofer yðe
2'	leton holm beran
1'	men ne cunnon . secgan hwa þæm hlæste onfeng .

The poet refers in 1 and 1' to the moment of Scyld's departure, in 2 and 2' to the retainers' committal of the body, in 3 and 3' to the sea which bore Scyld away as it had borne him in his infancy. The poet lists Scyld's titles in 4ab and b'a', mentions his ship in c and c', and describes it in d and d'. In unpublished lectures delivered in the University of Oxford the late Professor Alistair Campbell noted the apparent oddity of the adjective *isig* in line 33 and suggested that **ilig* 'speedy', cognate with Old High German *ilig*, Modern High German *eilig*, would give better sense. Confusion of long *s* with *l* would be a simple scribal blunder. The parallel diction of the passage lends plausiblity to a suggestion that the poet wrote something synonymous with *utfus*. The balance of diction throughout 4' is so obvious as to need no explanation. The crucial sentence of 4 ends with a punctuation point. The crux of 4' is marked by a punctuation point and a capital letter. Another punctuation point marks the end of 4', and a capital letter in *Nalæs* 43 introduces the last part of the chiastic verse paragraph, which ends with a punctuation point after *onfeng*. This concluding paragraph about Scyld occupies twenty-seven lines and contains 146 words. The first two lines about Scyld's departure into the Lord's keeping stand at the symmetrical centre of the Prologue. Counting lines, the golden section of 27 falls at 17 and 10. The tenth line from the beginning is 35, the caesura of which is the division between B'4 and 4'. The tenth line from the end is 43, *Nalæs hi hine læssan lacum teodan.*

Across the central proverb the poet joined parts B and B' in a chiasmus.

1 a	syððan ærest wearð feasceaft funden
b	ofer hronrade
2 a	geong
b	Liffre[ge]a
3	Scyldes eafera
3'	Scyld
2' a	felahror
b	on Fre[ge]an wære
1' a	hine æt frumsceafte forð onsendon
b	ofer yðe

As the fifty-two lines of the Prologue divide by extreme and mean ratio at 32 and 20, the golden section falls at the chiastic crux, at the proverb marked by a capital letter at line 20.

The hero of the Prologue is *Scyld* 4, whose name is the fifteenth word (5×3). After that *Scyldes* 19 is the seventy-fifth word (5×15). Between that and *Scyld* 26 there are thirty-five words (5×7). Between that and *Scyldinga* 30 there are twenty-five words (5 × 5). Between the first mention of *Scyld Scefing* 4a and the last *wine Scyldinga* 30b lie exactly half the verses of the Prologue, fifty-two of 104 half-lines, and half the words of the Prologue, 134 of 268. From the beginning to *Scyld Scefing* 4a inclusive there are thirty-two syllables, and from *wine Scyldinga* 30b inclusive to the end there are 221 syllables, together 253 syllables. Between *Scyld Scefing* and *wine Scyldinga* there are 257 syllables. Of the 134 words between *Scyld Scefing* and *wine Scyldinga* the central sixty-seventh word before *wine Scyldinga* is the first of *Beow wæs breme blæd wide sprang Scyldes eafera*. These sixty-seven words divide by symmetry at 34 and by extreme and mean ratio at 41 and 26. Between *Scyldes eafera* 19 and *Scyld* 26 there are thirty-four words. Between *Beow* 18 and *Scyld* 26 there are forty-one words.

Henry Bradley regretted the 'curiously irrelevant prologue' and believed that since it is unnumbered, 'there once existed a written text of the poem that did not include these lines'.[9] But they are stylistically identical with the verses of fit I lines 53–114. The poet mentions first the passage of time and second the begetting of Healfdene's four children. He mentions penultimately the begetting of four kinds of monster and finally the passage of time.

53	ða wæs on burgum Beow Scyldinga
	leof leodcyning longe þrage
56	oþþæt him onwoc heah Healfdene . . . ðæm feower bearn . . .
	wocun
	Heorogar 7 Hroðgar 7 Halga til . . . [Yrse On]elan cwen
111	þanon untydras ealle onwocon
	eotenas 7 ylfe 7 orcneas swylce gigantas
113	þa wið Gode wunnon lange þrage

The former passage occupies eleven lines (53–63) and fifty-six words, the latter four lines (111–14) and twenty-two words.

The poet divided the rest of the fit into two parts. The former relates the construction of Heorot in lines 64–79.

1	Þa wæs Hroðgare heresped gyfen wiges weorðmynd .
2	þæt him his winemagas georne hyrdon
3	him on mod bearn
4	þæt healreced hatan wolde . medoærn micel
5	men gewyrcean
6	þone yldo bearn æfre gefrunon .
7	7 eall gedælan buton folcscare 7 feorum gumena .
8	ða ic wide gefrægn weorc gebannan
7'	folcstede frætwan
6'	ædre mid yldum .
5'	þæt hit wearð ealgearo

[9] H. Bradley, 'Beowulf', *Encyclopaedia Britannica*, 11th edn (1910), III 758–61.

4' healærna mæst
3' scop him Heort naman
2' se þe his wordes geweald wide hæfde .

The poet refers in 1 to Hrothgar's prosperity, in 2 and 2' to his royal authority, in 3 and 3' to his conceiving and naming of Heorot, in 4 and 4' to the hall's magnificence, in 5 and 5' to men's building the hall and to its completion, in 6 and 6' to *yldo* and *yldum*, in 7 and 7' to the people, *folcscare* and *folcstede*, and at the crux in 8 to the ordering and construction of the hall.

The latter part occupies thirty-one lines 80–110, which are worth quoting in full.

	He beot ne aleh beagas dælde	80
	sinc æt symle Sele hlifade .	
	heah 7 horngeap heaðowylma bad	
	laðan liges ne wæs hit lenge þa gen	
	þæt se ecghete aþumswerian	
	æfter wælniðe wæcnan scolde .	85
	ða se ellengæst earfoðlice .	
	þrage geþolode se þe in þystrum bad	
	þæt he dogora gehwam dream gehyrde .	
	hludne in healle þær wæs hearpan sweg	
	swutol sang scopes Sægde se þe cuþe	90
VI	frumsceaft fira feorran reccan ..,	
III	cwæð þæt se Ælmihtiga eorðan worhte	
	wlitebeorhtne wang swa wæter bebugeð	
IV	gesette sigehreþig sunnan 7 monan	
IV	leoman to leohte landbuendum	95
III	7 gefrætwade foldan sceatas	
V	leomum 7 leafum lif eac gesceop	
	cynna gehwylcum þara ðe cwice hwyrfaþ .	
	Swa ða dryhtguman dreamum lifdon	
	eadiglice oððæt an ongan	100
	fyrene fremman feond on helle	
	wæs se grimma gæst Grendel hatan	
	mære mearcstapa se þe moras heold	
	fen 7 fæsten fifelcynnes eard	
	wonsælig wer weardode hwile	105
	siþðan him Scyppend forscrifen hæfde	
	in Caines cynne . þone cwealm gewræc	
	Ece Drihten þæs þe he Abel slog .	
	Ne gefeah he þære fæhðe ac he hine feor forwræc	
	Metod for þy mane mancynne fram	110

In lines 80–90a the poet alludes to the destruction of Heorot, next to the slaughter of kin which effected it, then to the dreadful *gæst* and his abode, and to men and their *dream*. In lines 99–110 he reverses the order, alluding to men and their *dream*, then to the *gæst* and his abode, next to the slaughter of kin, and finally to the desolation it effected. Capital letters in *He* 80 and *Swa* 99 introduce these passages, and a punctuation mark after *reccan* 91 concludes the former. The Creation Lay at the crux of the passage 90b–98 is the efficient cause of the action of the poem. Recitation of this lay enraged Grendel and incited his attack on Heorot. The lay bears some resemblance to *Aeneid* I 742 ff., but the primary model is Genesis I.9–27, which the poet has rearranged chiastically. He refers first to the creation of men, *frumsceaft fira*, which occurred on the sixth day, and last to *cynnum gehwilcum þara ðe cwice hwyrfaþ*, corresponding to *omnem animam viventem atque motabilem* (Genesis I.21), created on the fifth day. He refers second to earth and water, which God ordered on the third day, and he mentions penulti-mately limbs and leaves of trees, corresponding to *lignum pomiferum* (Genesis I.11), created also on the third day. At the crux he notes the *sunnan 7 monan*, the *luminare maius et luminare minus* (Genesis I.16) and their purpose, *leoman to leohte landbuendum, ut luceant in firmamento caeli et inluminent terram* (Genesis I.15), both established on the fourth day. The point of the reordering is that the Christian poet of *Beowulf* believed that God had created the universe as the Book of Genesis relates, but his pagan scop could not have known that account. The scop's Creation Lay is a creditable attempt by our Christian author to represent the distant pagan past without anachronism.

The entire passage has been punctiliously ordered in a seven-part narrative. The poet writes first of Heorot (80–82a) and alludes second to its end (82b–85). Returning to the point from which he began he states third that Grendel suffered for a long time (86–7) and relates fourth in a regression what caused that suffering (88–98). Returning again to the present he describes fifth the joy in Heorot and its interruption (99–101) and relates sixth in a regression Grendel's history (102–8). He ends by bringing the narrative back toward the period at which he began, describing seventh the descent of monsters from Cain (109–14). Within the regressions the narrative re-gresses. The lay which caused Grendel's suffering relates the events of the distant past, and the account of Grendel's history runs backward: Cain slew Abel (108b); then the Eternal Lord avenged the murder (107b–108a); subsequently He con-demned Grendel to the race of Cain (106–7a); thereafter Grendel dwelt in the moors (102–5). This may have been quite a common way to tell a story, but the present writer has noticed it only here and in Asser's *Life of King Alfred*.[10]

Fit I occupies sixty-two lines, eleven about the passage of time and the begetting of Healfdene's four children (53–63), sixteen about Hrothgar's prosperity and the building of Heorot (64–79), thirty-one about the Creation embedded in the history of Heorot and Grendel (80–110), and four about the begetting of four kinds of monster and the passage of time (111–14). The golden section of the sixteen lines about Hrothgar's prosperity falls at 10 and 6. Ten lines bring one to 74, the crux of the chiasmus. The golden section of the thirty-one lines about the Creation em-bedded in the history of Heorot and Grendel falls at 19.2 and 11.8. The Creation

---

[10] *Asser's Life of King Alfred*, ed. W. H. Stevenson, new impr. w. article on recent work by D. Whitelock (Oxford, 1959), §§ 11–16, 73–4, 95–7.

Lay begins in the eleventh line of the thirty-one-lined passage (90), and it ends in the nineteenth line (98). The Creation Lay occupies eight and one half lines, of which the golden section falls at 5.3 and 3.2. Five and one half lines from the beginning is the end of the crux of the chiasmus, describing the creation of lights (95). The number of introductory verses about Healfdene's children (11) added to that of the concluding verses about the monsters (4), plus that of the verses about the construction of Heorot (16) equals that of the verses about the Creation embedded in the history of Heorot and Grendel (31). The golden section of the number of lines in the fit, 62, falls at 38 and 24. The thirty-eighth line of the entire fit is 90, the beginning of the Creation Lay.

Fit I contains 341 words, fifty-six in the lines about the begetting of Healfdene's four children, ninety-one in the verses about Hrothgar's prosperity and the construction of Heorot, 172 in the verses about the Creation embedded in the history of Heorot and Grendel, and twenty-two in the concluding lines about the begetting of four kinds of monster. After the fifty-six words in lines 53–63 the fifty-fifth word is the beginning of the crux of the chiasmus in line 74, *ða ic wide gefrægn*. The golden section of the ninety-one words in lines 64–79 falls at 56 and 35, at *ða ic*. Of the fifty-four words in the Creation Lay the central are *sunnan 7 monan* at the crux of the chiasmus (94). The golden section of 341 falls at 211 and 130. The 211th word celebrates the creation of men, *frumsceaft fira*.

Counting the syllables one finds 162 in the lines about Hrothgar's prosperity and the construction of Heorot. The golden section of 162 falls at 100 and 62. The one hundredth syllable is *ða* at the beginning of the crux of the chiasmus. There are eighty-seven syllables in the Creation Lay, of which the central, forty-fourth, is the first of the word *sunnan*. The entire poem is composed like this.

Here then are the 'new' criteria for editing *Beowulf*, new only because unfamiliar to us. They are very old indeed, from a time long before St John the Evangelist, long before the author of the Hebrew text of Genesis I.1–II.4.[11] It matters not at all whether the *Beowulf* poet knew a word of Greek or Hebrew. He knew the Vulgate, which reproduces this mode of composition from both Hebrew Old Testament and Greek New Testament in minute particulars. He shared this mode of composition with scores of Celtic Latin and Anglo-Latin authors from the fifth century to the thirteenth, and with a large number of Old English and Middle English writers from the seventh century to the twelfth.[12]

An editor who wants to recover the text of *Beowulf* as it left the pen of its literate author almost exactly 1100 years ago needs only to listen to him, to note the parallel and chiastic shapes of his verse paragraphs and fits and groups of fits, to attend to the numbers of his lines, his words, and his syllables. He wrought his poem with an artistry that far exceeds the most extravagant claim yet made for it. He has left us criteria for recovering his *ipsissima verba*, perhaps his very orthography. But we can begin with the words.

---

[11] *Chiasmus in Antiquity, Structures, Analyses, Exegesis*, ed. J. W. Welch (Hildesheim, 1981).

[12] See my *British Books in Biblical Style* (forthcoming).

APPENDIX

The reason for mathematical composition of literary texts is that a writer imitates in his composition what he believes God to have done in the world. For evidence of belief that God created the universe as a mathematical act see my analysis of the story of Creation in Genesis I.1–II.4 as in note 5. Two other famous passages of the Old Testament and another in the Apocrypha present God's creation as a mathematical act of weighing, measuring, and balancing. In Job XXXVIII 4–7 God asks

ubi eras quando ponebam fundamenta terrae?	Where were you when I laid the foundations of the earth?
indica mihi si habes intellegentiam	Tell me, if you have understanding.
quis	Who
posuit	laid
mensuras eius	its measurements,
si nosti	if you know?
vel quis	Or who
tetendit	stretched
super eam lineam	the line upon it?
super quo bases illius	Upon what are its bases
solidatae sunt	grounded,
aut quis	or who
dimisit	laid down
lapidem angularem eius	its corner stone
cum me laudarent simul astra matutina	when the morning stars praised me together
et iubilarent omnes filii Dei.	and all the sons of God shouted for joy.

There are forty-six words in this account of the Creation, twenty-three in the first half and twenty-three in the second. There are fifty-three syllables in the first half and fifty-two in the second. There are 125 letters in the first half and 123 in the second.

Again in Isaiah XL 12 the prophet says that it is God

quis mensus est	Who has measured
pugillo	in the hollow of His hand
aquas	the waters
et	and
caelos	the heavens
palmo	in His palm
ponderavit	weighed
quis adpendit	Who has suspended
tribus digitis	with three fingers
molem terrae	the bulk of the earth
et libravit	and balanced

in pondere	with a weight
montes	the mountains
et	and
colles	the hills
in statera.	with a steelyard.

There are nine words in the first part and fifteen in the second, together twenty-four, which divide by extreme and mean ratio at 15 and 9. There are eighteen syllables in the first part and thirty in the second, together forty-eight, which divide by extreme and mean ratio at 30 and 18. There are forty-eight letters in the first part and seventy-eight in the second, together 126, which divide by extreme and mean ratio at 78 and 48.

Yet again in Sapientia XI 21 'Solomon' addressing the Creator says *sed omnia mensura et numero et pondere disposuisti* 'but You have disposed all things by measure and number and weight'. This arithmetic exactness extends also to the New Testament, in which Jesus states in Matthew X 30 *vestri autem et capilli capitis omnes numerati sunt* 'but even the hairs of your head are all numbered'.

There is explicit discussion in the Talmud of the counting of verses, words, and letters of the text of the Hebrew Bible.[13] In a dialogue which continued to be read in the Latin West Plato makes Timaeus discuss in minute particulars the mathematical creation of the world.[14]

In a golden section the number in the minor part (m) relates to the number in the major part (M) as the number in the major part relates to the number in the whole (m+M): $m/M = M/(m+M)$.[15] To calculate the golden section one needs only to follow Euclid, who describes in *Elements* II 11 and VI 30 how to divide a line in extreme and mean ratio,[16] or read Boethius *De Institutione Arithmetica* II 52.

Or one could multiply a number by 0.61803 to find the major part, and 0.38197 to find the minor part.

Or one could compile a table of Fibonacci numbers, each of which is the sum of the two to its left.

[13] *Kiddushin*, transl. Rabbi Dr H. Freedman, ch. I 30a–30b, in *The Babylonian Talmud: Seder Nashim*, ed. Rabbi Dr I. Epstein (London, 1936), Vol. VIII, pp. 144–6.

[14] Plato *Timaeus* §§ 31–32. For a Latin translation see *Timaeus a Calcidio Translatus Commentarioque Instructus*, ed. J.H. Waszink in *Corpus Platonicum Medii Aevi*, ed. R. Klibansky (London and Leiden, 1962), pp. 24–5. For specific discussion of the creation of the world by extreme and mean ratio see F.M. Cornford, *Plato's Cosmology* (London, 1937), p. 45.

[15] See F. Lasserre, *The Birth of Mathematics in the Age of Plato* (Larchmont NY, 1964); H.E. Huntley, *The Divine Proportion, A Study in Mathematical Beauty* (New York, 1970); R. Herz-Fischler, *A Mathematical History of Division in Extreme and Mean Ratio* (Waterloo, Ont., 1987).

[16] *The Thirteen Books of Euclid's Elements*, ed. 2 transl. T.L. Heath (Cambridge, 1956), I 137; *The First Latin Translation of Euclid's 'Elements' Commonly Ascribed to Adelard of Bath*, ed. H.L.L. Busard, Pontifical Institute of Mediaeval Studies, Studies and Texts LXIV (Toronto, 1983).

1	1	2	3	5	8	13	21	34	55	89	144	233	
1	2	3	5	8	13	21	34	55	89	144	233	377	
1	3	4	7	11	18	29	47	76	123	199	322	521	
1	4	5	9	14	23	37	60	97	157	254	411	665	
1	5	6	11	17	28	45	73	118	191	309	500	809	
1	6	7	13	20	33	53	86	139	225	364	589	953	
1	7	8	15	23	38	61	99	160	259	419	678	1097	
1	8	9	17	26	43	69	112	181	293	474	767	1241	
1	9	10	19	29	48	77	125	202	327	529	856	1385	
1	10	11	21	32	53	85	138	223	361	584	945	1529	
1	11	12	23	35	58	93	151	244	395	639	1034	1673	
1	12	13	25	38	63	101	164	265	429	694	1123	1817	

A writer who consults such a table sees that if he has composed a passage of eighty-nine words and wants its pair to exhibit extreme and mean ratio he must compose either fifty-five or 144 words.

Another way to calculate extreme and mean ratio is, as Dr John Blundell suggests, to divide a number successively by 2 and 3.

$n = 100$			$n = 196$			$n = 228$		
$\div2$	50	+ 50	$\div2$	98	+ 98	$\div2$	114	+ 114
$\div2$	25		$\div2$	49		$\div2$	57	
$\div2$	$12\frac{1}{2}$	+ $12\frac{1}{2}$	$\div2$	$24\frac{1}{2}$	+ $24\frac{1}{2}$	$\div2$	$28\frac{1}{2}$	+ $28\frac{1}{2}$
$\div2$	$6\frac{1}{4}$		$\div2$	$12\frac{1}{4}$		$\div2$	$14\frac{1}{4}$	
$\div3$	$2\frac{1}{12}$		$\div3$	$4\frac{9}{12}$		$\div3$	$5\frac{7}{12}$	
$\div3$	$\frac{25}{36}$	$- \frac{25}{36}$	$\div3$	$\frac{49}{36}$	$- 1\frac{13}{36}$	$\div3$	$1\frac{21}{36}$	$- 1\frac{21}{36}$
	=	$61\frac{29}{36}$		=	$121\frac{5}{36}$		=	$140\frac{33}{36}$

This form of calculation is equivalent to multiplication by $\frac{89}{144}$.

THE SEARCH FOR MEANING

Antonette diPaolo Healey

AT THE FIRST PLANNING CONFERENCE for the *Dictionary of Old English* in March 1969 one of the topics vigorously debated was whether to use manuscripts or printed editions as the citation base for the *Dictionary*. Arguments were mustered on either side. Those who favoured manuscripts saw them, like the Deity, as immutable and constant, and biblical rhythms were evoked to describe their stability: 'manuscripts are the same today as they were 1,000 years ago . . . and they will still be the same 1,000 years from now';[1] editions, by contrast, were seen as less fixed entities, varying according to the standards of the age in which they were produced. Those, on the other side, who favoured printed editions thought it 'a reckless procedure' to abandon the sound and occasionally superb scholarly editions of both past and present in favour of manuscripts rife with scribal error and characterized by indefiniteness about such modern concerns as punctuation and word division.[2] Angus Cameron, the founding editor of the *Dictionary of Old English*, was converted from the use of manuscripts to the use of editions, but reconciled what was best in each view: citations for the *Dictionary* were to be gathered from printed editions whose accuracy had been verified against manuscript.[3]

Six years ago, Ashley Crandell Amos reflected on this important decision taken at the start of the project, and it seemed to her in retrospect the only possible one: readers of the *Dictionary* would have editions, not manuscripts, on their bookshelves for handy reference, and editors of individual texts have pondered textual complexities with a thoroughness that lexicographers, surveying the whole, can never hope to duplicate.[4] With the experience of writing five letters of the *Dictionary* now behind us, it seems to me that the production of an historical dictionary is a lengthy enough task on its own without the lexicographer having to edit painstakingly from manuscript the very quotations to be cited – as a manuscript database would have entailed. Without question, the works of even a writer such as

---

[1] A. Cameron, R. Frank and J. Leyerle, eds, *Computers and Old English Concordances*, Toronto Old English Series 1 (Toronto, 1970), p. 65.

[2] *Ibid.* pp. 86–8; the quotation is from p. 86.

[3] A. Cameron, 'On the Making of the *Dictionary of Old English*', *Poetica* 15–16 (1983), 13–22, at 18.

[4] A.C. Amos, 'Dictionary of Old English: Prospects and Retrospects', unpublished paper delivered to the Seventh International Congress of the International Association for Neo-Latin Studies, Toronto, 9 August 1988.

Ælfric, who is a model of lucidity, are more easily accessible to us transcribed and analyzed by Skeat, Crawford, Pope and Godden,[5] than directly from the folios of London, British Library, Cotton Julius E.vii, Cotton Claudius B.iv, Cotton Vitellius C.v. and Cambridge, University Library, Gg.3.28. The source of the *Dictionary's* citations is edited texts and we would have it no other way. The 'List of Old English Texts and Index of Printed Editions' compiled by Angus Cameron,[6] the handbook accompanying *A Microfiche Concordance to Old English*,[7] and the Prefaces to the fascicles of the *Dictionary*[8] acknowledge our profound debt to the work of editors past and present. Without their scholarly editions there would be no new *Dictionary of Old English*. At every turn, we rely on them for expert knowledge, guidance and thoughtful argument.

Our intensive use of editions has made us very conscious of those features we find most valuable as we attempt to map out the shape of the language. The needs of the practising lexicographer may be slightly different from those of the ordinary scholar, but what we find useful for the writing of a dictionary may be generally useful for the field. All of my examples in this essay are drawn from the letter B, the letter of the *Dictionary of Old English* published in 1991.[9]

Dr A. J. Aitken, former editor of the *Dictionary of the Older Scottish Tongue*, once observed that 'for lexicographical purposes an accurate transcript was all that was necessary'.[10] For us it is the single most important feature in an edition. Before

---

5   *Ælfric's Lives of Saints Being A Set of Sermons on Saints' Days formerly observed by the English Church*, ed. W.W. Skeat, EETS os 76, 82, 94, 114 (London, 1881, 1885, 1890, 1900; repr. as 2 vols 1966); *The Old English Version of the Heptateuch, Ælfric's Treatise on the Old and New Testament and his Preface to Genesis*, ed. S.J. Crawford, EETS os 160 (London, 1922 [for 1921]); repr. with the text of two additional manuscripts transcribed by N.R. Ker, 1969); *Homilies of Ælfric: A Supplementary Collection*, ed. J.C. Pope, EETS os 259, 260 (London, 1967–8); *Ælfric's Catholic Homilies: The Second Series Text*, ed. M. Godden, EETS ss 5 (London, 1979).

6   A. Cameron, 'A List of Old English Texts and Index of Printed Editions', *A Plan for the Dictionary of Old English*, ed. R. Frank and A. Cameron, Toronto Old English Series 2 (Toronto, 1973), pp. 25–306.

7   A. diP. Healey and R.L. Venezky, *A Microfiche Concordance to Old English: The List of Texts and Index of Editions* (Toronto, 1980).

8   A. Cameron, A.C. Amos, and A. diP. Healey, co-eds, with S. Butler, J. Holland, D. McDougall and I. McDougall, *The Dictionary of Old English: D* (Toronto, 1986); A.C. Amos and A. diP. Healey, co-eds, with J. Holland, D. McDougall, I. McDougall, N. Porter and P. Thompson, *The Dictionary of Old English: C* (Toronto, 1988); A.C. Amos and A. diP. Healey, co-eds, with J. Holland, C. Franzen, D. McDougall, I. McDougall, N. Speirs and P. Thompson, *The Dictionary of Old English: B* (Toronto, 1991); A. diP. Healey, ed., with J. Holland, D. McDougall, I. McDougall, N. Speirs and P. Thompson, *The Dictionary of Old English: Æ* (Toronto, 1992); A. diP. Healey, ed., with J. Holland, D. McDougall, I. McDougall, N. Speirs and P. Thompson, *The Dictionary of Old English: A* (Toronto, 1994).

9   The writing of the letter B has been supported by the Social Sciences and Humanities Research Council of Canada, the Connaught Fund and the Provost's Office of the University of Toronto, and the Andrew W. Mellon Foundation of New York. The Xerox Corporation (USA) has supplied the project with hardware and software, and Xerox Canada Limited has maintained the equipment.

10 Frank and Cameron, *Plan*, p. 3.

we can search for a word's meaning, we need to admit it into the lexicon. And so my plea to editors is to show a tolerance for possible forms and an unwillingness to emend them out of existence. They can then be given status as headwords in the *Dictionary*.

Let me begin with the ill-treatment accorded the combined prefix *gebe-*. In the letter *B* there are over 500 headwords formed with the *be-* prefix.[11] There are also three headwords formed with the combined prefix *gebe-*, all attached to verbs: *gebegytan, gebelimpan* and *gebeniman*. The headword *gebegytan* does not appear in any dictionary. The relevant form is a dative infinitive attested only once in the *Life of St. Giles*, in Cambridge, Corpus Christi College 303, pp. 119–32. The manuscript is dated by Ker to the first half of the twelfth century.[12] The manuscript form *to gebegitanne* (p. 121, line 20) has been emended by Picard, its editor, to the more usual *to begitanne*.[13] She treats the manuscript reading as a scribal error, perhaps occurring under the influence of three other *ge-* forms in close proximity: *gebedu* in line 151, *gebletsod* in line 152, *geuðe* in line 153.[14] The citation is straightforward: **LS 9 (Giles)** 152: *sy his nama gebletsod on ecnesse þæt he us geuðe swilcne frofer of þe to **gebegitanne** 'Let his name be blessed in eternity that he may allow us to obtain such comfort from you'. The verb has the sense 'to obtain, secure (something)', a sense corresponding to one in *begytan*.

The next combined prefix is found in *gebelimpan*, a verb occurring in three versions of the West-Saxon Gospels in a rendering of Mark XIII.7: *oportet enim fieri* 'for such things must needs be' (Douay, KJV). The citation from the Corpus manuscript appears in the *Dictionary* in this way: **Mk (WSCp)** 13.7: *hit gebyrað þæt hit **gebelimpe**, ac þonne gyt nis ende* (BR *gebelimpe*, H *gelimpe*, LiRu *wosa*; cf. Mc: *oportet enim fieri*).[15] The Bodley and Royal manuscripts have the same form: *gebelimpe*.[16] The gospels in both Corpus and Bodley are dated by Ker to the first half of the eleventh century and that in Royal to the second half of the twelfth century.[17] Because of the close relationships among the manuscripts,[18] our three occurrences may provide only one independent witness to the form. Since Skeat in his edition lets the Corpus reading stand,[19] *gebelimpan* finds its way into the

---

[11] For a list of the *be-* prefixed words, see *Dictionary of Old English: B*, s.v. *be-*.

[12] N.R. Ker, *Catalogue of Manuscripts Containing Anglo-Saxon* (Oxford, 1957), No. 57, s.xii[1].

[13] B. Picard, *Das altenglische Aegidiusleben in MS CCCC 303*, Hochschul-Sammlung Philosophie Literaturwissenschaft 7 (Freiburg, 1980), p. 100, line 153.

[14] *Ibid*. p. 134, note to line 153.

[15] Cambridge, Corpus Christi College 140, fol. 65, line 5: 'it is fitting that such things happen, but then it is not yet the end'. The text is edited by W.W. Skeat, *The Gospel According to Saint Matthew and According to Saint Mark* (Cambridge, 1887 and 1871; repr. as one vol. Darmstadt, 1970), Mark XIII.7.

[16] Oxford, Bodleian Library, Bodley 441, 81v22; London, British Library, Royal I A.xiv, 25r15.

[17] Ker, Nos. 35 and 312, s.xi[1]; No. 245, s.xii[2].

[18] J.W. Bright, in *The Gospel of Saint John in West-Saxon* (Boston, 1906), p. xxii, concludes that neither Bodley nor Corpus is directly copied from the other, although they are closely related (p. xviii). Royal, according to Bright (p. xxi), is 'an unskilfully modernized transcript' of Bodley. I am grateful to Professor Eric Stanley for this reference.

[19] Skeat, *Mark*, p. 102, Mark XIII.7.

dictionaries, listed in both Clark Hall and Bosworth-Toller.[20] There is the possibility here, unlike *gebegytan*, that the prefixes *ge-* and *be-* may once have been alternative forms, and thereafter mistakenly copied as a unit to form the combined-prefixed verb. The sense of the new verb is clearly 'to happen, occur' corresponding to one of the two main senses of *belimpan*.

The last example is the earliest, occurring in the Corpus Glossary dated by Ker at the turn of the eighth and ninth centuries and by Bischoff and Parkes to the second quarter of the ninth century.[21] Here the Latin past participle *ademto* from *adimere* 'to take away' is glossed *gebinumini* 'taken away, deprived'. Like *gebegytan*, *gebeniman* does not appear in the dictionaries. Although Hessels does not emend the form, his note states that 'the scribe should have marked *ge* for erasure'.[22] Lindsay,[23] Wynn[24] and Hoad,[25] all emend, no doubt to make the Corpus form conform more closely to the reading of Épinal-Erfurt *binumni*.[26]

The evidence of the three forms in five manuscripts suggests that the combined prefix *gebe-* may have arisen as early as the ninth century and may still be found in late Old English texts of the twelfth century. In none of these occurrences does the word appear in transition between the end of one line and the start of the next. The reluctance of editors except Skeat to accept the combined prefix *gebe-* is probably based on grammatical statements such as Campbell's that the past participle usually has the prefix *ge-* as long as the verb does not have some other unaccented prefix,[27] and the fact that in Modern German *ge-* is not added to verbs with an unstressed prefix. However, as we have seen in the letter B, we have at least three clear and independent examples, and it is interesting to notice that what the grammars suggest is non-existent and editors are hesitant to record is formed from time to time until about the middle of the fifteenth century. C.T. Onions in the

[20] J.R. Clark Hall, *A Concise Anglo-Saxon Dictionary*, 4th edn with a Supplement by H.D. Meritt (Cambridge, 1960), s.v. +*belimpan* (his plus/minus sign means with or without preceding *ge-*); J. Bosworth and T.N. Toller, *An Anglo-Saxon Dictionary* (London, 1898), s.v. *gebelimpan*; there is no entry for *gebelimpan* in W. Somner, *Dictionarium Saxonico-Latino-Anglicum. Voces, phrasesque præcipuas Anglo-Saxonicas* (Oxford, 1659), nor in H. Sweet, *The Student's Dictionary of Anglo-Saxon* (Oxford, 1896); and there are no additional comments in T.N. Toller, *Supplement to An Anglo-Saxon Dictionary* (London, 1921), with *Enlarged Addenda and Corrigenda* by A. Campbell (Oxford, 1972).

[21] Cambridge, Corpus Christi College 144, 4r–64v; Ker No. 36, s.viii/ix; B. Bischoff and M.B. Parkes, 'Paleographical Commentary', *The Épinal, Erfurt, Werden, and Corpus Glossaries*, ed. B. Bischoff, M. Budny, G. Harlow, M.B. Parkes and J.D. Pheifer, EEMF 22 (Copenhagen, 1988), p. 25.

[22] *An Eighth-Century Latin-Anglo-Saxon Glossary*, ed. J.H. Hessels (Cambridge, 1890), p. 11, line 206 and note 7.

[23] *The Corpus Glossary*, ed. W.M. Lindsay (Cambridge, 1921), p. 5, A 206.

[24] J.B. Wynn, 'An Edition of the Anglo-Saxon Corpus Glosses' (unpubl. D.Phil. thesis, Oxford Univ., 1962), gloss 80.

[25] H. Sweet, *A Second Anglo-Saxon Reader: Archaic and Dialectal*, 2nd edn rev. by T.F. Hoad (Oxford, 1978), Corpus gloss 76.

[26] *Old English Glosses in the Épinal-Erfurt Glossary*, ed. J.D. Pheifer (Oxford, 1974), gloss 102.

[27] A. Campbell, *Old English Grammar* (Oxford, 1959), § 731 (h).

letter Y for the Oxford English Dictionary[28] cites the past participle *ybegunne* 'begun' from an anonymous translation dated 1432–50 of Higden's *Polychronicon*: 'the battle **ybegunne**, men of Persides . . . fledde'.[29] I do not want to overemphasize the three Old English *gebe-* forms. Perhaps they are mistakes, as the editors have taken them; but they also may be real words. We will withhold final judgement until we have proceeded further through the alphabet seeking corroborative evidence for other similarly unstressed prefixes. At the moment we try to signal for our readers the information we have found. Under the headword *gebegytan*, for example, there is a brief note pointing the user to the two other *gebe-* prefixes in the letter *B*. We have followed the same practice under *gebelimpan* and *gebeniman*. Our search for such forms would be easier if editors had preserved the manuscript readings.

Once we have an accurate transcript of the text, the next requirement for the lexicographer is a clear identification of the base manuscript and its folio numbers within the edition. This information should appear not only in the introduction but in the text itself. Clarity is particularly important if the base manuscript changes. Because of the nature of our work, we dip in and out of scores of editions a day, verifying citations, collecting variant readings, finding Latin sources, gleaning information from textual notes. For us to write entries efficiently, the most essential information must be immediately available. It may appear as if I am stating the obvious, but an extreme example of the problem for us is Miller's edition of Bede's *Ecclesiastical History*[30] where the base manuscript changes nineteen times among four manuscripts from the start of the text until its conclusion. Unless page xxii of the Introduction to Volume I.1 has been internalized, there is always uncertainty about the source of the printed text. Since Miller's edition is one from which we cite constantly, it would be most useful for us if there were running notes at the foot of each page: base = T or C or O or Ca. Miller, of course, comments when the base changes at the bottom of the appropriate page, but unless one is actually reading the page where the change occurs, there is doubt about the source of the printed text. Until a new edition of Bede is produced, a temporary solution is to mark up one's own copy of Bede, as we have done.

Another important feature of an edition to the lexicographer is the accurate recording of all lexical variants and the principal spelling variants. We would also be enormously helped by having folio numbers given for the variant readings. Hecht provides them in his edition of Gregory's *Dialogues*[31] for the variants from

---

[28] C.T. Onions, 'XYZ', *A New English Dictionary on Historical Principles*, ed. Sir J.A.H. Murray, H. Bradley, W.A. Craigie and C.T. Onions, vol. X, Part II. V–Z (Oxford, 1928), s.v. *ybegunne*.

[29] *Polychronicon Ranulphi Higden, Monachi Cestrensis; together with the English Translations of John of Trevisa and of an Unknown Writer in the 15th Century*, 9 vols, in *Rerum Brittanicarum Medii Ævi Scriptores or Chronicles and Memorials of Great Britain and Ireland during the Middle Ages* 41 (London, 1865–86), III, 147; Trevisa's translation is different: 'and whanne þe batailles come to gidres and gonne for to fiȝte, Cirus and þe Perses gonne forto flee' (III.147).

[30] *The Old English Version of Bede's Ecclesiastical History of the English People*, ed. T. Miller, EETS os 95, 96, 110, 111 (London, 1890–8; repr. 1959–63).

[31] *Bischof Wærferths von Worcester Übersetzung der Dialoge Gregors des Grossen*, ed. H. Hecht, Bibliothek der angelsächsischen Prosa 5 (Leipzig, 1900, Hamburg, 1907).

London, British Library, Cotton Otho C.i, and we find this information speeds up our work considerably. As variant manuscripts are our greatest source of new words for the *Dictionary*, we are constantly checking the manuscripts to ensure that the variant readings given in the editions actually do exist and to get a full sentence of context for quotation in the *Dictionary*. The folio number will hasten our search, and we do not find disruptive Hecht's typographical convention of enclosing the folio number within round brackets even in the middle of a word.[32] The convenience of having this information so readily available outweighs any concern with aesthetics.

One of the first questions asked when a new edition enters our office is 'Is there a glossary?'. If the answer is 'Yes', the second question asked is 'What kind of glossary is it?'. We are partial to a glossary which is not partial: an *index verborum* with full parsings and the significant morphological and syntactic information provided is best for us. It is also extremely useful for our work to have words not previously entered in the dictionaries signalled in some way and, similarly, to have new senses and new applications signalled. Of course, these are heavy demands for editors of large texts, but to those who edit smaller texts, perhaps not impossible, and to the dictionary-makers, invaluable. The lexicographer's greatest fear is to miss a word. Perhaps our second greatest fear is to overlook a meaning. An editor's attention to the status of his or her word and its meanings in the standard dictionaries, together with a willingness to point out what is new, will help ensure its recognition in the new *Dictionary of Old English*. John Pope's glossary to the *Homilies of Ælfric*[33] with its system of asterisks and square brackets is a model of clarity for calling attention to the vocabulary and meanings found only in the collection he has edited and for describing their status in the dictionaries. No doubt it was as invaluable to Alistair Campbell when he compiled his *Enlarged Addenda and Corrigenda* to Toller's *Supplement*, as it still is to us. A similar treatment of new vocabulary and meanings by editors of future texts would greatly further our work.

There are a few specialized areas I would like to mention briefly. If a text has a Latin source, and one's publisher is willing, it is most efficient for our work to have both the Old English text and Latin source published together in one volume, either as parallel texts or with the Latin keyed to the Old English as running footnotes. If there is no space for the Latin in the same volume, a carefully articulated system of reference to the source, such as Janet Bately's handling of Orosius' *History* in Zangemeister's edition, is extremely serviceable, as well as her richly full notes about the source material from which she often quotes or quotes whenever it seems desirable. A recent example of the help both source and note afforded us was in our attempt to define *bisceophād*, where we had to decide whether a figure in the *Orosius* was a Christian bishop, a high priest of the Jewish faith or a pagan priest.

---

[32] See, for example, Hecht, p. 112, note to line 15: *getim*(38a)*brode* O, where (38a) marks the change to a new folio number in the Otho manuscript.

[33] Pope, *Homilies of Ælfric*, II, 813–945.

Bately's succinct note[34] that the figure in question is later described in the *Orosius* as *sacerdotem Herculis* was the precise information we needed to assign the citation to the meaning 'office of authority of a pagan priest'[35] and it saved us many hours of searching.

When there is a paucity of material in Old English, it is necessary to seek help from the cognate Germanic languages, from Middle English and Modern English. We would find it very useful if editors would more frequently offer supporting evidence for meanings of poorly attested words. For example, when we defined the verb *behlīgan* instanced only once in a variant manuscript of the *Distichs of Cato*, its Old Frisian cognate *bihlia* 'to testify, testify against'[36] gave us some confidence in our definition 'to accuse (someone) of (something)'. The citation, from London, British Library, Cotton Vespasian D.xiv, appears thus in the *Dictionary* s.v. *behlīgan*: **Prov 1** (V) 1.10: *ðeh þe man hwylces yfeles* **belige**, *& þu þe unscyldigne wyte, ne rech þu hwæt heo ræden oððe runigen* (T *onhlige*, J *hlihge*; cf. Dist.Cat. 1.17 *ne cures si quis tacito sermone loquatur*).[37] Even though the proverb seemed clear ('if someone *accuses* you of some evil and you know yourself innocent, do not care [about] what they may plot or whisper'), there was no corresponding Latin to be a guide to the meaning. We had only the component elements of the verb, *be-* and *hlīgan*, the latter infrequently attested, and the Old Frisian cognate. Or again, when we were defining the masculine agent noun *bescēawere*, formed from the verb *bescēawian*, whose primary sense is 'to look, see', we were pleased to discover that the cognate Old High German form appeared in a context that closely matched our own. The unique occurrence of *bescēawere* is found in one of the glossed Hymns edited by Stevenson[38] from Durham, Cathedral Library B.III.32, and it glosses *speculator* 'looker out', who is God. The citation in the *Dictionary* reads: **HyGl 2** 24.4: *speculator astat desuper qui nos diebus omnibus actusque nostros prospicit* **besceawære** *ætwunaþ wiþufen se þe us dægum eallum & dæda ure besceawaþ* (HyGl 3 *sceawere*) 'the observer stands by above, he who watches us and our deeds in all days'. The cognate Old High German form is *biscouwāri*[39] glossing *circumspector* 'watcher' in a gloss to Ecclesiasticus VII.12 *circumspector deus* 'a God who sees all'. Here it would have been helpful if the editor had made the connection for us between the Old English and Old High German forms, and perhaps noted their identical referents. My third example is the verb *bellan* 'to

---

[34] *The Old English Orosius*, ed. J. Bately, EETS ss 6 (London, 1980), p. 275, note to p. 89, line 4.

[35] *Dictionary of Old English: B*, s.v. *bisceophād* sense 2.b.

[36] K.F. von Richthofen, *Altfriesisches Wörterbuch* (Göttingen, 1840), s.v. *bihlia*.

[37] See R.S. Cox, 'The Old English Dicts of Cato', *Anglia* 90 (1972), 1–42, esp. p. 18, note 10.

[38] *The Latin Hymns of the Anglo-Saxon Church*, ed. J. Stevenson, Surtees Society 23 (Durham, 1851), 24.4; the hymn has most recently been edited by Inge B. Milfull, 'Die lateinischen liturgischen Hymnen im angelsächsischen England und die Hymnenglossen der Handschrift, Durham Cathedral Library B.iii. 32', 2 vols (unpubl. Ph.D. dissertation, Univ. of Munich, 1990) II, 105–8; the citation in the *Dictionary* which followed Stevenson's edition should be corrected to Milfull: for Lat. *astat* read *adstat*; for OE *dægum* read *dagum*.

[39] T. Starck and J.C. Wells, *Althochdeutsches Glossenwörterbuch*, Fascicle *a-brunno* (Heidelberg, 1971), s.v. *biscouwāri*.

bellow, roar' which presented us with a different set of problems. Although there was one early cognate form Old High German *bellan*,[40] more information was available from the later history of the word. There are only two occurrences in Old English: one in Riddle 40 whose solution is 'creation',[41] the other in the Lindisfarne Prologue to Matthew.[42] In Riddle 40 *bellende* is used to describe the noise of a mast-fattened pig, a bellowing barrow pig: **Rid 40** 105 *mara ic eom ond fættra þonne amæsted swin, bearg **bellende**, <þe> on bocwuda, won wrotende wynnum lifde* 'I am bigger and fatter than a pig fed with mast, a dark, bellowing barrow pig who lived rooting in joy in the beechwood'. In Lindisfarne *bellende* forms part of a double gloss together with *rarende* glossing *rugiens* 'roaring'; here it is the voice of a lion roaring in the desert: **LiProlMt** 16 *secundum marcum in quo uox leonis in heremo rugientis auditur, æfter marc in ðæm stefn leas in woestern roeðe l rarende l **bellende** gehered bið* 'according to Mark in which the voice of a fierce lion is heard roaring or bellowing in the wasteland'. In the Middle English period, the verb is used mainly to describe the sound made by bulls and cattle,[43] and from 1486 on, according to Murray,[44] it describes specifically the voice of deer in rutting time. We can, of course, find such information for ourselves from the dictionaries; however, we are grateful when a textual note calls attention to the fact that a word rare in Old English has a later history and provides a brief description.

Even words which are frequently attested can profit from an editor's examination of the cognate evidence for specialized meanings. The verb *beþurfan* with about 150 occurrences has two main senses: 'to need'; 'to have a use (for)'. There was an interesting use of this verb in comparative constructions concerned with spiritual or other need which seemed to us ironic: something occurs which is more than or worse than is good for someone's need. In fact, the event which occurs is of no help or advantage at all. The first example is from Wulfstan's homily on *The Dedication of a Church* where we are told that a person who does anything useless either in word or deed performs the devil's will and angers his Lord *swiðor þonne he beþorfte* 'more than is good for his need'. The full citation reads: **WHom 18** 47: *and se þe þær deð ænig unnyt wordes oððon weorces, he dryhð deofles willan & abelhð his Drihtne swiðor þonne he **beþorfte**.*[45] A second instance is from the *Life of Paulinus* where we discover that after King Edwin was slain, Christianity cooled among the Northumbrians *swiðor þanne hi beþorfton* 'more than was good for their need'. The full citation reads: **LS 31 (Paulinus)** 8: *þa gelamp hit þæt se cyng Eadwine wærð ofslegen, and se cristendom mid Norðhembrum acolade swiðor*

---

40 *Ibid.* s.v. *bellan*.
41 G.P. Krapp and E.V. K. Dobbie, *The Exeter Book*, ASPR 3 (New York, 1936), Riddle 40, line 106.
42 Skeat, *Matthew*, p. 7, line 12.
43 H. Kurath and S. Kuhn, eds *Middle English Dictionary*, Part B.2 (Ann Arbor, 1957), s.v. *bellen* v. (2); cf. *belwen* v. sense c.
44 J.A.H. Murray, *A New English Dictionary on Historical Principles*, Vol. 1, A and B (Oxford, 1888), s.v. bell v.4 sense 2.
45 *The Homilies of Wulfstan*, ed. D. Bethurum (Oxford, 1957), p. 247, line 47.

þanne hi beþorfton.[46] The third example is from Ælfric's *Catholic Homilies* where we are told that it befell the wife of a pious man *wyrs ðonne he beðorfte* 'worse than was good for his need' when she was greatly afflicted with madness. The full citation reads: *ÆCHom* II, 10 85.138: *þa getimode his wife. wyrs ðonne he beðorfte. þæt heo ðurh wodnysse. micclum wæs gedreht.*[47] Dr Ian McDougall of the Dictionary staff found in Fritzner[48] a similar ironic use of Old West Norse *þurfa* with an added negative (functioning like the Old English examples with the comparative) which signifies that something is unneeded or superfluous, that one can gladly do without it. Recourse to the cognate evidence gave us confidence to label this particular construction in *beþurfan* as ironic.[49] It is the first construction so labelled in the *Dictionary*.

Another area where editors can help the lexicographer is by clearly stating in either the notes or the glossary when a definition is uncertain. In this case, a listing of the possibilities is very useful to us as well as the reasons for choosing one reading over another if any present themselves. For example in *Andreas* 1088, there is a striking personification of Hunger as a *blat beodgast*. The full context is: **And** 1085: *þa wearð forht manig for þam færspelle folces ræswa, hean, hygegeomor, hungres on wenum, blates beodgastes*[50] 'then on account of that sudden news the leader of the people became afraid, downcast, sad at heart, in expectation of Hunger, the *blat beodgast*'. Can we say for certain that Hunger is the 'pale guest at table'?[51] Must we not also admit the possibility that he is the 'pale ghost at table'? The interpretations are dependent on the second element of the compound, whether it is *gāst* 'ghost' or *giest* 'guest', and the forms are often confused. Verse particularly is open to this ambiguity, and both possibilities must be allowed.[52] As a colleague has suggested, Hunger is perhaps like Banquo at the feast, an unbidden guest, a pale ghost.[53]

A more complicated word in *B*, because both elements are uncertain, is *beormtēag*. It occurs in *Gerefa* in a single manuscript in a list of implements useful in the administration of a household and the cultivation of lands belonging to it: **LawGer** 17: *man sceal habban wængewædu, sulhgesidu, egeðgetigu & fela ðinga . . . cyste, mydercan, bearmteage, hlydan, sceamelas, stolas, læflas, leohtfæt,*

---

[46] K. Sisam, 'MSS. Bodley 340 and 342: Ælfric's *Catholic Homilies*', in his *Studies in the History of Old English Literature* (Oxford, 1953), pp. 148–98, at p. 151.

[47] Godden, *Ælfric's Catholic Homilies*, p. 85, line 138.

[48] J. Fritzner, *Ordbog over det Gamle Norske Sprog* (Oslo 1954), s.v. *þurfa*, sense unnumbered, 'ironic or elliptical'.

[49] *Dictionary of Old English: B*, s.v. *beþurfan* sense A.4. Cf. J.A. Simpson and E.S.C. Weiner, *The Oxford English Dictionary*, 2nd edn (Oxford, 1989) s.v. *need* v.2 sense 7.b from Yiddish *darf* (for MnG *bedarf*) similarly ironic. Professor Eric Stanley drew my attention to this use.

[50] *The Vercelli Book*, ed. G.P. Krapp, ASPR 2 (New York, 1932), *Andreas*, lines 1085–8.

[51] Thus defined by K.R. Brooks, *Andreas and the Fates of the Apostles* (Oxford, 1961), note to line 1088 and glossary.

[52] This is particularly true of *Andreas* where, as Brooks observes in his note to line 1000, there are 'no unambiguous forms of *giest*'.

[53] The Shakespearean parallel was suggested by Professor Eric Stanley.

blacern[54] 'one must have wagoncovers, ploughing gear, harrowing tackle and many things . . . chests, coffers, *bearmteage*, seats, stools, chairs, bowls, lamp, lantern'. The traditional definition of *bearmteage* is 'yeast-box', taking the first element *bearm* as a form of *beorma* 'yeast' and the second element *tēag* as meaning 'box, coffer'. Since *ea* forms for *beorma* 'yeast' do exist,[55] the traditional definition cannot be dismissed on phonological grounds. Professor Christine Fell suggested the possibility of 'lap-box', if the first element is *bearm* 'bosom, lap' and the second element means 'box, coffer', i.e., a personal box for keeping small valuables.[56] Another possibility is 'apron-string' or the like, if the first element is *bearm* 'bosom, lap' and the second element means 'tie, ribbon, string'. I do not believe that we will be able to say with certainty what this word means simply by examining the component elements because of the ambiguity of those elements. It may be only through other kinds of analysis, such as Professor Fell's examination of significant groupings in *Gerefa*,[57] that one possibility will present itself as likelier than another. However, at the moment it is our task to express doubt as to the meaning of the word by suggesting a range of possibilities and thus depose 'yeast box' from its single authoritative position in editions and the dictionaries.[58]

Let me conclude with an exemplum. It is a cautionary lesson both to editors and lexicographers on how a word can take on a life of its own if it is incorrectly treated. There is an occasional gloss in the Decisions of the Council of Chelsea (A.D. 816) edited by Haddan and Stubbs,[59] describing what services are to be performed for the soul of a dead bishop. The citation reads: *et xxx diebus canonicis horis expleto synaxeos **æt vii beltidum**, 'pater noster' pro eo cantetur* 'and for thirty days at the canonical hours "at the seven *beltidum*" when the meeting for prayer is over, a Pater Noster is to be recited for him'. The phrase *canonicis horis* is glossed *æt vii beltidum*. This is the sole occurrence of *belltid* in the Old English corpus, and Haddan and Stubbs get it right and provide a serviceable note on the word.[60] They correctly derive the word from its obvious elements: *belle* 'bell' and *tīd* 'time, hour', and explain it as referring to the seven canonical hours (*tidum*) at which the bell rang for prayer. Like Toller, we have followed their interpretation and have

---

54 *Die Gesetze der Angelsachsen*, ed. F. Liebermann, 3 vols (Halle, 1903–16), I, 455.

55 *Dictionary of Old English: B*, s.v. *beorma*, the spellings *bearman* and *bearma* are attested.

56 In personal communication to the editors of the *Dictionary*.

57 C.E. Fell, 'Some Domestic Problems' in *Sources and Relations: Studies in Honour of J.E. Cross*, ed. M. Collins, J. Price and A. Hamer, *Leeds Studies in English* 16 (1985), pp. 59–82, at p. 78, would group *beormtēag* in her Section 7: storage containers (of the lockable type?).

58 Liebermann, *Die Gesetze*, I, 455 'Hefekiste'; W.W. Skeat, '*Be Gesceadwisan Gerefan*' in *The Growth of English Industry and Commerce during the Early and Middle Ages*, 5th edn (Cambridge, 1915), ed. W. Cunningham, pp. 571–6 at p. 575 (17) 'yeast-box'; W. J. Sedgefield, 'Duties of a Reeve' in *Anglo-Saxon Prose Book* (Manchester, 1928), p. 406, note to lines 62 ff. 'yeast-box'; Clark Hall 'yeast-box'; Sweet 'yeast-box'; Bosworth-Toller *Supplement* 'a yeast-box'.

59 *Councils and Ecclesiastical Documents Relating to Great Britain and Ireland*, ed. A.W. Haddan and W. Stubbs, 3 vols (Oxford, 1869–71), III, 579–85. The gloss is found at III, 584.

60 *Ibid.* III, 585, note i.

defined the word as 'a canonical hour (marked by the ringing of a bell)'. This is, I think, the right history of the word – from its accurate treatment in an edition to its accurate documentation by the dictionaries. However, *belltid* exists in another form and has another life which Murray, with uncharacteristic lack of restraint within an *Oxford English Dictionary* entry, labels as 'one of the most grotesque blunders on record'. Under the word *belt* sb.1 after sense 5.d. he records in a separate paragraph an account of the history of the phrase *belt of pater-nosters or of Our Fathers*.[61] Herein lies the sad chronicle of the damage done to *beltidum* by its earliest editor Spelman[62] and the further travesty made of it by learned men. Spelman, misconstruing the Old English as Latin, caused the phrase *æt vii beltidum, pater noster* to metamorphose into 'a pater noster of seven belts', a phrase not immediately transparent, but which he explained was a 'rosary'.[63] According to Murray, the phrase was duly recorded by DuCange giving Spelman's explanation, although expressing some uncertainty about the existence of the rosary at that date (A.D. 816).[64] The phrase obviously captured a few imaginations and held them in thrall until at least 1849. Murray cites from Johnson the Nonjuror who in his *Ecclesiastical Laws* of 1720 describes 'belts' arranged with studs to be used as a rosary,[65] and he further documents the phrase's passage into 'modern mythology' by quoting John Lingard's *The History and Antiquities of the Anglo-Saxon Church* (1844): 'the frequent repetition of the Lord's Prayer, technically called a belt of Pater-nosters';[66]

61 W.H. Stevenson, 'Some Old-English Words Omitted or Imperfectly Explained in Dictionaries', *Transactions of the Philological Society* (1895–8), 528–42 at 530, appears to be the first Old English scholar to notice Murray's account 'of the erroneous connection of *beltidum* with a "belt of prayers".'

62 H. Spelman, 'Synodus apud Celichyth sub Wulfredo [An Christi 816]: Cap. 10 Vt Episcoporum fient exequiæ' in his *Concilia, decreta, leges, constitutiones, in re ecclesiarum orbis Britannici* (London, 1639), I, 331, line 5.

63 H. Spelman, *Archæologus in modum glossarii ad rem antiquam posteriorem* (London, 1626), s.v. *Beltis*: 'Rosarium, quo precantes usi sunt: à Sax: belt .i. cingulum'.

64 See C. DuCange, *Glossarium mediae et infimae Latinitatis*, 5 vols (Paris 1883–7), I, 623, s.v. *Beltis*: *Verum an Rosarii usus ea tempestate extiterit, Jure addubitari potest.*

65 J. Johnson, *A Collection of all the Ecclesiastical Laws, Canons, Answers, or Rescripts, with other Memorials concerning the Government, Discipline and Worship of the Church of England from its first Foundation to the Conquest, that have hitherto been publish'd in the Latin and Saxonic Tongues*, 2 Parts (London, 1720), Part I: A.D. DCCCXVI. Wulfred's Canons at Cealchythe, chapter 10, note b: '*VII Beltidum Pater Noster*: This seems to imply, that they had, in this Age, a certain Number of Studs fastned into their Belts, or Girdles, which were then us'd, as Strings of Beads now are, by the Papists, for the numbring of their Prayers: But with this Difference, that the Studs were all of one Size, and that every one of them stood for a Pater Noster; whereas the modern Fashion is, to have ten lesser Beads, which stand for Ave Maries, to one larger, which stands for a Pater Noster'.

66 J. Lingard, *The History and Antiquities of the Anglo-Saxon Church Containing an Account of its Origin, Government, Doctrines, Worship, Revenues and Clerical and Monastic Institutions*, 2 vols (London, 1845), II, 69, accompanied by an explanatory note 2: 'A belt of Pater-nosters appears to correspond with a string of beads of later times. How many Pater-nosters is contained, is not known. But, as it was substituted for the psalter, and the psalter was divided into three portions of fifty psalms each, it is probable that the same number was observed, and that the belt comprised fifty Pater-nosters'.

and Daniel Rock's *The Church of Our Fathers* (1849): 'seven "belts" of Our Fathers had to be sung for the deceased'.[67] To the lexicographer fell the task of recording the history of a non-existent word.

As we search for more perfect editions to help us write a more perfect dictionary, may both editor and lexicographer be spared from the worst evil of all: recording a ghost word and then fabricating a definition.[68]

---

[67] D. Rock, *The Church of Our Fathers As Seen in St. Osmund's Rite for the Cathedral of Salisbury*, a new edn in 4 vols ed. G.W. Hart and W.H. Frere (London, 1905), III, 6. Again because the phrase would have been opaque to Rock's audience, there is an explanatory note 8: '. . . This belt of "Pater Nosters" spoken of by one of our Anglo-Saxon councils . . . is the earliest notice, at least in western Christendom, of that pious usage of employing a string of some kind or another, the knots, notches, or knobs upon which might serve to tell, as the fingers went on holding one of them the while a certain prayer was said, exactly when the due number of such supplications had been gone over. What may have been the shape of, what the mode used, in bearing about with them this prayer-belt among the Anglo-Saxons, we do not know: perhaps the girdle worn around the waist by religious persons was of leather, and studded with small metal button-like bosses, or else deeply notched all along that end which, after being fastened by a buckle, hung loose almost to the ground at the wearer's side, so that it could be easily used for telling the "Our Fathers" at prayer-time. What may have been the precise number of such petitions forming a belt of "Pater Nosters," we are unable to guess . . .'.

[68] I am grateful to Dr David McDougall and Dr Ian McDougall for help on a number of particular points and to Dr Joan Holland, Dr Nancy Speirs, Dr Pauline Thompson and Professor Eric Stanley who read this paper in typescript. It has benefited greatly from their criticism.

WHOSE TEXT IS IT ANYWAY?
CONTEXTS FOR EDITING OLD ENGLISH PROSE

Clare A. Lees

THE HISTORY OF Anglo-Saxon studies as a discipline – its structures, premises, limits – is inescapably entwined with that of its students, its teachers, and its teaching.[1] In consequence, the history of the editing of Anglo-Saxon texts, particularly in the nineteenth century, is not simply part and parcel of the establishment of Anglo-Saxon studies *qua* discipline in the academies: newly discovered and edited texts often made their first appearance in textbooks.[2] As for the past so too the present. Teaching and research are still brought together by their common interest in the canon; by issues of what texts to edit for whom.

Textbooks, readers, and anthologies provide a fertile context for examining the relationship between editorial theory, practice, and the development of a canon of Old English texts, as has been recently suggested by the work of Allen J. Frantzen and Kevin S. Kiernan.[3] In general, however, Anglo-Saxonists have been little stimulated to examine this relationship and its implications. Indeed, a brief survey of the literature on teaching indicates that it finds its main outlet in the *Old English Newsletter* rather than in the more formal research journals, and underlines an apparent separation between teaching and research. Questions of choice – of what texts to edit and for whom – are necessarily implicated in questions of methodology

---

[1] The most recent study of the discipline is A.J. Frantzen, *Desire for Origins: New Language, Old English, and Teaching the Tradition* (New Brunswick and London, 1990), see especially pp. 1–83. For earlier studies, see E.N. Adams, *Old English Scholarship in England from 1566–1800* (New Haven: Yale University Press, 1917), and E.G. Stanley, 'The Scholarly Recovery of the Significance of Anglo-Saxon Records in Prose and Verse: A New Bibliography', *ASE* 9 (1981), 223–62. Michael Murphy also has some sporadic comments in 'Antiquary to Academic: The Progress of Anglo-Saxon Scholarship', *Anglo-Saxon Scholarship: The First Three Centuries*, ed. C.T. Berkhout and M. McC. Gatch (Boston, MA, 1982), pp. 1–17. For the history of English in American universities, see G. Graff, *Professing Literature: An Institutional History* (Chicago and London, 1987).

[2] See, for example, Benjamin Thorpe's editions of the *Lives* of *Cuthbert* and *Edmund* in *Analecta Anglo-Saxonica: A Selection in Prose and Verse from Anglo-Saxon Authors of Various Ages with A Glossary. Designed Chiefly as a First Book for Students* (London, 1834, 2nd edn 1846), pp. 74–84, 84–90. Henry Sweet edited Ælfric's *Life of Oswald* for the first edition of *An Anglo-Saxon Reader in Prose and Verse with Grammatical Introduction, Notes, and Glossary* (Oxford, 1876).

[3] Both examine the history of editing Cædmon's *Hymn*, while paying attention in textbook editions: see Frantzen, *Desire for Origins*, pp. 130–167 and K.S. Kiernan, 'Reading Cædmon's "Hymn" with Someone Else's Glosses', *Representations* 32 (1990), 157–74.

– of how to edit – and yet the former are rarely discussed.[4] One of the most important vehicles for discussion of editorial practice in recent years, for example, has been the invaluable Toronto *Dictionary of Old English*.[5] Equally importantly the *Dictionary* has enabled us all to take a much wider look at the corpus of Old English writing. In fact, although contemporary institutional practices can seem to encourage the separation of teaching and research, these two areas remain valuably linked in our daily professional lives as the many and varied discussions of both on ANSAXNET regularly witness. Rather than examine the implications of editorial practice and theory for either teaching or research, then, I want to explore the inter-relationship of all three and to suggest how this inter-relationship informs our presentation, and understanding, of contexts for Anglo-Saxon texts.

One important but largely untapped resource for exploring textbooks as contexts for the canon is the academic preface. By analyzing the image of Anglo-Saxon writing presented to students in the prefaces in relation to the contents of text-books, we gain a clearer sense of how textbooks participate in and are informed by our reconstruction of Anglo-Saxon culture. The function of books in material contexts is therefore an issue of central importance to Anglo-Saxon literary culture, linking editorial theory to research and pedagogic contexts – the present with the past.[6] To focus my discussion and make some preliminary observations on this

4   Representative of studies of Old English pedagogy are: P. Ridgewell, 'Metaparsing and Teaching Old English to Icelandic Undergraduates', *OEN* 14.2 (1981), 13–6; L. Harty, 'The Teaching of Old English to Students of English Literature 1981', *OEN* 16.2 (1983), 27–35; and R.F. Yeager, 'Some Turning Points in the History of Teaching Old English in America', *OEN* 13.2 (1980), 9–20. More recent are 'The Enjoyment and Teaching of Old and Middle English: The Current State of Play' by J. Simpson, *OEN* 25.3 (1992), 29–31; and A.J. Frantzen, 'A Recent Survey of the Teaching of Old English and Its Implications for Anglo-Saxon Studies,' *OEN* 26.1 (1992), 34–45, with a 'Response to the 1989 Survey' by R.F. Yeager on pp. 38–40. Becoming more common are discussions of computers and teaching; the most recent is 'Computer-Assisted Approaches to Teaching Old English,' by P.W. Conner, M. Deegan, and C.A. Lees, *OEN* 23.2 (1990), 30–5. *A Bibliography of Publications on Old English literature to the end of 1972*, ed. S.B. Greenfield and F.C. Robinson (Toronto and Manchester, 1980) does not consider textbooks or anthologies as worthy of attention; see the comments on pp. xiv, xvi. An increasingly valuable forum for Old English pedagogy is the electronic network, ANSAXNET, run by Patrick W. Conner. The so-called 'New Philology' issue of *Speculum*, edited by Stephen G. Nichols, which apparently seeks to renew interest in philology, pays scant attention to teaching (and none whatsoever to Anglo-Saxon); see, for example, L. Patterson's 'On the Margin: Postmodernism, Ironic History, and Medieval Studies', *Speculum* 65 (1990), 87–108, which makes the lame suggestion that non-medievalists should be encouraged to teach medieval courses (p. 104).

5   See H. Gneuss, 'Guide to the Editing and Preparation of Texts for the Dictionary of Old English', *A Plan for the Dictionary of Old English*, ed. R. Frank and A. Cameron (Toronto, 1973), pp. 11–24, reprinted above, pp. 7–26. Greater debate, however, has been stimulated by the Kane-Donaldson edition of *Piers Plowman*; see, for example, L. Patterson, 'The Logic of Textual Criticism and the Way of Genius: The Kane-Donaldson *Piers Plowman* in Historical Perspective', *Negotiating the Past: The Historical Study of Medieval Literature* (Madison, WI., 1987), pp. 77–113.

6   For studies of the material contexts of Old English writing, see F. C. Robinson, 'Old English in Its Most Immediate Context,' *Old English Literature in Context*, ed. J.D. Niles (Totowa, NJ, 1980), pp. 11–29, and K. O'Brien O'Keeffe, *Visible Song: Transitional Literacy in Old English Verse*, CSASE 4 (Cambridge, 1990) – both tend to concentrate on the poetry. For a broader study

area, I choose to concentrate on the provision of Old English prose in a few select textbooks. This study complements my earlier emphasis on research paradigms for Old English prose and their implications for pedagogy in general by concentrating instead on the teaching of prose hagiography.[7] In the light of the relative lack of attention paid to prose hagiography in some textbooks, I examine the significance of those texts that find their way into the canon and those that do not.

1. TEXTBOOKS AND THE CANON

For the editors of one of our most recent textbooks, *A Guide to Old English* by Bruce Mitchell and Fred C. Robinson, the canon is not an issue:

> The prose and verse texts selected are on the whole those which have tradition-ally been offered to beginning students to read. We have resisted the temptation to substitute novel selections for the familiar ones: such passages as King Alfred's Preface, the story of Cædmon, the conversion of Edwin, and Cyne-wulf and Cyneheard, have been chosen by generations of teachers and scholars as the appropriate introductory texts precisely because these are the essential ones for the proper orientation of beginners towards both the literature and culture of Anglo-Saxon England. Replacement of any or all of these with different selections might give the veteran teacher a refreshing change from the canon, but it would also deprive beginning students of important reference points in their initial study of Old English literature.[8]

Mitchell and Robinson's strong but circular appeal to tradition, together with a binarism that contrasts the 'novel' (the new, the entertaining) with the 'familiar' (the old, the instructive), present their own choice of texts as self-evident and beyond criticism. The contexts for teaching Old English, this Preface implies, have remained the same over generations. In fact, as Allen J. Frantzen has recently reminded us, contexts for Old English have been anything but stable.[9] The rhetoric of this Preface is easily unmasked: the 'tradition' to which Mitchell and Robinson here refer is rather new and, in the first instance, self-referential. The extract quoted above is taken from the Preface to the revised fifth edition of the *Guide*, published in 1992. It is identical with that reprinted in the revised fourth edition, published in 1986, which is itself a reprint from the third, revised in 1982. This third edition was the first edition to include *any* texts.[10] In fact, the *Guide* was

---

of the significance of the book, see S. Lerer, *Literacy and Power in Anglo-Saxon Literature* (Lincoln, NE, 1991).

[7] 'Working with Patristic Sources: Language and Context in Old English Homilies,' *Speaking Two Languages: Traditional Disciplines and Contemporary Theory in Medieval Studies*, ed. A.J. Frantzen (Albany, NY., 1990), pp. 157–81.

[8] B. Mitchell and F.C. Robinson, *A Guide to Old English* (Oxford, 1964; 5th edn, 1992), p. viii.

[9] See the useful summary in *Desire for Origins*, pp. 22–6.

[10] *A Guide to Old English* (Oxford, revised 3rd edn, 1982), p. viii.

originally published in 1964 as an introduction to the language only, written by Bruce Mitchell. The major difference between the third and the fourth editions is the introduction of eight *verse* texts (while the justification of its contents rests upon *prose* works): the selection of the prose works in these editions remains the same, with the fifth edition adding one new prose text – Ælfric's *Life of St Edmund*.[11] Notable too is the fact that the editors defend their choice of texts with an appeal to the canon when the *Guide*'s format of philology combined with reader is equally familiar, if not more traditional. The *Guide*'s primary concern remains teaching the language, as the opening sentences of all these Prefaces indicate:

> The *Guide* aims at making easier the initial steps in the learning of Old English. It is intended for beginners and will, it is hoped, prove especially useful for those wishing to acquire a reading knowledge of the language. But potential specialists in philology should find it a help in their preliminary studies of the essential grammar.[12]

Mitchell and Robinson's primary context for editing Old English texts for students is a linguistic one and their justifiably popular textbook is heavily weighted in favour of careful study of linguistic forms. Traditional methods of language learning combine with a conservative choice of texts for the students to translate – primer and reader have become one.[13] It is not so much the structure of the *Guide* that interests me, however, but the editors' defence of the canon that serves this structure.

Even the most cursory glance at earlier prefaces and textbooks suggests that the *Guide*'s casual justification of the canon – Alfred's Preface, Cædmon, Cynewulf and Cyneheard and so forth – rests on unstable foundations. Alfred J. Wyatt's Preface to his *Anglo-Saxon Reader*, first published in 1919, provides a useful contrast:

> The War has left its mark on this book. Five years ago I started to work at it with Bernard Pitt, late lieutenant in the Border Regiment, and we gave all our spare time in the winter months of 1914–15 to a review of the whole corpus of Anglo-Saxon literature with very distinct aims: to ascertain whether there was any suitable material that had not been drawn upon in earlier works of the same character; to attain to a greater variety of contents than was to be found in

---

[11] For the verse texts, see the fourth edition, pp. 215–79. There is no reference made to these new texts in the Preface to the fourth edition, although the Preface to the third announces them (p. viii). For the *Life of St Edmund* see the fifth edition, pp. 195–203.

[12] See the first edition of the *Guide*, p. vii; reprinted in all subsequent editions.

[13] Most of nineteenth-century English textbooks combine Grammar and Reader; see, for example, E.J. Vernon, *A Guide to the Anglo-Saxon Tongue: A Grammar After Erasmus Rask, Extracts in Prose and Verse, With Notes etc. for the Use of Learners and An Appendix* (London, 1846). The same model is adopted by Sweet in his *Reader*, until the publication of his *Primer*: see *An Anglo-Saxon Primer, with Grammar, Notes, and Glossary* (Oxford, 1882), p. v. The format, however, resurfaces in the eighth edition of the *Reader* (1894) to be deleted by C.T. Onions in the tenth (1946); see note 17 for further discussion.

some of the books then in use; to exclude, so far as possible, everything that was not intrinsically interesting; and finally to represent as many sides as we could of the life of our forefathers. We had just completed our survey and made a tentative list of contents, when Pitt, who thought "all is naught compared with the war," accepted a commission in the army. A year later, on the 30th April, 1916, he was killed in France. I am thankful to say that this book still bears traces of his work.[14]

In deciding whose text should be taught to whom, Wyatt and the late lieutenant Pitt were committed to a re-examination of the corpus of Old English works using several criteria: availability and suitability of material in other textbooks; an aesthetic of 'intrinsically interesting'; and as full as possible an exemplification of Anglo-Saxon culture. These criteria, together with the editors' poignant acknowledgement of their own historical context of the First World War (in striking contrast to the silence of most later prefaces about their historical circumstances), speak directly to the cultural significance of the *Reader*. Wyatt's rhetoric of patriotism is no mere anecdote.

Indeed, the more comprehensive selection of texts in this *Reader* is striking. Including what would now be called non-canonical works such as *Solomon and Saturn*, the *Benedictine Rule*, Gregory's *Dialogues*, the *Leechdoms*, and the *Apollonius*, the *Reader* illustrates the breadth of Anglo-Saxon culture (itself seen as 'the life of our forefathers') at a time when English studies was emerging as the main cultural discourse in the academies, explicitly challenging Philology and Anglo-Saxon. This sense of 'Englishness', as Brian Doyle terms it, and the desire to construct a cultural nationalism, although not exclusive to the inter-war years, gains a special poignancy here. Similiar factors contribute to the publication in 1921 of the Newbolt Report, just two years after that of Wyatt's textbook. Indeed, the Report remains one of the most influential statements on the discourse of English in English universities this century. In such a climate, the goals of Wyatt's wide-ranging *Reader* make perfect sense: they envisage a period of sustained engagement with Old English that many would envy today.[15]

In content and form, the parallels of Wyatt's *Reader* with the 'forefather' of all

---

[14] *An Anglo-Saxon Reader*, ed. A.J. Wyatt (Cambridge, 1919), p. v. A third scholar, G. Ainslie Hight, also figures in the production of this textbook, acknowledged on p. vi; neither Hight nor Pitt are credited on the title-page.

[15] An interesting contrast with Wyatt's textbook is offered by the American *The Elements of Old English*, ed. S. Moore and T.A. Knott (Ann Arbor: George Wahr, 1925), which offers a broad, though slightly idiosyncratic range of prose texts (including the Legend of St Andrew, the *Gospel of Nicodemus* as well as the ubiquitous Cædmon and Alfred's Preface) and a much smaller range of the poetry. For a general analysis of the Newbolt Report and its impact on English in British Universities, see B. Doyle, *English and Englishness* (London and New York, 1989), pp. 17–67. For the Report, see *The Teaching of English in England: Being the Report of the Departmental Committee Appointed by the President of the Board of Education to Inquire into the Position of English in the Educational System of England* (London, 1921). A brief account of the strained relationship between Philology (especially Anglo-Saxon) and English is given by Francis Mulhearn in *The Moment of 'Scrutiny'* (London, 1979), pp. 20–31. More recent

teaching anthologies, Sweet's *Anglo-Saxon Reader*, first published in 1876, are self-evident and fully acknowledged by Wyatt and Pitt. They are also superficial. The history of the changing shape of Sweet's *Reader* spans almost a century (if we include Whitelock's revisions in 1967), and merits more attention than I can give it here.[16] It is clear, however, that Sweet's primary goal in the production of the textbook was to place Anglo-Saxon Studies in Britain on a firmer institutional footing within English Philology and the emerging discipline of the History of the Language.[17] Sweet, like Wyatt, was ambitious for Old English, as his Preface to the first edition indicates. For both authors reader and primer are kept largely separate:

> There can be no question that the first object of all who occupy themselves with Old English literature, whether with the view to the literature itself, to historical investigations, or to a better understanding of the development of the English language generally, must be to acquire a sound elementary knowledge of the language itself.[18]

Although they are not necessarily the only prose texts, those selected by Mitchell and Robinson (with the exception of Bede's account of the conversion of Edwin) are indeed to be found in the majority of textbooks and readers, whatever their date.[19] What has changed, however, is their context: the discourse of the

---

controversies, that deal specifically with the teaching of Old English at Oxford are addressed in 'The Future of Old English: A Personal Essay', by P. Jackson, *OEN* 25.3 (1992), 24–8.

[16] Sweet's *Reader*, first published in 1876, has been through fifteen editions and numerous reprints. The first eight editions (1876–94) were produced by Sweet; C.T. Onions took charge of the ninth to the fourteenth edition (1922–59); and the fifteenth was revised by Dorothy Whitelock in 1967 (see her comments in the Preface to this edition, pp. iii–vii).

[17] For a general account of the creation of the History of the English Language, and some brief comments on Sweet's role in its formation, see T. Crowley, *The Politics of Discourse: The Standard Language Question in British Cultural Debates* (London, 1989), especially pp. 99–163.

[18] See the *Reader*, p. v, and his concluding comments in the Preface to the *Primer*, p. ix: 'In conclusion I may be allowed to express a hope that this little book may prove useful not only to young beginners, but also to some of our Professors of and Examiners in the English Language, most of whom are now beginning to see the importance of a sound elementary knowledge of "Anglo-Saxon". . . .'.

[19] And not only in Sweet's and Wyatt's textbooks. See, for example, J.W. Bright ed., *An Anglo-Saxon Reader* (New York, 1891), pp. 8–13 (Cædmon), 14–5 (Cynewulf), 26–9 (Alfred's Preface), 62–73 (Edwin) – all of these texts are repeated in *Bright's Old English Grammar and Reader*, ed. F.G. Cassidy and R.N. Ringler (New York, 3rd edn, 1971), pp. 109–24, 125–34, 138–42, 178–83; *An Anglo-Saxon Reader*, ed. G.P. Krapp and A.G. Kennedy (New York, 1929), pp. 33–8 (Cædmon), 48–52 (Alfred's Preface); R. Fowler, ed., *Old English Prose and Verse* (London, 1966), pp. 4–6 (Cynewulf), 15–8 (Alfred's Preface), 18–22 (Cædmon); R.E. Diamond, ed., *Old English: Grammar and Reader* (Detroit, 1970), pp. 82–5 (Cynewulf), 104–9 (Alfred's Preface), 111 (Cædmon's *Hymn*); *Beginning Old English: Materials for a One Year Course*, ed. J. Hill, A.R. Taylor, and R.L. Thomson, Leeds Studies in English (Leeds, 1977), pp. 40–1 (Cynewulf and Cyneheard), 42–4 (Cædmon), 45–8 (Alfred's Preface); and K. Crossley-Holland, ed. and trans., *The Anglo-Saxon World: An Anthology* (Oxford, 1982), pp. 37–9 (Cynewulf), 161–3 (Cædmon), 218–20 (Alfred's Preface). There are, of course, exceptions such as *Old English Literature*, ed. R. Quirk, V. Adams, and D. Davy (London, 1975), which includes none of these texts.

textbook and its relationship to the perceived structure of Anglo-Saxon studies, both of which vary over time. As Wyatt's and Sweet's Prefaces remind us, Anglo-Saxon studies in general, and textbooks in specific, participate in broader institutional questions such as the strengthening of Anglo-Saxon within the subject of Philology, the establishment of the History of the English Language, and the increasing significance of English Studies. In comparison, the reticence of Mitchell and Robinson about their historical context suggests that this 'tradition' has become self-evident – naturalized – and the debate about its linguistic and literary values apparently settled. In fact, the years since the first publication of the *Guide* have witnessed an increasing revival of scholarly debate about not only research methods and topics but also the institutional nature of the subject itself.[20]

What has also changed in the textbooks is the relative amount of attention paid to Old English prose in general. The range of prose works offered by Mitchell and Robinson as 'the proper orientation of beginners towards both the literature and culture of Anglo-Saxon' is narrow indeed. The sequence of Alfred's Preface, Cædmon, Edwin, Cynewulf and Cyneheard, even with the recent addition of Edmund, offers a very particular conception of Anglo-Saxon literary culture – one that privileges the aristocratic, the Christian, the poetic, and the warrior class (the masculine), implicitly complementing the equally familiar selection of verse texts in the *Guide*. This is a reductive but reasonable collection of the main reference points of the constructed text of Anglo-Saxon studies: what is subject to debate, however, is the extent to which the canon represents Anglo-Saxon literary culture, even for those students of language and literature who appear to be the main target market for the *Guide*. What this canon certainly does not do, at least according to the Preface, is offer beginning students a hint that there may be more to Anglo-Saxon than this received picture of the culture.

Some possible explanations for this narrowing of the textbook canon are suggested by again viewing Anglo-Saxon studies in broader historical perspective. In tandem with the increasing professionalization of the academies since World War 2, which has become the focus of increasing concern amongst educationalists, there has been a consonant compartmentalization of Anglo-Saxon studies.[21] Even though Dorothy Whitelock in 1967 rejects Sweet's well-known dictum that 'the principles which have guided me in selecting texts have also made me refrain as much as possible from antiquarian comment', the dominant paradigm through which textbooks are filtered remains that of the English Department.[22] To study

---

[20] For analogous comments about the relationship between aspects of the profession and the institution of Anglo-Saxon Studies, see Allen J. Frantzen's study of the bibliographies of the *Old English Newsletter* (which themselves are the most important guide to the changes in research topics and methods) in 'Value, Evaluation, and Twenty Years' Worth of Old English Studies', *Twenty Years of the 'Year's Work in Old English Studies'*, ed. K. O'Brien O'Keeffe, *OEN, Subsidia* 15 (1989), 43–57.

[21] See Doyle, *English and Englishness*, pp. 98–107.

[22] *Sweet's Anglo-Saxon Reader*, 15th edn, pp. vi–vii. See also Frantzen, 'Value, and Evaluation', pp. 50–2.

'the literature and culture' of the Anglo-Saxons (as Mitchell and Robinson suggest) means, in most cases, to study Old English language and literature (a term which, of course, had no resonance for the Anglo-Saxons). That study is itself increasingly the domain of the graduate school.

Granted that most students of Anglo-Saxon are students of English literature, there still remain some obvious shortcomings in the teaching canon – a problem that derives in part from the difficulty of establishing just what constitutes the 'literary' in Anglo-Saxon writings. One regular omission from the textbooks (although hardly the only one) is prose hagiography: not one anonymous Saint's life, and few of Ælfric's, have survived the selection criteria of successive generations of editors. This practice appears to parallel the opinions of some recent readers: in one recently published guide to the literature, for example, Michael Lapidge argues that prose hagiography has little literary merit. This view has at least the value of focussing the debate on 'literariness' for it is arguable how many Old English texts, prose or verse, display the post-Romantic sensibility that still seems to inform our definitions of the literary.[23] Whether by intention, oversight, or by virtue of the increasingly restricted courses that Anglo-Saxonists now often have to teach, hagiography is represented in the textbooks by one or two pious warrior kings (Edmund and the ubiquitous Oswald), and by the odd monastic saint (Cuthbert, Swithun).[24] It is not hard to see how this selection conforms to the image of Anglo-Saxon literary culture more generally promoted by the textbooks (or rather, by the discourse of the textbook) – the English kings, the English Church, the English monastic tradition. And this image of culture, in turn, conforms to that of the medieval period most usually offered by medievalists.[25] Also evident is the absence of any female Saint's life: Swanton's anthology of prose works in translation, which includes Ælfric's *Life of Agatha*, is merely the exception that proves the rule that twentieth-century versions of Anglo-Saxon culture have been most

[23] M. Lapidge, 'The saintly life in Anglo-Saxon England', *The Cambridge Companion to Old English Literature*, ed. M. Godden and M. Lapidge (Cambridge, 1991), pp. 243–61 (at 260–1).

[24] See, for example, Thorpe, *Analecta Anglo-Saxonica*, which includes the *Lives of Hilda, Cuthbert*, and *Edmund*. Sweet's *Reader* is largely responsible for the popularity of the *Life of Oswald*, see above, note 4; Bright's *Reader* originally included Bede's *Life of Edwin* (pp. 62–73), Ælfric's *Life of Gregory* (pp. 86–97), his *Life of Oswald* (pp. 98–106), and the anonymous *Life of Andrew* (pp. 113–28); the revised edition by Cassidy and Ringler includes only the *Life of Oswald* (pp. 239–49), as does Fowler in *Old English* (pp. 43–8). Wyatt's *Reader* includes only Ælfric's *Life of Cuthbert* (pp. 82–5), as does *Beginning Old English*, ed. Hill *et al.*, (extracts, pp. 50–1); Crossley-Holland translates Bede's *Life of Cuthbert* (pp. 163–72) and Ælfric's *Life of Edmund* (pp. 228–33); Mitchell and Robinson's *Guide* now includes Bede's account of the conversion of *Edwin* and Ælfric's *Life of Edmund* (fifth edition, pp. 195–203, 216–19). See also the *Lives* of *Oswald, Edmund*, and *Swithun* in *Ælfric: Lives of Three English Saints*, ed. G.I. Needham (London, 1966; repr. Exeter, 1976). I am delighted to note that Hugh Magennis has just edited the anonymous *Seven Sleepers* for Durham Medieval Texts; see below, p. 122.

[25] As Allen J. Frantzen notes, 'Prologue: Documents and Monuments: Difference and Interdisciplinarity in the Study of Medieval Culture', *Speaking Two Languages*, pp. 1–33 (especially pp. 14–5).

often realized as male.[26] Helen T. Bennett's recent discussion of the masculinist bias in the bibliographies of the *Old English Newsletter* also helps to open the debate about whether or not textbook canons can be related to research paradigms at least partly in terms of gender issues.[27]

The gender asymmetries of those texts anthologized are plain to see, but perhaps gender also plays another, less immediately obvious, role in selection criteria. Authored prose works (as opposed to anonymous prose works) are regular features of textbooks. Alfred, Bede, Ælfric, and, to a lesser extent, Wulfstan are prose authors with a relatively coherent corpus who all, not incidentally, have a definite place in the conventional literary history of our period. The concept of the author offered by this list of prose writers seems to conform to a quite different set of selection criteria to that of the poetry, which is of course largely anonymous. Indeed, Alfred's prose enjoys a critical popularity rarely granted to his poetry.[28] Recent theoretical work on how the concept of authorship factors into representations of literary history has some relevance here. It is possible, for example, that the function of the author, with its associations of corpus and control over both texts and meanings, is itself a literary construct, as Carolyn Dinshaw suggests in her analysis of the concept of the definitive masculine author in Chaucerian criticism.[29] And it is certainly the case that concepts of the author, corpus, and control play a more significant role in determining our understanding of Anglo-Saxon prose works than do those of anonymity, and compilation, for example.

Textbooks, then, are not just for students; they are products of and for the discipline. The low priority given to hagiography in the textbooks can be related to its status in the discipline in general. Greenfield and Calder's influential literary history, for example, pays scant attention to Ælfric's *Lives of Saints*, and the small but steady trickle of research has been mainly concerned with philological issues of textual criticism or New Critical readings.[30] This situation seems poised to

---

[26] *Anglo-Saxon Prose*, ed. and trans. M. Swanton (London and Melbourne, 1975), pp. 103–7.

[27] H.T. Bennett, 'From Peace Weaver to Text Weaver: Feminist Approaches to Old English Literature', in *Twenty Years of the 'Year's Work in Old English Studies'*, 23–42. The role of women scholars, such as the grammarian and editor Elizabeth Elstob (discussed by Kathryn Sutherland below, pp. 213–37), in the formation of Anglo-Saxon studies has yet to be fully assessed. Note, for example, that Miss Gunning and Miss Wilkinson are almost entirely responsible for the translations of Ælfric's *Lives of Saints* in W.W. Skeat, ed. *Ælfric's Lives of Saints*, vol. I, EETS os 76, 82, (Oxford, 1181, 1885; repr. as one vol., 1966); vol. II, EETS os 94, 114 (Oxford, 1890, 1900; repr. as one vol., 1966). For Skeat's acknowledgment, see vol. I, p. vii. All subsequent references to the *Lives of Saints* are to this edition, by page and line number.

[28] As James W. Earl notes in 'King Alfred's Talking Poems', *Pacific Coast Philology* 24 (1989), 49–61.

[29] C. Dinshaw, *Chaucer's Sexual Poetics* (Madison, WI, 1989), p. 37. For a theoretical analysis of the concept of the author that excludes the issue of gender, see M. Foucault, 'What is an Author?', *Language, Counter-Memory, Practice*, ed. D.F. Bouchard, trans. Bouchard and S. Simon (Ithaca, NY., 1977), pp. 113–38.

[30] S.B. Greenfield and D.G. Calder, *A New Critical History of Old English Literature* (New York and London, 1986), pp. 82–3: see also the comments on prose hagiography in the Vercelli Book, p. 75, although Latin hagiography is more fully treated by M. Lapidge, pp. 15–20. For source analysis of hagiographical texts, see especially J.E. Cross's studies on the *Old English Martyr-*

change, with renewed interest in the genre from editors, historians, feminists, and literary specialists.[31] All of this interest may succeed in modifying the canon. My emphasis on the relationship between pedagogic and research domains as contexts for editing texts, however, implies that the marginalization of certain texts and interests is as much an integral feature of the definition of the discipline as is the regular inclusion of others. Note, for example, how often Wulfstan's *Sermo Lupi* wanders in and out of anthologies and textbooks. Any attempt to edit the canon in one direction, in other words, will necessarily involve the silencing of texts in another. It seems to me that the crucial point here is the ideology of the canon itself as a continuing historical process.

In order to comprehend how textbooks can be viewed as more than teaching aids, I suggest that we need to pay further attention to their changing historical circumstances, to their own historical contexts and the canons they produce. In such a study, textbooks become cultural documents, which are products of specific, though extremely complex, socio-historical circumstances. The textbook, in other words, is never simply a reflection of the editor's preferences for certain language paradigms or for certain texts. The editor is no more insulated from history than the textbook and, as a result, it is possible to see many different issues and ideas about teaching, research, and culture converge in the production of a textbook.

Several avenues for future research emerge from my own prefatory exploration of editing contexts and the canon. As products of a particular society at a particular time, textbooks both encode *and* produce historically and culturally determined attitudes towards teaching and research – from which, certainly, my own attitudes are not excluded. The relation between textbook production and such attitudes can be studied in several ways, in relation to, for example: the paradigm of the discipline (the changing history of Anglo-Saxon studies in the nineteenth and twentieth

---

ology – a good introduction is his 'Saints' Lives in Old English: Latin Manuscripts and Vernacular Accounts: The *Old English Martyrology*', *Peritia* 1 (1982), 38–62; see also P.H. Zettel, 'Saints' Lives in Old English: Latin Manuscripts and Vernacular Accounts: Ælfric', *Peritia* 1 (1982), 17–37; and H. Magennis, 'On the Sources of Non-Ælfrician Lives in the Old English *Lives of Saints*, with Reference to the Cotton-Corpus Legendary', *N&Q* n.s. 32 (1985), 292–9. Dorothy Bethurum's 'The Form of Ælfric's *Lives of Saints*', *Studies in Philology* 29 (1932), 515–33 is the classic study of Ælfric's style; see also R. Waterhouse, 'Ælfric's Use of Discourse in Some Saints' Lives', *ASE* 7 (1978), 131–48; and B. Moloney, 'Another Look at Ælfric's Use of Discourse in Some Saints' Lives', *ES* 63 (1982), 13–9. The fullest New Critical account of Saints' Lives remains that by Rosemary Woolf, 'Saints' Lives', *Continuations and Beginnings: Studies in Old English Literature*, ed. E.G. Stanley (London, 1966), pp. 37–66. For a recent study of the anonymous *Lives* in Ælfric's collection, see H. Magennis, 'Contrasting Features in the Non-Ælfrician Lives in the Old English *Lives of Saints*', *Anglia* 104 (1986), 316–48.

[31] See, for example, S. Ridyard, *The Royal Saints of Anglo-Saxon England: A Study of West Saxon and East Anglian Cults* (Cambridge, 1988); D. Rollason, *Saints and Relics in Anglo-Saxon England* (Oxford, 1989); J.T. Schulenburg, 'Women's Monastic Communities: Patterns of Expansion and Decline', *Signs* 14 (1989), 261–92; and P.E. Szarmach, 'Ælfric's Women Saints: Eugenia', *New Readings on Women in Old English Literature*, ed. H. Damico and A.H. Olsen (Bloomington, IN., 1990), pp. 146–57.

centuries); the construction of aesthetic value (as is illustrated by both the Mitchell and Robinson and Wyatt Prefaces); literary criteria such as authorship (as is illustrated by the relative absence of anonymous prose texts in the canon); class and gender assumptions (as is suggested by the constructed image of Anglo-Saxon culture); not to mention the commerical demands of the publishing industry in relation to such a minority-appeal subject. Inevitably and unremarkably, the canon of texts represented in teaching anthologies says as much (if not more) about nineteenth- or twentieth-century attitudes towards Anglo-Saxon culture as it does about that culture itself. Factors influencing the production of the textbook not only need further study in their own right but, since it is the inter-relationship of teaching, editing, and research that particularly interests me, also suggest that we look again at our conceptions of the Anglo-Saxon author, the text, its contexts and its contents.

2. AUTHORS, PREFACES, TEXTS, AND CONTEXTS

The general issues raised by the functions of textbooks in material contexts have some relevance for our notions of texts and manuscripts produced by the Anglo-Saxons. They help to pose a challenge, as it were, to conventional textual criticism. The concepts of the author, preface, and corpus play a definite role in organizing the discourse of the textbook and, on examination, provide a point of entry into the web of relationships connecting the subject – Old English – with the methods of its study; the past with the present. Since this network of relationships extends to the research paradigms of the discipline, as I have already suggested, it is useful to reconsider how concepts such as that of the author structure our understanding of Anglo-Saxon texts at the research level. The genre of prose hagiography again provides a useful example. Without doubt, the concept of a vernacular author in relation to a clearly defined corpus of texts has been of enormous value in tracing the circulation of Ælfric's *Lives of Saints*, for example, and seems to fit neatly with his expressed intentions in the Preface to this Series.[32] Manuscripts, however, are not printed editions, and prefaces when considered in relation to the works that follow provide only a point of departure for understanding the manuscript, the texts, their cultural contexts, and their authors.

In view of the relative silence of Anglo-Saxon writers about their work, it is to be expected that scholars have fastened on Ælfric's Prefaces (including those to the two Series of the Catholic Homilies as well as to the *Lives of Saints*) for evidence of their author. These Prefaces are used to support three kinds of observations about Ælfric's work: his prose style; his methodology; and his intentions. In other words, analysis of the Prefaces tends to confirm already established insights into the relationship between this author and his work.[33] Valuable though such insights

[32] Skeat, vol. I, pp. 2–7.

[33] For the Prefaces to the Catholic Homilies, see *The Homilies of the Anglo-Saxon Church. The First Part, Containing the Sermones Catholici, or Homilies of Ælfric*, vol. I, ed. B. Thorpe

are, we need not forget other equally important considerations: authorial intention, for example, is expressed at least in part in this period by rhetorical convention, which must qualify our claims for an author's unique preferences; similarly, the Prefaces are themselves a formal genre, as is clear when they are considered as a group, which may qualify some of our claims for the uniqueness of any individual preface; equally, the limited circulation of the Prefaces must be considered in relation with the more extensive circulation of the texts (in various forms).[34]

Indeed, what fascinates me about the Preface to the *Lives of the Saints* is its complex relationship to the works that follow. The Preface opens with an assertion about style and intention that includes a confident reference back to an earlier work, which we can now identify as a version of the Cotton-Corpus legendary:

> Hunc quoque codicem transtulimus de Latinitate ad usitatam Anglican sermo-cinationem, studentes aliis prodesse edificando ad fidem lectione huius narra-tionis quibus-cumque placuerit huic operi operam dari, siue legendo, seu Audiendo.

> This book also have I translated from the Latin into the usual English speech, desiring to profit others by edifying them in the faith whenever they read this relation, as many, namely as are pleased to study this work, either by reading or hearing it read.[35]

This opening establishes a frame by which the Preface may be read: Ælfric here places the *Lives of Saints* against a set of expectations that he has envisaged in his intended audience. These expectations, in turn, can be measured against a know-ledge of the texts themselves. The limits of this collection, for example, are defined with reference both to an earlier Latin collection (the Cotton-Corpus legendary)

(London, 1844, rpr. Hildesheim, 1983), p. 1–9 (all subsequent references to the First Series are to this edition); and *Ælfric's Catholic Homilies: The Second Series Text*, ed. M. Godden, EETS ss 5 (Oxford, 1975), pp. 1–2. For discussion of the style of these Prefaces see, for example, A.E. Nichols, 'Ælfric's Prefaces: Rhetoric and Genre', *ES* 49 (1968), 215–23; and her 'Ælfric and the Brief Style,' *JEGP* 70 (1971): 1–12. A similar approach is taken by B.F. Huppé in 'Alfred and Ælfric: A Study of Two Prefaces', *The Old English Homily and Its Backgrounds*, ed. Huppé and Paul E. Szarmach (Albany, NY., 1978), pp. 119–37. Joyce Hill's comments on the 'self-explana-tory' nature of Ælfric's Prefaces in 'Ælfric, *Gelasius*, and St. George', *Mediaevalia* 11 (1989 for 1985), 1–17 (at p. 1) are representative of the standard interpretation. For a different perspective, see R. Waterhouse, 'Ælfric's "Usitatus": Use of Language in *Lives of Saints*', *Parergon* n.s. 7 (1989), 1–45. Jonathan Wilcox is currently preparing a critical edition of the Prefaces for Durham Medieval Texts.

34 The limited circulation of the Prefaces to the Catholic Homilies, in contrast to the texts, is made clear by Ker's comparative Table; see N.R. Ker, *Catalogue of Manuscripts Containing Anglo-Saxon* (Oxford, 1957), pp. 512–5. All subsequent references to the *Catalogue* are by editor, manuscript classification, and article number. The Preface to the *Lives of Saints* is preserved only in the two manuscript witnesses: London, British Library, Cotton Julius E. vii (Ker 162, arts. 1 and 2), and London, British Library, Cotton Otho B. x (Ker 177A, arts. 1 and 2).

35 Skeat, p. 2, lines 1–3, with a translation on the facing page. For discussion of the Cotton-Corpus Legendary, see Zettel, 'Saints' Lives in Old English'.

and to Ælfric's own earlier English collections, the First and Second series of the Catholic Homilies. The *Lives of Saints*, the Preface goes on to say, complements those Saints already honoured in the Catholic Homilies with those more specifically venerated in monastic circles, although this new selection is not intended to be comprehensive.[36] In fact, the *Lives of Saints* is one of the most comprehensive vernacular collections of saints' lives to survive. Ælfric continues by pointing out that the collection is not intended for a monastic audience alone so subtle doctrinal issues are avoided and the *Vitae Patrum* is not used. Yet the collection adapts a genre most familiar in monastic environments – the legendary – apparently for non-monastic use and invites us to speculate on the relation between the two.[37] If earlier collections, both Latin and English, provide one set of criteria for definition of the *Lives of Saints*, and theological appropriateness provides a second, then a third set of prescriptions concern method. Accordingly, Ælfric will not mention more than one ruler at any given time, nor translate literally (although sometimes he does), he says nothing new – although laymen do not know this, and so forth.[38] Nor should we ignore the paradox whereby Ælfric addresses the importance of writing in English in both Latin and English versions of the Preface.

Modesty topos and conventional denials aside, this series of descriptions and prescriptions does not simply define the *Lives of Saints* but also locates the Preface in a series of cultural discourses. These discourses include textual practices (the collection is defined in relation to other Latin and English ones); the language of spiritual behaviour (the Preface calls attention to the desire to revive a flagging faith – 'fide torpentes');[39] rhetoric; and assumptions about intended readers and/or listeners. The structure of the Preface is therefore a web of associations, inclusions, and exclusions. In its gesture towards Latin rhetoric and its use of a bilingual text (one Preface or two?), the Preface simultaneously points to the authenticating voice of Anglo-Latin, the emerging authority of English, Ælfric's own earlier prefaces, and the texts that follow.[40] Like the Catholic Homilies, this work also combines monastic, regular, and educated élite audiences with its dedication to Æthelweard and Æthelmær, its concern about content, and its theory of translation.[41] Scholars have yet to fully comprehend the complexity of its style and language switching – Latin, English plain prose, and English rhythmical prose – let alone the telling use of pronouns.[42] But I think that by now my point is clear: the

---

[36] Skeat, p. 2, lines 5–11.

[37] Skeat, p. 2, lines 12–17.

[38] Skeat, pp. 2–4, lines 18–19; p. 4, lines 22–3, 46–8.

[39] Skeat, p. 2, line 15.

[40] For discussion of Ælfric's bilingualism, see Waterhouse, 'Ælfric's "Usitatus" ', and Lees, 'Working with Patristic Sources', pp. 168–73.

[41] For the Preface, see Thorpe, pp. 1–9. For discussion, see M.R. Godden, 'The Development of Ælfric's Second Series of Catholic Homilies', *ES* 54 (1973), 209–16; and M. Clayton, 'Homiliaries and Preaching in Anglo-Saxon England', *Peritia* 4 (1985), 207–42.

[42] Ælfric, for example, uses the first person pronoun 'ic' to open and conclude the English version of the Preface, but uses the plural 'we' with in the body of the text; see Skeat, pp. 4–6.

Preface can be viewed as a textual event precisely because it refers away from the *Lives* as often as it does toward them. As a direct result of this web of cultural associations, the Preface's relationship to the collection known as the *Lives of Saints* and the author, Ælfric, is by no means clear-cut.[43]

Indeed, as is so often the case with medieval books, the works that follow this Preface continue, at least in part, the challenge to our habitual associations of author, preface, and text. As is well-known, the manuscript recensions of the *Lives of Saints* indicate that Ælfric's control over his material was not total. The utterly obvious answer to the question of whose text is the collection in London, BL, Cotton Julius E. vii is that they are Ælfric's, *but they're not all Ælfric's*. As is equally well-known, four texts are anonymous works: Skeat XXIII, *The Seven Sleepers*; XXIIIB, *Mary of Eygpt*; XXX, *Eustace*; and XXXIII, *Euphrosyne*.[44] Nor are all the *Lives of Saints* simply *Saints' Lives* initially or 'originally' intended for this collection; also included are: one commissioned Life (Skeat XXXI, *Martin*); several homilies, some of which have connections with earlier Catholic Homilies (Skeat I, XII, XIII, XVI, XVII, XVIII); and three final *obiter dicta*, apparently tacked onto the end of the manuscript and not edited by Skeat (versions of the *Interrogationes Sigewulfi* and the *De Falsis Diis* – the third, the *De Duodecim Abusivis* is missing from the set).[45] Put simply, what survives as the text, or manuscript, of Ælfric's *Lives of Saints* is neither finished nor definitive, however much it may appear so in its edited, printed form. Since the manuscript collection now known as the *Lives of Saints* involves more than one author and more than one generic principle as well as more than one manuscript, we are in the presence of a textual process which defies our notions of the definitive text or context, author, editor, or reader. As in the case of the Catholic Homilies, subsequent compilers took extracts from the collection to include in other texts and manuscripts in a process which further modifies and re-defines our notion of context and authorship.[46]

Nor are our notions of contexts for this collection exhausted by textual considerations. Another context suggested by Ælfric in his Preface to the *Lives* is that of the

---

[43] For a brief discussion of texts as events, see Lees, 'Working with Patristic Sources', p. 165 and note 35. For an exploration of the paradox of the genre of the preface, which purports to mark boundaries between texts as well as capture authorial intention, see J. Derrida, *Dissemination*, trans. B. Johnson (Chicago, 1981), pp. 1–59 ('Outwork, prefacing').

[44] Ker 162, arts. 30, 31, 41, and 44.

[45] For a description of the manuscript, see Ker 162. The fullest textual criticism of the *Lives of Saints* remains that of P. Clemoes, 'The Chronology of Ælfric's Works', *The Anglo-Saxons: Studies in some Aspects of their History and Culture presented to Bruce Dickens*, ed. P. Clemoes (London, 1959), pp. 213–47. See also *Homilies of Ælfric: A Supplementary Collection*, ed. J.C. Pope, vol. I, EETS 259 (Oxford, 1967), pp. 83–5.

[46] See, for example, Wulfstan's version of the *De Falsis Diis*, edited by D. Bethurum, *The Homilies of Wulfstan* (Oxford, 1957), pp. 221–24. For an example of this well-known process involving the Catholic Homilies, see Lees, 'Theme and Echo in an Anonymous Old English Homily for Easter', *Traditio* 42 (1986), 115–42.

monastic legendary adapted for a wider audience, which invites general consideration of the formal structure and sequence of the items in this liturgical frame. In fact, the order of items in Julius E. vii is not always strictly according to the calendar while the notion of a calendar itself implies that there is only one that could be followed. The anonymous *Life of Euphrosyne* (Skeat XXXIII), although assigned to February 11th, appears amongst a group of items for November, for example, and Ælfric's own *Life of Eugenia* is assigned to December 25th – a day unusual for her *Life* to judge from other Anglo-Saxon calendars.[47] More generally, Peter Clemoes has argued convincingly that Skeat XVI, on the *Memory of the Saints*, was intended to introduce the set.[48] Our understanding of the shape of this collection, in other words, is modulated by several factors: the general adaptation of a liturgical frame beyond its most obvious monastic context; Ælfric's specific interpretation of a particular sequence for his own structure; and subsequent compilers' re-interpretation of that sequence, not to mention later editorial reconstruction of these processes.

Even cursory examination of the main manuscript for the *Lives of Saints* thus complicates our notions of the definitive author and his well-defined English legendary. Criteria such as authorship, genre, and structure are sometimes in a far more fluid relationship than we would care to admit. One apposite example of the forces of contingency in the unfolding process of this Anglo-Saxon book is the re-positioning of the anonymous *Life of Euphrosyne* in London, British Library, Cotton Otho B. x. In this badly burned and fragmentary manuscript, *Euphrosyne* apparently followed the *Life of Eugenia*: the two texts are now contextually and calendrically related.[49] They are also related generically – a consideration perhaps more important than their different authorship in this particular context. The Ælfrician *Eugenia* and the anonymous *Euphrosyne* have remarkable similarities in their subject of female saintly transvestism. Both are graphic instances of the means whereby a woman's sexuality is erased by her transformation to sanctity – not simply by their becoming not-woman, but also not-man and even not-person; as Ælfric puts it (of Eugenia): 'and sæde hyre gewislice / hwæt heo man ne wæs'.[50] What this amounts to, in these *Lives* as in other female *Lives* of saints, is the degree to which women are *not* the subject of their *Lives*. If the text of the *Lives of Saints* turns out to be not just Ælfric's, then the text of the female saints' *Lives* is not at all the saints – a distinction that itself might be carefully considered in relation to the male *Lives* in the set.[51] The real issue for the purposes of this discussion, however,

---

[47] Indeed, there is no celebration for Eugenia on this day in the extant calendars; see *English Kalendars Before A.D. 1100*, ed. F. Wormald, Henry Bradshaw Society 72 (1934, repr 1988).

[48] Ker 162 art. 44. For Skeat XVI, see Clemoes, 'Chronology', p. 222.

[49] Ker 177A, arts. 9 and 10.

[50] 'and said to her assuredly how she was no man'; Skeat, vol. I, p. 28, lines 77–8.

[51] My point that female saints may be represented as experiencing their spirituality differently as a result of their different sex is made neither by Magennis nor Szarmach in their studies of *Eugenia*: H. Magennis, 'Contrasting Features in the Non-Ælfrician Lives in the Old English *Lives of Saints*', pp. 320–7; and P. Szarmach, 'Ælfric's Women Saints: Eugenia'.

is how to edit this process, this multi-layered Anglo-Saxon book. Or to put it bluntly, should the anonymous *Euphrosyne* continue to be included in Ælfric's *Lives of Saints*, as Skeat did, or are the criteria of genre and structure and compilation to play a greater role in the editing process than is often the case?

3. EDITING CONTEXTS

Both textbooks and Anglo-Saxon manuscripts provide contexts for comprehending and influencing our notions of Anglo-Saxon literary culture. In the examples that I have discussed, assumptions about authorship and prefaces clearly connect the textbook to the manuscript. It seems to me, therefore, that an examination of the construction of subjectivity in the female saints' *Lives* is just one procedure in an overall re-assessment of the dichotomies of conventional textual criticism: text and context, author and editor, preface and collection, corpus and canon, edition and anthology, masculine and feminine. In viewing the *Lives of Saints* as a material process, involving a succession of inter-related events that change over time, I am not simply historicizing the relationship between Ælfric's Preface and the collection of texts it frames but examining the function of the medieval book/collection and our relationship to it. We can 'eliminate' the non-Ælfrician texts in editing the collection, as Peter Clemoes persuasively argues on the criterion of authorship.[52] We can create an authorial text; after all, we know far more about Ælfric than Skeat did. But we might note that such an edition would derive its theoretical underpinning from the familiar moral rhetoric of philology – that of the 'corrupt' manuscript.[53] We might also recognize that such an edition, unlike its manuscripts, would have a very peculiar status as evidence.

In addition, the separation of the anonymous works from the already more prestigious Ælfrician texts will doubtless contribute to the likelihood of even less anonymous prose works finding their way into textbooks. The authorial text is only one element of the dynamic of the collection of texts that now goes by the name of the *Lives of Saints*. Another complementary and equally important project might be to re-assemble the relationship between the non-Ælfrician texts, as well as that between the Ælfrician and the anonymous: it is here that I see the value of electronic editing that can help us to explore some of the paths of reception and circulation indicated by the collection.[54] Textbooks are asked to fulfil many different demands by their readers, as is patently obvious from my argument. The real value of electronic editions is their interactive nature, which enables us to be more

---

[52] Clemoes, 'Chronology', p. 219.

[53] See Dinshaw's brief but pertinent comments in *Chaucer's Sexual Poetics*, p. 13.

[54] For a discussion of conventional editorial theory in relation to electronic editing, see P.M.W. Robinson, 'The Collation and Textual Criticism of Icelandic Manuscripts', *Literary and Linguistic Computing* 4 (1989), 99–105, 179–81. The value of electronic editions in relation to Old English is discussed by Marilyn Deegan and Robinson above, pp. 27–37.

fully aware of our often conflicting interests in reconstructing a text at the same time as mapping the interests of others.

Editing texts for students is often presented as a special case for the editor, but I wonder whether the difference is one of degree rather than of kind: the editor is, after all, also a teacher. The concept of the 'author' is a vital theoretical construct in the process whereby the manuscript becomes the context, the background, for the authoritative edition. This is invaluable in the ranking and interpretation of the many potential layers of a medieval book but remains only one way to interpret the manuscript evidence. The edition, in turn, is an important factor in the process of canon formation – a point of departure for the textbook. After all, the critical literature on the *Lives of Saints* neatly illustrates how authored works carry more weight in the canon than anonymous. The fact remains, however, that most Old English texts are anonymous and the division into authored versus anonymous works is sometimes no more than a convenient methodological fiction in the canon, textbook, or even edition.[55] The failure to consider our theories of the Anglo-Saxon book and consequently our theories of textual criticism makes it only too easy to ignore, for example, *Euphrosyne* when talking about *Eugenia* and easier still to forget both when presenting Old English texts to students.[56] To put it bluntly, the Old English hagiographical tradition as represented by the *Lives of Saints* or the Catholic Homilies – let alone the anonymous texts – contains far more than just English male aristocrats.[57]

Important for our understanding of editing contexts is the extent to which the fundamental materiality of the text – any text – as a product of specific historical and cultural processes is sometimes under-estimated in our reconstructed editions. Debates about editing practices tend to centre on the advantages and disadvantages of the degree of editorial intervention in the text. Both sides have important cases to present and there is no need for attitudes to fossilize in one direction or the other: different methods of editing highlight different interpretations of the evidence. Similarly, the canon is not a static and unchanging given but is a dynamic process involving more than prefaces and texts. I propose therefore that we stop arguing whose text is it anyway – the tradition's, the author's, the editor's, or the reader's – and start to examine the processes that create the contexts for these texts. We might adopt some of the spirit of Wyatt and Pitt in the winter of 1914–15, who fully acknowledged their own context, even as we note that their notion of intrinsic interest evokes the totalizing functions of the early twentieth-century textbook – the need to gather together all the literature most necessary for men to know, to

---

55 For further discussion see Lees, 'Working with Patristic Sources', pp. 160–8.

56 I am grateful to Paul E. Szarmach for allowing me to read his forthcoming study of *Euphrosyne*, 'St. Euphrosyne: Holy Transvestite', which draws attention to this much neglected *Life*.

57 The best guide to prose hagiography (rather than the canon of prose hagiography) is D.G. Scragg, 'The Corpus of Vernacular Homilies and Prose Saints' Lives before Ælfric', *ASE* 8 (1979), 223–77.

paraphrase another famous educator. By addressing the question, 'whose text is it anyway', we recognize that the canon is as necessarily subject to change and interpretation as the textbook, the edition, and the manuscript: all are of vital importance to our evolving understanding of Anglo-Saxon culture and all require a flexibility of response as we collaborate on the process of editing texts for our changing readers.[58]

[58] My research for this article was greatly assisted by a faculty grant from Fordham University; I also wish to thank Allen Frantzen for his helpful comments during its preparation. This is for Jean Geary.

OLD ENGLISH TEXTS FOR STUDENT USE

Hugh Magennis

THE TOPIC UNDER CONSIDERATION in this essay has a number of facets, since the phrase 'for student use' is an indiscriminate one, having reference to a wide range of types of courses and levels of study. To say anything useful about what Old English editions for student use should be like or what new editions might be required at present, we need to be aware of the functions such editions are intended to fulfil in particular types of study programme. The implicit contrast in the phrase 'for student use' is with 'scholarly' editions, such as those in the Early English Text Society series, but scholarly editions too are invaluable in the classroom and, though not primarily intended as such, these can also be regarded as types of edition for student use. A particular edition designed for student use will reflect certain educational objectives, consciously or unconsciously espoused by the editor, and will be suitable for some teaching purposes but not others. Our topic needs to be broken down, therefore, and approached from the perspective of objectives and levels of study rather than from that of a monolithic concept of an ideal all-purpose edition.

A guiding principle, however, which should be seen as applying universally, is that Old English editions designed for student use should be interesting to students as well as to professional Anglo-Saxonists and should be as 'user-friendly' as possible. These requirements may seem to a disinterested observer perfectly obvious, but tutors who have had to struggle with Sweet's *Anglo-Saxon Reader* remember their difficulties in promoting the subject of Old English among students and unsympathetic colleagues. Indeed, the lack of satisfactory teaching materials, reflecting a paucity of innovation in approaches to Anglo-Saxon studies at a time when other aspects of university English courses were changing radically, has contributed in no small way to the decline of Old English as a teaching subject in the past twenty years. There is still no edition of *Beowulf* that most student users find helpful for close understanding of the original text.

The attachment to uncritical perpetuation of the interests and methods of the past, for which Anglo-Saxonists are still castigated by opponents,[1] has in fact now

---

[1] As in the recent attacks on Old English in the British media. Among these is Valentine Cunningham's assertion that Old English is not worth studying at all, being 'educationally, linguistically, historically . . . a *cul-de-sac*' (*Times Literary Supplement*, 30.8.1991). The hostile attitude to Old English of many modernists in America is described by A.J. Frantzen: 'Anglo-Saxon language and literature recall both the oppression of philological discipline – translation and memorization

been replaced among teachers of Old English by a highly self- conscious pre-occupation with what they do and how they do it. The place and content of Old English courses are being examined by teachers and the principles underlying 'traditional' courses are being reassessed and deconstructed. Traditional philology-based courses continue to be taught, but in many universities survey courses, mostly or partly using modern translations of Anglo-Saxon texts, now provide the most widely-chosen Old English options. These survey courses, of a kind unknown to previous generations of students, can be used as stepping-stones to philologi-cally-based courses, but new types of non-introductory Anglo-Saxon literary courses, focusing on such questions as gender, reception, ideology and politics, are also becoming available. In the British Isles what looks like a new assertiveness among Old English teachers is indicated by the appearance of recent articles in *CUE News* dealing with the teaching of Old English[2] and the formation of an association of teachers in the field, TOEBI (Teachers of Old English in Britain and Ireland).[3]

In this fluid and developing teaching context, after the relative uniformity of the past, a wide range of types of published Old English edition are in use, reflecting the variety in learning objectives alluded to above. Many course organizers also construct their own improvised teaching packages. Though not usually thought of as such, modern English translations represent one type of edition, widely used in survey courses. Thus, the popular anthology *The Anglo-Saxon World* is (to quote the title page) 'edited and translated' by Kevin Crossley-Holland;[4] the Everyman *Anglo-Saxon Poetry* is 'translated and edited' by S.A.J. Bradley.[5] In such editions students receive the Anglo-Saxon work entirely at second hand, but even this they can find exciting and rewarding. More useful, however, for encouraging informed appreciation of the literature is the guided use of the second type of edition available to Old English teachers, the parallel-text edition, such as Richard Hamer's *A Choice of Anglo-Saxon Verse*,[6] T.A. Shippey's *Poems of Wisdom and Learning in Old English*[7] and Michael Swanton's *Beowulf*.[8] From the point of view of the Old English teacher the current Early English Text Society policy of not

    – and the vague, violent primitivism that cliché has attached to Anglo-Saxon culture' (*Desire for Origins: New Language, Old English, and Teaching the Tradition* (New Brunswick and London, 1990), p. 2).

2 J. Smith and J. Wogan-Brown, 'New Accents in Old English Studies', *CUE News: The Newsletter of the Council for University English* 4.1 (1991), 11–13; J. Simpson, 'The Enjoyment and Teaching of Old and Middle English: the Current State of Play', *CUE News*, 4.2 (1992), 3–5; repr. *OEN* 25.3 (1992), 29–31.

3 Teachers of Old English in Britain and Ireland: secretary, Dr J.J. Smith, Department of English Language, University of Glasgow.

4 K. Crossley-Holland, trans., *The Anglo-Saxon World*, The World's Classics (Oxford, 1984).

5 S.A.J. Bradley, trans., *Anglo-Saxon Poetry* (London, 1982).

6 *A Choice of Anglo-Saxon Verse*, ed. and trans. R. Hamer (London, 1970).

7 *Poems of Wisdom and Learning in Old English*, ed. and trans. T.A. Shippey (Cambridge and Totowa, NJ, 1976).

8 *Beowulf*, ed. and trans. M. Swanton (Manchester, 1978).

supplying facing translations presents a considerable limitation on the use of these volumes for teaching purposes. In the new types of non-philology Anglo-Saxon courses that have been emerging in recent years parallel-text editions are a major resource. Their more widespread production would be welcomed by those teachers who create their own dual-language editions using scissors, paste and photocopier.

In modern translations and parallel texts the emphasis is on rendering accessible to the non-specialist material written in an unfamiliar language. Such editions lend themselves to 'ideas' courses rather than to the types of close-reading approaches followed in more traditional programmes. First-hand study of Old English literature, however, requires the cultivation of linguistic skills on the part of the reader and entails the use of original-language editions in which comprehension is not entirely dependent on access to a translation. The supply of editions of this kind, particularly for beginning students, is an area to which teachers of Old English are devoting much attention at present, as the textbooks inherited from previous generations are now unsatisfactory, assuming a training in Latin grammar that students no longer possess.

The most obviously innovative way in which teachers are devoting attention to new types of edition for use in 'original-language' Old English courses is in the creation of computer workstation packages. The account of the 'electronic edition' given above by Marilyn Deegan and Peter Robinson[9] indicates the extent of the editing possiblitites offered to the Old English scholar by the computer. Not only in the study, however, but also in the classroom Anglo-Saxonists have been exploiting computer technology in a range of ways. From the production and use of interactive exercise programs, aimed at building lexical and grammatical proficiency, to experimentation in the study of literary texts with the assistance of 'Hypercard' and 'Windows' packages, teachers of Old English have been in the vanguard of those interested in applying computer technology in the teaching of the humanities.

In the classroom, computers have so far been used principally in ways which reflect a desire to make the traditional discipline of Old English more exciting for a new generation of computer-literate and would-be computer-literate students. Such teaching has the broader effect of consolidating familiarity with computers, itself an educational talisman in a society increasingly dependent on information technology. On-screen exercises, such as those created by the Glasgow STELLA initiative,[10] are the digital equivalent of the pen and paper slot-filling games used in traditional language teaching (the significant difference being that students interact with the computer, at their own pace, rather than with a tutor). Hypercard and Windows packages, such as the well-known '*Beowulf* Workstation'[11] and 'Wulf',[12]

---

[9] 'The Electronic Edition', above, pp. 27–37.

[10] STELLA Project, University of Glasgow (E-mail: STELLA@UK.AC.GLASGOW.VME). STELLA is an acronym for Software for the Teaching of English Language and Literature and its Assessment.

[11] Authored by P.W. Conner (West Virginia University). For an account of this see P.W. Conner and M. Deegan, 'Computer-Assisted Approaches to Teaching Old English', *OEN* 23.2 (1990), 30–5.

[12] Authored by J. Dillon and J. Jesch (University of Nottingham). For an account of this see the

are the digital equivalent of the print student edition of an Old English text. These Hypercard and Windows packages are electronic editions, thus representing a novel aspect of the enterprise of editing Old English texts for student use.

The electronic student edition differs from the print student edition in the range of information it renders immediately accessible to users and in the productive ways it allows them to experiment with translation. One of the stated aims, indeed, of the 'Wulf' program is 'actively to subvert students' attempts to learn a "correct" translation'.[13] The electronic student edition comes with an on-board library, through which the user can selectively browse, limited only (as in any teaching package, electronic or print) by the built-in parameters of the program. Users are spared many of the frustrations of struggling with Old English in the non-interactive medium of print and can proceed at their own pace with a sense of progress.

Such packages are usually devised as means to an end rather than as ends in themselves. They are intended to encourage the student into the discipline of Old English. There would be no educational point in producing separate Hypercard editions of all Old English literature, as the limitations of the packages become apparent when the student begins to move to more advanced work. But computer-assisted teaching can also make possible new types of learning, 'adding a dimension not available from books'.[14] As the teaching agenda changes and non-traditional approaches to Old English are introduced, the computer is coming into its own in the classroom as well as the study, as a powerful and liberating tool. Students can be encouraged to use electronic corpora to make discoveries about the literature and language in a way that is not an electronic equivalent of a print-technology procedure but instead represents active learning in areas in which the 'right answer' has not already been codified in some monument of philological scholarship. Collocations, formulas and images are among the aspects of literary study that benefit from such research. More advanced courses in Old English could be enriched by this kind of exploitation of the computer, but Joy Jenkyns has recently demonstrated how the use of electronic 'search' facilities can also provide interesting insights for Old English students in first-year groups.[15]

Although electronic student editions provide an interesting dimension to the learning of Old English, the main emphasis in class for the foreseeable future will continue to be on printed editions. Students studying Old English texts in the original language meet them in two main types of printed edition, the reader and the separate edition of one text or of a small number of texts. In both types there has been some innovation and experiment in recent and current work, and there is much scope for future development. Mitchell and Robinson's *A Guide to Old*

authors' 'Wulf', in *The STELLA Symposium: Computers in Teaching and Research in English*, proceedings of conference, held June 14–15, 1991, at the University of Glasgow, ed. J. Anderson and S. Lee, pp. 32–4.

[13] Dillon and Jesch, 'Wulf', p. 32.

[14] Dillon and Jesch, 'Wulf', *ibid*.

[15] J. Jenkyns, 'Anglo-Saxon Riddles', *The STELLA Symposium*, pp. 34–6 (esp. p. 36).

English has become the most widely used reader, eclipsing the anachronistic Sweet's *Anglo-Saxon Reader*. The *Guide* has itself been an evolving and developing project, now in its fifth edition.[16] Even so, many teachers have not found it a congenial textbook for today's students, and other readers with less linguistic superstructure have been produced.[17] Mitchell and Robinson's *Guide* is excellent for courses in which some linguistic basis has already been laid, but has proved unsatisfactory as an introductory reader. Awareness of the problems that some students are experiencing in using the *Reader* has led Mitchell to the preparation of a more elementary textbook, his forthcoming *An Invitation to Old English*.[18]

With regard to separate editions of Old English texts, an important project in recent years has been the reprinting in the Exeter Medieval Texts series of the old Methuen's Old English Library. This has made many valuable editions available again and is to be applauded by all Anglo-Saxonists. On the other hand, this enterprise also transmits a conservatism about the presentation of texts and about what kind of editions we need, which does not reflect the changes in the subject of Old English noted above. In recent 'new' Old English editions of separate texts and selections there has been some innovation in approach, though it is to be hoped that this area will develop much more in the future. New research findings are opening up questions about the significance of the manuscript presentation of Old English works and about their textuality,[19] and there is room for editorial experiment with layout and punctuation.[20] In their printed form Old English poems look essentially like modern poems. The experience of approaching them with attention to their manuscript form is quite different from that of reading them in a printed edition, as students fully appreciate when given the opportunity to do so. This dimension, however, is abstracted away in the typical edition.

Attractiveness of presentation and clarity in explication and editorial support combine in Bernard Muir's *Leoð: Six Old English Poems* to produce the kind of 'user-friendly' student edition referred to at the beginning of the present chapter.[21] Muir also includes in his edition complete manuscript facsimiles of each poem in the collection. This editor is modest in the amount of critical and interpretive commentary he provides, preferring to steer the reader in the direction of further study by means of an extensive bibliography. Muir's book developed from the

---

16 B. Mitchell and F.C. Robinson, *A Guide to Old English*, 5th edn (Oxford, 1992).

17 For example, H. Magennis and I. Herbison, *Discovering Old English: Guided Readings* (Belfast, 1990); J.J. Smith, *Introduction to Old English*, Department of English Language, Univerity of Glasgow, teaching material, 4th edn (1991).

18 As announced by Bruce Mitchell in a paper, 'An Invitation to Old English', at TOEBI Annual General Meeting, Oxford University Computing Centre, February 8, 1992.

19 See especially K. O'Brien O'Keeffe, *Visible Song: Transitional Literacy in Old English Verse*, CSASE 4 (Cambridge, 1990); M. Irvine, 'Medieval Textuality and the Archaeology of Textual Culture', in *Speaking Two Languages: Traditional Disciplines and Contemporary Theory in Medieval Studies*, ed. A.J. Frantzen (Albany, NY, 1991), pp. 181–210, 276–84.

20 See B. Mitchell, 'The Dangers of Disguise: Old English Texts in Modern Punctuation', *RES* 31 (1980), 385–413; Mitchell and Robinson, *Guide*, pp. 297–300.

21 B.J. Muir, *Leoð: Six Old English Poems: A Handbook* (New York, 1989).

experience of teaching the particular poems in the classroom.[22] On a smaller scale is Peter S. Baker's admirable *'Wulf and Eadwacer: A Classroom Edition'*.[23] This edition helpfully draws the student into the interpretation of the poem, presenting the critical problems without oversimplification but without mystification. Neither Muir nor Baker provides a translation of the Old English texts, but both have detailed glossaries incorporating much interpretive guidance.

Such editions furnish valuable teaching material for use in original-language courses. They provide up-to-date editions of texts that have been staple elements in the traditional canon of Old English literature, and they facilitate the consideration of current issues in the criticism of the edited poems. The canon of Old English literature, however, has itself now become a debating point among Anglo-Saxonists. The chapter in the present volume by Clare Lees suggests something of the limitations of this canon.[24] The readers in current use still concentrate on the texts 'canonized' in the previous century, with the same selections recurring; and most of the recent separate editions, including those by Muir and Baker, are of familiar favourites. As the perspectives of Old English literary studies expand, however, we also need editions of texts ignored or stigmatized in the past. For example, prose hagiography is poorly represented in accessible editions, with the exception of certain canonized examples by Ælfric. But prose hagiography is now recognized as a major early medieval genre and as a key medium for the expression of ideological ideas. It also brings an important dimension to the study of the textual culture[25] of Anglo-Saxon England and to questions of literary transmission and reception. As well as new editions of 'old' texts, therefore, there is also a need for attractive editions of 'new' texts.

Hagiography also represents a useful area for classroom study for the down-to-earth reason that it contains a wealth of good stories. At the beginning of this chapter it was suggested as a guiding principle for producing student editions that the material should be interesting to students, not just to their teachers. The kind of lively narrative exemplified in many saints' lives, amply fulfils this criterion. Non-narrative homilies, on the other hand, though they have much to tell us about early medieval spirituality and values, prove to be best taken in small doses in the classroom.

Prose hagiography is one example of Old English writing whose increased study would enliven the subject in new ways. Editions of other types of writing at present not accessible would also be highly desirable. Selections from King Alfred's *Boethius*, for example, or from the Old English *Bede* could form the bases of exploratory courses on Anglo-Saxon literary topics. Michael Swanton already

---

[22] See *Leoð*, Preface, p. ix.

[23] P.S. Baker, *'Wulf and Eadwacer: A Classroom Edition'*, *OEN* 16.2 (1983), Appendix, pp. 1–8.

[24] 'Whose Text is it Anyway? Contexts for Editing Old English Prose', above, pp. 97–114. See also Lees's chapter, 'Working with Patristic Sources: Language and Context in Old English Homilies', in *Speaking Two Languages*, ed. Frantzen, pp. 157–80, 264–76.

[25] On textual culture see M. Irvine, 'Medieval Textuality and the Archaeology of Textual Culture'.

presents a useful but extremely limited selection from the *Anglo-Saxon Chronicle* for use in introductory courses.[26] The forthcoming edition of prefaces by Ælfric from Durham Medieval Texts is greatly to be welcomed.[27]

The editorial strategy and approach chosen by the producer of the text will depend on the level of study for which it is intended and the objectives it sets out to meet. The policy for editing Old English (and Latin) texts in the recently established series Cambridge Studies in Anglo-Saxon England is to provide facing modern translation with no glossary. The forthcoming editions in this series will not be aimed primarily at classroom study but their emphasis on immediate comprehensibility will render them particularly suitable to a wide range of types of Anglo-Saxon studies course. The one type of course for which they will not be satisfactory is that in which the emphasis is on close study of the original language.

Editions whose main objectives include developing knowledge of Old English on the part of the user do not require facing translations. Some indeed would argue that the inclusion of such translations is counterproductive, distracting attention away from the Old English text itself. What is essential, however, in an edition which is aimed at getting students to read and understand Old English is the provision of a detailed and well signposted glossary. In this kind of edition indeed the glossary is to an important extent the linchpin of the whole enterprise, for the usefulness of the glossary is a key indicator of how successful the edition is (as in the editions by Muir and Baker discussed above).

The balancing act in which the editor is engaged is in presenting the Old English work with fidelity to its existence as a product of manuscript textuality, without at the same time erecting barriers between the reader and the text. For example, normalization of manuscript spelling is helpful only in elementary readers, and even then should be phased out as the student progresses to more difficult passages. It should not be employed in separate editions of Old English works, though spelling inconsistencies should receive some attention in commentary or glossary. On the other hand, most current practitioners agree that for prose texts there is little benefit to be gained from not using modern punctuation, including capitalization and quotation marks, as recommended in the important discussion of editing techniques by Helmut Gneuss.[28] The same principle is usually applied to the editing of poetry, though here it would also be interesting to see experimentation in the presentation of texts.

With regard to emendation, the editor's strategy will be determined to a significant degree by the state of the original text, but the current consensus among Old English scholars is for as little emendation as possible, and this should apply to student editions as well as to 'scholarly' editions. People can disagree, of course,

---

26 *An Anglo-Saxon Chronicle*, ed. M. Swanton, revised edn (Exeter, 1990). *The Parker Chronicle*, ed. A.H. Smith, revised edn (Exeter, 1981) proves unhelpful for today's literary students.

27 Currently being prepared by Jonathan Wilcox.

28 H. Gneuss, 'A Guide to the Preparation of Texts for the Dictionary of Old English', in *A Plan for the Dictionary of Old English*, ed. R. Frank and A. Cameron (Toronto, 1973), pp. 11–23 (reprinted above, pp. 7–26).

with any kind of editorial strategy. What is more important than the strategy is that the edition must make clear the status of all textual material. It is necessary to give the reader relevant textual information in all Old English editions, even those intended for student use (even if most students ignore the *apparatus criticus*). Good students can also be encouraged to respond to some of the editorial decisions in a critical way and to understand something of the provisional nature of the whole business of editing, although this kind of encouragement is perhaps more the province of the teacher than of the editor.

Many students ignore the introductions to Old English editions, as they find them uncongenial and unhelpful. The introduction to Wrenn's *Beowulf*, for example, remains largely unread even though this edition is widely in current use.[29] What should be in an introduction depends, as with other aspects of the edition, on the objectives it is envisaged as fulfilling. The introduction should set the work in its relevant contexts, but with a firm sense of its intended readership. Traditionally, sections on language have been *de rigueur* in Old English editions, but these are necessary only in those editions in which the language itself is seen as primary focus of study. As we have seen, the focus on language is no longer paramount in many Anglo-Saxon study programmes. Even in those editions that set out to develop knowledge of Old English it is not helpful to today's students exhaustively to trace the development of each phonological feature in the text in the old-fashioned way. There are only a few lines on language in Muir's *Leoð*. And the present writer in a recent student edition of *The Legend of the Seven Sleepers* intended for original-language study[30] has chosen to concentrate on such practicalities as the treatment of inflexion in this Old English text. The introduction to *The Legend of the Seven Sleepers* also adds two headings to the discussion of language that do not normally appear in editions of Old English texts. There is a section on vocabulary, influenced particularly by the researches of Helmut Gneuss and Walter Hofstetter on Winchester vocabulary;[31] and one on syntax, greatly aided by the work of Bruce Mitchell, whose *Old English Syntax* has opened out this aspect of language study.[32]

A key aim of student editions, whether intended for original-language study or not, and whether realized in print or electronically, is that readers should be encouraged to explore the edited work for themselves. The editor's role in student editions should be as a facilitator, opening out the text for a non-expert audience.

---

[29] *Beowulf with the Finnesburg Fragment*, ed. C.L. Wrenn and W. F. Bolton, revised edn (Exeter, 1988).

[30] *The Anonymous Old English Legend of the Seven Sleepers*, ed. H. Magennis, Durham Medieval Texts 7 (Durham, 1994).

[31] See H. Gneuss, 'The Origin of Standard Old English and Æthelwold's School at Winchester', *ASE* 1 (1972), 63–83; and W. Hofstetter, *Winchester und der spätaltenglische Sprachgebrauch*, Münchener Universitäts-Schriften, Philosophische Facultät 16 (Munich, 1987); see also M. Gretsch, 'Æthelwold's Translation of the "Regula Sancti Benedicti" ', *ASE* 3 (1974), 149–51.

[32] B. Mitchell, *Old English Syntax*, 2 vols (Oxford, 1985).

Student editions should be sound and scholarly, of course, but should not over-burden the reader with scholarly explication. It is through such carefully prepared editions that new generations of students are to be introduced to the excitement and dynamism of contemporary Anglo-Saxon studies.

EDITING OLD ENGLISH ORAL/WRITTEN TEXTS:
PROBLEMS OF METHOD
(WITH AN ILLUSTRATIVE EDITION OF
CHARM 4, *WIÐ FÆRSTICE*)

A.N. Doane

WE ARE SO USED TO poetic texts arranged in metrical lines, emended, punctuated, and annotated, that we have perhaps overlooked that editions can serve other purposes than defining *the* text. The 'critical' text is an essential but perhaps preliminary stage towards understanding Old English poetry as it has been preserved, that is, in relation to the materiality of its production. Magoun's texts of *Beowulf* and the *Vercelli Book* of the last generation helped students by stripping the text of critical apparatus and normalizing them for reading. Translations such as Raffel's and Greenfield's of *Beowulf* have experimented with sound and metre.[1] But 'scholarly' texts have been so long narrowly focussed on the 'look' of the printed texts and their philological impeccability that little attention has been paid either to their performance or their distinguishing manuscript format, that is, to how they *might* sound or *do* look – even though sound and sight were and are the only two ways a text can be directly received. Rather, texts are prepared as evidences of the editor's interpretations of a whole tradition of modern reception (i.e. scholarship) in order to facilitate the continuation of this (modern) tradition. The consideration of the manuscript as any more than a largely disruptive middleman between the real text and its serious reception plays only a marginal role in this process. In this paper I want to talk about editing texts for how they might sound from how they do look; or, to put it another way, how their edited look might respond to their manuscript look in order to centre the text on present-day voiced reading. That is, I will not pass over the manifest features of the manuscript in order to discover a 'virtual' or ideal text 'beyond' the manuscript, nor will I present the edited text as final, but as a prompt meant to encourage a variety of responses that might continue the *mouvance* in which this kind of text historically lived.

In the following pages when I use the term 'orality' I do not refer to oral-formulaic

---

[1] F.P. Magoun, *The Anglo-Saxon Poems in Bright's Anglo-Saxon Reader, Done in a Normalized Orthography* (Cambridge, MA, 1956); idem., *Beowulf and Judith Done in a Normalized Orthography and Edited* (Cambridge, MA, 1959); idem., *The Vercelli Book Poems: Done in a Normalized Orthography* (Cambridge, MA, 1960); B. Raffel, *Beowulf: A New Translation with an Introduction* (New York, 1963); S.B. Greenfield, *A Readable Beowulf: The Old English Epic Newly Translated* (Carbondale and Edwardsville IL, 1982).

theory as we are familiar with it. It was oral-formulaic theory, to be sure, that first taught us to take the orality of Anglo-Saxon poetry seriously. But as it has been worked out, this theory is marked by naïve textualism, reducing, by a fairly unexamined process, texts once oral to written texts. Even in the case of modern oral songs gathered under field conditions, oralists have canonized, concorded, and regularized these sounds-objects into texts as objects for the eye (as for example in the monumental *Serbo-Croation Heroic Songs* of Parry, Lord and Bynum), and then have proceeded to deal with them as with any other texts (just telling a different story about their origins).[2]

What I mean here by orality is the 'voice' of orality, or simply *vocality*, as Zumthor has named it.[3] This concept of vocality does not depend upon distinctions and justifications that require irrefutable knowledge that a text was or was not composed according to the pure theory, that is, extemporaneously, using traditional memory techniques and oral formulas, without writing and without a concept of a fixed text. What we are rather considering here is the *fact* of vocality, regardless of whether the text was originally composed with the use of writing. We know that in the Middle Ages many texts, and especially vernacular texts, were intended to be voiced, be it through the means of extemporized oral composition, memorized recitation from a fixed text, or reading from a book, or any mixture of these techniques. D.H. Green has recently reminded us that the mutual interpenetration of textuality and orality is the norm in the Middle Ages and that scholars committed to either side of the 'literacy/orality' debate tend to forget this symbiosis.[4] Medieval texts are visible prominences in what was once a vast sea of orality: some texts were islands that might have remained relatively high and dry, but most were shoals that were constantly awash in vocality.

Now, neither oral-formulaicists, nor other scholars of Old English, have seriously tackled the profoundly different register in which vocalized texts exist. Everyone who studies Old English professionally is already a committed textualist, and in practice behaves as though an oral text read silently is the same as an oral text heard. And indeed, how could we do otherwise, since all our training and trust is devoted to the eye and only suspicion is accorded to the ear. And in no group of scholars is this distrust of the ear and valorization of the eye more powerful and ingrained than among textual editors. To my knowledge, editors have given very little consideration, rather they have tended to be actively hostile, to the idea that vocality might have implications for the texts they edit. At most, vocality has been thought of as a corrupting influence, as the source of 'aural error'.[5]

---

[2] The implications of these remarks are discussed more fully by me in 'Oral Texts, Intertexts, and Intratexts: Editing Old English' in *Influence and Intertextuality*, ed. E. Rothstein and J.B. Clayton, Jr. (Madison, 1991), pp. 75–113.

[3] See in particular P. Zumthor, 'The Text and the Voice', *New Literary History* 16 (1984), 67–92, esp. p. 74.

[4] 'Orality and Reading: The State of Research in Medieval Studies', *Speculum* 65 (1990), 268–80.

[5] See, for example, W. Krogmann, 'Hörfehler in der altsächsischen Genesis', *Jahrbuch des Vereins für Niederdeutsch* 81 (1958), 10–13.

It might be objected that metre, with which most editors are very much concerned, does bring in ear-considerations. But, on the contrary, metre as it is commonly understood by Old English scholars and as it is utilized by editors for the purposes of textual criticism, is an eye-concept, answering certain textualist demands and obeying certain external, silent rules. What is actually heard when Old English poetry is read aloud is not metre but a rhetorical heightening of selected stylized speech patterns marked by alliterative stress-pulses at irregular intervals. Unless some sort of unnatural delivery technique is employed (that is, one carefully worked out and defended by a theory of metre usually comprehensible and practicable mainly to its progenitor), we do not hear the lines and half-lines of Old English verse as inevitably as we see them in print, nor do we hear the Old English line patterns as regularly as we do in most English 'metrical' poetry since the twelfth century. The impression of heightening is given by the rule-bound restriction of patterns but the restriction does not, as in metre, result in the limitation of the pattern to a single one. Metre is somewhat visible in some Anglo-Saxon manuscripts because of discreet artificial textualist devices such as pointing or extra spacing, but this is far from omnipresent or systematic. In modern editions there is the more grossly intrusive textual device of 'caesuras' and 'lines'. What we *see* is 'metre' but we do not *hear* it as such, despite the ingenuity of the isometricists.[6]

Discussions about orality have taken place and continue to take place using texts formed before the advent of orality studies in Old English, on the assumption that Old English texts are *only* writing, with single authors (even if unknown), and definite, intended meanings (even if irrecoverable). The idealized, uniform, deracinated Old English texts that we read in the Anglo-Saxon Poetic Records, set out in impeccable modern textual dress, and which the oral-formulaicists, first with the help of Grein's *Sprachschatz* and then Bessinger's concordance, relied on as their Bible, is the site where the textualists and the oralists have agreed to conduct their conspiracy of silence.

So what is at issue is the relation of vocality and textuality and the implications of these notions for editorial methods in Old English. In particular I want to consider the problematics of *the production of oral texts*, an ambiguous phrase which refers equally to the primary setting (a setting of genuine vocality, of actual speaking or singing), the secondary setting (the making of chirographs that descend from vocalized production), and the tertiary setting (the making of edited, printed texts from chirographs[7] putatively related to vocal production). And finally,

---

[6] John D. Niles in a forthcoming paper in *Oral Tradition* makes a similar point about the metre of genuine oral texts, using the case of British ballads.

[7] I take the use of the term 'chirograph(ic)' from W.J. Ong, *Orality and Literacy: The Technologizing of the Word* (London, 1982), since the Latinate equivalent, 'manuscript(ic)', is already entirely occupied by its denotation of the physical product of handwriting, whereas I want to denominate the activity and productivity of handwriting. The normal paleographical meaning of 'chirograph', a document deliberately separated into several parts for the purposes of later verification, is not relevant here.

the phrase raises the question of how this editorial production is to be used and what further productions it might lead to.

The editorial method usually applied to Old English poetic texts, which are in most cases preserved in unique copies, is an intertextual method. By intertextuality I mean an editor's ability to refer beyond a text as it appears in a manuscript to two intertextual resources: a primary intertext or 'hypertext' constructed into a concordance from a wide variety of sources; and a secondary intertext consisting of all previous editorial conjectures about a given text. Intertextuality bestows upon the editor the power to make selections of variant 'readings' where the actual manuscript tradition of particular texts provides no basis for such choice, because there are, in fact, no variants. These editorial intertexts, one a large but fixed idealized 'primary' intertextual reservoir composed of ancient texts of various sorts, the other a 'secondary' intertextual grid of scholarly commentary continually increasing in density and weight, take the place of the *traditio* that exists for texts preserved in multiple copies.

But these normalizing editorial resources are not normal for the speaking person nor for the medieval vernacular scribe, neither of whom have the power of consciously scanning a vast written *traditio*. Of course, the editorial intertexts are indispensable because they take the place of the *langue* of natural language, the unconscious competence of the speaker and the scribe. But the editor is not a *producer* of utterance; the editor is searching for and claims to find the 'ideal', 'intended', or 'virtual', text that has always been there all along, the text of which a manuscript is only a distorted reflection; from the already produced speech of the manuscript he moves to the already produced speech of the intertexts. To do this he must turn away from the performative factors, the peculiarities and singularities, the elements that shift from performance to performance, from copy to copy that are there to be found in the 'actual text', the text as it appears in the manuscript. Of course Old English editors depend upon the actual text in the first instance but not in the last resort. For the intertextual method allows an Old English editor to disregard the manuscript whenever convenient and in the end to discard it by a programmatic step, stripping the manuscript text of all its individual features precisely because they are individual, deposing it in favour of a 'virtual' text that claims to go beyond and/or behind the single witness.

Lee Patterson has made clear the binary thinking inherent in editorial processes.[8] An editor works by arranging the data so that it can be selected by a process of progressively narrower either/or choices. All editorial methods – stemmatic, 'best-text', eclectic – represent a protracted series of on/off digital decisions. This process is heightened by an editor's need to move from 'script to print'; whatever other considerations apply as to the best reading, in the last analysis an editor has always to come up with a single reading that will be unambiguously either this

---

[8] 'The Logic of Textual Criticism and the Way of Genius: The Kane-Donaldson *Piers Plowman* in Historical Perspective' in *Negotiating the Past: The Historical Understanding of Medieval Literature* (Madison, 1987), pp. 77–113, esp. 80–96.

letter or that letter as represented in already-existing type-fonts set into an entirely preformed spatial grid (thus such frequent editorial comments as, 'between these letters there is space for 4 letters').

Such editorial processes stem not from the nature of the manuscript being edited but from the nature of the printed text that is the ultimate receptor of the edited text. Printed text is inherently digital or binary in the sense that a letter in a font is itself or another, but not both, a single ASCII number. When looking at printed text, a reader scans a series of pre-set visual patterns; chirographs do not allow such easy scanning because letters subtly differ even when the 'same' and patterns often occur which contradict expectations or baffle the eye. The editor resolves this by making binary choices which resolve the textual hot spot[9] into a definite reading that can be scanned. This letter, which looks like an *e* – no, an *o* – is resolved into one or the other on the basis of the intertext, what makes sense in terms of lexis, grammar, or dialect. The editor produces a modern text, and like all modern (printed) text the edited text becomes foreseeable in the sense that all the possibilities are already known, are already extant in the pre-made font, and already explained in the dictionaries and grammars. The so-called 'oral formulas' themselves are apprehended as nothing other than pre-known textualized phonemic strings; in fact all printed text could be said to be inherently more formulaic than any vocal utterance, however formulaic and repetitive, or any chirographic text.

The model for text-editors as well as their medium is mechanized typography that always presents the already known letter, the letter that is there before the word or the phrase or even before the writer, always ready in limitless profusion and all-embracing potential, while the utterance only exists on a breath, some certain breath. No one can speak it again, because 'it' will be a different utterance, but anyone can tomorrow or next month write it 'the same', print it 'even more the same', and read it years hence as 'exactly the same'.

Voice is not digitalized as print is: it is part of a flow. It consists of indefinite gradations from one overlaid set of sounds (timbre, pitch, etc.) to another, and most of the sounds of speech are not phonemic; and even phonemes flow into one another and interact more than the literalized speech of writing does. No two utterances are identical either from the same speaker or different ones the way the 'same' text is always irreducibly the same. Within an utterance, the flow is modulating the semantic and affective burden of the message. Therefore utterance is not 'foreseeable' in the way text is (in the head of a text composer or in the phonemic strings of grammar or the prescriptions of dictionaries) and neither is it 'forespeakable' since no one, not even the utterer, knows what the utterance will be until it has been uttered. Frederick Smith (writing about Swift's 'Tale of a Tub'), has made an elegant distinction between *syntax*, 'the static structure of a completed thought',

---

[9] The term in this sense is used by J. Dagenais, 'That Bothersome Residue: Towards a Theory of the Physical Text', in *Vox Intexta: Orality and Textuality in the Middle Ages*, ed. A.N. Doane and C.B. Pasternack (Madison, 1991), 254.

and *rhythm*, 'the movement of thought through the mind'.[10] We can make a similar distinction between the already uttered, static, syntactic *text* whose elements can be categorized and the rhythmic flow of the utterance in process as it comes from the mind through the mouth to the ear, never finished, yet always subject to negotiation between interlocutors, as well as modified by faulty hearing and bad remembrance.

The chirographic representation of text is also different from printed or mechanized text in that it retains some of the features of speech. Like an utterance each manuscript is unique and is the result of a somatic gesture. Manuscript writing is not digital but analogue, a flow with indefinite gradations and indeterminacies. As such it both resembles speech in a general way and may actually preserve the particulars of a given speech (record it) beyond the mere phonemic string. That is, those elements of speech which are particular to speech may show through the chirographic 'text' because the chirograph is always itself a performance, a doing.

Nevertheless, the two registers, text and voice, different as they are, are hardly sealed from each other because writing is, to use Yuri Lotman's term (as cited by Ong[11]), a secondary modelling system dependent on speech. Ong says that writing (at the moment of production or consumption) must always be at least internally voiced. This is at least theoretically and practically true of alphabetical writing.[12] That is, there is an area within reception of text where text goes back to utterance and becomes once again untextlike. But it must be said that modern writers are only subliminally aware of this most of the time. Writing that derives from genuine oral utterance is not a secondary modelling system in exactly the same way (one must leave aside, even if thinking of, 'grammatological' writing at this point). Writing is playing catch up to the speech, not controlling and modelling it. The problem is not that as moderns we do not voice the text, but that as editors we do not account either for how the text was produced via vocality and what that means, nor do we much worry about how our textualist operations will affect the *inevitable*

---

[10] F. Smith, *Language and Reality in Swift's Tale of a Tub* (Columbus, 1979), p. 71.

[11] Ong, *Orality and Literacy*, p. 8.

[12] Eric Havelock also makes the point: 'The acoustic efficiency of the script had a result which was psychological: once it was learned you did not have to think about it. Though a visible thing, a series of marks, it ceased to interpose itself as an object of thought between the reader and his recollection of the spoken tongue. The script therefore came to resemble an electric current communicating a recollection of the sounds of the spoken word directly to the brain so that the meaning resounded as it were in the consciousness without reference to the properties of the letters used. The script was reduced to a gimmick; it had no intrinsic value in itself as a script and this marked it off from all previous systems' (*Origins of Western Literacy: Four Lectures Delivered at the Ontario Institute for Studies in Education, Toronto, March 25, 26, 27, 28, 1974* Ontario Institute for Studies in Education 14 [Toronto, 1976], 46). Havelock also says that the Greek alphabetic system revealed that speech is not a continuous flow as syllabaries seem to imply, but a series of finite particles (phonemes). But here Havelock seems to be carried away by a textualist bias. First, the alphabet only imperfectly analyzes the phonemes of any given language. Second, even if the alphabet can analyze speech into parts, that does not mean that these parts have more than a theoretic existence. As Havelock himself says, the empirical basis of speech is the experience of speech as a continuum. And it is on this empirical basis that ancient writing, even alphabetic writing is still based.

subsequent voicings. In other words, we do not make the fuss about the 'shifting and inessential' vocality of our texts that we do about their 'essential' phonemic strings.

Yet it cannot be said that it is tact that prevents us from searching for voice, that we do not do it because we do not know what Old English sounded like. In the boldest and most confident way, and with untheoretized assumptions that doing so bears some relation to how the text should be apprehended, we mark longs and shorts, delineate uniform caesuras, and provide punctuation according to more or less current local conventions. Indeed, the entire venerable structure of historical phonology as applied to dead languages, the linchpin of Germanic philology, hardly bears thinking about as one begins to contemplate actual speech versus the problems of grapholectics.

To put it more directly, what I am proposing is that a manuscript is a record not only of a phonemic string (the 'text') but also of certain *performative factors*. These are of two sorts: first, the scribe's record of an actual performance, if he is copying from a voice, or his scoring for a voice if that is his intention; this would include not only the actual 'text' spoken, the phonemic string that can be alphabetically transcribed, but also such mistakes, hesitations, repetitions, phrasings, pitches, resolutions, and stalls as might be heard and might influence the transcription. However, I am not willing to argue very hard that such texts exist or ever existed, since apart from factual considerations, this is just another road to the 'virtual text'. I am much more concerned with the second sort, the evidences in the existing material texts which show an activity much more essential and intimate: the scribe's own acting out of the vocality of the text as he writes, as the outward somatic activity took place even when the scribe was copying from a written exemplar, as he 'reperforms', 'revocalizes', the script. This bodily reflection of aural, vocal activity ought to produce marks and arrangements in the chirograph itself, however individual, ad hoc, and difficult of interpretation they may be or, to state the other side, even if the writing is the product of a scribe trained in the production of a stylized script of a particular school or scriptorium. It is always the product of a variable human hand connected to an individualized conciousness possessing a competence in the language and an inner ear. In any case, textual signs are produced that are different from and less regular than the printed, standardized symbols into which the chirographs must be translated by editors. These non-standardized signs in the chirograph, a product of a performance as unique and individuated as any act of speech, are the very traces that the oralist claims to be, and ought to be, looking for. Paying attention to them may mean that an editor may have to give up the idea of the 'definitive' edition in Old English in order to produce a 'definite' edition, an edition that will reflect a single textual performance rather than an idealized text disconnected from its material localization.

These unique marks, which I will call performative for the sake of the argument, are not necessarily meant to convey a meaning to a reader; they are rather the by-products of a meaning that has been apprehended by ear and/or eye, interpreted as speech, and that has asserted itself in a supererogatory motion of the scribe's hand. The marks are thus usually erratic and incompletely carried through, like non-phonemic speech features. But they are there and can be reckoned with.

The editor tends to strip away the 'random' marks of a manuscript that do not accord with modern notions of textuality; indeed a conscientious editor sees that as part of the job of editing – to recover the original phonemic string, elevating it to the status of a modern text, while effacing the non-modern textuality; that is, he or she in bringing out the text reforms the textuality. Now this is almost the exact opposite of the editing rules of W. W. Greg for editions of early modern texts, who prescribes that we must preserve the textuality (or 'accidents' – spelling and punctuation) of the copy-text but are free to emend the text itself, the 'substantives', the 'readings' of the text as commonly understood.

Why not, then, diplomatic editions? These have their clear uses, especially, as in the case, say, of Zupitza's *Beowulf*, for making decisions about a manuscript for those without immediate access to it. But there are problems. One is that a diplomatic edition, as a mechanizing of the chirographic record, enforces the flow of handwriting into a preset grid. Another is that, by the nature of it, all ambiguities are resolved, not necessarily in favour of sense and the good reading, as in a definitive edition, but nevertheless away from indeterminacy. Another is that editorial interpretation does inevitably enter in (the editor 'performs') but in covert and unacknowledged ways that privilege our established sense of textuality (such as supplying line numbers, italics and dots for 'missing' letters). The main problem, however, is that a diplomatic edition fails to interpret the textuality that is being produced. Layout becomes more formalized, idiosyncratic features (such as capital letters) tend to become regularized (perhaps for economic and typographical reasons) and indeterminate space becomes set space. Certain textual marks (such as points and indentations) already having a certain set of meanings for modern textualists, are reproduced without their significance as representations of the manuscript marks being made clear, even if we happen to know what that might be.[13]

Modern editors have their notions of textuality and ancient scribes had theirs. Among the ideas of modern editors are conventional standards for lineation and caesuras (based on rules of metre) that produce the 'river' down the middle of Old English verse lines, modern norms of punctuation (light, twentieth century Anglo-American, or heavy, nineteenth century German), of paragraphing, and of capitalization (beginnings of all sentences, proper names). As usually done in editions, none of these modern textual features bear much relation to the same technical features in the manuscripts and certainly serve different functions. Certainly few

---

[13] See the interesting remarks on diplomatic editions by J.E. Knirk, 'The Role of the Editor of a Diplomatic Edition', *The Sixth International Saga Conference, 28.7 – 2.8, 1985: Workshop Papers II* (Copenhagen, 1985), pp. 603–12. While he makes the important point that in our culture a feature in a manuscript does not become seeable or discussable, that is, an object of contention, until it has been put into modern textual form (i.e. published/printed) (p. 604), he also argues that systematic non-modern features of manuscript textuality should be stripped away from the diplomatic text (p. 608).

modern editors feel obliged to put their ideas of textuality aside in favour of the scribe's, even if they consciously note the difference.

Unlike modern editors, whose textual practices tend to be strong and systematic but highly conventional, the textual practices of Anglo-Saxon scribes tend to be weak and wavering, but often revealingly idiosyncratic and inventive.[14] Furthermore, medieval calligraphic craft literacy placed value on the written marks as unique and powerful things in themselves, as objects to be considered. Amongst all the marks and blots, we can generalize that these scribes, rather than worrying about metrical lineation, structural paragraphing, articulated rhetorical punctuation, and capitalization based on phrase-and-word categories, tended to transmit three other textual factors, word-group spacing, non-syntactic pointing, and 'accent' marks. These three features are found in many manuscripts, but none of them, it must be said at once, are used in quite the same way by any two scribes and seldom by any scribe with rigorous consistency. (Not that pointing, etc., was not somewhat theoretized by medieval writers; but we are talking about scribal practice.) These marks do seem strikingly analogous to three well-recognized features of vocality which modern textuality does not take much into account: spoken phrasing, pause, and pitch.

Editing by and for the ear is perhaps a new concept. Certainly it is an underdeveloped one. Betsy Bowden has made a beginning in *Chaucer Aloud*,[15] where she asks many readers, expert and lay, to voice select Chaucer texts according to their understanding of the texts. Editing is not her aim, but she brings to mind at least one method, the collation of many voicings where the collation of multiple manuscript copies is not possible. Another suggestive avenue is scientific phonetics, the precise mechanical measurement of voice, its production and effects. Certainly, an informed awareness of the mechanics of speech would be a useful tool for an editor of the vocalized text, analogous to the textual editor's knowledge of scientific etymology. But, given the average Old English editor's training, interests, and experience, his or her best resource may be an inner one: aural intuition, the text that resounds in the ear of the seasoned Old English scholar. It is the same sort of instinct that at the beginning of modern Old English studies allowed Kemble, by hunches, to set out *Beowulf* correctly in lines 'according to metre', long before the metre had been theoretically worked out. This instinct, deriving from experience, was of course subjective and not scientific. An instinct about sounds, while based as much as possible on what little we do know of Old English sounds, intonation, pitch, and so forth, must also take its stand on what we feel about sounds after long experience and experiment with them as speakers of a West-Germanic dialect. English as a spoken language has changed in the past thousand years, but probably less than the corresponding senses of textuality have, and we seldom interrogate our sense of textuality. In the end, relying on hunches about sound is probably no

---

[14] See P. Clemoes, 'Language in Context: *Her* in the 890 Anglo-Saxon Chronicle', *Leeds Studies in English* 16 (1985), 27–36.

[15] B. Bowden, *Chaucer Aloud: The Varieties of Textual Interpretation* (Philadelphia, 1987).

less or more scientific than the textual editor's proud reliance on 'hunches' and intuition when he or she chooses to make an emendation away from what the manuscript presents or decides where to place a comma. Both methods involve leaps in the dark: both are performances – of editors, not scribes – and should be valued and evaluated as such.

In order to illustrate, if not justify, the preceding rather abstract remarks, I undertook a brief editing project according to 'oral' principles, by and for the ear, however crude and exploratory the results. I selected a charm from the *Lacnunga* in London, British Library, Harley 585, *Wið Færstice*, 'For a sudden stitch', Charm 4 in Dobbie's *Anglo-Saxon Minor Poems*. I chose a charm since they normally must have been intended for vocalization (by whatever means composed or preserved) since a charm has no efficacy unless spoken;[16] and the charms in the Harley 585 collection of herbal recipes and charms are certainly not literary (as may be, say, the charm-like structure of *The Wife's Lament*). Like all the material in that little medical/magical *vade mecum* it was clearly intended for practical use to cure some ailment. Moreover, the concentration of a charm is on the power of the voice itself, as a kind of physical force, to coerce the malignant powers to obey: charms do not rely on logic, but on manner and efficacy of delivery. A concentration on the logic and intertextual sanitariness of the *text* of a charm to the exclusion of such interactive elements as *manner of presentation* seems intrinsically incongruous. So, if there is little reason to object to recovering according to traditional methods the correct text, if it can be recovered, there should be even less reason to object to the representation in an edition of such features of vocalization as can be inferred from the exact written context in all its peculiarities, for the writer of a charm must have felt through his/her body while writing the power of it in other ways than as a pure, formal phonemic string.

Our scribe, one of several who contributed to this book of medical recipes, seems to have a particularly weak sense of textuality. His writing does not strike the eye as organized or formal or regular. But he has a very strong sense of word spacing, which I am interpreting as reflecting suprasegmentals, the rhythms of spoken phrases. If one reads this piece aloud *from the manuscript*, paying attention to the spacing, and to our trained ear's sense of the rhetorical movement of the words and the level of importance of the ideas, it is possible to produce a textualized version that looks and reads aloud differently and, I think, better than one

---

[16] L.M.C. Weston has recently stressed the practical rhetoric of the 'double structure' of many charms, 'to transfer power in a specific direction and to a specific purpose' ('The Language of Magic in Two Old English Metrical Charms', *NM* 86 [1985], 176–86, at 177) and Howell Chickering has stressed the dramatic verbal performance quality of the charms, *Færstice* in particular ('The Literary Magic of "Wið Færstice"', *Viator* 2 [1971], 83–104). Stanley Hauer overstresses the autonomous 'literary' quality of this charm ('Structure and Unity in the Old English Charm *Wið Færstice*', *English Language Notes* 15 [1978], 389–401). There indeed are charm-like texts that are 'talismanic', that is, not requiring to be spoken in order to be efficacious: the most spectacular example is the Latin prayer inscribed twice on the crest of the recently discovered Coppergate helmet from York, doubtless intended to protect the wearer during battle (see D. Tweddle, *The Coppergate Helmet* [York, 1984], 17–18).

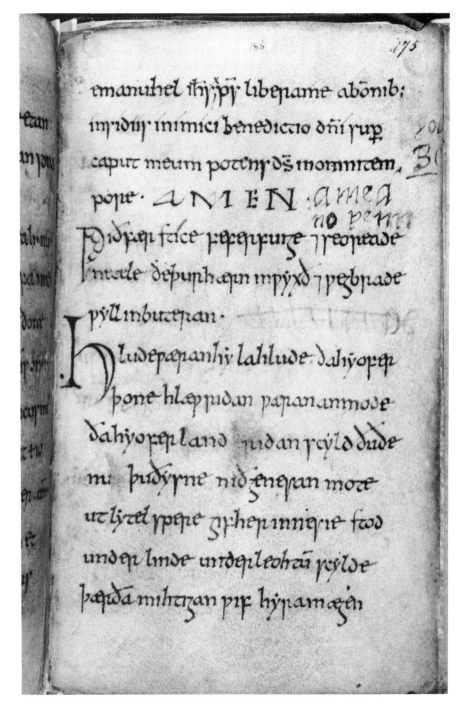

Fig. 1.   London, British Library, Harley 585, fol. 175r

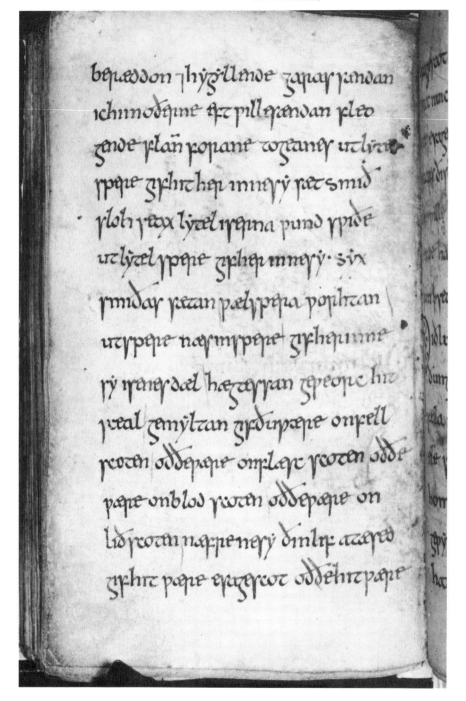

Fig. 2. London, British Library, Harley 585, fol. 175v

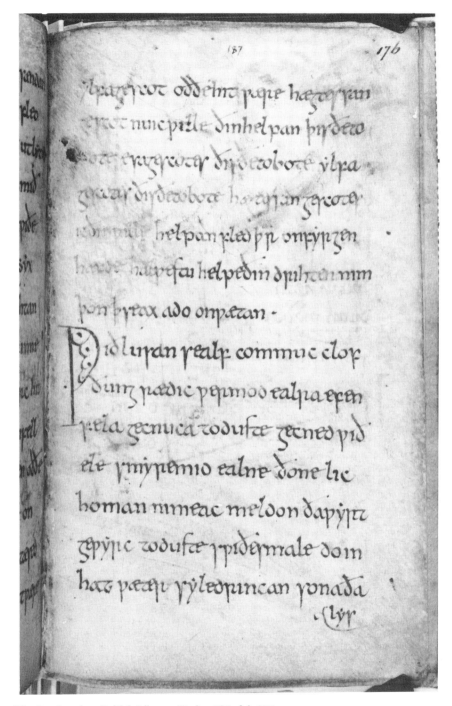

Fig. 3. London, British Library, Harley 585, fol. 176r

edited to the usual norms of Old English poetry. My actual method was to read aloud from the manuscript into a tape recorder many times until I achieved a reading that seemed to me to reflect in its pauses and breathings the spacings of the manuscript text that I was interpreting as suprasegmentally significant, and then to transcribe that reading back as a written document, taking account of the pauses, intonations, and stresses of the voice. Lines represent speech utterances separated by audible pauses. Spaces within the lines represent a slowing down of the pace. Unspaced points between words indicate words written without spaces in the manuscript which I take as indicating single suprasegmental phrases. What I take to be 'instructions to the charmer' (i.e., not to be spoken) are in italics.

I hope this format has produced a readable text (I have introduced no emendations in the text itself). It should be stressed that this is not represented as a 'diplomatic edition'. The facsimiles of the manuscript are provided for reference and should serve the purpose of indicating the scribal text much more accurately. And while it may appear to the reader that some things strange to our sense of textuality have been imposed on the text, I can only say that these impositions seem to me authorized by the textuality of Harley 585, fols. 175r, 175v, 176r. At the same time, the edition avoids a different kind of imposition: that of 'regular' poetic lineation (by the lights of modern textual editors of Old English) on a text that plainly resists it. One immediate gain, as it turns out, is the elimination of any need to posit gaps and scribal errors in several places where they are traditionally posited (e.g., ASPR, lines 14, 27); another is the highlighting of the natural rhetorical repetitions and parallelisms. To clarify the details I have included as an appendix to this article an 'Intertextual Commentary' (by which I mean the editorial intertext as discussed above), a fairly traditional-looking commentary, to justify some of the editorial decisions taken here, point out some of the features of the text that thus emerges, and discuss the most important of the established editorial concerns about this text.

In any case, this procedure produces a text that makes best sense when read aloud, while maintaining to the eye something of the scribe's arrangement (the scribe's line-arrangements are regarded as non-significant, determined simply by the width of the leaf). The only other liberty with the scribe's performance that I have allowed myself (apart from any errors on my part that may remain) is to consistently carry out the same arrangements of spacing that prevail in parallel utterances in places where the scribe has been inconsistent.

HARLEY 585 fol. 175r

Wið.fær stice	*feferfuige and.seo.reade.netele*	1
ðe.þurh.ærn	*inwyxð* *and wegbrade.*	
Wyll in.buteran.		

	Hlude.wæran.hy	
la.hlude		5
	ða.hy.ofer þone hlæw ridan	
wæran anmode		
	ða.hy.ofer.land ridan	
scyld ðu.ðe nu		
þu ðysne nið.genesan mote		10
ut.lytel.spere gif.her inne.sie		
stod under linde		
under.leohtum scyld		
ðær.ða mihtigan wif hyra.mægen / beræddon		[fol. 175v]
and.hy.gyllende		15
garas sændan		
ic.him.oðerne eft wille.sændan		
fleogende flan forane togeanes		ASPR 10
ut.lyte.spere gif.hit her.inne.sy		
sæt smið		20
sloh seax lytel iserna		
wund swiðe		
ut.lytel.spere gif.her.inne.sy		
syx smiðas sætan		
wæl.spera worhtan		25
ut.spere		
næs.in.spere gif.her.inne.sy		
isenes dæl hægtessan geweorc		
hit sceal gemyltan		
gif.ðu.wære on.fell scoten		ASPR 20
oððe.wære on.flæsc scoten	31	
oððe.wære on.blod scoten		
oððe.wære on.lið scoten		
næfre.ne.sy ðin.lif atæsed		
gif.hit wære esa.gescot		35
oððe.hit wære / ylfa.gescot		[fol. 176r]
oððe.hit wære hægtessen.gescot		
nu.ic will ðin.helpan		
þis.ðe.to.bote esa.gescotes		
ðis.ðe.to.bote ylfa.gescotes		40
ðis.ðe.to.bote hægtessan gescotes		

ic.ðin.wille helpan
    fled þære on.fyrgen hæfde
hal.westu
    helpe.ðin drihten   45

nim þonne þæt seax
ado on.wætan.

What is the status of a text like this?[17] Is it descriptive, a record, of the manuscript textuality? Or is it prescriptive, a score, showing how any oral reading of the text ought to go, like a poem of Charles Olson? Or rather is it a prompt, encouraging a multiplication of further vocal performances, all unique because not restricted to the visual register? It is my hope that it is something of all of these, but especially the last. Perhaps 'performative' editions such as this one have the potential of loosening the textual bonds, of giving permission for oral readings that respond to the movements of the text; readings informed and responsible to the manuscript evidence but responsive and individualized as vocalizations. Perhaps it will turn out that the 'true' text will be something that can meet the ear as well as the eye.

At the same time, the unfamiliar lineation, which breaks away from the half-line structure of Dobbie's edition[18] produces its own textuality and makes the phrasing immediately visible while also highlighting the uniqueness of the rhetorical constitution of this text. To give one example, the lineation of the ASPR edition, lines 20–22a, makes the following lines merely defective:

        gif ðu wære on fell scoten   oððe wære on flæsc scoten
        oððe wære on blod scoten
        oðð wære on lið scoten. . . .

On the other hand, the 'oral' edition (lines 30–3) shows the rhythm and parallelism at a glance and encourages a rhythmic reading:

        gif.ðu.wære   on.fell scoten
            oððe.wære   on.flæsc scoten
            oððe.wære   on.blod scoten
            oððe.wære   on.lið scoten

The present edition is intended to respond to the most evident 'oral' feature of this text as we have it in this manuscript, its relatively thoroughgoing marking of

---

[17] The presentation of this paper at the Manchester conference was accompanied by a tape of my reading the charm as here edited, played once as the audience visually scanned a facsimile of the manuscript and played again as they scanned this edition.

[18] *The Anglo-Saxon Minor Poems*, ed. E. Van Kirk Dobbie, ASPR 6 (New York, 1942), Charm 4, 'For a Sudden Stitch', pp. 122–3.

suprasegmentals.[19] The spacing and the resulting visually obvious parallelism arise from following the relative spacing of the manuscript text and then arranging it on the page as 'verse' rather than as a block of 'prose'. Other features that seem not to be marked in the manuscript, such as stress, pitch, dynamics and rhetorical rhythm, are not marked in this edition. Yet an 'oral' edition might, after comparison of generically similar works in all the extant manuscript contexts, in consort with controlled oral reading performances, as here, venture to mark such features as further help to readers. The phonemic text also might in some instances contain clues for performance that could be marked, such as dynamic markers for the opening in this charm, 'La HLUDE'. And the spelling of texts might be emphasized in ways that might better accord with what seems the 'performative' or scribal pronunciation: for example, in our charm, rather than normalizing MS *isenes* (line 28 of our text = ASPR 18a) to *isernes*, as Dobbie does, one might present the manuscript form as the more difficult reading and hence as the one more likely to be reflecting the scribe's pronunciation and 'emend' our line 21 (= ASPR 14a) *iserna* to *isena*.[20] Whatever performative features an editor might *add* to an edition, taking clues both from a given manuscript and from other performances in generically similar texts, nevertheless the oral editor must remain sensitive to the uniqueness of the individual performance and avoid homogenizing all performances to a single system or attempting to produce an entirely hypothetical 'ideal' performance. That would merely introduce into the editing of Old English oral texts a new dimension of totalizing at variance with the basic premise of this project.

APPENDIX: INTERTEXTUAL COMMENTARY TO *FÆRSTICE*

1/ASPR 1 Wið.fær stice a large accent added over *i* of *stice*. *Færstice*, it is generally agreed, means 'sudden sharp pain'. It is not agreed of what sort. J. Grimm (*Teutonic Mythology*, 4th edn, tr. J. S. Stallybrass [London, 1882–8], p. 1243) thought 'stitch in the side'; A. Heusler (*Die altgermanischen Dichtung* [Potsdam, 1926], p. 59) thought headache. Others (F. Grendon, 'The Anglo-Saxon Charms', *Journal of American Folklore* 22 [1909], p. 214; G. Storms, *Anglo-Saxon Magic* [The Hague, 1948] p. 142; H. Chickering, 'The Literary Magic of *Wið Færstice*', *Viator* 2 [1971], p. 83) supposed rheumatism. The first two seem unlikely since a charm would not be invoked for a pain of short duration and the charm seems to be associated with the body, not the head (the arguments are summarized by G.W. Abernethy 'The Germanic Metrical Charms', Unpubl. PhD

---

[19] A feature studied in relation to Old English poetry by R.D. Stevick, *Suprasegmentals, Meter, and the Manuscript of Beowulf*, Janua Linguarum: Series Practica 71 (The Hague, 1968).

[20] See A. Campbell, *Old English Grammar*, Oxford, 1959, § 475. For possible translations of 21–22, see the commentary.

diss, Univ. of Wisconsin, 1983, pp. 93–4). The mention of nettles as a cure suggests that the tactic is to attack the pain by applying a countering pain. According to the OED, 'feverfew', as the name suggests, was a traditional remedy for fever, and 'waybread' (plantain) for swelling and redness. These implied features of the ailment, combined with sudden pain, and the deliberate application of an irritant to the skin, suggest that the charm may be against some painful skin eruption, perhaps what we would call 'allergic reaction', the kind showing sudden onset, pain, itching, heat, redness, and swelling. This might explain the battle imagery, as of armies encountering with spears (itching combatted by scratching); and it might help to explain the difficult line 43/ASPR 27 (see below).

T.O. Cockayne (*Leechdoms, Wortcunning, and Starcraft of Early England*, [London, 1864–9, repr. 1961]) thought that lines 1–2/ASPR 1–2 formed a charm by themselves. This is a reasonable guess in view of the way these lines are laid out on fol. 175 (see the facsimile). But this section seems to indicate the preparation of a salve that is referred to again at the end of the charm (*wætan* 47/ASPR 29) in an utterance that is clearly part of *Færstice* as written. Therefore it seems best to regard lines 1–2, with H. Stuart ('Utterance Instructions in the Anglo-Saxon Charms', *Parergon* n.s. 3 [1985], p. 35), as an 'implied utterance instruction' that the scribe deliberately set apart from the 'spoken' part of the charm.

2/ASPR 2 þurh.ærn has been explained as *ærn* 'house' by Cockayne, and *ærn* < **ern* 'barley' (cf. OHG *aren/arn* 'harvest') by F.P. Magoun ('Zu den altenglischen Zaubersprüchen', *Archiv* 171 [1937], 19). The latter is favoured by editors and would presumably mean 'the nettle which grows in the field and protrudes among the grain'. The former would perhaps mean, with A.R. Skemp ('The Old English Charms', *Modern Language Review* 6 [1911], 291), 'the nettle that grows into the house through the (loose wattle) walls'.

3/ASPR 2 wyll in.buteran. Point after *buteran*. 'Boil in butter', a frequent instruction in the herbals (cf. A. DiPaolo Healey and R.L. Venezky, *A Microfiche Concordance to Old English* [Toronto, 1980], W055 277–89, W025 15–28).

4/ASPR 3 la.hlude These words heavily inked and a smudged (added?) point after *hlude*.

6/ASPR 4 ridan Preterite plural; the scribe prefers forms in *-an* (cf. *beræddon* 14/ASPR 8).

7/ASPR 4a wæran anmode The arrangement, following the scribe's phrasing, obviates the 'lack of alliteration' noted in ASPR 4 and elsewhere and points up the rhythmic, semantic, rhyming parallelism of lines 6 and 8.

10/ASPR 5 þu ðysne nið.genesan mote The construction is asyndetic, '(shield yourself now) – you might be able to escape this attack'. There is no need to supply a conjunctive before *þu* (such as *þæt* [*Sweet's Anglo-Saxon Reader in Prose and Verse*, rev. D. Whitelock (Oxford, 1967)], *gif* [F. Holthausen, 'Zur Textkritik alt- and mittelenglischer Gedichte', *Archiv* 188 [1951], 100]).

14/ASPR 8 beræddon The normal meaning is 'deprive', 'dispossess' but with accusative of person and/or genitive of thing. The word may mean what it seems to say, the 'mighty women deprived (themselves) of power', though it is difficult to explain why they would do this; or it may mean 'the mighty women deprived (them: others) of their power' but then it is difficult to see to whom the reference is. To avoid such unclarity of reference, various ad hoc translations of *beræddon* have been offered: 'to consult about' (T. N. Toller, *An Anglo-Saxon Dictionary Supplement* [Oxford, 1921]); 'prepare' (Grendon; W. Horn, 'Der ae. Zauberspruch gegen den Hexenschuss', in *Probleme der englischen Sprache und Kultur, F/S Hoops* [Heidelberg, 1925]; J. H. G. Grattan and C. Singer, *Anglo-Saxon Magic and Medicine* [London, 1952]); cf. *rædan* 'to prepare'); 'talked up (their strength)' (Chickering, 'Literary Magic', 84).

15/ASPR 9a and hy gyllende The scribe's suprasegmental division shows clearly that *gyllende* belongs with *hy*, the women (so Cockayne and Storms), and not with *garas* ('screaming spears'), as the majority of editors construe.

18/ASPR 11 flan (= flane) Accusative singular feminine; presumably, by metonomy one of the 'spears' of 16, the accusative singular masculine *oðerne* (17) forming a grammatical bridge between the two terms.

19/ASPR 12b gif.hit her.inne.sy Note that *hit* does not occur in the other similar versions of this phrase (11/ASPR 6b; 23/ASPR 15b). Presumably the variation between the lines is a 'spoken' feature rather than a conscious 'insertion' or correction by the scribe (so Grattan and Singer). M. Rieger regularized by omitting *hit* in 19 (*Alt- und as. Lesebuch* [Giessen, 1861], p. 142).

21/ASPR 13b seax lytel Presumably this little knife is connected with the instructions at the end, *nim þonne þæt seax*.

22/ASPR 14 iserna wund swiðe This is not easy to construe and, if regarded from the point of view of metre, is obviously defective. Dobbie, following L. Ettmüller (*Engla and Seaxna Scopas and Boceras* [Quedlinburg, 1850], p. 302) and others, prints * * * *iserna, wundrum swiðe*, positing one hiatus to space out the on-verse and emending the off-verse to provide the extra syllable that the proposal creates a demand for. Grattan and Singer took *iserna* as nominative singular masculine weak 'small the iron', but *isern* is otherwise a strong noun (Abernethy, 108). Disregarding regular metre, and following the suprasegmentals as written, *iserna* can be construed with *seax lytel* 'little knife (made) of iron', followed by the interjection 'great wound'; or, more grammatically, '(a smith) struck/forged a little knife of iron (parts) (that was) strong (to make) wounds', taking *wund-swiþ* as weak neuter accusative; for the formation, cf. *þryþ-swiþ*, *Beowulf* 131, 736. The arrangement *iserna wund swiðe* can also be construed, but with more strain: 'great the wound of iron' (i.e., 'wound caused by iron'). The latter arrangement sets up a semantic/rhythmic parallelism: 'forged a knife small: the wound of iron great'.

23/ASPR 15 gif.her.inne.sy Point after *sy*. It is taken as marking a hiatus.

25–33 Another hand has made drypoint vertical divisions in this part of the text: they do not necessarily correspond to conventional metrical or rhetorical units. They occur after *sætan* 24, *worhtan* 25, *spere* 27, *dæl* 28, *sceal* 29, *fell scoten* 30, *flæsc scoten* 31, *blod scoten* 32, *lið scoten* 33. Did somebody once strike the manuscript with rhythmical apotropaic gestures made with 'a little knife'?

25/ASPR 16b wæl.spera worhtan *spera* = *speru* accusative plural neuter. Related to the scribe's habit of writing the preterite plural as *-an* (as in this phrase), where unaccented *-a*, *-o*, *-u* have fallen together in pronunciation (A. Campbell, *Old English Grammar* [Oxford, 1959], § 49). *worhtan* could be construed as an infinitive, but given the scribe's practice, is better taken as preterite plural.

28/ASPR 19a hægtessan Variously glossed *Phinotissa* [= Pythonissa], *Parce*, *Striga*, *Furia*, *Eumenides* (see *Microfiche Concordance* H002 8–9, s.v. haegtess[e], hæhtis[se]). It is paired with *hellerune* in one gloss, suggesting a demonic, underworld (feminine) figure, more (or less) than human. The isolated gloss in the set is *striga* 'witch'. In this text *hægtessa(n)* are the associates of the demonic *ylfa* and *esa*.

32/ASPR 21 Sweet/Whitelock, following Grimm, makes up a 'missing' half line by supplying *oððe wære on ban scoten*.

35/ASPR 23a esa Nominative *ōs*, corresponding to ON *áss*, *æsir*. These are presumably no longer gods in the full sense.

36/ASPR 23b ylfa.gescot W. Bonser (*The Medical Background of Anglo-Saxon England* [London, 1963], pp. 158–62) explains that 'shot', 'shooting' means frequently 'shooting pain' and is especially associated with elves.

43/ASPR 27 fled þær on.fyrgen hæfde MS: *þr*. This line is the most troublesome in the text. It is worth noting that some charms introduce deliberately nonsensical incantations, of which this might be one, portentous sounding words meaning little (see Grendon, pp. 124ff.). Dobbie's version sums up the problems (and partial solutions): *Fleoh þær * * * on fyrgenheafde*. He takes *fled* as a miswriting for a verb *fleoh*, imperative (so Grattan, 'Three Anglo-Saxon Charms from the *Lacunga*', *Modern Language Review* 22 [1927], 2, who emended to *fleah*, preterite), allowing *hæfde* to function as a noun, which he then, following Sweet's *Anglo-Saxon Reader*, compounds with *fyrgen* because the latter never occurs in Old English as a simplex. He then posits some missing words in the on-verse. Forms of this version are now the commonly accepted reading: 'flee there . . . onto the mountaintop' (cf. Charm 2, 21 'Fleoh þu nu, atttorlaðe', the intertext of this emendation). According to the OED, the past tense *fled* does not appear in English until about 1350 and may be via Scandinavian; it is not impossible, but not likely, that this is a very early instance of it. Abernethy (p. 112) points out that there is no need to actually emend *hæfde* since that is a common variant spelling of *heafde*. But it is worth looking at the end of the line again. Though *fyrgen* does not elsewhere appear in Old English as a simplex, the variety of compounds it participates in as first element implies its continuing generative force as a simplex. It occurs as a simplex in Gothic *fairquni* 'mountain' and ON *Fjörgin* 'earth'. We may have then the simplex here. This would leave *hæfde* as verb of the sentence. Or if we cannot accept the simplex, *hæfde* might better be taken as the verb anyway and the loss placed thus: *on fyrgen- * * * hæfde*. With *hæfde* functioning as the verb, *fled* can be taken as a noun, *flēd(e)* 'flood', 'tide'. The whole line can thus be taken as written (with or without an elision after *fyrgen*) as '(it) had a flood on the mountain'. Thus, if this mysterious sentence can be construed at all, it may be alluding to the eruption of a hive or boil in connection with the ailment being charmed, probably the bursting being seen here as the outer sign of the effected cure.

46/ASPR 29 nim þonne þæt seax MS *þōn*. Unlike the clearly marked-off opening instructions, there is no textual indication that the closing instructions have begun at this place.

47/ASPR 29 ado on wætan. It is not clear what is meant and M. Doskow, 'Poetic Structure and the Problems of the Smiths in *Wið Færstice*', *Papers on Language and Literature* 12 (1976), 325, cautions against speculation. Most commentators have taken the *wætan* to refer to the buttery ointment mentioned in the opening, with the knife being used to apply the medicine to the affected place (so, e.g., Skemp, p. 290). But Abernethy (p. 113), suggesting that the knife might be used to scrape off the ointment after it has done its work and noting such phrases in the medical recipes as *ado of ða buteran*, suggests *ado of* 'take off (the knife)' but he does not emend his text accordingly. If my explanation of the 'mountain' in the previous note is right, the *wætan* might not refer to the salve but to the watery issue from a rash, boil, or hive, the placing of the knife in it being a magical gesture of finality as the ailment is 'killed'.

EDITING AND THE MATERIAL TEXT

Katherine O'Brien O'Keeffe

THE YOKING OF 'material' and 'text' has the whiff of oxymoron about it. If 'material' is a word whose referent evokes the world in its most concrete forms, 'text' is a word whose referent has become all but disembodied.[1] It is precisely to counter the modern literate disembodiment of text that I wish to consider the materiality of an Old English text and its implications for editorial strategies. To illustrate both these issues, I have chosen *Solomon and Saturn I*, a poem whose survival in two manuscripts presents some challenges to the traditional practice of textual editing for Old English verse.

The problems raised by the two manuscript texts of *Solomon and Saturn I* lie at the heart of the standard practice used in editing Old English verse. Cambridge, Corpus Christi College 422, pp. 1–26 (=A), copied in the mid-tenth century,[2] has provided the base text for all four independent editions.[3] The other, later text preserved in Cambridge, Corpus Christi College 41 (=B),[4] functions as a supplement by supplying the first thirty lines of the present *Solomon and Saturn I* (lines unreadable on the damaged page 1 of CCCC 422) and appearing thereafter as a witness in the apparatus. Kemble's dismissive evaluation of B apparently prevailed in subsequent editions: 'As the only interest of this second codex is derived from the lines which it furnishes to the first, and the various readings, it requires no further remark'.[5] Kemble's judgment of B, so reasonable within the rubrics under which he edited the poem, raises issues about the practices of editing Old English verse in multiple manuscripts, among them the relative significance of two manuscript records, the question of manuscript authority, and the validity of a composite text or, indeed, of an authoritative edition.

---

1 On the distinction between work and text see Roland Barthes, 'From Work to Text', in *The Rustle of Language*, trans. Richard Howard (New York, 1986), pp. 56–64. For Barthes's deconstructive emphasis on 'intertextuality' see Vincent B. Leitch, *Deconstructive Criticism: An Advanced Introduction* (New York, 1983), pp. 106–7 and more generally pp. 121–2.
2 N.R. Ker, *Catalogue of Manuscripts Containing Anglo-Saxon* (Oxford, 1957), no. 70, s. x^med.
3 These are in chronological order: *The Dialogue of Salomon and Saturn*, ed. J. M. Kemble (London, 1848); *Salomo und Saturn*, ed. B. Assmann, Bibliothek der angelsächsischen Poesie, 3.2 (Leipzig, 1898), pp. 58–82 (304–28) and 237–8 (483–4); *The Poetical Dialogues of Solomon and Saturn*, ed. Robert J. Menner (New York and London, 1941); *The Anglo-Saxon Minor Poems*, ed. Elliott Van Kirk Dobbie, ASPR 6 (New York and London, 1942), pp. 38–48 and 164–70.
4 Ker, *Catalogue*, p. 45, 's. xi^1 or xi^med'.
5 *Salomon and Saturn*, ed. Kemble, p. 133.

Three fundamental assumptions underlie my approach to the editing of *Solomon and Saturn I*. In the interest of economy, I should like simply to state them as a way of indicating the grounds of my argument. First, I take as a given that manuscripts of Old English verse preserve a form of literacy different from our own. Elsewhere I have argued the case for regarding such literacy as 'transitional', that is, still deeply influenced by its situation in a residually oral culture.[6] This influence is exhibited in textual transmission by forms of variance generally associated with the circumstances of oral performance and by a textual array comparatively low in interpretative visual cues. Such 'transitional' literacy is an important feature of the contemporary reception of verse texts and is a crucial component in their transmission. Second, my argument assumes that the psychological and cultural forms of our own literacy are historical phenomena and as such are not culture-neutral. Literacy thus cannot constitute a transcendent category of perception (akin, for example, to Kant's categorical claims for time and space) through which we apprehend without barrier the writing of a previous age. Literacy as we know it (or perhaps, more accurately, live it) constitutes, in fact, an ideological formation. My third assumption flows naturally from the first two – that the disembodiment of text, which is both a reflex and a strategy of modern literate ideology, limits the optimum recovery of medieval texts and their contexts.

This last point, perhaps, requires further elaboration. To term the disembodiment of text 'reflex' and 'strategy' is to view it from two complementary historical perspectives. It is the reflex of a literacy characterized by suppression of the early somatic elements of reading (where lips and fingers, sound and touch supplemented sight) and of writing (where the reminder of the bodily and the individual always present in the handwritten textual object disappears before the uniformity of print).[7] Reading and writing are, quite simply, much less 'bodily' than they were in early literate settings. The disembodiment of text is strategic when viewed in terms of its usefulness in rendering a text manipulable: when the 'real' text is purely conceptual, existing apart from and before any realization of it in manuscript or print, such a text is subject to endless reconstructions and appropriations. Whether viewed as reflex or strategy, however, the disembodiment of text is the efficient product of a modern literacy whose ideological force is all-pervasive.[8] Functioning as ideology, our literacy blinds us to its own historical and cultural dimensions, presenting itself as a window on the past rather than as a lens. My argument, then, is that the window (the temptation to accept literacy as the transparent, trans-historical access to the past) is paradoxically more distorting

---

[6] Katherine O'Brien O'Keeffe, *Visible Song: Transitional Literacy in Old English Verse*, CSASE 4 (Cambridge, 1990), pp. 8–14; 191–4.

[7] The hand and wrist pain of carpal tunnel syndrome, affecting (among others) longterm users of word processors, provides an unfortunate backward link to the physical complaints of professional scribes.

[8] See Katherine O'Brien O'Keeffe, 'Texts and Works: Some Historical Questions on the Editing of Old English Verse', in *New Historical Literary Study*, ed. J.N. Cox and L.J. Reynolds (Princeton, 1993), pp. 54–68.

than the lens (the acceptance of the historical situatedness of our own literacy). The latter stance, acknowledging the historicity of literacy, requires the negotiation of a fundamental difference between ourselves as readers and the medieval readers for whom the texts we study were produced. The first step in this process of negotiation lies in our methods of editing.

Kemble's 1847 edition of the Solomon and Saturn poetic dialogues established and presented the text according to the then developing philological principles.[9] In context, the edition formed one part of a larger historical survey of the appearance of the Solomon and Marcolf legend in the Middle Ages. Kemble based his text on A, supplementing it with the first thirty lines from B. A modest apparatus records some but not all of his departures from A and some variants from B. Kemble indicates long vowels with an accent mark (though neither consistently nor always accurately and by no means following the manuscript). He modernizes capitalization and punctuation, regularizes spelling (blithely interchanging thorn and eth), and lays out the text in hemistichs with a facing Modern English translation. And Kemble's edition of *Solomon and Saturn I* abandons English 'blackletter' for the modern print conventions of the Old English alphabet.

The differences between Kemble's edition and Assmann's, published some fifty years later as part of Wülker's revision of Grein's *Bibliothek*, are instructive. Assmann's edition is a deliberate technical improvement on those of Kemble and Grein, intended to present the text with greatest accuracy. A is the base text with emendations now and again from B.[10] All expanded abbreviations are indicated by italics.[11] The full apparatus records all variants from the edition as well as earlier editorial readings. The modern typographic version of the Old English alphabet is expanded to include insular *g* and the abbreviation for *ond*. Nonetheless, Assmann disregards manuscript capitalization, punctuation and accents, and he presents the text in two-stave lines (though without a space marking the caesura).

The two twentieth-century editions depart from Assmann's text less in textual readings (although technical advances had allowed the recovery of some further readings) than in the conception of the editions. Menner designed his edition as the last word on the subject. Its introduction covers history, palaeography, language, and sources. Textual notes and a full glossary accompany the edition, which presents facing texts of A and B. Various kinds of emendation are signalled typographically: replaced letters in italics, added letters in square brackets, conjectures for faded letters in parenthesis. The full apparatus gives all manuscript readings and selected critical readings. Abbreviations are expanded silently, though so-called 'unusual' abbreviations are indicated in the apparatus. The text itself was

---

[9] Kemble's edition of *Solomon and Saturn* proper was first published as no. 13 of the Ælfric Society in 1847. The publication dates of the full three parts of *Anglo-Saxon Dialogues of Salomon and Saturn* (paginated consecutively) were 1845, 1847, 1848.

[10] E.g., at 35a *ungesibb* (A: *ungelic*); at 56a *scyldum* (A: *scyldigum*); at 63b emended from B to *astæned*.

[11] These include -u*m*, ðon*ne*, and þ*æt*.

prepared from photostats and from a transcript of the manuscripts made by J.C. Pope in 1933. Menner notes that 'the capitalization and punctuation of the MSS are disregarded in the text, but recorded in the apparatus when they might possibly be significant. The accents of the MSS are not recorded'.[12] Menner emends as well to improve sense. His most startling departure from the tradition of editing the text, however, is his moving of lines 170–8 in *Solomon and Saturn I* to the end of *Solomon and Saturn II*, following a suggestion made by Vincenti.[13] Dobbie's edition, made in cooperation with Menner, conforms to the constraints of the ASPR format. Emendation is minimal, and the apparatus limited to manuscript variants from the printed text. Punctuation and capitalization are modern.

Dissatisfaction at this wealth of editorial scholarship on *Solomon and Saturn I* appears ungrateful, perhaps perverse. But I will risk such an appearance to discuss a pervasive failure in both the presentation of manuscript evidence and the construction of a usable and responsible text. In all of these editions, a significant body of information disappears when the modern text is made. The information to which I refer is manuscript format, spacing, capitalization and punctuation. Of the four editors, Menner is the only one to refer to such matters, and then only to acknowledge that he has ignored them. His acknowledgement is not made as a confession of shortcoming but rather as a statement of conformance with general editorial principle.[14]

Such principle conceives of the text as essentially separable from the manuscripts which transmit it. The text is an abstraction, conceived in the mind of its author, damaged in its incarnation, and in need of redemption by its modern editor. This act of redemption strips away the mundane, the scribal, in order to restore the text (as far as possible) to a state close to that in which it entered the world. For this to be an intellectually responsible exercise, variants, format, spacing, capitalization and punctuation must be some or all of the following: extratextual, inherently meaningless or signs of (presumably scribal) corruption. The assumptions I have outlined are virtually axiomatic. For variants, one thinks of Kenneth Sisam's warning that the judge (our editor) must not surrender to the (presumably impeachable) witness.[15] For punctuation, one thinks of Krapp's indictment of the 'heedlessness of scribes in transmitting what may have been originally a more systematic style of punctuation'.[16]

These editorial postures represent, in fact, a flight from history, since they strive to erase the intervening time and events between the now and the moment of composition – an attempt which presumes that the relationship of medieval author

---

[12] *Poetical Dialogues*, ed. Menner, p. 79.

[13] Menner, pp. 10–12, following A.R. von Vincenti, *Die altenglischen Dialoge von Salomon und Saturn*, Münchner Beiträge zur romanischen und englischen Philologie 31 (Leipzig, 1904), 64.

[14] On the development of editing practices in Old English see J.R. Hall, 'Scholarly Editing in Medieval English Studies: Old English', in *Scholarly Editing: An Introduction to Research*, ed. D.C. Greetham (New York, forthcoming).

[15] K. Sisam, *Studies in the History of Old English Literature* (Oxford, 1953), p. 34.

[16] *The Vercelli Book*, ed. G.P. Krapp, ASPR 2 (New York, 1932), p. xxxi.

and modern reader can be unmediated. However, the attempt to produce this kind of 'faithful' version of a poem is necessarily doomed to failure by the very denial of historicity that motivates the desire for an unmediated textual recovery. What is wrong with this picture? It disregards the material text.

The material text is the poetic work-in-the-world. It is an incarnation of what is otherwise merely an idea, or perhaps more accurately, an abstraction. Because a poem cannot exist apart from its transmitting manuscripts, what we call a poem is actually a complex of individual manifestations. The material text, that is, the poem as transmitted and presented in an individual manuscript, is the fundamental unit in which the poem appears in the world. Its materiality extends beyond the obvious fact that an object, the transmitting manuscript, is the vehicle by which the poem acts in the world. Much more important is the less obvious fact that the array of a poem in the manuscript constitutes in itself a body of information. (If you think it does not, recall how irritating it is for us to read a diplomatic edition – irritating precisely because such an edition lacks the visual information necessary for *us* in the twentieth century to read easily.) Material texts remind us that the poem is a work. Its integral connection with the transmitting manuscript locks it in a social, economic and historical matrix, binding together authors, scribes, editors and readers.

Thinking about the materiality of a text requires reconceiving our notion of the nature of an Old English poem and its mode of being. The poem, whether surviving in a single manuscript or in two or more, is not a unitary phenomenon at all but rather a complex composed of all of its individual manifestations in manuscript form. These manifestations are *realized* texts: each manuscript text is place and time specific and embodies the poem as a particular reading. The poem cannot exist without the medium which transmits it.

By applying this conception of material text to *Solomon and Saturn I*, we can observe that the promotion of A to base text actually diminishes our larger understanding of the poem. What survives of the poem survives from two different times and contexts. The first, that realized text in A, travels with other Solomon and Saturn material, perhaps conceived with them as a single work. The second, the text in B, was always fragmentary, and survives with an odd assortment of texts in the margins of a copy of the *Historia ecclesiastica*.[17] In the sixty-three lines they have in common, these realized texts contain some ten metrically, lexically and syntactically appropriate variants. Such variants pose a problem, since there is no editorial strategy for choosing between them which does not finally come down to individual preference.[18] Nor can it be argued that the older text is entirely reliable.

---

[17] On the importance of context in the understanding of an Old English poem see Fred C. Robinson, 'Old English Literature in its Most Immediate Context', in *Old English Literature in Context*, ed. J.D. Niles (Bury St Edmunds, 1980), pp. 11–29 and 157–61, and Fred C. Robinson, ' "Bede's" Envoi to the Old English *History*: an Experiment in Editing', *Studies in Philology* 78.5 (1981), 4–19.

[18] See O'Keeffe, *Visible Song*, pp. 64–6.

A represents a version of the poem to which runes have been added, almost certainly after original composition.[19] The orthography, capitalization and punctuation of the two realized texts differ. In the capitalization and punctuation particularly we see the poem brought forth at two separate moments in the development of literacy in Anglo-Saxon England. As a case in point, the capitalization in *Solomon and Saturn I* in itself constitutes a discrete reading of the text, since by varying the size and elaborateness of individual capitals the scribes indicate a perception of the relative importance of the two contestants in the dialogue.

I have made the argument that the material text constitutes a fundamental part of a poem's existence and that the cost of ignoring a poem's material existence is no less than abandoning crucial elements of its historical meaning. This is so, in part, because the Old English poetic work has an intrinsic visual dimension which cannot be translated from the manuscript. Recognizing the poem's materiality effectively counters the literate ideology behind our visual assumptions about meaning and counters as well the flight from history that idealist conceptions of the poem presuppose. Representing the material existence of an Old English poem in an edition, then, is necessary if we are to gain access to the visual information which grounds the poem in the world.

Modes of literacy are historical phenomena, and there are excellent reasons why we present Old English poems in the form we currently do. Foremost among these reasons is that our current methods produce a readable poem. My argument, then, is not to abandon these methods, but to supplement them with an equally informative one, which will counter the idealized text with a realized one.

My own approach to editing *Solomon and Saturn I* has taken the form of an experiment with strategies to represent the material texts of the poem. Most important of these is the separate presentation of each manuscript version in facing text format: on the left side of the opening a full, critical textual edition, on the right an 'archaeological' diplomatic text which in effects maps in print the visuals of each manuscript page.[20] Since these editions are given in parallel, the information on the manuscript page determines how much text is offered per page in critically-edited format. To the extent that the diplomatic text is 'archaeological', it obviates, I believe, the need for a critical apparatus. Because a scrupulous diplomatic text performs an analytical mapping of the manuscript, it offers more particular information than a facsimile, which may often be visually ambiguous.[21]

The second major strategy is the presentation of each material text in its manuscript context.[22] For A this requires presenting *Solomon and Saturn I* with its two

---

[19] Kenneth Sisam, review of *Poetical Dialogues*, ed. Menner, *Medium Ævum* 13 (1944), 35.

[20] See F. Masai, 'Principes et Conventions de l'Édition Diplomatique', *Scriptorium* 4 (1950), 177–93.

[21] Obviously, such a diplomatic text cannot claim to be 'objective', since its construction depends on a series of interpretations of physical and visual evidence. But such interpretations limit themselves to the 'translation' of physical and visual evidence from manuscript to print and ought not to concern themselves with the creation of 'meaning'.

[22] See F.C. Robinson, ' "Bede's" Envoi', 1–19.

companion texts, the prose *Solomon and Saturn* and the second verse text, *Solomon and Saturn II*. For B manuscript context requires presentation of *Solomon and Saturn I* along with the text it surrounds, Bede's account of the apostasy of Sighere and the East Saxons.[23]

The historical editing I propose accounts for the work-in-the-world. It does not freeze the text in an arbitrary moment, the desired moment of authorial creation (for the reasons outlined above always an illusion), but seeks to chart the work's path in the world, to trace its encounters, watch the effects it has and the developments it undergoes. It endeavours to read the text as part of a matrix, one most easily and concretely located in the text's material condition.[24] As an object, the text (in its manifestation as work) persists in pointing us to the facts of its production and reproduction, of its 'literal' appearance in the world, the arrays by which it encodes meaning. The individual manuscript text insists on its otherness. Regard for its materiality prohibits our translating its spatial array into modern print form, for in terms of visual array, presentation in the normal editorial conventions of lineation, regular spacing of words, capitalization, punctuation is as much translation as a shift in language.

The attraction and, indeed, the strength of standard editing are that it presents the text in a form most accessible to *us*. But it is readable only because it has been reduced and reconstituted as a modern written message. In the process of reduction and reconstitution, the individual realized text loses its history in a necessary bifurcation: in the recovery of an original text (if not authorial at least made 'authoritative'), the process which cleanses the realized text of traces of its action in the world is a move to *undo* history, and the companion process which provides the now disembodied text with a visual array to ensure its modern readability is a move to accelerate history to its present form. These twin moves both situate the work in the present (effectively an historical move) and deny the value of its situatedness in any intervening moments (in whatever moments its texts were realized in surviving copies).

Regard for an author prompts the recovery of an authorial text. Regard for the work urges a sympathetic presentation of its material form. The editor who would produce an edition of a text works in relation to the text and its 'truth' analogously to the scribes who copy and make changes in transmitting the text. Both work, labour on the text, affect it and change it in accordance with describable rules. Thus any copy, reproduction, transmission or version will always

---

[23] See *The Old English Version of Bede's Ecclesiastical History of the English People*, ed. T. Miller, 4 vols, EETS os 95–6, 110–11 (London, 1890–98), I, 250 (III.22).

[24] See M.M. Bakhtin and P.N. Medvedev, *The Formal Method in Literary Scholarship*, trans. A.J. Wehrle (Cambridge, MA, and London, 1985): 'All the products of ideological creation – works of art, scientific works, religious symbols and rites, etc. – are material things, part of the practical reality that surrounds man. It is true that these are things of a special nature, having significance, meaning, inner value. But these meanings and values are embodied in material things and actions. They cannot be realized outside of some developed material', p. 7. See also pp. 12 and 17.

be a collaboration with the author (insofar as it makes sense, in an anonymous tradition, to speak of one).

It is precisely the material text which allows the poetic work to perform its criticism of the present through its insistent otherness. Decisions on editorial practice of the kind we are exploring here are of the first importance, because the editing of a text determines the limits of the criticism that may be conducted on that text. In many ways, our discipline's decisions on editing practice will determine the very viability of our subject. We may properly ask: 'Does the text still live?' The answer is yes, if we understand the text to exist in a dialogue with the present. In this way the text persists in affecting the world, since it comments on the world which receives it. Our editing should make possible such dialogical study, where the edited poetic work presses our reading community to reflect on itself in reflecting on the text.

TEXT AND CONTEXT IN EDITING OLD ENGLISH: THE CASE OF THE POETRY IN CAMBRIDGE, CORPUS CHRISTI COLLEGE 201

Graham D. Caie

THE MODERN SCHOLAR who extracts a single work from an Anglo-Saxon manuscript to edit it is akin to the archaeologist who selects a single artifact from a composite site, cleans it, restores missing pieces, names it and presents it in a pristine modern setting as an isolated phenomenon. Old English editors ought to feel a responsibility to convey the context, both codicological and sociohistorical, of the work they edit. Not only does the modern editor give a sense of clinical tidiness that is not in the original, but also influences the reader's interpretation by emendations and by supplying titles.[1] Rarely is the feel of the manuscript context conveyed in the modern edition that frequently includes no facsimile or description of the items surrounding the chosen text. One can learn much about the work and its application by asking if it is in a well-worn, utilitarian book, if it is illustrated, and if the text is punctuated or glossed. Editors ought to ask such questions as: does this item begin a new section in the manuscript? Is it in the same hand as the previous and following items? What is the nature of the surrounding works, e.g., are they prose or poetry, secular or religious? A similar plea for the study of Old English poems in their codicological context was recently made by Fred C. Robinson in ' "The Rewards of Piety": Two Old English Poems in their Manuscript Context'.[2] He points out that many works have no clear divisions, most have no titles and, as an example, he convincingly demonstrates how *An Exhortation to Christian Living* (hereafter *Exhortation*) and *Summons to Prayer* (*Summons*) in CCCC 201 are in fact one and the same poem.[3] The first editor thought that the macaronic section must constitute a new item and his decision was never queried, probably because the manuscript was not consulted.

I should like to take Fred Robinson's argument further and examine the 'five' (now four) poems that appear together in CCCC 201, as I believe that, in spite of

---

[1] An example of a misleading title is *The Benedictine Office* which is neither strictly Benedictine nor an Office.

[2] In *Hermeneutics and Medieval Culture*, ed. P.J. Gallacher and H. Damico (New York, 1989), pp. 193–200, at 193. The paper read at the Manchester Conference was in fact written before I had read Professor Robinson's article.

[3] I suggested a similar unity in an earlier article, 'The Vernacular Poems in MS CCCC 201 as Penitential Literature', *A Literary Miscellany Presented to Eric Jacobsen*, ed. G.D. Caie and H. Nørgaard (Copenhagen, 1988), pp. 72–8.

being written in two different hands and periods, they function as a group in that manuscript and that the compiler might well have had good reason for placing them together. The five poems are *Judgment Day II* (*Jdg II*), *Exhortation, Summons, Lord's Prayer II* (*LP II*) and *Gloria I* (*Glo I*) on pages 161–70 of the manuscript.[4]

Jdg II begins on a new page with a large green capital which generally in CCCC 201 indicates a new and separate item. Its rubric also announces clearly that it is a new work: 'Incipit versus Bede presbiter. De Die Iudicii. Inter florigeras fecundi cespites herbas flamine uentorum resonantibus undique ramis', the latter part comprising the initial hexameters of Bede's work. The poem concludes with a colophon: 'Her endað þeos boc þe hatte inter florigeras. ðæt is on englisc betwyx blowende þe to godes rice farað and hu þa þrowiað þe to helle farað' ('Here ends this book that is called *inter florigeras*, that is in English, between the blossoming ones which journey to God's kingdom and how those who travel to hell fare'). This most definitely indicates the conclusion of a poem, or at least an end to the translation of Bede, yet, as the same scribe immediately continues with *Exhortation*, there is a visual link between the two. There is no line separation, no indication of a break and no green capital to suggest a new work. It is as if the scribe is pointing out to the reader that at this point the Bede translation concludes and an original but related work immediately follows.

Exhortation is more didactic and less imaginative than *Jdg II*: its message is one of repentance with fasting, prayer and good works as preparation. But in spite of the colophon and change in tone and mood, there are both verbal and thematic links between *Jdg II* and *Exhortation* that suggest that they were intended as companion pieces. *Exhortation* begins with a front-shifted connective 'Nu' that implies that the next stage is commencing:

> Nu lære ic þe swa man leofne sceal
> gif þu wille þæt blowende rice gestigan.

> 'Now I shall teach you, dear man, what you must do, if you
> wish to climb to the blossoming kingdom.'   (lines 1–2)[5]

The poet seems to be saying: 'You have heard about the blossoming kingdom of heaven from Bede, now I shall tell you how to reach it.' The *blowende rice* of *Exhortation* must refer both to the colophon's *blowende*, mentioned above, which in turn is a direct translation of Bede's *florigeras*, and to the many references to flowers at the conclusion of *Jdg II* where the prophets and martyrs are described in terms of red flowers and the virgins white. The poet of *Exhortation*, therefore,

---

4   See the edition by E.V.K. Dobbie, *The Anglo-Saxon Minor Poems*, ASPR VI (New York, 1942); other editions are by Hans Löhe, *Be Domes Dæge*, Bonner Beiträge zur Anglistik 22 (Bonn, 1907), and J.R. Lumby, *Be Domes Dæge*, EETS os 65 (London, 1876). I have a new edition of *Jdg II* in preparation.
5   I have changed Dobbie's punctuation in my forthcoming edition and omitted the period between these lines.

assumes that we know what the blossoming kingdom is and thereby creates a deliberate link with the preceding work, as he also does with the theme of Dooms-day: 'þeos woruld is æt ende . . .' ('this world is at its end'). He addresses the listener in the second person singular 'þu', as does the *Jdg II* poet, which suggests that *Exhortation* is meant as a devotional exercise to be read aloud by a priest addressing a single penitent as 'dear man' and 'thou'.

There then follows what was previously thought to be a new poem, *Summons*, in which the familiar 'þu' continues, and the poet-priest leaves a space with the abbreviation 'N' for 'Nomen', for the name of the penitent to be added.[6] The *Summons* section begins immediately after *Exhortation* with no separating line, no green capital and the initial Þ is the same size and colour as initials at the beginning of other paragraphs in these poems. Identical punctuation marks are found throughout the three poems. The links between *Jdg II* and *Exhortation* are similar to those between *Exhortation* and *Summons*, which starts with the connective 'þænne' and continues with the confessor's 'gemiltsað þe', echoing common prose absolutions. *Summons* is a macaronic Old English and Latin poem based on the *confiteor* pattern.[7] Only because of the macaronic section was it considered a separate poem, yet a poem such as *The Phoenix*, as Professor Robinson has pointed out, also concludes with a macaronic section and begins with an Old English translation of a Latin work.[8] Leslie Whitbread suggests that there might be an established and symmetrical design to the three poems, as they begin and end with Latin.[9]

The use of macaronic verse also links these three poems with the final two, *LP II* and *Glo I*, although there are major problems to be faced before discussing any connection between the first three poems and final two. The *Summons* scribe clearly concludes his poem on page 167 with the word 'c a e l o r u m' evenly spaced over a full line before adding an elongated punctus versus. There is a one-line manuscript break before *LP II*, which is in a different hand and probably written at a later period. The first three poems are in an early eleventh-century, pointed hand, that of scribe A, who was responsible for the initial section of the manuscript after the Parkerian table of contents and up to page 7.[10] The larger and more rounded hand of the scribe who is responsible for the majority of items in CCCC 201 resumes on page 167. Ker has described this hand as belonging to the mid-eleventh century.[11]

---

[6] See the facsimile of CCCC 201, p. 166, overleaf. *Summons* is said to begin nine lines from the foot of the page

[7] I am greatly indebted to Leslie Whitbread for his comments in 'Notes on Two Minor Old English Poems', *Studia Neophilologica* 29 (1957), 126.

[8] Robinson, ' "The Rewards of Piety" ', p. 196.

[9] L. Whitbread states that 'whoever added *Exhortation* and *Summons* in that order to *Jdg II* was attempting to copy a complex technical convention', 'Notes on Two Minor Old English Poems', 128.

[10] This initial section of CCCC 201 contains an Old English translation of the *Regularis Concordia*.

[11] N.R. Ker, *Catalogue of Manuscripts Containing Anglo-Saxon* (Oxford, 1957), p. 82.

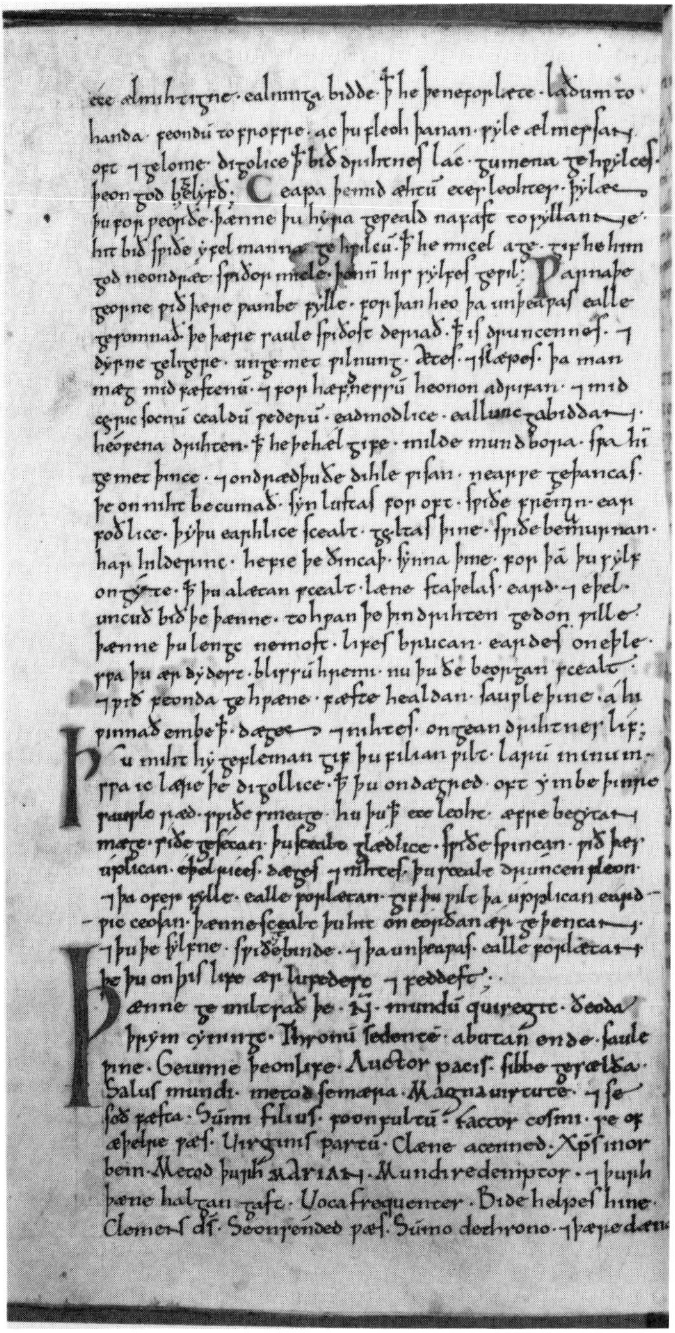

Fig. 4. Cambridge, Corpus Christi College 201, p. 166

There are, however, very strong verbal links between *LP II* and *Glo I* apart from the scribal.[12] Both are didactic, devotional exercises, based on the two prayers, each taking one line of the liturgical prayer and elaborating on it. There are also sufficient numbers of verbal echoes to suggest common authorship: e.g.,

> Sy þe þanc and lof þinre mildse
> wuldor and willa

'Thanks and praise be to you for mercy, glory and will' (*LP II*, lines 58–59) is echoed in the first two lines of *Glo I*:

> Sy þe wuldor and lof wide geopenod
> geond ealle þeoda, þanc and wylla   (*Glo I*, lines 1–2).

Similarly, line 21 of *Glo I*: 'and tosyndrodost hig syððon on mænego; / . . . ealle gesceafta.' ('and you separate them then in many: . . . all creation . . .') is probably by the same poet who wrote 'and ealle gesceafta, / and tosyndrodest hig siððan on manega' (*LP II*, line 65).[13]

We have, then, two distinct groups of poems in CCCC 201: *Jdg II*, *Exhortation* and *Summons* creating the first, and *LP II* and *Glo I* the second. Yet, although the two groups are written in a different hand and possibly at a different time, one should investigate the possibility that the later scribe or manuscript compiler had some reason for placing them together, other than the fact that they constitute the only vernacular poetic texts in the manuscript and contain eschatological material (e.g. *LP II*, lines 90–2). A codicological clue might be the fact that *LP II* begins immediately after *Summons* with the top of the capital 'P' and 'Þ' of 'Pater' and 'Þu' reaching the last line of the previous poem. External evidence is found in the fact that both groups have the same function and audience as penitential material.

A further link is to be found in a Doomsday homily which Napier printed as no. XXIX in his collection of the homilies of Wulfstan, and which is found in Oxford, Bodleian Library, Hatton 113, folios 68ʳ–70ᵛ.[14] It begins with the rubric 'Her is

---

[12] See L. Whitbread, 'The Old English Poems of the "Benedictine Office" and Some Related Questions', *Anglia* 80 (1962), 37–49, at 41, where he calls *LP II* and *Glo I* 'companion pieces by the same author at the same time'.

[13] There are many more verbal echoes which James Ure mentions, e.g. *LP II*, 35–36 and *Glo I*, 1–2; *LP II*, 51–53 and *Glo I* 42–43; *LP II*, 73 and *Glo I*, 14; see *The Benedictine Office: An Old English Text*, ed. J. Ure (Edinburgh, 1957), pp. 53ff. Ure goes further and claims that these two poems were written as organic parts of the Benedictine Office and even written specifically for the Office. See also P. Clemoes, 'The Old English Benedictine Office, Corpus Christi College Cambridge, MS. 190, and the Relations Between Ælfric and Wulfstan: A Reconsideration', *Anglia* 78 (1960), 265–83.

[14] This homily is edited by A.S. Napier, *Wulfstan: Sammlung der ihm zugeschriebenen Homilien*. Sammlung englischer Denkmäler in kritischen Ausgaben, 4 (Berlin, 1883); repr. with bibliographical supplement by Klaus Ostheeren (Dublin and Zurich, 1967), no. XXIX, pp. 134–43. This is a late eleventh-century Worcester manuscript. The homily is pseudo-Wulfstan and appears in this manuscript with those homilies generally accepted to be the work of Wulfstan. See

halwendlic lar and ðearflic læwedum mannum, þe þæt læden ne cunnon . . .': 'Here is healing and necessary instruction to the laity who know no Latin'. This Wulfstanian homily contains a substantial section of *Jdg II* as well as direct, didactic teaching on penance. It is clear that the homilist is preparing his audience for confession: he selects those passages from *Jdg II* that would instil the greatest fear into his audience and omits much about the reciprocal joys of heaven. In both manuscripts the translation of the Bede poem appears as an imaginative means of catching the audience's attention before launching into the strictly didactic section.

The five poems appear to have the same function as a penitential sermon, but in the form of devotional exercises for an individual, thence the second person singular pronouns of the poetry are replaced by plurals in the homily. CCCC 201, which contains all Wulfstan's homilies and many other works considered to be by him, such as substantial parts of *The Institutes of Polity, The Canons of Edgar, The Benedictine Office*, and his revision of Ælfric's first pastoral letter, certainly reflects Wulfstan's interests and responsibilities.[15] He placed great importance on the significance of penance and the clergy's need to instruct the laity on this matter. It would, therefore, be in keeping that this Wulfstanian manuscript provided the priest with a series of poems that would help him lead the penitent from a state of sin to final absolution – and it is not surprising that the compiler adds forms of absolution in the *De Confessione*, a work that follows *Glo I* on page 170. Allen Frantzen[16] mentions the need for confessors to deal not only with the *theory* of penance, but also the vernacular literature that he calls devotional exercises that would lead to the *practice* of penance at a time when private penance was recommended. The handbooks were specific and contained the orthodox formula for penance, but there was a growing need for vernacular literature that was catechetical, that prepared one for penance and put one in the correct spiritual mood beforehand and afterwards: 'The heightened spiritual awareness achieved in confession was sustained by means of prayer, preaching and poetry. These literary forms, discursive and devotional, were better able than the penitentials to supply themes and images to reinforce the sinner's conversion. . . . Much medieval literature seeks to guide its audience along this path, but only certain texts do so with explicit references to confession and penance, and these materials – homilies and prayers and poems – join with the handbooks to constitute "penitential literature".'[17] These poems, then, are better understood in the light of the late Anglo-Saxon penitential

Donald G. Scragg, 'Napier's "Wulfstan" homily XXX: Its Sources, Its Relationship to the Vercelli Book and Its Style', *ASE* 6 (1977), 197–211, at 209–10, and Donald G. Scragg, 'The Corpus of Vernacular Homilies and Prose Saints' Lives Before Ælfric', *ASE* 8 (1979), 223–77, at 259.

[15] Dorothy Whitelock suggested that manuscripts such as Oxford, Bodleian Library, Junius 121, Cambridge, Corpus Christi College 190 and Oxford, Bodleian Library, Hatton 113/114 (which contains the prose version of *Jdg II*) must have been based on Wulfstan's commonplace book and that the compiler of CCCC 201 'had access to material collected by Wulfstan'; see *Sermo Lupi ad Anglos*, ed. D. Whitelock, 3rd edn (London, 1963), p. 27.

[16] A.J. Frantzen, *The Literature of Penance in Anglo-Saxon England* (New Brunswick, N.J., 1983).

[17] See *Ibid.* pp. 11–12.

tradition. They were catechetical works that might be read by the individual layman or, as the macaronic *Summons* and the forms of absolution might suggest, by the priest to the laity.[18]

As suggested above, editors have influenced the reading of Old English poems by the titles given, and *Jdg II* is no exception. Only 80 of the 300 lines of *Jdg II* are actually about Doomsday and a more appropriate title might be 'Pilgrimage of Penance'. It begins with devotional confession and leads through contrition to the eschatological vision that prepares the reader for the exhortation that is to follow. Just as the Napier XXIX homilist saw this poem's potential for catching his audience's imagination and creating a mood of fear and introspection that was necessary for compunction, so also the author of *Exhortation*, or the manuscript compiler, might have viewed the Old English translation of Bede's poem as a fitting introduction for this spiritual pilgrimage.

Jdg II begins with the much-praised lyrical description of a paradisal and protected garden in which the persona sits alone.[19] Then the tormented skies and wind evoke the fear of Doom and the need to remember past sins. The individual stages of penance are clearly traced in the next section that owes much to the soul and body topos, another important theme in penitential works: one must weep tears of remorse, pray, beat one's breast, open one's heart and reveal all sins now rather than wait for their public revelation at Doomsday. Christ is presented as the Physician who will heal with plasters the wounds of sin. The poet therefore traces the necessary pilgrimage of the soul from the pleasant place, the garden of this world, through the psychological torments that make one reconsider the meaning of life to the eternal garden of paradise. The horrors of Doom and other terrors promised are goads that will bring about the necessary contrition and confession. As in *Christ III*, *Judgment Day I* and so many Ælfrician and Wulfstanian homilies, the torments of hell are graphically and vividly described in great detail, surely the most common and effective psychological method of scaring one into changing one's ways.[20] The description of the joys of heaven pales in comparison in all Doomsday literature and indeed no Christian poet, not even Dante or Milton, has been able make heaven more attractive than hell.

Jdg II provides the perfect, lyrical introduction, gently leading the listener from his complacent state to one made receptive by fear. The eschatological imagery at the beginning of Bede's poem is expanded and made more obvious in the vernacular one which was intended for the laity,[21] while the absence of any mention of confession to a priest can be explained by the eighth-century practice of private

---

[18] See *Ibid.* pp. 181–7.

[19] See the descriptions of the poem as a lyric in G.K. Anderson, *The Literature of the Anglo-Saxons* (Princeton, 1966), p. 166, and C.W. Kennedy, *Early English Christian Poetry* (New York, 1963), p. 252.

[20] I have expanded on this topic in my *The Judgment Day Theme in Old English Poetry* (Copenhagen, 1976), pp. 115–59.

[21] See my 'The Vernacular Poems', pp. 72–8, for a more detailed comparison between the two introductions.

confession. Frantzen calls this a work of 'devotional confession – a form of confession which was, throughout the early medieval period, an accepted method of obtaining remission for the punishment due to sin'.[22] By the tenth century priestly confession was obligatory and therefore, once the reader is in the correct, receptive penitential mood, the *Exhortation* poet is more explicitly didactic: 'Now I shall teach you, dear man . . .'. The poet is no longer a fellow sinner, but a priest addressing a penitent. And so the collection of poems continues with direct, unadorned exhortation to repent, leading in *Summons* to absolution. Finally, as is necessary, the penitent is asked to say and contemplate on the Lord's Prayer and, in this case, the expanded form of the Gloria instead of the Creed. In this way the manuscript compiler puts together a collection of devotional exercises with a clear, chronological purpose – from worldly sin to final absolution.

Such a collection would have an important place in any work associated with Archbishop Wulfstan especially with his concern for the instruction of the laity, in particular the lay clergy, as can be seen, for example, in his *Canons of Edgar* where he urges all Christian men to know their Creed and Pater Noster, if not in Latin at least in English. The fact that *Summons* requires some knowledge of Latin might also point to the lay clergy as its intended audience. The monastic reform of the tenth century with its emphasis on penance, and the work and ideals of Wulfstan in the eleventh, create the spiritual and cultural setting in which this manuscript was created. By looking at the poems in their manuscript and cultural context and by considering the aims of the manuscript compiler, the poems in CCCC 201 can be seen as a unified devotional exercise connected with the sacrament of penance, and not a 'hodge-podge' of isolated works.

---

[22] Frantzen, *The Literature of Penance*, p. 185.

EDITING OLD ENGLISH
AND THE PROBLEM OF ALFRED'S *BOETHIUS*

M.R. Godden

HISTORICALLY, the motive force behind the editing of Old English texts, especially prose, has been an interest in language. It was the need to provide material for the New English Dictionary which prompted the creation of the Early English Text Society, itself responsible for the majority of editions of Old English prose, and similar concerns lay behind other Victorian editions, such as the Ælfric Society series. The interest in language and especially in spelling and inflexions strongly influenced the way in which editors tackled their work. There is much here to be grateful for, but looking back one is also conscious of the limitations and deficiencies of such approaches: the repeated failures to provide the promised second volume of commentary, the lack of interest in the text's content or the author's thought, the presentation of texts in ways which made few concessions to readers who were looking for the sense rather than the spellings. Too many texts have been fettered rather than freed by their editors. One Alfredian text can be taken as an example for many.

King Alfred's version of Boethius's *Consolation of Philosophy* is one of the most important works in Old English prose, the major achievement of a major figure in English literary history, but the standard edition, indeed the only full one, is one of the minor tragedies of Anglo-Saxon literary scholarship. Produced by W.J. Sedgefield in 1899,[1] it is accurate and painstaking, a monument to philological dedication, carefully reproducing the text of different manuscripts letter-by-letter; but the resulting pages present an almost impenetrable barrier to King Alfred's own thoughts and expression, with their daunting array of roman and italic type, round and square brackets and superscript numbers. But the problem is not simply that the presentation of the text on the page is so opaque; it is also, as we will see, that the text so presented is a hybrid, a composite of different authorial versions based on untested critical principles, and that it gives only the most limited impression of the second and more interesting of the two versions. In fact, neither the structure of the second version nor the precise relationship of the two has ever been examined in sufficient detail. Yet one has to admit that the textual situation is very complicated and it is hard to find a satisfactory solution.

The manuscript situation in its essentials is probably familiar to most Anglo-

---

[1] *King Alfred's Old English Version of Boethius De Consolatione Philosophiae*, ed. W.J. Sedgefield (Oxford, 1899).

Saxon scholars, but it would help to examine it afresh. There are just two medieval manuscripts of the work extant.[2] The later one, Oxford, Bodleian Library, Bodley 180, was written in the first half of the twelfth century, more than two centuries after its composition. It contains the *Consolation* in Old English prose, clearly written, well-preserved and complete. The other copy is in London, British Library, Cotton Otho A.vi. This is a manuscript of the middle of the tenth century, quite close in time to Alfred, and has verse and prose alternating in the text. The manuscript was very badly damaged in the Cotton fire of 1731: several leaves were destroyed, mainly at the beginning, and all others were charred at the edges, and the text is often illegible. Before the fire, Francis Junius had made a copy of the Bodley manuscript and collated it with Cotton. His transcript, still in the Bodleian library,[3] has selected variants from Cotton entered in the margins, and where Cotton had whole passages different from Bodley these are transcribed on separate pages, now pasted in.

The text in the Bodley manuscript begins with a preface which immediately poses problems. It identifies Alfred as the author, mentions the preoccupations of his reign and then describes the two successive versions which he made of the translation:

> Ælfred kuning wæs wealhstod ðisse bec, and hie of boclædene on englisc wende, swa hio nu is gedon. Hwilum he sette word be worde, hwilum andgit of andgite, swa swa he hit þa sweotolost and andgitfullicast gereccan mihte for þam mistlicum and manigfealdum wordum and bisgum þe hine oft ægðer ge on mode ge on lichoman bisgodan. Ða bisgu us sint swiþe earfoþrime þe on his dagum on þa ricu becoman þe he underfangen hæfde, and þeah ða þas boc hæfde geleornode and of lædene to engliscum spelle gewende, and geworhte hi eft to leoðe, swa swa heo nu gedon is; and nu bit and for Godes naman he halsað ælcne þara þe þas boc rædan lyste, þæt he for hine gebidde, and him ne wite gif he hit rihtlicor ongite þonne he mihte; forþamþe ælc mon sceal be his andgites mæðe and be his æmettan sprecan þæt he sprecð, and don þæt þæt he deþ.[4]

<hr/>

2   There is a detailed description of the two manuscripts in N.R. Ker, *Catalogue of Manuscripts Containing Anglo-Saxon* (Oxford, 1957), nos. 167 and 305.

3   Oxford, Bodleian Library, Junius 12.

4   'King Alfred was the translator of this book, and turned it from Latin into English, as it is now done. Sometimes he put word for word, sometimes sense for sense, as clearly and intelligibly as he could render it on account of the various and manifold words and anxieties [*probably an error for* worldly anxieties, *the reading of the other MS*] which often busied him both in mind and body. The anxieties which came upon the kingdom which he had undertaken in his days are very difficult for us to number, and yet when he had learnt this book and turned it from Latin into English discourse and shaped it [*the other MS has* then he shaped it afterwards] into verse, as it is now done; and now he prays and for God's sake beseeches everyone who takes pleasure in reading this book that he should pray for him, and not blame him if he understands it more correctly than he was able to; for everyone must say what he says and do what he does according to the power of his understanding and his leisure.'

Although the preface refers to Alfred in the third person it is generally, and surely rightly, accepted as his own work: there are close similarities to his other prefaces; the humble request at the end for prayers and the closing modesty topos indicate Alfred himself as author; and the statement that he first produced a prose translation and then turned it (or part of it) into verse fits with the internal evidence of the two versions. The difficulty is that this preface seems to have been written to introduce the second of the two versions which it describes, the one using verse, but the text which follows in this manuscript is entirely in prose. The same preface appears in the other manuscript and one must presume that Alfred wrote it for this subsequent version and that it was later transferred, by Alfred himself or another, to a copy of the earlier prose version.

The preface is followed in the Bodley manuscript by a long table of contents in Old English, which divides the work into forty-two sections or chapters and describes in some detail the action and argument of each chapter. The chapter divisions have no parallel in any known copy of the Latin text, and do not correspond with either the book-divisions of the Latin or, in general, the boundaries between prose and verse in it; indeed, Alfred's version is at times so independent of the Latin that the chapter division and table of contents can only have originated with the Old English text. The table shows an intelligent understanding of the underlying themes of the translation and is probably by Alfred himself,[5] perhaps inspired by the similar table of contents taken from his Latin source in his previous translation, the *Pastoral Care*. The text of the Old English *Consolation* then follows in the Bodley manuscript, beginning with an introductory account by Alfred of Theoderic and Boethius and then loosely rendering the Latin original. The text is all in prose and divided into sections by large coloured initials, or spaces for them which have not been filled in. The forty-two chapters indicated by the table of contents are all marked in this way, and many of them are numbered; there are also a number of further sections or sub-sections marked in a similar way. Presumably, the manuscript preserves an arrangement laid down by Alfred himself more than two hundred years earlier.

In the Cotton manuscript the crucial opening leaves have been destroyed and it is only with some difficulty that the original shape of this version can be reconstructed from Junius's notes and collations.[6] It appears to have run as follows:

1. The prose preface already seen in Bodley 180, with slight variations of wording.

2. A brief verse preface of ten lines, not in the Bodley manuscript. It tells how Alfred composed the work in verse, making it pleasant so that his teaching would not be ignored; though it begins by referring to Alfred in the third

---

5 As argued by K. Otten, *König Alfreds Boethius* (Tubingen, 1964), pp. 11–13.
6 A reconstruction of the text of the opening pages of the Cotton version is given below in an appendix.

person it shifts at the end to first-person reference to the author, and the personal tone suggests that it is Alfred's own voice and his own work.

3. An introductory account of Theoderic and Boethius in eighty-four lines of verse, paralleling the similar prose account in Bodley. It gives rather more information on the Goths than the prose, and a slightly more favourable slant on them.

4. An Old English verse rendering of the metre or song with which the Latin text begins.

5. An Old English prose rendering of the first prose section of the Latin text, corresponding closely with the version in Bodley.

Thereafter verse and prose alternate, with the verse being used for most of those sections which correspond to metres in the Latin text. There appears to have been no table of contents in the Cotton manuscript: the Junius transcript has no collations for the table, and a note in Junius's hand, subsequently crossed through, reports its absence. Nor is there any trace in the text of the division into forty-two chapters seen in Bodley. Instead, the text appears to have been divided up into some sixty-three sections, with a new line and space for a large three-line initial each time the text changes from verse to prose or back again (and also at the beginning of a new book of the Latin text). These divisions often correspond with the chapter divisions in the Bodley manuscript, but there are also many cases where they do not match at all: that is, there are many section divisions which do not correspond to chapter divisions in Bodley, and there are chapter divisions in Bodley which do not correspond to boundaries in Cotton. Traces of the Bodley arrangement are perhaps evident in the slightly enlarged capital within the manuscript line which occurs in Cotton at the point where chapter xviii begins in Bodley and again where chapter xix begins, suggesting that the Cotton arrangement goes back ultimately to a copy containing something like the Bodley manuscript's organization.

The Cotton text is a quite substantially different version of the work, though it is difficult to see how different until one reconstructs it with scissors and paste. It is not simply that the parts of the prose version which correspond to the Latin metres have been turned into verse. The new verse preface, the long introductory account in verse and then the first metre together mean that after the opening prose preface we have nearly 120 lines of verse before we return to prose, and then for only twenty lines or so before we resume with verse. This is a work which announces itself, both in the prefaces and in the form of its opening, as a poem not a prose text. Its structural principles are also very different. The elaborate forty-two chapter arrangement with matching table of contents, cutting across the prose and verse divisions of the Latin text, is replaced by an arrangement which emphasizes the alternation of verse and prose in the English text.

How do these two versions relate to each other? The prefaces assert that both versions were the work of Alfred himself and that the verse was based on the prose. Both statements seem now to be generally accepted: the long debate about Alfred's authorship of the verse, beginning in the last century, largely ended with Sisam's article of 1953.[7] Two contrasting theories have been proposed for the relationship of the two versions. In his edition Sedgefield gave a stemma to show the relationship of the two extant copies and a third brief fragment that is now lost. The stemma would appear to suggest that Alfred produced a collection of the verse portions which was transmitted separately from the main text, and that someone in the middle of the tenth century then substituted these verse passages for the equivalent prose in a copy of the prose version, to produce what we find in the Cotton manuscript. Sedgefield did not give his reasons for this view, unless they are implied by his comments about dialect, but there seems little to be said for it. The verse portions can have had no point or meaning as an independent collection, and it would have been very difficult, probably impossible, for someone unconnected with Alfred to substitute them successfully in the correct places in the prose version. The two prefaces make it clear that Alfred himself designed and issued a version of his work incorporating the verse; the natural assumption is that the Cotton copy derives from that.

A very different view from Sedgefield's was proposed by Kenneth Sisam, who suggested that Alfred may have formally published or issued only one version, the verse and prose one from which Cotton derives, and that the prose version was just a preliminary stage and never meant to be circulated or read.[8] Somehow, he speculated, a copy was made of that prose draft and that was the ancestor of the Bodley copy. He did not elaborate his reasons for this view, but was perhaps relying on the fact that the prose version lacks a preface of its own, at least in the surviving copy, and the possible hint in the prose preface that the prose version was just a stage on the way to the verse. The suggestion does not account for the evidence, however. As we have seen, the prose version is carefully divided into forty-two chapters described in a detailed table of contents, all probably by Alfred himself. Such work can only have been undertaken with the intention of copying and circulating the text for others to read. But the divisions and descriptions seem to have been designed for the prose version, rather than the verse, taking no account of the verse and prose alternation in Cotton and its different structure, or indeed of its differences of expression: thus the phrase 'þone smyltan sæ' in the entry for chapter ix corresponds to the 'smyltan sæ' of the prose text rather than the 'ruman sæ' of the verse. There is no sign of the chapter divisions in the Cotton text:

---

[7] K. Sisam, *Studies in the History of Old English Literature* (Oxford, 1953), pp. 293–7. More recent studies include J.W. Conlee, 'A Note on Verse Composition in the *Meters of Boethius*', *NM* 71 (1970), 576–85; A.A. Metcalf, 'On the Authorship and Originality of the *Meters of Boethius*', *NM* 71 (1970), 185–7, and *Poetic Diction in the Old English Meters of Boethius* (The Hague and Paris, 1973); P-E. Monnin, 'Poetic Improvements in the Old English *Meters of Boethius*', *English Studies* 60 (1979), 346–60 (based on a chapter of his dissertation 'The Making of the Old English *Meters of Boethius*' (University of Massachusetts, 1975), for which see *Dissertation Abstracts* 36 (1976), 6117A). Metcalf accepts Alfred's authorship, Monnin questions it, suggesting that the true author may have been an illiterate singer.

[8] Sisam, *Studies*, pp. 294–5.

indeed, it seems very likely that Alfred dispensed with the forty-two chapter arrangement for his revised version, because it clashed with the new set of divisions between verse and prose, which become the dominant structure in Cotton. Further evidence is the fact that Ælfric a century later refers to Alfred's translation and borrows from it, and it is clearly the all-prose version that he used.[9] The evidence indicates that the two manuscripts derive from two successive versions of the whole text produced and issued by Alfred, one all in prose and the other alternating verse and prose. As the evidence of the continued copying and use of the prose version might suggest, we do not have to assume that the second version was designed to supplant the first; the wording of the verse preface might be taken to imply that Alfred was simply recasting the work for a different kind of readership or audience.

Thanks partly to Junius, it is the prose version which has dominated the editorial history of Alfred's Boethius. The earliest edition, by Rawlinson in 1698,[10] relied heavily on Junius's transcript for both text and arrangement: it presented the prose text of Bodley 180 with an apparatus giving the variant readings from Cotton's prose sections recorded by Junius and an appendix containing Cotton's verse portions, similarly drawn from Junius. The edition by Cardale in 1829 gave the prose text only: it was closely based on Rawlinson but incorporated some of his Cotton variants into the main text and supplied a number of conjectural emendations.[11] The 1864 edition by Fox was based in turn on Cardale, but supplied fresh collations of his text with the two manuscripts, and added the verse portions in an appendix.[12] One might add that the separate editions of the verse portions by Fox and Krapp have continued the tradition set by Rawlinson of treating the verse as in some way extraneous to the *Consolation*.[13]

Sedgefield's edition of 1899 is a much more complicated phenomenon, though it too reflected the historical emphasis on the prose version. He set out to present the testimony of the Cotton manuscript, which had recently been reassembled, and he made this his primary copytext, presumably because its early date made it an important witness to Old English language. But like all his predecessors he nevertheless presented the work as a whole in the form of the earlier of the two versions,

[9] On Ælfric's use of Alfred's Boethius see W.F. Bolton, 'The Alfredian Boethius in Ælfric's Lives of Saint I', *N&Q* n.s. xix (1972), 406–7, and M.R. Godden, 'Anglo-Saxons on the Mind', in *Learning and Literature in Anglo-Saxon England: Studies presented to Peter Clemoes*, ed. M. Lapidge and H. Gneuss (Cambridge, 1985), pp. 271–98, esp. pp. 278 and 296–9.

[10] *An. Manl. Sever. Boethi Consolationis Philosophiae Libri V. Anglo-Saxonice redditi ab Alfredo, Inclyto Anglo-Saxonum Rege. Ad apographum Junianum expressos*, ed. C. Rawlinson (Oxford, 1698).

[11] *King Alfred's Anglo-Saxon Version of Boethius De Consolatione Philosophiae with an English translation and notes*, ed. J.S. Cardale (London, 1829).

[12] *King Alfred's Anglo-Saxon Version of Boethius De Consolatione Philosophiae with a literal English translation, notes and glossary*, ed. S. Fox (London, 1864).

[13] *King Alfred's Anglo-Saxon Version of the Metres of Boethius*, ed. S. Fox (London, 1835); *The Paris Psalter and the Meters of Boethius*, ed. G.P. Krapp, ASPR 5 (New York, 1932).

the all-prose, forty-two chapter form witnessed by Bodley 180, and consigned the verse passages from the Cotton version to an appendix. Thus for the prose passages which are common to both versions he reproduced the readings of Cotton wherever it could still be read, recording the Bodley variations somewhat selectively in the footnotes, signalled by superscript numbers in the body of the text; occasionally he substituted Bodley readings for Cotton in the text. Where Cotton could not be read or was entirely destroyed, he reproduced the Bodley text, in italic type and enclosed in brackets, and added in the footnotes the readings recorded from the Cotton manuscript by Junius, though occasionally he introduced these variants into the text, apparently where the Bodley reading was thought not to make sense. For the sections where the two manuscripts do not correspond, that is where Bodley has prose and Cotton has verse, he reproduced the Bodley version, though again presenting the text in italics and within brackets. Thus Sedgefield's editorial creation is a curious kind of composite: it combines the all-prose forty-two chapter arrangement of the first version with the prose preface which really belongs in the second version and alternates between the texts of the two different versions, emending on a rather ad hoc basis while leaving serious errors uncorrected. It is very unsatisfactory in other ways too. In its layout of the text it relies heavily on the tradition established by Junius without reporting the evidence of the manuscripts: thus Sedgefield does not record which of the chapter numbers are from the Bodley manuscript and which editorial, and he follows Junius in imposing on the text a system of numbered paragraph divisions, often in unlikely places: thus the division at I ii–iii (Sedgefield p. 9) is not at all strongly marked in the manuscript, while the one between §§iii and iv is inserted at a point which, in terms of the manuscript layout and the sense, appears to be the middle of a sentence. Moreover, Sedgefield's decision to use as copytext a manuscript which does not in fact contain the version he was editing created a text that was heavily concealed beneath editorial signals.

There is a pressing need for a new edition, and particularly one that presents a full text of Alfred's later, poetic version of the *Consolation*. As the basis of an edition, the prose version does have distinct advantages: it has the table of contents amounting to an analytical index and a clear numbered structure, and it perhaps provides better evidence for Alfred's handling of Boethius's ideas. But the second version represents Alfred's later thoughts, it is the version to which the prefaces refer, it is in some sense the more literary version, with two contrasting styles of writing, and it is often clearer and sharper and more emotive in expression. Any attempt to edit the Cotton version must first meet some difficult questions of method and principle, however. Firstly, there is the problem of differences of detail between the two manuscripts, in the prose portions which are common to both versions. A decision to edit the Cotton version does not necessarily imply a commitment to all the readings of the Cotton manuscript. Sedgefield and his predecessors were surely right to attempt a critical text, but the process needs to be pursued in much more comprehensive fashion. Cotton is a much earlier manuscript but it does have copying errors which could be corrected by reference to Bodley (a point demonstrated by Sisam using Napier's transcript of the lost fragment).[14] Thus at Sedgefield 25/25–6 the edited text, following Cotton, reads: 'Forðæm ic ðe mindgige þæt þu ongite þætte nan gesælð nis on þis andweardan life ðonne seo gesceadwisnes'. This makes very poor sense and syntax, and Bodley's additional clause after *life*, 'ac onget ðæt nauht nis betere on þis andweardum life', is clearly correct: the repetition of *life* could easily have caused an accidental omission by a scribe in the Cotton tradition. Other variations are more difficult. Thus at 51/27 Cotton has *aræd* and Bodley has *areht*; Sedgefield prints the former. Either is possible in context, but *areht* is Alfred's standard usage in such senses and *aræd* is not used elsewhere in the Boethius. There is also the possibility that not all differences in the prose portions are scribal. When Alfred recast parts of the text as verse he must surely have at least re-read the parts that he left as prose, and it is very likely that he altered details of expression as he did so. A possible case is the following pair:

63/18 C wenstu mæge his wela and his rice hine þær on londe wyrðne don?
       B *lacks* his wela and
63/28 C ... þæt se anwald and se wela sie þæt hehste good
       B *lacks* and se wela

There are several doublets like C's in this section, some found in both manuscripts, and one can easily see their point: Alfred is trying to analyse the problem of *honores* or *dignitates* and it is difficult to find an exact equivalent in Old English. Did the Bodley scribe omit *wela* each time because it was a confusing term (here it means good fortune in general, but elsewhere in the text it denotes monetary wealth in particular)? Or did Alfred decide to add *wela* when producing the second version, to make the sense more precise? A clearer case is 68/17, where B has 'þeah mon nu hwone godra mid rihte herige' and C has the additional phrase 'soð an seggað'. B is closer to the Latin and the C reading does not make sense unless one adds an initial 'and' (as Sedgefield does when incorporating the C reading into the text). Was the phrase omitted by the scribe of B or added by a scribe of C; or is it possibly Alfred's own (miscopied) revision or explanatory gloss, defining 'praising a man with justice' more precisely as telling the truth about someone? These may be cases where both readings are authorial.

More serious is the problem of dealing with the text that is no longer legible in the Cotton manuscript. The missing verse sections can be taken from Junius's transcriptions and the missing prose can be reconstructed by using the Bodley copy and substituting the Cotton variants recorded by Junius, but Junius's transcriptions and collations are in various ways limited in their usefulness and reliability. Firstly, Junius was selective in his recording of spelling variants: he seems to have listed about three-quarters of them, but the principle of exclusion is hard to see. He seems also to have missed the occasional variation of substance: thus at Sedgefield

[14] Sisam, *Studies*, p. 294 n. 2.

141/23 he failed to record Cotton's reading *men* (and presumably as a result of this Sedgefield himself failed to record Bodley's omission of the word). Secondly, he tended to normalize, emend and sometimes miscopy when transcribing rather than recording precisely the manuscript reading: thus on the first page of his transcript of the Bodley manuscript, he supplies an additional *he*, corrects *hæse* to *hæfda*, copies *deð* as *deþ* and renders the sequence *bi . . . be . . . be* as *bi . . . bi . . . bi*. Thirdly, he seems to have been little interested in recording differences of layout – he does not record the absence of chapter divisions and numbers in Cotton for instance – and his system of recording collations did not allow for clear marking of omitted passages. Thus chapter 3 of the prose text renders a sequence of Latin prosa 1, Latin metra 2 and Latin prosa 2 all as prose. Junius's collations show that at the point where the Latin verse began the Cotton manuscript had instead a rendering in Old English verse (printed as Metre iii). But he does not indicate the point at which Cotton turned back to the prose text. One would normally assume it was at the point where the substance of the Latin metre ends and where the prose signals the end of Wisdom's song: 'þa se wisdom þa and seo Gesceadwisnes ðis leoð asungen hæfdon, þa ongan he eft sprecan and cwæð to þan Mode: Ic geseo þæt þe is nu frofres mare þearf þonne unrotnesse'. But Junius records no Cotton variants against this sentence and its final words seem to be incorporated into the last half-line of the Old English metre: 'him is frofre ðearf'. (Similarly, in the Old English metres vi, vii and viii the preamble to the song is incorporated into the verse.) It seems probable that part at least of this sentence was absent from the Cotton version, but the omission is not recorded.

Reconstructing Alfred's second version of the *Consolation* from the surviving parts of the Cotton manuscript, from the Bodley manuscript and from Junius's transcriptions and collations would evidently be no easy task and would involve a fair degree of editorial intervention. In matters of the overall structure and the main elements of the text it can nevertheless be done. In matters of detailed readings and especially spellings the task would be marred by the selectiveness of Junius's collations and the occasional inaccuracy of his transcriptions, but not to the extent of making the result worthless. But this raises further questions about the presentation of the text on the page, the point with which this paper started. Sedgefield saw himself as meeting the needs of what he called 'the scientific investigator of Old English'[15] and it was for his sake that he so painstakingly reproduced the fragmentary text of the Cotton manuscript and rigorously distinguished it, at the level of individual letters, from the readings of Bodley or Junius. Sedgefield's other intended reader, 'the student of our literature', seems to have taken a lower place in his concerns. For such a reader, concerned more with Alfred's style and thought than his (or his scribes') spelling, what is needed is a clean and readable text of the second version, preferably with a consistent system of spelling and inflexion. But would a critical reconstruction of the kind described, supplementing Cotton with

---

[15] See the preface to his edition, p. vii.

readings from Bodley and from the seventeenth-century transcripts and collations of Junius, satisfy scholarly decorum – and especially philological decorum – without the array of protective brackets and italics that erect such a barrier to readers of Sedgefield's edition?

We have the materials to produce a radically different Alfredian Boethius from the one familiar to us, closer to what Alfred the *poet* wrote: a version that is much more ambitious in literary terms and would be of consuming interest to those who care about Old English literature. But it is not found in any extant manuscript – though we know a great deal about the manuscript in which it was preserved before the Cotton fire. The kinds of editorial activity needed to do it, reconstructing original structures and accidentals, were once quite common with editions of Old English poetry.[16] But scholarly anxiety about manuscript testimony and philological precision has always lain heavier on Old English prose, and the current climate is more hostile to editorial adventurousness than in the past. The editorial history of Alfred's Boethius has left a great deal still to be done.[17]

APPENDIX

KING ALFRED'S BOETHIUS: VERSE AND PROSE VERSION

THE OPENING SECTION

Ælfred kuning wæs wealhstod ðisse bec. and hie of boclædene on Englisc wende swa hio nu is gedon. Hwilum he sette word be worde, hwilum andgit of andgite, swa swa he hit þa sweotolost and andgitfullicast gereccan mihte for þam mislicum and manigfealdum weoruldbisgum þe hine oft ægðer ge on mode ge on lichoman bisgodan. ða bisgu us sint swiþe earfoþrimu þe on his dagum on þa ricu becoman þe he underfangen hæfde, and þeah ða he þas boc hæfde geleornode and of lædene to engliscum spelle gewende, þa geworhte he hi eft to leoðe, swa swa heo nu gedon is; and nu bit and for Godes naman he healsað ælcne þara þe þas boc rædan lyste, þæt he for hine gebidde, and him ne wite gif he hit rihtlicor ongite þonne he meahte, forþamþe ælc mon sceal be his andgites mæðe and be his æmettan sprecan þæt he sprecð and done þæt þæt he deþ.

> ÐUS Ælfred us ealdspell reahte,
> cyning Westsexna, cræft meldode,
> leoðwyrhta list. Him wæs lust micel

---

[16] One might cite, for instance, *Beowulf with the Finnsburg Fragment*, ed. C.L. Wrenn (London, 1953), or J.R.R. Tolkien, *The Old English Exodus: Text, Translation, and Commentary* ed. J. Turville-Petre (Oxford, 1981), esp. pp. 36 and 43.

[17] As has perhaps become clear, the present contributor hopes to produce a new edition of Alfred's Boethius (when he has completed his long-delayed volume of commentary for his edition of Ælfric).

ðæt he ðiossum leodum leoð spellode,
monnum myrgen, mislice cwidas,
þy læs ælinge ut adrife
selflicne secg, þonne he swelces lyt
gymð for his gilpe. Ic sceal giet sprecan,
fón on fitte, folccuðne ræd
haleðum secgean; hliste se þe wille.

Hit wæs geara iu ðætte Gotan eastan
of Sciððia sceldas læddon,
þreate geþrungon þeodlond monig.
Setton suðweardes sigeþeoda twa;
Gotene rice gearmælum weox.
Hæfdan him gecynde cyningas twegen,
Rædgod 7 Aleric; rice geþungon.
Þa wæs ofer Muntgiop monig atyhted
Gota gylpes full, guðe gelysted
folcgewinnes. Fana hwearfode
scir on sceafte; sceotend þohton
Italia ealle gegongan,
lindwigende; hi gelæstan swua
efne from Muntgiop oð þone mæran wearoð
þær Sicilia sæstreamum in
eglond micel eðel mærsað.
Ða wæs Romana rice gewunnen,
abrocen burga cyst. Beadurincum wæs
Rom gerymed. Rædgot 7 Aleric
foron on ðæt fæsten. Feah casere
mid þam æþelingum ut on Crecas.
Ne meahte þa seo wealaf wige forstandan
Gotan mid guðe. Giomonna gestrion
sealdon unwillum eþelweardas,
halige aðas; wæs gehwæðeres waa.
Þeah wæs magorinca mod mid Crecum,
gif hi leodfruman læstan dorsten.
Stod þrage on ðam; þeod wæs gewunnen
wintræ mænigo, oðþæt wyrd gescraf
þæt þe ðeodrice þegnas 7 eorlas
heran sceoldan. Wæs se heretema
criste gecnoden; cyning selfa onfeng
fulluhtþeawum. Fægnodon ealle
Romwara bearn, 7 him recene to
friðes wilnedon. He him fæste gehet
þæt hy ealdrihta ælces mosten
wyrðe gewunigen on þære welegan byrig
ðenden God wuolde þæt he Gotena geweald
agan moste. He þæt eall aleag;

wæs þæm æþelinge Arrianes
gedwola leofre þonne Drihtnes æ.
Het Iohannes godne papan
heafde beheawon; næs ðæt hærlic dæd.
Eac þam wæs unrim oðres manes
þæt se Gota fremede godra gehwilcum.

Ða wæs ricra sum on Rome byrig
ahefen heretoga, hlaforde leof,
þenden cynestole Creacas wioldon.
Þæt wæs rihtwis rinc; næs mid Romwarum
sincgeofa sella, siððan longe.
He wæs for weorulde wis, weorðmynða georn,
beorn boca gleaw. Boitius
se hæle hatte; se þone hlisan geþah.
Wæs him on gemynde mæla gehwilce
yfel 7 edwit þæt him elðeodge
kyningas cyðdon. Wæs on Creacas hold;
gemunde þara ara 7 ealdrihta
þe his eldran mid him ahton longe,
lufan 7 lissa. Angan þa listum ymbe
ðencean þearflice, hu he ðider meahte
Crecas oncerran, þæt se casere eft
anwald ofer hi agan moste.
Sende ærendgewrit ealdhlafordum
degelice, 7 hi for Drihtne bæd,
ealdum treowum, ðæt hi æft to him
comen on þa ceastre, lete Creca witan
rædan Romwarum, rihtes wyrðe
lete þone leodscipe. Ða þa lare ongeat
Ðeodric Amuling, 7 þone þegn oferfeng,
heht fæstlice folcgesiðas
healdon þone hererinc. Wæs him hreoh sefa,
ege from ðam eorle. He hine inne heht
on carcernes cluster belucan.
Þa wæs modsefa miclum gedrefed
Boetius. Breac longe ær
wlencea under wolcnum; he þy wyrs meahte
þolian þa þrage, þa hio swa þearl becom.
Wæs þa ormod eorl, are ne wende,
ne on þam fæstene frofre gemunde;
ac he neowol astreaht niðer ofdune
feol on þa flore. Fela worda spræc,
forþoht ðearle; ne wende þonan æfre
cuman of ðæm clammum. Cleopode to Drihtne
geomran stemne, gyddode þus.

Hwæt, ic lioða fela lustlice geo
sanc on sælum. Nu sceal siofigende,
wope gewæged, wreccea giomor,
singan sarcwidas. Me þios siccetung hafað
agæled, ðes geocsa, þæt ic þa ged ne mæg
gefegean swa fægre, þeah ic fela gio þa
sette soðcwida, þonne ic on sælum wæs.
Oft ic nu miscyrre cuðe spræce,
7 þeah uncuðre ær hwilum fond.
Me þas woruldsælða welhwæs blindne
on ðis dimme hol dysine forlæddon,
7 me þa berypton rædes 7 frofre
for heora untreowum, þe ic him æfre betst
truwian sceolde. Hi me to wendon
heora bacu bitere, 7 heora blisse from.
Forhwam wolde ge, weoruldfrynd mine,
secgan oððe singan þæt ic gesællic mon
wære on weorulde? Ne synt þa word soð
nu þa gesælða ne magon simle gewunigan.

Þa ic þa þis leoð, cwæð Boetius, geomriende asungen hæfde, þa com þær gan in to
me heofencund wisdom, and þæt min murnende mod mid his wordum gegrette,
and þus cwæð: Hu ne eart ðu se mon þe on minre scole wære afeded and gelæred?
Ac hwonon wurde þu mid þissum woruldsorgum þus swiðe geswenced? Buton ic
wat þæt þu hæfst þara wæpna to hraðe forgiten þe ic þe ær sealde. Ða cleopode se
wisdom and cwæð: Gewitaþ nu awirgede woruldsorga of mines þegenes mode,
forþam ge sind þa mæstan sceaþan. Lætaþ hine eft hweorfan to minum larum. Ða
eode se wisdom near, cwæð Boetius, minum hreowsiendum geþohte, and hit swa
niowul hwæthwugu uparærde; adrigde þa mines modes eagan, and hit frægn liðum
wordum hwæðer hit oncneowe his fostermodor. Mid þam þe ða þæt mod wið his
bewende, þa gecneow hit swiðe sweotele his agene modor; þæt wæs se wisdom ðe
hit lange ær tyde and lærde. Ac hit ongeat his lare swiðe totorene and swiðe
tobrogdene mid dysigra hondum, and hine þa frægn hu þæt gewurde. Ða andwyrde
se wisdom him and sæde þæt his gingran hæfdon hine swa totorenne, þær þær hi
teohhodon þæt hi hine eallne habban sceoldon; ac hi gegaderiað monifeald dysig
on ðære fortruwunga and on þam gilpe, butan heora hwelc eft to rihtre bote
gecirre. Ða ongan se wisdom hreowsian for þæs modes tydernese, and ongan þa
giddian and þus cwæð:

Æala, on hu grimmum 7 hu grundleasum
seaðe swinceð þæt sweorcende mod
Þonne hit þa strongan stormas beatað
weoruldbisgunga. þonne hit winnende
his agen leoht anforlæteð,
7 mid uua forgit þone ecan gefean,
ðringð on þa ðiostro ðisse worulde,

175

sorgum geswenced. Swa is þissum nu
mode gelumpen; nu hit mare ne wat
for Gode godes buton gnornunge
fremdre worulde. Him is frofre ðearf.

ÆLFRIC, AUTHORIAL IDENTITY AND THE CHANGING TEXT

Joyce Hill

I

'THE IDEAL OF textual criticism is to present the text which the author intended.' This confident statement, the central tenet of Thorpe's *Principles of Textual Criticism*,[1] is a principle widely accepted by modern editors and it is one which has shaped editorial policy even for the manuscript culture of the Middle Ages, when concepts of authorship and textual integrity were markedly different from our own. For the Anglo-Saxon period the editorial striving for the often elusive original has been executed in two ways: conjectural emendation and, in the case of multi-copy survivals, the giving of editorial priority to the text which is judged, on the grounds of early date and relative textual purity, to be the closest to 'the text which the author intended'. The first of these responses was popular in the nineteenth century and in the early part of the twentieth century, but it has fallen out of favour in recent decades and has been replaced by a determinedly conservative approach, which gives priority to the manuscript reading, even when this is problematic. Various justifications have been offered for this current avoidance of emendation: that many texts survive in single copies only, so that the methodologies of textual criticism which were developed for the emendation of classical texts cannot be properly deployed; that conjectural emendation removes the linguistic interest of the surviving copy or copies; and that, however 'sleepy and careless' a scribe may have been, he knew his Old English better than the best modern editor of Old English can ever do.[2] More recently, in making a case for the exploitation of modern critical theory in the study of Old English literature, Allen Frantzen has argued against conjectural emendation on the grounds that it produces a supposedly originary and authoritative text for which there is no direct evidence, and for conservative editing because it is the means by which the editor and reader can come to understand what is extant as a moment in the texts' progressive history or

---

[1] J. Thorpe, *Principles of Textual Criticism* (San Marino, CA, 1972), p. 50.

[2] The case for a conservative approach in editing Old English poetry is argued by E.G. Stanley, 'Unideal Principles of Editing Old English Verse', *Proceedings of the British Academy* 70 (1984), 231–73. The quotation is on p. 257. See also the case put forward by H. Gneuss, 'Guide to the Editing and Preparation of Texts for the Dictionary of Old English', *A Plan for the Dictionary of Old English*, ed. R. Frank and A. Cameron (Toronto, 1973), pp. 9–24, reprinted above, pp. 7–26, where, however, Gneuss was principally concerned with the editorial practices suitable for preparing editions to meet a particular need.

worldly eventfulness.[3] In practice, editors of multi-copy texts have continued to exercise the principles of textual criticism in order to be able to present the nearest survival to the textual starting point. But in recent years some scholars have begun to pay attention to texts which derive from earlier ones,[4] and modern editors now recognize and discuss, even if for practical reasons their editions cannot directly demonstrate, that the text edited is but one stage in a continuing development. Thus Malcolm Godden, in editing the Second Series of Ælfric's *Catholic Homilies* from a first recension manuscript very close to the author (Cambridge, University Library, Gg. 3. 28), presents what may be presumed to be substantially 'the text which the author intended', but he explains that Ælfric subsequently developed the collection and issued several different copies.[5]

Objections to the conservative approach have been voiced by Michael Lapidge, who reminds us that this editorial practice does not hold sway in the editing of Anglo-Latin literature, which ought properly to be inseparable from Old English in our study of Anglo-Saxon culture.[6] He argues forcefully that editors have a responsibility to emend Old English texts in instances where there is demonstrably

---

[3] A.J. Frantzen and C.L. Venegoni, 'The Desire for Origins: An Archaeology of Anglo-Saxon Studies', *Style* 20 (1986), 142–56, objected vigorously to the 'pursuit of pure origins' on the grounds that the modern construction of 'the uncorrupted version of a mythical Ur-text' means that editors 'seek to erase centuries of history that surround the texts they study' (p. 152). The case for studying the text as transmitted, rather than creating an apparently authoritative one, has since been more fully argued by Frantzen in *Desire for Origins: New Language, Old English, and Teaching the Tradition* (New Brunswick and London, 1990). Frantzen argues in particular for the applicability of reception theory. For the relevance of this theory and the concept of textual 'eventfulness' to traditional studies of textual transmission within the manuscript culture of medieval England, see J. Hill, 'The preservation and transmission of Ælfric's saints' lives: reader-response in the early Middle Ages' (forthcoming). For the concept of the 'eventful text', see especially H.R. Jauss, *Toward an Aesthetic of Reception,* transl. by Timothy Bahti, with an introduction by Paul de Man (Minneapolis, 1982), pp. 32–6 (Thesis 5). For the concept of a text's 'worldliness', see E.W. Said, *The World, The Text and the Critic* (Boston 1983; London, 1984), p. 35.

[4] See, for example, the articles cited below in note 14.

[5] *Ælfric's Catholic Homilies: The Second Series. Text*, ed. M. Godden, EETS ss 5 (London, 1979). Godden's entire introduction is informed by the fact that 'more than one authentic form of the *Catholic Homilies* has come down to us' (p. xx). See also P.A.M. Clemoes, 'The Chronology of Ælfric's Works', *The Anglo-Saxons: Studies in Some Aspects of their History and Culture presented to Bruce Dickins*, ed. P. Clemoes (London, 1959), pp. 212–47. For the closeness of CUL Gg. 3. 28 to Ælfric, see Godden, p. xliii. As we see from N.R. Ker, *Catalogue of Manuscripts Containing Anglo-Saxon* (Oxford, 1957), there were many reworkings of Ælfric's texts by others, just as there were commonly reworkings of texts by other writers throughout the period.

[6] M. Lapidge, 'Textual Criticism and the Literature of Anglo-Saxon England', *Bulletin of the John Rylands Library*, 73 (1991), 17–45, and 'The Edition, Emendation and Reconstruction of Anglo-Saxon Texts', *The Politics of Editing Medieval Texts*, ed. R. Frank (New York, 1992), pp. 131–57. For further discussion of the relative merits of the conservative and emending approaches, see S. Wenzel, 'Reflections on (New) Philology', *Speculum* 65 (1990), 11–18, and for valuable comments with regard to Middle English, see D. Pearsall, 'Editing Medieval Texts: Some Developments and Some Problems', *Textual Criticism and Literary Interpretation*, ed. J. J. McGann (Chicago, 1985), pp. 92–106.

evidence of scribal error and where this can be rectified in ways which must reasonably be considered to take us closer to the good sense that an intelligent author would have intended. The transmitted text, which Lapidge would be willing to emend, is the text which a conservative editor and an advocate of reception theory would wish to preserve. But important distinctions need to be made in relation to each of these positions. Lapidge's arguments in favour of emendation are concerned mainly with the removal of textual corruption caused by scribal error, whether on a large or small scale. Reception theorists, on the other hand, are more concerned with the *rewritten text* which, in the Middle Ages, included the actual rewriting of text and context by subsequent users, as well as the cerebral 'rewriting' of a given text by every individual who reads or hears ('receives') the text within his or her circumstantially determined moment. Sleepy and careless scribes who introduced errors rewrote the text inadvertently, but alongside this we have to take account of the habit of a manuscript culture to rewrite deliberately, perhaps with the intention of 'improving' the text, of adapting it to particular circumstances, or of laying claim through appropriation within a new context to existing work which was recognized as having authoritative value. It is with this deliberate form of textual eventfulness that I am principally concerned in the present paper in considering authorial identity and the changing text. The question of emendation is consequently not an immediate issue here, although in focusing on Ælfric's Pastoral Letters (section III below), I shall in fact be dealing with texts whose survival in more than one copy makes possible the practice of textual criticism, which has traditionally been the basis for editorial emendation.

In Ælfric's case, one of the distinctive characteristics to which we can readily respond is that he has a strong sense of authorial identity and apparently some notion of the definitive text, so that it is easy to justify proceeding, as one might with a more modern author, by giving editorial priority to the author's original. But this begs several questions. How close was Ælfric's sense of authorial identity and the definitive text to that of the present day? What should the editorial response be to his own revisions?[7] And are we doing justice to the literary and intellectual history of the period if we pay less attention to the subsequent non-authorial modifications? The purpose of the discussion which follows is to demonstrate, by reference to Ælfric, that modern concepts of authorship and textual integrity are not applicable to the Anglo-Saxon period, *even when they appear to be present*, and thus to argue that editorial activity should properly be extended to revisions, derivatives and composites.

---

[7] Some of Ælfric's augmentations and expansions of particular homilies are separately edited by J.C. Pope, *Homilies of Ælfric: a Supplementary Collection*, 2 vols, EETS os 259 and 260 (London, 1967–68); others (to homilies in the Second Series only) are noted in *Ælfric's Catholic Homilies*, ed. Godden, p. xxi, and commented on in the textual notes to Godden homilies III, VII, XVI, and XIX. Invaluable though this is, it provides only part of what we need and it has the disadvantage that the evidence of the revisions and the discussions of them are divided between a number of publications.

II

Ælfric names himself as author in his prefaces and commonly gives some explanation of how he came to write the work in question; he may also make reference to other works he has written, thus revealing a consciousness of his cumulating oeuvre and, incidentally, providing modern scholars with important evidence towards the establishment of the chronology of his canon. But, detailed though this factual self-identification is by comparison with other Old English writers, there is much more to Ælfric's authorial persona than this, for throughout his prefaces and in the body of most of his works he sustains a strong sense of authorial presence, rhetorically by appropriate modes of address and intellectually by referring, directly and indirectly, to his authorial responsibilities – to the biblical text, to his sources, to religious orthodoxy, to the contemporary church, to his teacher Æþelwold and to his immediate audience. Furthermore, we find him insisting on accurate scribal copying and on the transmission of his work in distinctively Ælfrician manuscripts, unmodified and uncontaminated by juxtaposition with the work of others.

However, as has been suggested already, the situation is not quite what it seems to be. Ælfric was not concerned with textual accuracy, textual integrity and authorial identity as such, in what one might call a 'modern' sense, but with accuracy, integrity and authorship as agents and guarantors of theological reliability in a context where, from a committed reformist viewpoint, he saw around him much that was inadequate, unreliable and outside the tradition with which he identified. Thus, in the Old English preface to the *Catholic Homilies*, his injunction to scribes to be accurate in copying is justified by associating it with the introduction of doctrinal error, for which he uses *gedwyld*, a word customarily employed by him to denote departures from orthodoxy:

> Mycel yfel deð seðe leas writ, buton he hit gerihte, swylce he gebringe þa soðan lare to leasum gedwylde: forþi sceal gehwa gerihtlæcan þæt þæt he ær to woge gebigde, gif he on Godes dome unscyldig beon wile.[8]

---

[8] *The Homilies of the Anglo-Saxon Church. The First Part, containing the Sermones Catholici or Homilies of Ælfric*, ed. B. Thorpe, 2 vols (London, 1844–46) I, 8. 'He does great evil who writes false, unless he correct it; it is as though he turn true doctrine to false error; therefore should everyone make that straight which he before bent crooked, if he will be guiltless at God's doom' (Thorpe's translation, p. 9). The same injunction is repeated verbatim in the preface to the Second Series: *Ælfric's Catholic Homilies*, ed. Godden, p. 2. On Ælfric's exploitation of his authorial identity in order to guarantee his texts and thereby to promote a polemical position in fostering the Benedictine Reform, see also J. Hill, 'Reform and Resistance: Preaching Styles in Late Anglo-Saxon England', *De l'homélie au sermon: Histoire de la prédication médiévale. Actes du Colloque internationale de Louvain-la-Neuve (9–11 juillet 1992)*, ed. J. Hamesse and X. Hermand (Louvain-la-Neuve, 1993), pp. 15–46.

Later injunctions to copyists, in the prefaces to the *Grammar*,[9] *Genesis*, the *Lives of Saints* and in the *Libellus de ueteri testamento et nouo*, are much briefer and do not spell out the connection with doctrinal error in the same way, but the context is clear: Ælfric, in all cases, has just defined his position, either by contrast with others, or by association with the Benedictine reform, or both, and concludes with the injunction in an attempt to guarantee that the position he puts forward is preserved in transmission. His recurrent use of *leas* to characterize the error introduced by careless scribes is suggestive of the doctrinal motivation, since it is a regular term in his writings for matters heretical.

It is likewise his belief in the tradition to which he belongs coupled with his doubts about other traditions, rather than a desire to preserve authorial identity as such, which motivates the pleas for uncontaminated transmission at the end of the Second Series of *Catholic Homilies* and the Old English preface to the *Lives of Saints*:

> Gif hwa ma awendan wille. ðonne bidde ic hine for godes lufon þæt he gesette his boc onsundron. fram ðam twam bocum ðe we awend habbað we truwiað þurh godes diht.[10]

> Ic bidde nu on godes naman gif hwa þas boc awritan wille . þæt he hi wel gerihte be þære bysne . and þær namare betwux ne sette þonne we awendon.[11]

In fact, in a way that is entirely characteristic of his age, Ælfric did not have a notion of a fixed text. He designed the First and Second Series of *Catholic Homilies* as two cycles and refers to them in the Old English preface to the Second Series and in the injunction quoted above, as 'two books', yet in the Latin letter to Archbishop Sigeric which accompanies the First Series he gives permission to the two to be re-ordered into one book[12] and, as noted above (p. 178), he subsequently developed the collection himself, issuing revised versions.

Ælfric was ready to alter his text for the same reason that others were to alter it: because it was a utilitarian collection. The limit that he attempted to set upon the changes, that they should not go beyond what he himself devised, has the effect of

---

9   It might be thought that the *Grammar* is in a different category from the rest because it deals with rules of language rather than with matters of faith, but the Old English preface, which includes the injunction to copyists, fulfils the same function as the others discussed here: *Ælfrics Grammatik und Glossar*, ed. J. Zupitza (Berlin, 1880), pp. 2–3. Ælfric explains in the preface that he sees grammar as the key to religious understanding and in the course of the work he makes some doctrinal points as, for example, in his comments on Latin *sum* (p. 201).

10 *Ælfric's Catholic Homilies*, ed. Godden, p. 345. 'If anyone wishes to translate more, then I beseech him, for the love of God, that he set down his book separately from the two books which we have translated, we trust through God's guidance.'

11 *Ælfric's Lives of Saints*, ed. W.W. Skeat, 2 vols in 4 parts, EETS os 76, 82, 94, 114 (London, 1881–1900), repr. as 2 vols (London, 1966), I, 6. 'I pray now in God's name, if any man desire to transcribe this book, that he correct it well according to the copy; and set down therein no more than we have translated' (Skeat's translation, p. 7).

12 *The Homilies of the Anglo-Saxon Church*, ed. Thorpe, I, 2.

aligning him with the modern author, who might also revise and reissue. But the limitation was unusual for its time and, as we have seen, it had a medieval motivation. More significantly for the present discussion, it was a limitation imposed against the odds, for the prevailing practice was not to observe textual integrity and authorial identity, but to reuse texts as the need arose, even if this meant altering the context in which they were transmitted or used, adapting the texts, or plundering them for composite compilations. Ælfric's various pleas were made precisely because he knew that such practices were the norm. But the norm could not be gainsaid and his two major collections, the *Catholic Homilies* and the *Lives of Saints*, were very soon transmitted in ways that he did not intend[13] and were used by some as if the items in them were on a par with all other Old English homilies.

If we prioritize 'the text which the author intended', these instances of non-authorial re-use can be seen as degradations of the Ælfrician tradition and we may be sure that Ælfric would have viewed them thus. But ecclesiastical and theological activity in the eleventh and early twelfth century cannot be understood if these adapted texts are not examined. Some work has already been done in this field by Whitbread, Szarmach, Godden and Lees,[14] who variously discuss homily redactions which draw upon wholly anonymous texts (Whitbread and Lees), and those which combine Ælfric with anonymous material (Szarmach and Godden), but there is room for more study of changing manuscript contexts[15] and of individual

---

[13] For example, Oxford, Bodleian Library, Bodley 340, from the beginning of the eleventh century, is an anthology organized mainly in the order of the church's year, using both series of *Catholic Homilies* (as Ælfric had allowed), but combining its Ælfrician selection with a number of anonymous homilies, three of them even providing for the last three days of Holy Week, despite Ælfric's statement in both series that no homilies should be preached on these days. For a discussion of the manuscript and a list of its contents, see *Ælfric's Catholic Homilies*, ed. Godden, pp. xxv–xxviii; for details of the ignoring of Ælfric's pronouncements about not preaching on Maundy Thursday, Good Friday and Holy Saturday, see J. Hill, 'Ælfric's "Silent Days" ', *Leeds Studies in English*, ns 16 (1985), 118–31. Similarly, the *Lives of Saints* collection was in circulation at the beginning of the eleventh century already incorporating non-Ælfric items; London, British Library, Cotton Julius E. vii, is the closest extant manuscript to Ælfric's original collection and gives us his statement of authorship in the preface and the injunction about maintaining the integrity of the collection, even though in practice the manuscript ignores both. On this manuscript and the subsequent treatment of its Ælfrician saints' lives, see J. Hill, 'The Dissemination of Ælfric's Lives of Saints: A Preliminary Survey', *Holy Men and Holy Women: Old English Prose Saints' Lives and Their Contexts*, ed. P.E. Szarmach (forthcoming).

[14] L. Whitbread, ' "Wulfstan" Homilies XXIX, XXX and some related Texts', *Anglia* 81 (1963), 347–64 (corrected in the concluding section of D.G. Scragg, 'Napier's "Wulfstan" homily xxx: its sources, its relationship to the Vercelli Book and its style', *ASE* 6 (1977), 197–211); P.E. Szarmach, 'Three versions of the Jonah story: an investigation of narrative technique in Old English homilies', *ASE* 1 (1972), 183–92; M.R. Godden, 'Old English composite homilies from Winchester', *ASE* 4 (1975), 57–65; C.A. Lees, 'The Blickling Palm Sunday Homily and its Revised Version', *Leeds Studies in English*, ns 19 (1988), 1–30.

[15] For the poetry we generally have evidence of only one moment in the history of what was perhaps a changing text and almost certainly a changing manuscript context. Even so, although the circumstances of survival are different from the sorts of prose text discussed here, it is relevant to note the arguments put forward by F.C. Robinson, 'Old English Literature in Its Most Immediate Context', *Old English Literature in Context: Ten Essays*, ed. J.D. Niles (Cambridge

adapted and composite texts. To us, with our notions of authorial identity and textual integrity, the changing text may seem to be of secondary importance, even though we are well aware of its existence and of the cultural circumstances which brought it about. But it did not have a secondary status in the Middle Ages and examination of it in its various forms, singly and in comparison with all other texts to which it is related, can yield important primary evidence for Anglo-Saxon literary and intellectual activity.[16]

III

The complexities of textual integrity and authorial identity, with their attendant editorial problems, have so far been exemplified by works originally issued by Ælfric in his own name. By contrast his Pastoral Letters, one for Wulfsige, bishop of Sherborne c.993–1002, and four for Wulfstan, bishop of Worcester 1002–1016 and archbishop of York 1002–1023, were not issued in his name or written in his own person.[17] The deliberate submergence in these letters of his otherwise apparently strong authorial identity and the letters' textual history at the hands of Ælfric and others complement the evidence so far discussed and demonstrate with particular clarity the way in which, even in Ælfric's case, Anglo-Saxon attitudes to textual integrity and authorial identity differ from our own and so call into question some of the customary principles of modern editorial practice.

In common with other works, the Pastoral Letters are texts designed for circulation, but with the significant difference that the initiators of the circulation were to be the bishops, not Ælfric, so that it was a sense of episcopal authority which was needed to validate the texts for the secular clergy. The two bishops and Ælfric had a reformist monastic background in common but the authority of the letters could not be overtly grounded upon this tradition, even if all three men were inspired by it,[18] and in consequence Ælfric avoided the process of self-identification within the public text through which, as we have seen, he laid claim to the tradition elsewhere. Instead, responding to the life that these texts were to have in the public domain, he

---

and Totowa, 1980), pp. 11–29, in particular his belief that 'a return to manuscript contexts might suggest new ways to examine old questions about authorship and textual integrity' (p. 29).

[16] For the view that this is a direction for future editorial activity, see M. Godden 'Old English', *Editing Medieval Texts*, ed. A.G. Rigg (New York and London, 1977), pp. 9–33, esp. p. 29.

[17] *Die Hirtenbriefe Ælfrics*, ed. B. Fehr, Bibliothek der angelsächsischen Prosa IX (Hamburg, 1914), reprinted with a supplementary introduction by P.A.M. Clemoes (Darmstadt, 1964). Reference will be made to the letters by page and paragraph number as appropriate. The question of authorial identity is, of course, peculiarly complex in the Pastoral Letters, since Ælfric was engaged in 'ghost-writing', but although he submerged his own identity to the extent of using appropriately episcopal turns of phrase (see below, p. 184), the actual voice that we hear is recognizably that of the reformist monk, masspriest and abbot, as I show in 'Monastic Reform and the Secular Church: Ælfric's Pastoral Letters in Context', *England in the Eleventh Century: Proceedings of the 1990 Harlaxton Symposium*, ed. C. Hicks (Stamford, 1992), pp. 103–17.

[18] I discuss this further in 'Monastic Reform and the Secular Church'.

composes throughout, as he explains to Wulfsige, 'quasi ex tuo ore dictata sit *et* locutus esses ad clericos tibi subditos',[19] and he maintains a sense of the episcopal voice, and thus of episcopal authority, by a range of rhetorical devices, notably successions of impersonal declarative statements which establish an appropriate regulatory tone, the apt use of imperatives and plural address, and the occasional use of the superior 'we', reinforced in the Old English letters by direct identification in such phrases as 'we biscepas' and 'Vs bisceopum gedafenað'.[20]

Ælfric's authorship of the Old English letter for Wulfsige, the earliest of the five, is personally acknowledged, but in a way which is markedly different from the statements of authorship discussed so far. It occurs as a private communication in a detachable Latin preface which is in the form of a personal covering letter to Wulfsige, which Wulfsige, quite properly, did not circulate when he issued the letter in his own person.[21] Furthermore, Ælfric's acknowledgement of authorship is here merely circumstantial, revealed in the epistolary form of address, 'Ælfricus humilis frater uenerabili ep*isocopo W*ulfsino salute*m* in d*omi*no',[22] and it is thus non-functional. It is not a means of identifying the tradition to which Ælfric belongs, it does not serve as a guarantor of theological reliability, and it does not lead at any point to the corollary injunction that scribes should be accurate in copying and the text be transmitted in uncontaminated form.

Precisely the same observations can be made with regard to the Wulfstan letters. Here we have one authorial statement only, which alludes to all four letters (two Latin and two Old English). This stands at the head of the first Old English letter and explains how, having written two letters in Latin for Wulfstan, Ælfric is now sending, at Wulfstan's request, versions of each in English. Ælfric's name occurs only in the form of address, 'Aelfricus Abbas uulfstano Venerabili archiepiscopo salutem in Christo',[23] and the information about authorship is confined to the private letter, distinguished from what follows, as in the Wulfsige example, by choice of language and by style.

Effectively, therefore, Ælfric surrenders authorial identity. The contrast with the examples discussed earlier clarifies and confirms what we have deduced to be Ælfric's position: that the establishment of authorial identity was for him a functional device, motivated by a sense of theological responsibility, rather than being a concern to claim authorship as such. In the Pastoral Letters the responsibility was

---

[19] *Die Hirtenbriefe Ælfrics*, ed. Fehr, p. 1: 'as if it [the letter] had been dictated from your mouth and you had been speaking to the clergy under you'.

[20] *Ibid.* pp. 133 (Wulfsige letter) 'we bishops' and 168 (first Old English letter for Wulfstan) 'It is fitting for us bishops'. The second Old English letter for Wulfstan makes a direct connection with the identification in the first by beginning: 'Eala ge mæsse-preostas, mine gebroþra! We secgað eow nu þæt we ær ne sædon'. ('My brother masspriests! We now declare to you what we did not declare before').

[21] See below, p. 187.

[22] *Die Hirtenbriefe Ælfrics*, ed. Fehr, p.1: 'Ælfricus, a humble brother, to the venerable bishop Wulfinus, greeting in the Lord'.

[23] *Die Hirtenbriefe Ælfrics*, ed. Fehr, p. 69: 'Abbot Ælfric to the venerable archbishop Wulfstan, greeting in Christ'.

that of the bishops and it is thus their voices that we hear; in the *Catholic Homilies*, by contrast, the responsibility was Ælfric's own, so that he took care to guarantee the text by particularizing his identity in the Old English preface and by maintaining a sense of his presence, in attitude though not in name, throughout the collection.[24]

The omission of injunctions to copyists in the Pastoral Letters likewise contrasts with Ælfric's practice in several other works and similarly clarifies and confirms what has already been deduced: that Ælfric made such statements, not prompted by what would have been an anachronistic desire for a definitive authorial text, but as part of his identification with a particular tradition, which was itself motivated by a sense of theological responsibility. For the Pastoral Letters, issued by others, open to alteration by them before issue and of course susceptible to alteration and juxtaposition with other material once distributed, an attempt at control in his own person would have been inappropriate.[25] Ælfric, in this case, was allowing for the operation of normal practices; in the cases where he expresses the wish for control he implicitly identifies what the normal practices were. In all of these cases the definitive text as we understand it is a modern illusion, but whereas with large and complex works the editing of the changing text as well as the starting text presents practical difficulties, the Pastoral Letters are short enough for the different versions to be presented simultaneously, as Fehr recognised when editing them in 1914. The benefit of his procedure is that we are directly provided with evidence showing firstly, that it is not necessarily possible to be specific about 'the text which the author intended', even when we have available a good range of manuscripts which lend themselves to textual criticism, and secondly that, if Fehr had limited his edition to an editorially determined 'best text', we should have been denied valuable evidence for Ælfric's working methods, Wulfstan's intellectual response to his first Old English letter, and the ways in which the letters were used by others.

The textual relationships of each letter are too involved to be presented here in any detail, but the summary which follows illustrates the complexities of authorship and exemplifies the kinds of problem that the changing text poses for the editor, whether in choosing what to edit, if choice should be made, or in deciding upon how to present the full sequence of the textual progression.[26]

Ælfric wrote the two Latin letters for Wulfstan in 1005 and apparently sent them

---

[24] The Old English preface survives as a preface only in one manuscript (although part of it occurs elsewhere, adapted for homiletic use) and it is debatable whether it was written some time after the homily collection was drawn up: see K. Sisam, *Studies in the History of Old English Literature* (Oxford, 1953), pp. 170–71. But the unique survival is in CUL Gg. 3. 28, and the injunction to copyists, which comes at the end, would have been pointless if Ælfric had not intended the preface to circulate with the homilies.

[25] As P. Clemoes notes, 'The Old English Benedictine Office, Corpus Christi College, Cambridge, MS 190, and the Relations Between Ælfric and Wulfstan: a Reconsideration', *Anglia* 78 (1960), 265–83, at p. 272, n. 6: ' . . . pastoral letters, by their nature, were particularly liable to revision and supplementation while in use – their text is much less stable than that of a homily for instance . . .'.

[26] In discussing the changing texts of the letters I draw upon Fehr's introduction to *Die Hirtenbriefe*

to him immediately. The three extant copies of each are all in Wulfstan common-place-book manuscripts:[27] Cambridge, Corpus Christi College, 190, Part A (s. xi^1); Copenhagen, Kongelike Bibliotek, Gl. Kgl. Sam. 1595 (s. xi^1); Cambridge, Corpus Christi College 265 (s. xi^{med}). Of these, the Copenhagen manuscript, from Worcester or York, is thought to show Wulfstan's own hand.[28] Yet, in addition to a certain amount of scribal error, the copies show signs of modification, which Clemoes deduces took place whilst the letters were in Wulfstan's possession, even though both letters in all three manuscripts appear to share an exemplar which may have been the manuscript, or a copy of the manuscript, which Ælfric himself sent to Wulfstan.[29] If the modifications are Wulfstan's own, then one could argue – scribal error apart – that the Latin letters are in some sense 'original' in being in the form determined by their apparent episcopal author, since it is not unreasonable for Wulfstan to have modified what was written in his persona. But we certainly do not have the letters as originally written by their actual author, nor do we have the means of reconstructing them, despite our ability to see that some modification has taken place.

The two Old English letters for Wulfstan, although closely related to the Latin ones and often translations of them, in fact represent a further stage in Ælfric's thinking and also exemplify his careful adjustment to a not very learned audience, so that the material is expanded, explained, added, omitted and rearranged. Beyond that we find that Wulfstan rewrote the first of these two letters and that extracts from both of Ælfric's Old English texts came to be used as free-standing passages.

The Wulfsige letter survives in three manuscripts: Cambridge, University Library, Gg. 3. 28 (s. x/xi); Oxford, Bodleian Library, Junius 121 (s. xi $^{3rd\ quarter}$); Cambridge, Corpus Christi College 190 (additional quires s. xi^2). The version in CUL Gg. 3. 28 is probably to be seen as a copy of Ælfric's 'file text'; it comes after the *Catholic Homilies* and its position in the manuscript, together with the closeness of the manuscript to Ælfric, suggest that Ælfric had the letter copied for safe-keeping onto spare leaves at the end of a manuscript of the Second Series of *Catholic Homilies* which served here as the exemplar for CUL Gg. 3. 28.[30]

Ælfrics, pp. x–xxii (description of manuscripts) and pp. liv–lxiv (textual relationships), and in particular pp. cxxvii–cxlv of the supplementary introduction by Clemoes.

27 D. Bethurum, 'Archbishop Wulfstan's Commonplace Book', *Publications of the Modern Language Association of America* 57 (1942), 916–29; D. Whitelock, 'Archbishop Wulfstan, Homilist and Statesman', *Transactions of the Royal Historical Society 4th ser.* 24 (1942), 25–45.

28 Ker, *Catalogue*, p. 140, and N. Ker, 'The Handwriting of Archbishop Wulfstan', *England Before the Conquest: Studies in Primary Sources presented to Dorothy Whitelock*, ed. P. Clemoes and K. Hughes (Cambridge, 1971), pp. 315–31. A detailed account of the instances of Wulfstan's hand in the Copenhagen manuscript is given on pp. 319–21. See now *The Copenhagen Wulfstan: Copenhagen Kongelike Bibliotek Gl. Kgl. Sam. 1595 (quarto)*, ed. J.E. Cross and J. Morrish Tunberg, EEMF 25 (Copenhagen, 1993).

29 *Die Hirtenbriefe Ælfrics*, ed. Fehr, p. cxxxvii (Clemoes).

30 For the closeness of the manuscript to Ælfric, see above, p. 178, and *Ælfric's Catholic Homilies*, ed. Godden, p. xliii. It must be remembered, however, that it is not the 'original manuscript' of the *Catholic Homilies*: see Sisam, *Studies in the History of Old English Literature*, pp. 182–3, and the incorporation of Latin notes, listed by Ker, *Catalogue*, p. 13.

Unfortunately, however, it breaks off after 'gegremedon' in Fehr §108 because of the loss of leaves from the manuscript. Junius 121 is a Wulfstan commonplace-book manuscript[31] and the copy in it presumably derives from one sent to Wulfstan by Ælfric. Both of these copies have the explanatory prefatory letter to Wulfsige. The copy in CCCC 190, although now part of a commonplace-book manuscript, is not on pages which were part of the original nucleus of the manuscript, but is included amongst material on three quires, mainly in one hand of Exeter type, which were added in the second half of the eleventh century.[32] It lacks the prefatory Latin letter found in the two copies directly traceable to Ælfric and it is likely that the copy in CCCC 190 derives, perhaps by transmission between neighbouring dioceses, from the version of the letter as issued by Wulfsige. In the present context, however, what is significant is the pattern of modification, both authorial and non-authorial, for CCCC 190 does not include a revision traceable to Ælfric (Fehr §§105–10) and recorded in his file copy in CUL Gg. 3. 28 (although incomplete through loss of leaves) and in Junius 121, whilst it *does* include apparently unauthorized additional material (Fehr §§150–61), not found in Junius 121.[33] The sequence seems to be that Ælfric sent a copy of his original letter to Wulfsige, who issued it without the prefatory letter, and that at some stage this public version acquired additional non-authorial material, perhaps in part derived from a synodical decision.[34] From this comes the copy in CCCC 190. Having sent the letter to Wulfsige, Ælfric revised it, had a copy of this revision written out for reference at the end of an existing manuscript of the Second Series of *Catholic Homilies* and, perhaps at the time when they were in correspondence about pastoral letters, sent a copy of this version to Wulfstan for reference, therefore retaining the explanatory preface. It is apparently from these stages of recording and transmission that the copies in CUL Gg. 3. 28 and Junius 121 are respectively derived.[35] Thus, if we wish to edit 'the text that the author intended', we are confronted with a difficulty: the manuscript closest to the author (CUL Gg. 3. 28) gives us an

---

[31] See note 27 above.

[32] Ker, *Catalogue*, pp. 70–73, especially p. 73.

[33] The end of CUL Gg. 3. 28 is lost, as already noted, and so this manuscript is no help here. Fehr, *Die Hirtenbriefe Ælfrics*, p. xxii, thought that the letter in Junius 121 contained §§150–61 but that these leaves had been lost. Clemoes, *ibid*. p. cxxxi, shows that there are no leaves missing from Junius 121 at this point, so that the letter must always have ended at Fehr §149, as it now does. However, Whitelock, in *Councils and Synods with other Documents relating to the English Church, I, A.D. 871–1204: Part I: 871–1066*, ed. D. Whitelock, M. Brett and C.N.L. Brooke (Oxford, 1981), pp. 193–5, argues that §149 could not have been the original conclusion, and she suggests that Fehr §§159–61, now only in CCCC 190, was Ælfric's original ending, moved to come after the unauthorized insertion.

[34] Suggested by Whitelock, *Councils and Synods*, p. 195, on the strength of Fehr §157, p. 33: '*And we bisceopas geræddon, þa we ætgædere wæron . . .*', 'And we bishops decreed, when we were together . . .'.

[35] The copy in Junius 121 was believed by Fehr to share a common line of transmission with that in CUL Gg. 3. 28, but Clemoes shows that this is not so and that, in addition, Junius's text has been 'subject to unauthorised revision (e.g. sect. 16a) and a little minor corruption (e.g. in sect. 7)': *Die Hirtenbriefe Ælfrics*, ed. Fehr, p. cxxxv.

authorially revised text and is accidentally incomplete, so that its missing portion would need to be supplied from Junius 121, always supposing that Junius 121 is unmodified at this point; CCCC 190 is closer to Ælfric's original in that it does not have the revision, but it lacks the prefatory letter, it has acquired non-authorial material at the end, and it has a small accidental omission (Fehr §73), although this is an obvious case of eye-skip and could reasonably be supplied from one of the other manuscripts. Given that the text is fairly short, the solution in this case can be the editorial presentation of all three simultaneously, but if it were a long text, the editor's dilemma would be a real one, since each copy has useful evidential value, singly and comparatively, and an 'original' could be created only by editorial conjecture.

IV

In an essay published in 1981, entitled ' "Bede's" Envoi to the Old English *History*: an Experiment in Editing', Fred C. Robinson questioned the modern assumption that 'whenever one medieval author expands or completes the work of another the editor has a responsibility to disengage the two writers' contributions and present them to readers as two independent compositions'.[36] Robinson's 'experiment in editing' was 'to present a text of complex authorship . . . in the composite, integral state that its last shaper intended it to have'.[37] In so doing, he confronts us with the need to attend to the changing text and not to allow our editorial practices to be limited by modern notions of authorship and textual integrity even when, as in this instance, we have two clear starting points to which an editor can revert: the original Latin text, in which Bede establishes his authorial identity; and the version in Old English, which retains Bede's statement of authorial identity, but which in fact adapts the text, largely by omission.[38]

In the Bedan example, as with Ælfric, the establishment of authorial identity functions as a statement of the author's scholarly credentials, but in both cases the subsequent treatment by others defines the difference between our concepts of authorship and textual integrity and those of the Middle Ages. In the field of Old English prose, at least, we have some opportunities for responding to that difference editorially, by presenting versions of the changing text. That much would thereby be learnt about Anglo-Saxon literary and intellectual activity is evident from Robinson's modest 'experiment' and from the studies of composite homilies already undertaken.[39] While it is right to exercise editorial skills in favour of the

---

[36] F.C. Robinson, ' "Bede's" Envoi to the Old English *History*: An Experiment in Editing', *Studies in Philology* 78 (1981), 4–19, at p. 6.

[37] *Ibid*. p. 7.

[38] D. Whitelock, 'The OE Bede', *Proceedings of the British Academy* 48 (1962), 57–90.

[39] See above, p. 182, and consider now *The Vercelli Homilies and Related Texts*, ed. D.G. Scragg, EETS 300 (London, 1992).

original text, if we have suitable material for doing so, this activity needs to be complemented by editorial interest in the text subsequently intended, whether by the author or by others, since the philosophy of the time, as even Ælfric's case-history shows, was that neatly summed up by a tenth-century scribe in a maxim which may be applied metaphorically to the written artefact: 'A scæl gelæred smið swa he gelicost mæg, be bisne wyrcan buton he bet cunne'.[40]

---

[40] Quoted by Robinson, ' "Bede's" Envoi to the Old English History', p. 6: 'A learned artificer must always work from his exemplar as closely as he can, unless he knows how to work better' (Robinson's translation). Found on 15r of Leningrad [now St Petersburg], Public Library, Lat. O. v. XVI. I, along with Latin and Old English scribbles following a grammatical text in Latin written in Anglo-Saxon minuscule (s. x[in]): N.R. Ker, 'A supplement to *Catalogue of Manuscripts Containing Anglo-Saxon*', *ASE* 5 (1976), 121–31, at 127.

ÆLFRIC'S *LIVES OF SAINTS* I AND THE BOULOGNE SERMON: EDITORIAL, AUTHORIAL AND TEXTUAL PROBLEMS

Theodore H. Leinbaugh

Ælfric's *Lives of Saints* presents a number of editorial and textual problems. The chief manuscript witness to the collection – London, British Library, Cotton Julius E.vii – contains several items not written by Ælfric. And other items in the manuscript, such as the five liturgical homilies (four for the Proper of the Season, one for an unspecified occasion), though genuinely by Ælfric, do not seem to conform with the Latin preface that specifies a collection of saints' lives, 'passiones uel uitas sanctorum', celebrated by monks in their festivals.[1] Skeat faithfully – some would argue slavishly – followed the Julius manuscript in his pioneering edition of Ælfric's *Lives of Saints* (= *LS*). Since neither Skeat's edition nor the Julius manuscript accurately represents the original contents of the *Lives*, the first problem confronting an editor or student of the set is establishing which texts Ælfric originally authorized for the set. It is easy enough to exclude non-Ælfrician pieces, such as the story concerning the Seven Sleepers and the life of the actress and courtesan St Mary of Egypt (*LS* XXIII and XXIII B), but it is more difficult to determine whether Ælfric intended to include the liturgical homilies as part of his collection and, if so, in what order.

Peter Clemoes has persuasively argued that the liturgical homilies found in the Julius manuscript form an authentic part of the *Lives* and justifies their inclusion by arguing that homilies 'directly dependent on the liturgy' were unsuitable for Ælfric's 'non-liturgical reading-book', whereas homilies on general themes, such as those found in *LS*, were acceptable.[2] Clemoes even suggests that a liturgical homily from this latter category – item XVI, a general sermon for the memory of the saints – not only initiated Ælfric's plan to compile a volume of *Lives* but also

---

[1] *Ælfric's Lives of Saints*, ed. W.W. Skeat, EETS os 76, 82, 94 and 114 (London, 1881–1900, rptd as two vols 1966) I, 4; references to individual sermons will be identified as *LS* followed by item number and line number; other references will be to Skeat, volume number and page. The Julius manuscript is the only extant copy of the set as a whole.

[2] P. Clemoes has noted that Ælfric makes a formal distinction between narratives not intended for reading as part of the liturgy and liturgical homilies: 'in the latter there is always a reference to the anniversary *today*'. See his article 'The Chronology of Ælfric's Works', *The Anglo-Saxons: Studies in Some Aspects of Their History and Culture Presented to Bruce Dickins*, ed. Peter Clemoes (London, 1959), pp. 212–47, especially p. 221, which is quoted here. A corrected reprint is also available: *The Chronology of Ælfric's Works*, *OEN* Subsidia 5 (Binghamton, New York, 1980). Clemoes discusses the texts included in Skeat's edition that are not by Ælfric on p. 219.

was 'written to serve as a general introduction to it' (p. 222). I would agree that Ælfric included homilies (rather than just saints' lives) in his original plan for the *Lives*. Yet the possibility that *LS* XVI was designed to introduce the set (as, I suppose, a type of preface that might have preceded *LS* I) seems to me more a matter of conjecture than the role assigned to *LS* I, which, I believe, was consciously designed by Ælfric to open the collection proper. *LS* I, I would argue, correctly opens both the Julius manuscript and Skeat's edition and therefore merits attention as the cornerstone of the *Lives of Saints*.

In this essay I will examine the relationship between *LS* I and four affiliated texts, most notably the complex relationship between *LS* I and a Latin sermon found in Boulogne-sur-Mer, Bibliothèque Municipale 63. Some have argued that Ælfric himself compiled the Boulogne sermon, but I intend to reexamine the basis for this claim, which rests largely on the seemingly paradoxical proposition that the Latin sermon is both a source for and a translation of *LS* I. My analysis of the editorial and textual problems that link *LS* I and the Boulogne sermon raises important questions about determining the authorship of the Boulogne sermon but nevertheless sheds some light on the question of Ælfric's intended placement of *LS* I within the *Lives of Saints*.

I. *LS* I AND ITS RELATED TEXTS

Although *LS* I appears in the Julius manuscript under the title *Nativitas Domini Nostri Iesu Christi*, only the introductory portion of this homily designated for Christmas deals with the birth of Christ. Ælfric later revised *LS* I, and this revised version survives in only one manuscript, where no title is given. When A. O. Belfour edited this text, he supplied the title *In Natali Domini* (see item IX in his edition of *Twelfth-Century Homilies in MS. Bodley 343*), but this title also seems somewhat inappropriate since *In Natali Domini*, like *LS* I, mentions the birth of Christ only briefly.[3]

LS I is related to a second text, a largely parallel Latin sermon often attributed to Ælfric and found in Boulogne-sur-Mer 63. The title of the sermon, *Sermo in Natale Domini et de Ratione Anime*,[4] accurately reflects its content and in fact better describes the content of *LS* I and Belfour IX than the titles currently attached to these texts, which deal more substantively with the nature of the soul than with the birth of Christ. The suitability of the Boulogne sermon's title for these Old

---

[3] *Twelfth-Century Homilies in MS. Bodley 343*, ed. A.O. Belfour, Part 1, Text and Translation, EETS os 137 (1909; rpt. London, 1962). References to individual sermons will be by Belfour's item number, followed by his page and line number. The title of Belfour's collection of homilies is itself something of a misnomer since *Twelfth-Century Homilies in MS. Bodley 343* actually contains not homilies originally composed in the twelfth century but rather pre-Conquest material with a heavy dose of twelfth-century spellings.

[4] E.M. Raynes discusses the sermon and calls it a source of *LS* I in her article 'MS. Boulogne-sur-Mer 63 and Ælfric', *Medium Ævum* 26 (1957), 65–73, esp. p. 68. I have edited the sermon in my doctoral dissertation: 'The Liturgical Homilies in *Ælfric's Lives of Saints*' (unpublished Ph.D. dissertation, Harvard Univ., 1980).

English texts springs not from coincidence but from a shared heritage: *LS* I, Belfour IX and the Boulogne sermon all ultimately derive from a brief treatise by Alcuin that explains the nature of the human soul: *De Ratione Animae ad Eulaliam Virginem*.[5] The references to Christmas and the birth of Christ found in the Boulogne sermon, *LS* I and Belfour IX form no part of Alcuin's original text and came as later interpolations to a base text that originally dealt exclusively with the nature of the human soul.

In addition to its ties with Alcuin's *De Ratione Animae*, the Boulogne sermon and Belfour IX, *LS* I shares resonances with a fourth text, King Alfred's version of Boethius's *Consolation of Philosophy*, which W.F. Bolton has argued provides a source for several sentences in *LS* I and Belfour IX.[6] A brief analysis of these texts will reveal the complexities of their interrelations.

II. *LS* I AND BELFOUR IX

Skeat published the first installment of his edition of the *Lives of Saints* in 1861 and only later discovered the existence of another manuscript witness to *LS* I. He dismissed Ælfric's revised version of the homily found in Bodley 343 as a 'late and inferior text' (Skeat, I, 544). Although the manuscript of the revised version post-dates that of *LS* I by some 150 years, the text is by no means inferior. The rhythmical prose that distinguishes Belfour IX from *LS* I compares favourably in style with the other work of Ælfric's middle and late career, and the textual readings are usually sound. The language of the text is what might reasonably be expected from a twelfth-century copy of an earlier Anglo-Saxon text, and Belfour IX merits further study in its own right.

LS I begins with a reference to Christ's birth, but moves almost immediately to a discussion of heretics who question Christ's coeternity with the Father. After a few remarks on the three orders of being within the universe (the beasts, grouped with soulless things; the angels, grouped with the souls of men; and, lastly, the eternal Lord), the homily takes up the topic of the Holy Trinity. A lengthy discussion

---

5 Eulalia is Alcuin's affectionate nickname for Gundrada, the cousin of Charlemagne and the sister of Abbot Adalhard of Corbie. The source in Alcuin was first noted by Clemoes in his article '*Mens absentia cogitans* in *The Seafarer* and *The Wanderer*', *Medieval Literature and Civilization: Studies in Memory of G. N. Garmonsway*, ed. D.A. Pearsall and R.A. Waldron (London, 1969), pp. 62–77; see particularly p. 63, n. 2. Alcuin's treatise on the soul, which can be dated to the last years of his life (801–4), has been edited by J. Curry, 'Alcuin, *De Ratione Animae*: A Text with Introduction, Critical Apparatus, and Translation' (unpublished Ph.D. dissertation, Cornell Univ., 1966); the text is more readily available in PL 101, cols 639–47.

6 The connection between the two works was noted in 'The Alfredian Boethius in Ælfric's "Lives of Saints" I', *N&Q* 19 (1972), 406–7. Bolton suggests in his article that the borrowings from Alfred imply that Ælfric's Old English homily, not the Boulogne Latin text, must have been composed first. *LS* I is also related to Ælfric's *De Creatore et Creatura*. Clemoes has noted ('Chronology', p. 239) that *LS* I was 'rewritten as Belfour IX before *De Creatore et Creatura* drew on the latter'. For further information on the relation between *De Creatore et Creatura* and the texts discussed here, see pp. 89–93 of my doctoral dissertation and my article 'A Damaged Passage in Ælfric's *De Creatore et Creatura*: Methods of Recovery', *Anglia* 104 (1986), 104–14.

follows on the subject of man's soul, which Ælfric likens to the Trinity in its threefold structure comprised of memory, understanding and will.[7] The homily concludes with a description of the soul's beauty, which, we are told, consists in 'loving wisdom'.

Belfour IX generally follows the pattern of *LS* I. The slightly longer opening section of Belfour IX stresses the benefits of the Incarnation for mankind. Then Belfour IX takes up roughly the same topics found in *LS* I: the coeternity of Christ with the Father, the various orders of being within God's creation, the nature of the Trinity and the nature of man's soul. There are, of course, differences between the two texts. Belfour IX adds material not found in *LS* I, and in several instances this material acts as a reminder of the occasion for which the homily was intended. At one point Christ is described as 'þe liflice laf þe of heofene astah, 7 nu todæg wærð ácenned of þam clæne mædene' (Belfour, p. 84, lines 19–20). No reference to Christ's birth appears in the corresponding section of *LS* I.

In addition to these differences, there are similarities between the two texts that have not yet been noted. Skeat, speaking of the relation of Belfour IX to his text of *LS* I, said that the 'wording at first differs from that of the text, but gradually approaches it' (Skeat I, 544). And Neil Ker has more precisely observed the close agreement between the final two-thirds of each homily. Yet the parallels in the opening sections must not be overlooked. The same phrases frequently appear in both texts, and where they do not parallel each other word for word, they often parallel each other *sensum ex sensu*. For example, lines 2 and 3 of *LS* I, 'on soðre menniscnysse acenned wæs of þæm halgan mædene marian' ('was born in true human nature of the holy Virgin Mary'), parallel lines 4 and 5 of Belfour IX (p. 78): 'on soðe menniscnesse ácenned of Mariæ þet halige mæden' ('born in true human nature of Mary that holy virgin'). Further parallels could be cited, but clearly Belfour IX, even in its opening sections, closely agrees in content with *LS* I.

Given this similarity, Ælfric's motivation for revising his homily might be questioned. The answer is straightforward: Ælfric revised the homily in order to make it

---

[7] The tripartite structure of the soul is a commonplace that can be traced to classical writings, though Ælfric's source is Alcuin's *De Ratione Animae ad Eulaliam Virginem* as transmitted via the Boulogne sermon. Alcuin notes that the soul is made in the image of the Holy Trinity insofar as it possesses understanding, will and memory ('intelligentiam, voluntatem, et memoriam habet'). Earlier in his treatise Alcuin relies on a Platonic division of the tripartite soul into a rational part, a passionate part and an appetitive part ('pars rationalis, irascibilis, et concupiscibilis'), but here he adopts the Augustinian tripartite division as found in Augustine's *De Trinitate* X, 11, 18. The passage in *De Trinitate* is cited by F. Moriones, *Enchiridion Theologicum Sancti Augustini* (Madrid, 1961), in his section called 'De analogiis Sanctissimae Trinitatis': 'Haec igitur tria, memoria, intelligentia, voluntas, quoniam non sunt tres vitae, sed una vita' ('Since, therefore, these three, memory, understanding and will, are not three lives, but one life'; p. 138). See also K. Werner, 'Der Entwickelungsgang der mittelalterlichen Psychologie von Alcuin bis Albertus Magnus', *Denkschriften der kaiserlichen Akademie der Wissenschaften, philosophisch-historische Classe* 25 (Vienna, 1876), 69–150. More recent work on the topic includes G. Ladner's 'Eine karolingische Modifizierung der psychologischen Trinitätsanalogien des hl. Augustinus', *Aus Kirche und Reich: Studien zu Theologie, Politik und Recht im Mittelalter. Festschrift für Friedrich Kempf*, ed. H. Mordek (Sigmaringen, 1983), pp. 45–53.

stylistically compatible with the other writings of his middle and late career by transforming much of the ordinary prose of *LS* I into the kind of rhythmical prose found in Belfour IX. In those places where there is some substantive rather than stylistic alteration, the source can usually be traced to the Boulogne sermon. The Old English phrase quoted earlier, for example, describing Christ as 'the living bread, who descended from heaven and on this very day was born of the immaculate Virgin', is not found in *LS* I but is present in the Boulogne sermon.

III. THE BOULOGNE SERMON

The relationship between the Boulogne sermon and the two Old English homilies has been raised before but deserves closer scrutiny. Enid Raynes first suggested that the Boulogne sermon provides the main source for *LS* I. Clemoes subsequently discovered that the second half of the Boulogne sermon was taken from Alcuin's *De Ratione Animae* and also reported that *LS* I and Belfour IX were 'verbally identical almost throughout their rendering of that part of the Latin homily [i.e., the Boulogne sermon] which is derived from Alcuin' (Clemoes, '*Mens absentia cogitans*', p. 63, n. 2). The relationship between the first half of the Boulogne sermon (lines 1–142) and *LS* I appears to be more complicated. I have quoted above a passage from Belfour IX that finds its source in the first half of the Latin text. No equivalent passage can be found in *LS* I, and Malcolm Godden has cited further instances where Belfour IX more closely follows the Boulogne text.[8] In his article's addendum, 'Note on the relationship of LS, no. i, Belfour, no. ix and the Boulogne Latin version', Godden examines parallel versions of the texts related to *LS* I. I reproduce his comparisons in abbreviated form in order to review his explanation of the relationship between the texts.

IV. THE FIVE RELATED TEXTS

1. Boethius, *De Consolatione Philosophiae* V, met. v:
  Quam uariis terras animalia permeant figuris!
   Namque alia extento sunt corpore pulueremque uerrunt
    Continuumque trahunt ui pectoris incitata sulcum.[9]

2. Alfred's Boethius (Sedgefield, p. 147/2–10):
  Hwæt, þu miht ongitan þæt manig wyht is mistlice ferende geond eorþan, and sint swiðe ungelices hiwes, and ungelice farað. Sume licgað mid eallon

---

[8] M.R. Godden, 'Anglo-Saxons on the Mind', *Learning and Literature in Anglo-Saxon England: Studies Presented to Peter Clemoes*, ed. Michael Lapidge and Helmut Gneuss (Cambridge, 1985), pp. 271–98.

[9] 'In what varied shapes the animals traverse the earth! For indeed there are some with a body stretched out, and they scrape over the dust and, stirred by the strength in their breast, they make a continuous furrow.' Boethius, *De Consolatione Philosophiae* V, met. v, ed. L. Bieler, CCSL 94 (Turnhout, 1957), 100; unless otherwise noted, translations from Latin and Old English are my own.

lichoman on eorþan, and swa smuhende farað þæt him nauþer ne fet ne fiðeras ne fultumað.[10]

3.   *LS* I, lines 49–55:

Ða gesceafta þe þæs an scyppend gesceop synden mænig-fealde, and mis-lices hiwes, and ungelice farað. Sume sindon ungesewenlice gastas butan lichoman, swa swa synd ænglas on heofonum. Sume syndan creopende on eorðan mid eallum lichoman, swa swa wurmas doð. Sume gað on twam fotum, sume on feower fotum. Sume fleoð mid fyðerum, sume on flodum swimmað.[11]

4.   the Boulogne text (Leinbaugh, pp. 115–16, lines 74–88):

Creaturae uero quas unus Creator creauit multiplices sunt et uariae figurae, et non uno modo uiuunt; ex quibus quaedam sunt incorporalia et inuisibilia, ut angeli in caelo nullo terreno cibo utentes. . . . [Q]uaedam etiam natatilia sunt ut pissces in mari, et in amne uagantia, quae sine aquis uiuere nequeunt, et nos in aquis suffocamu[r]. . . . Sed homo solus recta statura ambulat, qui ad imaginem Dei creatus est et proprio incessu significat quod debet plus de celestibus meditari quam de terrenis.[12]

5.   Belfour IX, pp. 82/29–84/5:

Nu beoð þa gesceaftæ þe þe an Scyppend iscop mislice heowes and moni-fealdes cyndes; and heo alle ne libbæð na on ane wisæ. Summe heo beoð unlichamlice and eac unsegenlice swa beoð englæs; he nabbæð nænne li-chame, and heo libbæð on heofene, swiðe bliþful on Godes isihðe, and heo eorðlice mætes næfre ne brucæð. . . . Þa fixas nabbæþ nan lif buton wætere; ne we ne magon libban noht longe on watere.[13]

---

[10] 'See, you are able to perceive that many a creature goes travelling about the earth in different ways, and they are very unlike in appearance, and they move in different ways. Some lie with all of their body on the earth, and so go crawling so that neither feet nor feathers assist them.' *King Alfred's Old English Version of Boethius De Consolatione Philosophiae*, ed. W.J. Sedgefield (Oxford, 1899; rpt. Darmstadt, 1968); I have silently expanded the abbreviations in Sedgefield's text.

[11] 'The creatures that this one Creator shaped are of many kinds and of varied appearance, and move differently. Some are invisible spirits without a body, just as the angels are in heaven. Some go crawling on the earth with their entire body, just as worms do. Some go on two feet, some on four feet. Some fly with feathers, some swim in flowing waters.'

[12] 'Truly the creatures that the sole Creator created are of different and varied shape and they do not live in one manner. Of these, certain ones are incorporeal and invisible, such as the angels in heaven who partake of no earthly food. . . . And certain ones are also swimming creatures like the fish in the sea and those wandering in the river, which cannot live without water, whereas we are suffocated in water. . . . But man alone, who was created in the image of God, walks with an upright stature and by his special manner of walking signifies that he ought to think more about heavenly than earthly matters.'

[13] 'Now those creatures that the single Creator shaped are of varied appearance and diverse nature. And by no means do they all live in one manner. Some of them are incorporeal and also invisible, as are the angels. They have no body and they live in heaven, very blissful in God's

Godden argues that this sequence of texts represents the order of composition as it pertains to the opening portion of *LS* I:

> Alfred is clearly paraphrasing Boethius's Latin text here, and there is no need to posit any further source or influence for him. Ælfric adapts and expands that paraphrase in LS, no. i, while retaining many close verbal parallels that attest the directness of the debt; the Boulogne Latin text, resembling LS, no. i, rather than Alfred's version, but expanding the references to angels and fish which Ælfric had added in recasting Alfred, must be a translation and expansion of the LS, no. i passage. (pp. 297–8)

Godden's analysis seems convincing, but I question the conclusion that the Boulogne text 'must' be a translation of the *LS* I passage; I would revise the word 'must' to a more modest 'may', since I believe we are dealing with a plausible hypothesis rather than an incontrovertible proof. My quibble over wording would mean little except for the fact that Godden relies on this 'must' to make his more important argument that the Boulogne Latin text 'must have been written by Ælfric' (p. 298).

V. AN ALTERNATIVE SEQUENCE OF COMPOSITION

If the sequence Godden has proposed is true, then Ælfric's authorship of the Boulogne sermon seems certain. Yet I believe that it is possible to posit an alternative sequence that places the composition of the Boulogne sermon before that of *LS* I; such a sequence would, of course, undermine Godden's particular line of proof for Ælfric's authorship of the Boulogne sermon.[14] Godden's argument rests in part on the assumption that the Boulogne Latin text must have been written after *LS* I because the Latin text apparently expands the references to angels and fish found in *LS* I. It seems theoretically possible, however, that the reverse is true: Ælfric may have condensed the references to angels and fish found in his Latin source when translating it into Old English.

Godden has also surmised that *LS* I must precede the Boulogne sermon because *LS* I apparently borrows several Old English sentences directly from Alfred's Boethius. This seems a logical sequence, and yet it is still conceivable that the Boulogne sermon was composed first. It seems possible that while translating the Boulogne sermon, Ælfric could have spotted several key passages that reminded him of quite similar passages in Alfred's Boethius, which he appropriated for his own translation.

The alternative sequence I propose for the composition of these texts suggests

---

sight, and they never partake of earthly food. . . . The fish have no life outside of the water; nor can we live long at all in water.'

[14] I confess at the outset that I raise these questions in the role of an *advocatus diaboli* who, as a *promotor fidei*, may in fact champion the canonization or beatification that he is charged to argue against: I share common ground with Godden in believing that Ælfric may have composed the Boulogne sermon. Yet I hesitate to assign the text to Ælfric without further proof.

that Ælfric (or another author) decided to write a homily in Latin on the Catholic faith and on the nature of the human soul. He used as his chief source Alcuin's *De Ratione Animae*, which he followed closely but rearranged in order to form the last two-thirds of the Boulogne sermon. The opening third of *LS* I has no source in Alcuin, and Godden argues that this portion of the homily was freely composed in Old English and subsequently translated into Latin to form the opening third of the Boulogne sermon. Yet it seems possible to theorize that the opening third of the Boulogne sermon may originally have been composed from Latin rather than Old English sources: Latin patristic material on heretical matters concerning the coeternity of Christ with the Father, various biblical citations selected from the Vulgate, other Latin material (patristic and non-patristic) concerning the nature of the soul and material with strong classical precedents on man's place in the universe. Traditional topoi on the diversity of creation and the importance of man's erect stature also form part of the opening section of the Boulogne sermon and may well derive from Latin rather than Old English sources. These Latin materials could have provided Ælfric with a primary source, which he augmented with several sentences from Alfred's Boethius.

This alternative sequence could be confirmed by the discovery of a direct Latin source for the opening portion of the Boulogne sermon. The absence of identifiable sources makes Godden's posited sequence for these texts more attractive, yet it should be noted that reasonably close Latin parallels for several topoi in the first third of the Boulogne text do exist and may adumbrate the discovery of closer parallels or even direct sources. The symbolic importance of man's erect stature can be traced back to the writings of Xenophon, Plato (*Symposium*, *Republic* and *Timaeus*), Aristotle and Heraclitus; Cicero also takes up the topic and his Latin rendering mentions heavenly concerns (*caelestium*) in much the same way as the Boulogne sermon's reference to the heavens (*celestibus*).[15]

Later Christian writers avidly adopted the topic: Lactantius refers to the significance of man's stature more than a dozen times in his writings.[16] And it seems

---

[15] The belief that by his erect posture and gait, man reveals that he should think more about heavenly than earthly things (in contrast to the brute animals, which are inclined towards the earth) was popularized by Stoic philosophers, but was a commonplace even from the time of Xenophon (*Memorabilia* 1, 4, 11); a number of examples are collected in S. O. Dickerman's *De Argumentis quibusdam apud Xenophontem, Platonem, Aristotelem obviis e Structura Hominis et Animalium petitis* (Halis Saxonum, 1909), pp. 93–101. In addition to parallels found in Plato and Aristotle, Dickerman quotes Cicero, who asserts that the gods made men tall and erect, raised up from the ground, so that they might be able to take in knowledge of the gods while gazing at the heavens: 'Qui primum eos humo excitatos celsos et erectos constituit, ut deorum cognitionem caelum intuentes capere possent' ('Who [=Nature] in the beginning lifted them up from the earth, raised them up tall and erect, so that they might be able to receive knowledge of the gods while contemplating the vault of heaven'; *De Natura Deorum*, 2.56.140; *M. Tulli Ciceronis De Natura Deorum*, ed. A.S. Pease, 2 vols [Cambridge, MA, 1955–8], pp. 913–15). Further parallels are listed in Pease, II, 914–15, notes.

[16] Lactantius uses the idea repeatedly in his *Divinae Institutiones*: 'nam cum ceterae animantes pronis corporibus in humum spectent, quia rationem ac sapientiam non acceperunt, nobis autem status rectus, sublimis vultus ab artifice deo datus sit, apparet istas religiones deorum non esse

relevant to note that Alcuin's *De Animae Ratione* – the Boulogne sermon's chief source – borrows several passages verbatim from Lactantius, which demonstrates that ideas from Lactantius might readily have found their way into the text of *LS* I. Isidore, Augustine and Ambrose also refer to the topic in ways that may be more closely related to the Boulogne sermon's Latin than to Alfred's Old English translation of Boethius.[17]

In short, either the opening portion of *LS* I was translated from the Boulogne sermon (with the possible exception of some lines adopted directly from Alfred's Boethius) or, as Godden has argued, the opening portion of *LS* I was composed freely in Old English without the benefit of Latin sources and then translated into Latin to form the opening portion of the Boulogne sermon. Both alternatives seem possible. Godden's hypothesis hinges on the relatively plausible inference that since *LS* I seemingly draws directly upon Alfred's Old English version of Boethius, Ælfric must have freely composed *LS* I with Alfred's text in front of him before translating the homily into Latin. Yet it does not seem utterly implausible to assume that the Latin text came first and that Ælfric translated this Latin text and incorporated a few sentences from Alfred's Boethius that were suggested by their closeness to the Latin. One other possibility ought to be considered: perhaps Ælfric did not use Alfred's Boethius as a source, but rather both Alfred and Ælfric made use of the same Latin source and, as they translated, they both produced remarkably similar Old English translations.

rationis humanae, quia curvant caeleste animal ad veneranda terrena' ('for although other living creatures with prone bodies gaze towards the earth because they have not received reason and wisdom, to us, however, a standing posture and a face lifted aloft have been given by God the Creator. It is plain that those religious practices involving pagan gods are not for the man of reason, because they reduce the celestial creature to mere earthly worship'; Lib. II, 1, 14, ed. S. Brandt, *CSEL* 19, 97–8). The same general notion is repeated in Lib. II, 2, 19; Lib. II, 17, 9; Lib. II, 18, 1, 6; Lib. III, 12, 26; Lib. III, 20, 11; Lib. III, 27, 16; Lib. III, 28, 16; and several times elsewhere in the work. Lactantius repeats the idea in his other works: 'De Opificio Dei' 8, 2; 10, 26; 19, 10; 'De Ira Dei' 14, 1; 20, 10; etc.; cf. Dickerman, p. 98.

[17] Augustine writes that man was not created as the irrational animals who look towards the earth, but rather erect in order that this bodily form might admonish us to know the things that are above: 'Non enim ut animalia rationis expertia prona esse videmus in terram, ita creatus est homo; sed erecta in caelum corporis forma admonet eum quae sursum sunt sapere' ('For truly we see that man was not created just as the animals that are bent towards the ground and devoid of reason, but rather the erect shape of man's body, directed toward the sky, admonishes him to know the things that are above'; *De Civitate Dei* 22, 24; *CCSL* 48, ed. B. Dombart and A. Kalb [Turnholti, 1955], pp. 849–50, lines 127–9). Similar ideas are expressed in Augustine's *De Genesi contra Manichaeos* I, 17, 28 (PL 34, cols 186–7); *De Trinitate* XII 1, 1 (PL 42, cols 997–9); *De Genesi ad Litteram* VI 12, 22 (PL 34, col. 348); and *De Diversis Quaestionibus* LI, 3 (*CCSL* 44 A, ed. A. Mutzenbecher, [Turnholti, 1975], p. 80, lines 55 ff.; PL 40, col. 33). The same idea occurs several times in Isidore's work; see, for example, *Libri Differentiarum* II 16, 46: '[animalia] prona sunt, et ad terram vergentia; nobis naturaliter vultus in coelum erectus est; illis otium et opulentia; nobis ratio et sermo concessus est, per quae intelligere et Deum confiteri possimus' ('Animals are prone and incline towards the earth; for us the face is by nature raised up toward heaven; to those creatures leisure and power have been granted; to us, reason and language, through which we are able to discern and acknowledge God'; PL 83, col. 77). See also Isidore's *Etymologiae* XI 1, 5 (PL 82, col. 397).

VI. A COMMON LATIN SOURCE FOR ALFRED'S BOETHIUS AND ÆLFRIC'S *LS* I

I believe that in several instances a common Latin source accounts for similarities in phrasing between *LS* I and Alfred's Boethius that might otherwise be attributed to Ælfric's direct knowledge and use of Alfred's text. I believe I can offer proof that at times Ælfric's translation of his Latin source uncannily matches Alfred's phrasing not because Ælfric directly copied from Alfred, but rather because both Ælfric and Alfred followed the same Latin source. The following three passages presumably represent Ælfric's use of Alfred's Boethius as a source for *LS* I and Belfour IX:

Forþi ic cwæð þæt sio sawul wære þreofeald, for þa(m) þe uðwitan secgað þ(æt) hio hæbbe þrio gecynd. An ðara gecynda is þ(æt) heo bið wilnigende, oðer þ(æt) hio bið irsiende, þridde þ(æt) hio bið gesceadwis. Twa þara gecynda habbað netenu swa same swa men; oðer þara is wilnung, oðer is irsung. Ac se mon ana hæfð gesceadwisnesse, nalles nan oðru gesceaft.	Uþwytan sæcgað. þæt þære sawle gecynd is ðryfeald. An dæl is on hire gewylnigendlic. oðer yrsigendlic. þrydde gesceadwislic. Twægen þissera dæla habbað deor and nytenu mid us. þæt is gewylnunge and yrre.	Uðwiten, þæt beoð wisæ lareowæs, secgæð þæt ðare sawle gecunde is þreofeald: an dæl on hire is wilnigendlic, oðer [yrsigendlic, ðriddæ] sceadwislic. Twegen þisseræ dæle habbæð deor and nyten mid us, þæt is wilnunge and yrre.
(Alfred's Boethius, p. 81, Sedgefield; cf. Bolton, p. 406)[18]	(Ælfric, *LS* I, lines 96–9)[19]	(Belfour IX, p. 86, lines 29–32)[20]

[18] 'Therefore I said that the soul was threefold, because philosophers say that it has three natures. One of those natures is that it has will, the second, that it has passion, the third, that it is rational. Two of those natures beasts have in the same fashion as men; one of those is will, the other is passion. But man alone has rationality, by no means any other creature.'

[19] 'Philosophers say that the nature of the soul is threefold. One part in it has will, the second passion, the third rationality. Two of these parts beasts and cattle have in common with us, that is, will and passion.'

[20] 'Philosophers, that is, wise teachers, say that the nature of the soul is threefold. One part in it has will, the second passion, the third rationality. Two of these parts beasts and cattle have in common with us, that is, will and passion.'

Ælfric's phrasing in *LS* I (middle column) closely approximates Alfred's Boethius (first column), and the phrasing in Belfour IX (last column) follows that of *LS* I. At first glance this looks like another instance of Ælfric's direct borrowing from Alfred's Boethius, as Bolton suggests in his article. And this apparent borrowing might well seem to buttress Godden's argument that Ælfric first worked with Alfred's Old English text in composing *LS* I before translating *LS* I into Latin.

Yet a comparison of the same passage in *LS* I with the Latin text of Alcuin's *De Ratione Animae* and the Latin text of the Boulogne sermon suggests an entirely different sequence for the composition of these texts:

Triplex est enim	Triplex est enim	Uþwytan sæcgað.
animae, ut	animae, ut	þæt þære sawle
philosophi	philosophi	gecynd is
volunt, natura:	uolunt, natura:	ðryfeald. An
est in ea quaedam	est in ea quaedam	dæl is on hire
pars	pars	
concupiscibilis,	concupisscibilis,	gewylnigendlic.
alia	alia	oðer
rationalis	rationabilis,	yrsigendlic.
[Al.rationabilis]		
tertia	tertia	þrydde
irascibilis.	irascibilis.	gesceadwislic.
Duas enim habent	Duas enim habent	Twægen þissera
harum partes	harum partes	dæla habbað
nobiscum bestiae	nobiscum bestiae	deor and
et animalia	et animalia	nytenu mid us.
communes, id est,	communes, id est,	þæt is
concupiscentiam,	concupiscentiam	gewylnunge and
et iram.	et iram.	yrre.
(Alcuin, *De Rat.* III; Migne, Patrologia Latina, 101, cols 639–40)[21]	(Boulogne, Leinbaugh, p. 121, lines 156–60)[22]	(Ælfric, *LS* I, lines 96–9)[23]

Here, with the Latin texts available for comparison, it is indisputable that the Boulogne sermon copies Alcuin's text (first column) verbatim and that the direct source for *LS* I would clearly seem to be the Boulogne sermon (second column) instead of Alfred's Boethius as previously suggested. Despite barriers imposed by the differences in language, Ælfric's Old English text more closely follows the Latin of the Boulogne text than the Old English of Alfred's Boethius. For example,

---

[21] 'The nature of the soul is, indeed, threefold, as the philosophers maintain. There is in it a certain appetitive part, a second rational part and a third passionate part. Two of these parts, to be sure, beasts and animals have in common with us, that is, appetite and passion.'

[22] The translation is identical to the preceding passage from Alcuin.

[23] See note 19.

Ælfric translates the Boulogne sermon's Latin doublet *bestiae et animalia* with a closely matching doublet, *deor and nytenu*, whereas Alfred's Boethius gives merely the single word *netenu*. Apparently Alcuin's ninth-century Latin text preserves a text that serves as a source for both Old English texts: Alfred's ninth-century rendering of Boethius and Ælfric's tenth-century translation of Alcuin's text as transmitted via the Boulogne sermon, *LS* I. The similarities in phrasing between the Old English texts of Alfred and Ælfric derive not from the fact that Ælfric copied Alfred directly, but rather from the fact that the two Old English texts share a common Latin source. If these Latin texts had not survived – or had gone unnoticed – scholars would no doubt have erroneously surmised that Ælfric borrowed directly from Alfred.

It is interesting to note that Godden tacitly accepts the primacy of the Boulogne sermon instead of Alfred's Boethius in this particular instance in spite of the fact that this sequence (Alcuin – Boulogne sermon – *LS* I) seemingly contradicts his argument that *LS* I was written before the Boulogne sermon: I emphasize the word *seemingly*, since Godden offers an explanation for this apparent anomaly that I discuss below.

Although I have argued that the Boulogne sermon provides Ælfric's direct source for *LS* I in this particular example, I note one caveat: Ælfric does not follow Alcuin's precise order in his list of the three constituent parts of the soul. Alcuin lists first the appetitive or concupiscent (*concupiscibilis*), then the rational (*rationalis*) and, finally, the passionate or irascible (*irascibilis*). Ælfric instead follows the traditional sequence – in ascending order from the lowest to the highest functions of the soul – as given in Alfred's Boethius: first, the appetitive or concupiscent (Alfred's *wilnigende*, Ælfric's *gewylnigendlic*), then the passionate or irascible (Alfred's *irsiende*, Ælfric's *yrsigendlic*) and, finally, the rational (Alfred's *gesceadwis*, Ælfric's *gesceadwislic*). If Alcuin, as transmitted by the Boulogne sermon, is indeed Ælfric's source for this passage, the shift in the order of this list would seem to require some explanation.

It might be possible to suppose that Ælfric simultaneously consulted the Boulogne sermon and Alfred's Boethius while composing *LS* I or that Ælfric deviated from the Boulogne sermon when translating it and independently arrived at the order found in Alfred's Boethius for the three parts of the soul. Perhaps the case for coincidental parallels between Alfred and Ælfric could be strengthened by arguing that Ælfric's alteration of the sequence found in the Boulogne sermon gives better rhetorical sense: placing man's reason at the end of the list emphasizes the division between reason and those components of the soul held in common by man and beast, the passionate and appetitive modes. Other possibilities exist: Ælfric's list of the component parts of the soul, which might be taken as a commonplace, could be indebted to sources or influences other than the Boulogne sermon or Alfred's Boethius. These competing possibilities emphasize the difficulty of assessing Ælfric's sources and trying to assign priority to them.

Godden writes with some assurance that the 'successive recastings of *De consolatione Philosophiae* . . . show clearly the relative order of the three versions [*LS* I

– Boulogne – Belfour IX] and their relationship to each other' (p. 296). Yet I believe that the arguments and examples adduced above call into question our ability to know clearly the relative order of these versions. Until the alternative hypotheses can be decisively ruled out, the precise relationship between these various texts will remain open to question.

The evidence for Ælfric's direct borrowing from Alfred looks convincing in several of the instances cited by Bolton (and particularly the one instance echoed by Godden), but the examples and arguments I have put forward demonstrate that Ælfric's passage on the constituent parts of soul derives from the Boulogne sermon and that Alfred's text need not have been consulted at all: the strong verbal parallels between Ælfric and Alfred appear to be coincidental. I have alluded to the fact that Godden tacitly supports this same conclusion, and that is because my example of a shared Latin source comes from the final two-thirds of *LS* I. Godden has argued that Ælfric composed the opening third of *LS* I in Old English and then translated this text into Latin to form the beginning of the Boulogne sermon; yet for the remaining two-thirds of *LS* I, Godden reverses his argument and argues that the Boulogne sermon serves as the direct source:

A quite different relationship must be posited for the remainder of the homily. The ultimate source here is Alcuin's *De animae ratione*, and the very close verbal agreement between Alcuin's wording and the Boulogne Latin text of the homily shows that no English version could have intervened between them; the Boulogne text must be an adaptation and abridgement of Alcuin's treatise. The LS, no. i English version, closely resembling the Boulogne text but showing some further slight adaptation and small additions, and revealing no independent use of Alcuin's treatise, must be an adapted translation of the Boulogne text. Belfour, no. ix, incorporating the changes made by LS, no. i and showing many verbal parallels with it, must be based on LS, no. i itself. Thus for this second and longer part of the homily, the relationship is: Alcuin (Latin) – Boulogne text (Latin) – LS, no. i (Old English) – Belfour, no. ix (Old English). Whatever explanation one offers for this complex set of relationships, it seems clear that the Boulogne Latin text, being partly based on LS, no. i, as well as serving as source for both LS, no. i and Belfour, no. ix, must have been written by Ælfric, like the two Old English texts. (p. 298)

I fully accept the sequence of composition put forward by Godden for the second and longer part of the homily. I have merely tried to argue that this same sequence might well apply to the first part of the homily. Godden's notion that the Boulogne sermon serves as both a translation of and a source for *LS* I seems paradoxical, but he offers a plausible explanation for these unusual and seemingly illogical circumstances:

I would suppose that at some early stage Ælfric made a Latin abridgement and adaptation of Alcuin's treatise, probably in the knowledge that he would not be able to obtain access to the treatise at a later date. . . . Subsequently, I take it,

Ælfric used this précis as the basis of LS, no. i., prefaced with new material which was partly his own and partly drawn from Alfred's Boethius. When he later was called on to produce a Latin version of LS, no. i (perhaps for a different readership; Ælfric also produced parallel Latin and English versions of his pastoral letters), he naturally used his original Latin adaptation of Alcuin for the second part rather than retranslating that part of LS, no. i. (p. 298)

On the one hand this scenario seems reasonable enough, but, on the other hand, it also seems possible to assume that Latin prefatory matter (taken from unidentified sources) was added to this précis of Alcuin to produce the Boulogne sermon *before* Ælfric translated the entire piece – with some abridgements – into *LS* I. As Ælfric wrote in the Latin preface to his *Lives of Saints*: 'prolixiores passiones breuiamus uerbis, non adeo sensu, ne fastidiosis ingeratur tedium si tanta prolixitas erit in propria lingua quanta est in latina' – that is, 'we condense the longer narratives, not with regard to sense but rather words, lest tedium be inflicted upon the fastidious' (Skeat, I, 4). Certainly the pattern of translating and condensing Latin sources aptly characterizes the pattern of Ælfric's career, which was primarily dedicated to disseminating the knowledge concealed in Latin texts to a wider audience, particularly to the uneducated majority of his countrymen. It seems inherently more likely that Ælfric should follow this same pattern in translating the Boulogne sermon from Latin into Old English; it seems more problematic to assume that he would have translated *LS* I into Latin 'perhaps for a different readership'. That latter assumption raises a number of difficult questions about that 'different readership': would such a readership, learned and skilled in reading Latin, have required a Latin translation of an Old English sermon? Under what circumstances would such a Latin sermon have been delivered, read or recited? Other texts in the Boulogne manuscript have been documented as sources for Ælfric's Old English writings; why would this text have been treated in a different manner? There may be reasonably plausible answers to these and similar questions, but it is great rarity to find Ælfric translating a sermon from Old English into Latin: the reverse generally holds true.

VII. LATIN ANALOGUES FOR *LS* I

Two other matters concerning the relative sequence of these texts deserve scrutiny. I have already pointed out some previously unnoticed Latin precedents for portions of the first third of the Boulogne sermon, and I offer one more example that may lend support to the possible existence of Latin sources for that portion of the sermon. Ælfric exploits an analogy based on the sun to counter those who would raise doubts about the triune nature of God:

Seo sunne þe onliht ealne mideard is godes gesceaft. and we magon understandan þæt hyre leoht is of hyre. na heo of þam leohte. and seo hætu gæð of þære sunnan. and of hire leohte gelice. Swa eac þæs ælmihtigan godes sunu is æfre of þæm fæder acenned. soð leoht. and soð wisdom. and se halga gast is æfre of him bam. na acenned. ac forðsteppende. (*LS* I, lines 71–7)[24]

This traditional image and argument can be traced as far back as the fourth-century writings of Athanasius, whose defence of the coeternity of the Father and the Son sounds remarkably similar to Ælfric's:

The sun and the radiance are two lights, or different substances; or to say that the radiance accrued to it over and above and is not a single and uncompounded offspring from the sun; such, that sun and radiance are two, but the light one, because the radiance is an offspring from the sun. [25]

A Latin text formerly ascribed to Bede, and now known as *De Substantiis* (PL 90, col. 1116), even more closely approximates the phrasing found in the Boulogne sermon. *De Substantiis* equates God the Father (*personam Patris*) with the sun, the Son (*personam filii*) with the light of the sun, and the Holy Spirit (*personam Spiritus sancti*) with the heat of the sun. The phrasing is insufficiently close to qualify *De Substantiis* as the direct source, but closer Latin parallels may yet surface. Vercelli homily XVI shows that this commonplace circulated elsewhere in the vernacular, though the Vercelli text employs the more general example of fire (rather than the sun) as a Trinitarian analogue.[26]

One last matter concerning the sequence of these Ælfrician texts must be considered. Godden has argued that Ælfric wrote the first third of *LS* I in Old English, translated this text into Latin and subsequently translated this Latin text to produce Belfour IX:

Belfour, no. ix very closely resembles the Latin version of Boulogne rather than LS, no. i, and the complete absence of significant verbal similarities between the two Old English versions suggests that Belfour, no. ix is a retranslation of the Boulogne Latin text, not an intermediary between LS, no. i, and Boulogne'. (p. 298)

Here Godden suggests that Belfour IX's reliance on the Boulogne text produces close parallels in phrasing. Yet even though Belfour IX usually does come closer than *LS* I to rendering the Latin of the Boulogne text, this does not always hold true. For example, lines 3–9 of *LS* I are closer to the Latin text in both sequence and wording than Belfour IX. In line 9 of *LS* I we find the straightforward

[24] 'The sun that illumines the whole earth is God's creation, and we can understand that her light is from herself and not she from the light, and that heat proceeds equally from the sun and from the light. So likewise the son of Almighty God is eternally begotten of the Father, true light and true wisdom; and the Holy Ghost is eternally of them both, not begotten but proceeding'.
[25] *Select Treatises of S. Athanasius, Archbishop of Alexandria, in Controversy with the Arians, A Library of Fathers of the Holy Catholic Church*, vol. viii (Oxford, 1842), pp. 154–5.
[26] See *Vercelli Homilies IX–XXIII*, ed. P.E. Szarmach, Toronto Old English Series 7 (Toronto, 1981), pp. 45–6, and *The Vercelli Homilies and Related Texts*, ed. D.G. Scragg, EETS os 300 (Oxford, 1992), pp. 272 and 276, and references on p. 276.

statement: 'þa iudeiscan axodon crist hwæt he wære' ('The Jews asked Christ who He was'). This closely follows the Latin's 'Iudei namque interrogauerunt Christum dicentes: *Tu quis es?*' ('For truly the Jews questioned Christ, saying "Who are you?" '; Leinbaugh, p. 110, lines 11–12). Belfour IX strays further from the Latin: 'Nu mage ge ihyren hu þe Hælend andswerede þam arlease Iudeis þe him syððan acwaldon, þa ða heo him axodon mid onde and cwæden, "Sæge us, la! hwæt eart ðu" ' ('Now you can hear how the Saviour answered the impious Jews who afterwards killed him, when they with spite questioned him and said, "Tell us, lo!, who are you?" '; p. 78, lines 21–3). In these examples, contrary to expectation, *LS* I more closely approximates the Boulogne sermon.

Although I share Godden's belief that the Boulogne sermon may well have been compiled by Ælfric, it seems to me that a proof or claim for his authorship based on the relative sequence of these texts is premature: too many unresolved questions remain. Until those questions are settled, Ælfric's authorship of the Boulogne sermon must remain simply a good possibility. Perhaps proof for Ælfric's authorship may come from other channels; an analysis of the way in which Alcuin's text has been reworked, for example, might reveal a pattern characteristic of Ælfric's methods elsewhere. Or perhaps the Boulogne sermon itself might reveal stylistic habits peculiar to Ælfric. Although I do not propose to address these issues directly, I will now turn briefly to a few textual and editorial problems that may have a bearing on the Boulogne sermon's relationship to Ælfric's Old English texts.

VIII. EDITORIAL AND TEXTUAL PROBLEMS

Lines 160–2 of the Boulogne sermon read:

> Homo solus inter *inrationabiles* ratione uiget, consilio ualet, intellegentia antecellit. ('Man alone among *irrational beings* thrives by reason, flourishes by taking counsel, excels by intelligence'; I have added italics here and in the following quotations for emphasis)

The reading *inrationabiles* makes no sense; the Boulogne sermon's source for these lines, Alcuin's text of *De Ratione Animae*, far more sensibly reads:

> Homo solus inter *mortales* ratione viget, consilio valet, intelligentia antecellit. (PL 101, col. 640)

Alcuin's correct reading, 'Man alone among *mortal* beings . . .', clearly reveals the error of the Boulogne sermon. Although both *LS* I and Belfour IX avoid the misreading of the Boulogne sermon, neither of these two Old English texts includes the correct wording from Alcuin that singles out man among all *mortal* beings:

> Se man ana hæfð gesceád. and ræd. and andgit. ('Man alone has reason, and counsel and intelligence'; *LS* I, 99–100; cf. Belfour IX, p. 86, line 33)

Ælfric's Old English text attempts to emend the error of the Boulogne text by omitting the misreading, and his statement that 'man alone has reason, and counsel and intelligence' seems true enough. Yet from a wider perspective, Ælfric's Old English text contains an error: angels also have the traits here attributed to man alone, an error that Alcuin avoids by limiting his comment to *mortal* creatures. If Ælfric did indeed compile the Boulogne text and was himself responsible for the reading *inrationabiles*, it would follow that he either introduced the error himself or mechanically copied a defective text of Alcuin. And it would appear that Ælfric subsequently attempted to correct the error when he came to translate the Boulogne sermon to produce *LS* I and Belfour IX. If, however, Ælfric's authorship of the Boulogne sermon is questioned, it might be argued that he prudently condensed his Old English translation in order to eliminate an error he detected in his Latin source – a source he apparently viewed with a critical eye and sought to correct.

I have previously discussed the passage that equates the Trinity of the Godhead – the Father, the Son and the Holy Ghost – with the trinity of the soul's structure – comprised of memory, understanding and will. The passage occurs in both Alcuin's *De Ratione Animae* and the Boulogne sermon. Alcuin's text briefly discusses the separate faculties of the soul and argues that they have a certain unity:

> Sed in his tribus unitas quaedam est: Intelligo me intelligere, velle et memi-
> nisse; et volo me intelligere et meminisse et velle; et memini me intelligere et
> velle et meminisse. (PL 101, cols 641–2)[27]

Alcuin's text is carefully structured; each faculty of the soul is related in turn to the soul's triune structure. Yet the Boulogne version of Alcuin's text disrupts Alcuin's precise formulation:

> Nam in his tribus unitas quaedam est. .... Intellego me intellegere, uelle, et
> meminisse; et uolo me intellegere et meminisse et uelle; et *minime* intellegere
> uel uelle uel meminisse. (Leinbaugh, p. 123, lines 180–5)[28]

Minime is a corruption of Alcuin's *memini me*, the initial letters *me-* having dropped out. The Boulogne reading mars the syntactical parallels of the original by introducing an anomalous clause lacking the expected reference to memory (*memini*, 'I remember'). If we accept Ælfric's authorship of the Boulogne sermon, we might assume that he again slipped or unthinkingly followed a corrupt text and later tried to correct this irregularity when writing his Old English version:

---

[27] 'Yet there exists a certain unity among the three; I understand that I understand, will and remember; and I will that I understand and remember and will; and I remember that I understand and will and remember'.

[28] 'For there exists a certain unity among the three. .... I understand that I understand, will and remember; and I will that I understand and remember and will; and by no means [?] understand or will or remember'.

and þas ðreo þing habbað annysse him betwynan. Ic undergyte. þæt ic wylle undergytan and gemunan. and ic wylle þæt ic undergyte and gemune. þær þær þæt gemynd bið. þær bið þæt andgyt and se wylla. (*LS* I, 119–22; cf. Belfour IX, p. 88, 18–21)[29]

There is nothing in Ælfric's Old English translation that answers to the Boulogne reading *et minime intellegere* or to Alcuin's *et memini me intellegere*. Ælfric concludes his translation with something of a compromise between these two readings. As in Alcuin's text, there is a reference to memory (*gemynd*) coming after the earlier references to understanding and will, but Ælfric more closely follows the Boulogne text in abandoning the syntactic parallels carefully established by Alcuin. Alcuin emphasizes the interdependence of understanding, will and memory through these syntactic parallels; he uses rhetoric to emphasize the theological point that these three components mirror the triune nature of God. Ælfric closely follows Alcuin's *Intelligo* (mirrored in the Boulogne's *Intellego*) with the words *Ic undergyte*, and he again closely follows Alcuin's *et volo* (mirrored in the Boulogne's *uolo*) with the words *and ic wylle*, but nothing in Ælfric's Old English text corresponds to Alcuin's reading *et memini me* (mangled by the Boulogne's reading *et minime*).

In his translation of this passage, Ælfric establishes a pattern by identifying the soul's first two components with an appropriate verb – *ic undergyte*; *ic wylle* – and this pattern calls for a third Old English verb – *ic gemune* – corresponding to the Latin phrase *et memini me*, 'and I remember that I'. Instead of that expected verb, however, the noun *gemynd* is deployed in a syntactic structure that abandons the careful parallelism used to describe understanding and will: 'þær þær þæt gemynd bið. þær bið þæt andgyt and se wylla' ('There where memory is, there is understanding and will'). Ælfric's use of the noun *gemynd* improves the faulty text found in the Boulogne sermon by completing the sequence of references to understanding and will with an appropriate reference to memory. Yet the faulty parallelism in Ælfric's Old English seems obtrusive and suspect. We may draw the same conclusion as in the previous example: if Ælfric himself composed the Boulogne sermon, he either introduced an error when working with Alcuin's text or copied a faulty text of Alcuin with the zeal of an amateur. When he came to write the Old English homilies, he seems to have avoided once again the pitfall of his Latin text's corrupt reading *et minime intellegere*. If, however, Ælfric's authorship of the Boulogne text is questioned, his handling of the translation shows that he recognized an error and tried to avoid it in his Old English translation.

A third and final example conforms to the same pattern established in the two previous examples. Once again, an incorrect or irregular reading from the Boulogne text does not appear in Ælfric's Old English translation, and, once again,

---

[29] 'And these three things have a unity between them. I understand that which I will to understand and to remember. And I will that which I understand and remember. There where memory is, there is understanding and will'.

Ælfric's Old English translation indicates a departure from Alcuin's text. The Boulogne sermon succinctly defines the soul in this manner:

> Hoc modo anima definiri potest, iuxta suae proprietatem naturae: anima est spiritus intellectualis, rationalis, semper *inmota*, semper uiuens, bonae maleque uoluntatis capax. (Leinbaugh, p. 126, lines 233–5)[30]

The Latin word *immotus* (or *inmotus*), 'unmoved, immovable, motionless', seems inappropriate to apply to the soul, particularly after previous references to the soul's swiftness (Leinbaugh, p. 124, lines 195 ff.); perhaps a copyist may have thought that spiritual things do not have motion in the same way as physical things, and though the reading is clearly an error, some sense – even if somewhat tortured – can be made of the misreading. The source for these lines in Alcuin reads *semper in motu*, 'always in motion' (PL 101, col. 644). These diametrically opposed readings differ, however, by only one letter, the final *a* of *inmota*, 'motionless', vs. the final *u* of *in motu*, 'in motion'. A scribe or Ælfric himself could easily have slipped in erroneously writing a final *a* in place of *u* (or writing a poorly formed *u* that was taken as an *a*), thus subverting the sense of the passage. Once again Ælfric avoids this error when translating the Boulogne sermon into Old English. The Latin text records that the soul is 'spiritus . . . rationalis, semper *inmota*, semper uiuens'; Ælfric simply omits the corrupt 'semper *inmota*' but faithfully reproduces the other attributes ascribed to the soul, namely, that it is a rational spirit that is always living:

> Seo sawul is gesceadwis gast ['spiritus . . . rationalis']. æfre cucu ['semper uiuens'] and mæg underfon ge godne wyllan. and yfelne. æfter agenum cyre. (*LS* I, 171–2; cf. Belfour IX, p. 92, 4–6)[31]

Ælfric here appears to be translating the Boulogne text *verbum ex verbo* rather than *sensum ex sensu*, and the absence of any reference in Ælfric's Old English to either *inmota* or *in motu* seems telling.

In my opinion, in each of these three instances Ælfric studiously avoids the errors of the Boulogne sermon not through his fidelity to the original source in Alcuin but rather through what appears to be shrewd improvisation stimulated by the defects in the Boulogne compilation. I believe that Ælfric recognized and sought to correct textual deficiencies in his copy of the Boulogne sermon, that these same deficiencies appear in the text preserved in the Boulogne manuscript and that these deficiencies were either of Ælfric's own making or were made by an earlier compiler.

The fact that Ælfric so carefully avoids the defects of the Boulogne sermon

---

[30] 'The soul can be defined in this way, according to its own nature: the soul is an intellectual, rational spirit, always *motionless*, always living, capable of the desire for good or evil'.

[31] 'The soul is a rational spirit, always living, and can follow either a good or evil desire according to its own choice'.

might be construed by some as evidence that he did not compose the sermon: it might seem rather unlikely that he copied or introduced errors into his own Latin compilation and later avoided these selfsame errors when turning the compilation into English. Any attempt to assign the Boulogne sermon's authorship to Ælfric must satisfactorily explain why the textual corruptions found there are so conspicuously absent from Ælfric's Old English translations of the text.

If the textual problems of the Boulogne text betray an intimate connection with Ælfric's Old English homilies, it cannot necessarily be inferred that this evidence brings us any closer to establishing Ælfric's authorship of the Boulogne text. Ælfric may have been the author of the Boulogne text, but the textual evidence adduced here seems open to various interpretations. The available facts inspire caution rather than conviction: Ælfric's authorship of the Boulogne sermon remains a matter of conjecture.

IX. THE PLACE OF *LS* I WITHIN THE *LIVES*

The complex relations between *LS* I, Belfour IX and the Boulogne sermon present unresolved, complex difficulties, but these difficulties should not obscure the importance of *LS* I (and Ælfric's other liturgical homilies) to the *Lives of Saints*. As I noted earlier, Clemoes has observed that the composition of item XVI in the *Lives*, a general sermon for the memory of the saints, perhaps marks the beginning of Ælfric's plan for the *Lives of Saints*. I would, however, modify his speculation that *LS* XVI was meant to introduce the collection. One of the most salient facts to emerge from a study of *LS* I and its related texts is that the chief source for *LS* I, Alcuin's *De Ratione Animae*, is not a Christmas homily. Either Ælfric himself grafted this Christmas material onto Alcuin's text or he recognized the importance of the Christmas material in the Boulogne sermon. Since Ælfric begins his liturgical year with Christmas rather than Advent in both sets of the *Catholic Homilies*, it seems entirely appropriate that he would select a Christmas homily to open his third major collection of pious readings.

The *Lives of Saints*, following the same sequence of the liturgical year established in both volumes of the *Catholic Homilies*, opens with the Christmas sermon, *LS* I, followed by Saint Eugenia (honoured on December 25), Saint Basil (January 1), Saint Julian (January 9), Saint Sebastian (January 20), and so on through the calendar. It seems reasonable to conclude that the Julius manuscript, which follows the cycle of the liturgical year, adheres to Ælfric's intended plan for the *Lives of Saints* collection with greater accuracy than the interpolation of several non-Ælfrician items might otherwise lead us to suspect. *LS* XVI might still be considered as a kind of preface to the *Lives of Saints* in much the same way that *De Initio Creaturae*, a sermon *quando volueris*, precedes *De Natale Domini*, the Christmas homily that opens the liturgical cycle in *Catholic Homilies* I. The second volume of the *Catholic Homilies* lacks a prefatory homily and immediately opens with the Christmas homily titled *Nativitas Domini*. In the *Lives of Saints*, Ælfric may or may not have intended that a prefatory homily precede *LS* I. *LS* XVI, as a 'homily for any occasion' ('Spel loca hwænne mann wille'), stands outside the liturgical cycle, and it may well be, just as its rubric suggests, a sermon for the Common of the Saints ('Sermo de memoria Sanctorum'). In my opinion, *LS* I was meant to open Ælfric's *Lives of Saints* proper – whether or not preceded by a prefatory piece – not merely because Christmas homilies also open the *Catholic Homilies* but also because Ælfric unquestionably regarded Christ's life as the supreme exemplar of sanctity and therefore the proper cornerstone on which to build his collection of pious lives.

Only after acknowledging the pivotal role and the complex editorial and textual problems presented by the liturgical homilies in Ælfric's *Lives of Saints* can we begin to understand to what extent the Julius manuscript represents Ælfric's original plan for his collection of saints' lives. Any future attempt to re-edit Skeat's pioneering edition must take into account the important and perhaps seminal role of the liturgical homilies. Although they are not saints' lives, they form an integral part of Ælfric's collection: *LS* I plays an especially crucial role in opening the liturgical cycle that provides the very framework for the *Lives of Saints*.

EDITING FOR A NEW CENTURY:
ELIZABETH ELSTOB'S ANGLO-SAXON MANIFESTO
AND ÆLFRIC'S ST GREGORY HOMILY

Kathryn Sutherland

THE PUBLICATION in 1709 of Elizabeth Elstob's edition of Ælfric's *An English-Saxon Homily on the birth-day of St Gregory . . . Translated into Modern English* appeared to some among her contemporaries to threaten a dangerous act of cultural and political re-imagination. Thomas Hearne, the Oxford antiquary, noted in his diary for 20 October of that year: 'this small Work is designed to promote and advance Saxon Knowledge; but I am much mistaken if it will not have a quite different effect, and make it look mean and little.' He condemned Elstob's intimate and personal presentation of her material, remarking peevishly that '[t]he long, tedious Dedication and Preface, containing above three-score Pages', and 'the Bedrol of Subscribers' names at the End' 'are such odd Flights of Vanity that they do and will make the Book ridiculous'. And, having censured the production as 'this Farrago of Vanity', he, paradoxically and for good measure, claimed that Elstob could not herself be responsible for it anyway: 'Which Book tho' it bear the Name of Mrs Elstob yet is chiefly owing to her Brother Mr William Elstob, lately Fellow of University College, and now Rector of St Swithun's in London.'[1]

Elizabeth Elstob (1683–1756) and Thomas Hearne (1678–1735) stand on opposite sides of an apparently unbridgeable divide: he a university scholar, and she a self-taught woman; he an adherent of an obsolescent order, a fervent Non-juror, who in 1715 would lose his academic appointments because of his open support for the exiled Stuart monarchy;[2] and she an advocate of the future, a realist at least in matters of the monarchy, and an enthusiastic champion of educational opportunities for women. The atmosphere of party politics and topical polemic in which Saxon studies were pursued until well into the eighteenth century may help the modern researcher to re-instate a lost truth – that the past which is attested to by early records is no simple model disinterestedly reconstructed but is itself at the service of the historical determinants of that present in which it is 'recovered'. Evidence about the past, like other social evidences, gains consent by virtue of its

I am grateful to Dr Marilyn Deegan and Professor Malcolm Godden for reading this essay and giving me the benefit of their Old English scholarship.

[1] *The Remains of Thomas Hearne: Reliquiae Hearnianae, being extracts from his MS. diaries,* ed. J. Buchanan-Brown (London, 1966), pp. 78–9.

[2] For details of Hearne's biography, see D.C. Douglas, *English Scholars 1660–1730,* 2nd edn (London, 1951), pp. 178–94.

adaptability to a present need already inscribed within the historical inquiry. This, in some form, holds as true for the researches of the late twentieth century as for those of the early eighteenth century. What the examples of both Hearne and Elstob reveal is that the editing of old works embodies an act of imagination which delivers to the modern age the idea of the past *via* a theory of texts. For Hearne, the imaginative strategy is implicit and covert; in Elstob's case, it takes the form of an overt intervention into the frame of the edited material. Hearne is remembered for, among other things, the first printed text of that fragment of English nationalist tragic poetry *The Battle of Maldon*; and the bias of his Saxon scholarship is towards proving and celebrating the legitimate descent in unbroken line of the last defenders of the recent Stuart monarchy from those Saxon warriors who died in defence of King Alfred's rightful heirs and patrimony. As their chronicler, Hearne, too, belongs to the same extended family. He observed in his diary entry for 11 April 1727:

> A° 1067 Wm Conq. besieged Oxford, and took it. The North side being weakest, he laid siege to it on that Part. It seems the Scholars and others, that remained there, were for Edgar Atheling, and were therefore the same as we now-a-days call Non-Jurors.[3]

It was Elizabeth Elstob's ambitious purpose to fashion anew the informing method of history, and so to make the present resignify, by shifting the ground of conventional historical inquiry from the martial deeds of heroes to the learning and piety of famous women. She stamps women's authority on the Saxon homiletic tradition even in her title-page; and her propagandist zeal does not flag until she has explained the full implications of its extended description – *An English-Saxon Homily on the Birth-Day of St Gregory: Anciently used in the English-Saxon Church. Giving an Account of the Conversion of the English from Paganism to Christianity. Translated into Modern English.* For, the Preface informs us, it was 'by the Endeavours of a Pious Lady; *Berhta* the first Christian Queen of *England*', that the English were converted to Christianity. Beginning with Helena, mother of Constantine, and herself in all probability an Englishwoman, the list of 'illustrious Women' extends through the Saxon Princesses, on to Queen Elizabeth, and down to the eighteenth-century Queen Anne of Great Britain, female monarchs celebrated 'for Wisdom and Piety, and constant Success in their Affairs'.[4]

It is the confidence which flows to Elstob through this feminized Christian genealogy which authorized her own significant contribution to Old English scholarship. In the two volumes which represent her published Saxon research –

---

[3] *Remarks and Collections of Thomas Hearne*, IX (10 Aug. 1725–26 March 1728), Oxford Historical Society, 65 (Oxford, 1914), 296. See, too, my essay 'Byrhtnoth's Eighteenth-Century Context', in *The Battle of Maldon AD 991*, ed. D.G. Scragg (Oxford, 1991), pp. 183–95.

[4] E. Elstob, *An English-Saxon Homily on the Birth-Day of St Gregory: Anciently used in the English-Saxon Church . . . Translated into Modern English, with notes, &c.* (London, 1709), pp. lviii–lix.

the 1709 modern English edition of the St Gregory homily and the 1715 *Rudiments of Grammar for the English-Saxon Tongue*, with its important prefatory 'An Apology for the Study of Northern Antiquities' – Elstob proposed and locally effected a linguistic revolution which was also an act of women's self-appropriation in history. She was the first scholar to present the language of the Anglo-Saxons in its originative relation to the English spoken in her own day; she compiled the first critical edition of one of Ælfric's sermons, complete with a parallel English translation and notes; and she produced the first Old English-Modern English grammar. Her most ambitious project, her edition of both series of Ælfric's *Catholic Homilies*, a project begun with the edition of the St Gregory homily, remains, apart from a thirty-six-page proof specimen, in manuscript form. At least one contemporary account suggests that she lost what financial security she possessed in her unsuccessful attempt to see the edition through the press.[5] Importantly, and at every point, Elstob's Saxon researches have an analogue in her concern to establish a scholarly tradition and a place in history for women.

Sadly, what knowledge we have of Elstob's life and work is patchy and tantalizingly inconclusive. Born in Newcastle-upon-Tyne in 1683, she was orphaned by the age of eight and subsequently lived with her uncle, the Rev. Charles Elstob, prebendary of Canterbury. Later and most productively, she set up home with her elder brother William, an Oxford scholar and Saxonist. Through him she was accepted into the society of such scholars and antiquarians as George Hickes, John Hudson, Humphrey Wanley, and Ralph Thoresby. From being the pet and female prodigy of the male Anglo-Saxon establishment, first in Oxford and then in London, where the brother and sister moved in 1702, and the acquaintance at least of an extensive circle of literary women, Elstob disappeared, in about 1718, for twenty years until her late post (from 1739) as governess to the Duchess of Portland's children restored her in some measure at least to that former world of learning. As the daughter of Edward Harley, Earl of Oxford, the Duchess of Portland presented the opportunity for renewed access to the rich resources of the Harleian Library as well as desperately needed financial support. But if Elstob's new security was welcome, the restoration of scholarly links came too late.[6]

---

5   Most of Elstob's work for her edition of Ælfric's *Catholic Homilies* survives as London, British Library, Lansdowne 370–4 and Egerton 838. Elstob's financial problems are referred to at several points in Hearne's diaries and in the correspondence of her friends. They are discussed in S.H. Collins, 'The Elstobs and the End of the Saxon Revival', *Anglo-Saxon Scholarship: the first three centuries*, ed. C.T. Berkhout and M. McC. Gatch (Boston, MA, 1982) pp. 107–18, at pp. 114–15.

6   Accounts of Elstob's life and work began to appear in print towards the end of the eighteenth century. They tend to rework the same few personal details, drawn largely from the papers of George Ballard (see below), and the same observations on the fate of learned women. See S. Pegge, 'An Historical Account of . . . the Textus Roffensis; including memoirs of W. Elstob and his sister', *Bibliotheca Topographica Britannica* 25 (London, 1784). J. Nichols, *Literary Anecdotes of the Eighteenth Century*, 6 vols (London, 1812) IV, 112–40, draws his account of the Elstobs from Ballard and Pegge and includes several of Elizabeth's letters. Among more modern accounts, the most detailed is C.A. White, 'Elizabeth Elstob, the Saxonist. Outlines of the Life of a Learned Lady, in the (so-called) Augustan Age of English Literature', *Sharpe's London*

Weighed down by financial problems and recurrent disappointments in her publishing ventures, Elstob had literally vanished from the world of Saxon scholarship a few years after her brother's death in 1715; it was not until the summer of 1735 that George Ballard, a staymaker by trade and an antiquarian by inclination, discovered her running the humblest of elementary schools in Evesham, Worcestershire. Elstob's correspondence with Ballard, preserved from 17 August 1735 in Oxford, Bodleian Library, Ballard 43, is our only insight into those twenty lost years. In a short note dated 2 October 1735 anticipating Ballard's visit to her the following Saturday, Elstob writes: 'I propose to my self a a[sic] great deal of Satisfaction. Not having had for near twenty years the Conversation of one Antiquary, I won't say of one Learned Man, but even of them a very few.' A few months later, on 7 March 1736, she informs him, 'But I must acquaint you that mine, may truely be term'd, a life of disappointments, from my Cradle till now, nor do I expect any other while I live.'[7]

Elstob's letters to Ballard reveal long years of physical and intellectual privation borne with stoicism and Christian fortitude. Illnesses are many; in particular, a recurrent complaint, which she describes as 'my old Nervous Fever'[8] and which affects head, eyes, and hands, prevents her from writing and suggests in part at least a psychosomatic origin. When she fled from London and her unpaid debts, in or soon after 1718, Elstob had to abandon her precious books and manuscripts, and she never recovered them again. Losing them, losing track of her greatest project – her transcript of Ælfric's *Catholic Homilies* – and losing all opportunity for scholarship in the necessity of earning a bare living, Elstob also seems to have lost all sense of herself as having existed as that resourceful and ambitious young female scholar. She is now, she informs Ballard, 'a poor little contemptible old maid generally Vapour'd up to the ears, but very chearfull, when she meets with an agreeable conversation.'[9] Writing on 21 July 1748 of her lost books, she concludes: 'it is at least thirty years since this happen'd to me, and you may reasonably think it has made me very unhappy ever since, which if my Friends were sensible of, I must believe they wou'd avoid all occasions of bringing it to my remembrance.'[10] In the teasingly short memoir which she was eventually persuaded to make of her life for Ballard, she wrote detachedly in the third person and firmly in the past tense.

Elstob's achievements as a Saxonist are impressive. She herself dates her interest in Old English to 1698, when she was fifteen. It was then that her brother William transcribed the Old English version of Orosius which so caught her imagination.[11]

Magazine, n.s. 35 (1869), 180–90; 243–7; 304–10; n.s. 36 (1869–70), 26–32, 95–9; 147–53; 190–5; 251–4. White's is a fulsome, novelistic treatment, but is also densely informative. See, too, S.H. Collins, 'Elizabeth Elstob: a Biography' (unpubl. PhD dissertation, Indiana University, 1970), which usefully draws together earlier sources.

7   Oxford, Bodleian Library, Ballard 43, 7^r; 17^v.

8   *Ibid.* 51^r, a letter of 10 April 1738.

9   *Ibid.* 5^v, a letter of 29 August 1735.

10   *Ibid.* 72^r.

11   See Elstob's account of this in *An English-Saxon Homily*, p. vi.

The *English-Saxon Homily on . . . St Gregory* appeared when she was twenty-six and *Rudiments of Grammar* when she was thirty-two. She spent her late twenties and early thirties on the ill-fated edition of Ælfric's homilies. By then her career was over. In her late memoir Elstob lovingly acknowledges the support given to her early researches by a brother 'who very joyfully and readily assisted and encourag'd her, in her Studies, with whom she labour'd very hard as long as he liv'd'. She continues with a summary of her scholarly activities from the time she settled with him:

> In that time she translated and Published, An Essay on Glory written in French by the Celebrated Mademoiselle de Scudery. And Publish'd An English-Saxon Homily on the Birth Day of St Gregory, with an English Translation and Notes &c. Also the Rudiments of Grammar for the English Saxon Tongue. She design'd if ill fortune had not prevented her to have Publish'd all Alfricks Homilies, of which she had made an entire Transcript with the various readings from other Manuscripts, and had translated several of them into English. She likewise took an exact Copy of the Textus Roffensis upon Vellum, now in the Library of that Great and Generous encourager of Learning, the Right Honourable the Earl of Oxford. And transcribed all the Hymns, from an Ancient Manuscript belonging to the Church of Sarum. She had several other designs, but was unhappily hinder'd, by a necessity of getting her Bread, which with much difficulty, labour, and ill health, she has endeavour'd to do for many Years, with very indifferent success.[12]

Brief though her career was, it is possible to isolate certain formative influences on Elstob's work and to evaluate her editorial practice in their light. There is first the high esteem in which she was held by George Hickes. Hickes's scholarly and personal authority over late seventeenth- and early eighteenth-century Saxon studies was massive; but in Elstob's case it derives in part at least from his long and open sympathy with the cause of women's education. When in 1715 both Hickes and William died, Elstob lost her two greatest supporters. Secondly, there is Elstob's relation to the Christian feminist philosophies of Mary Astell and the circle of literary women in which she moved. Thirdly, there is the less tangible but no less significant effect upon her studies of a felt, personal connection with an impersonal past. Elstob was convinced that editing is a kind of dialogue between the past and the present through which both are enlivened; for her, Saxon studies was a route to self-discovery as a woman living in the eighteenth century. It is sadly ironic that, so reticent as she eventually became, she should have propounded so openly engaged and idiosyncratic a relation to textual studies. It would appear that only by inhabiting the past did she animate herself.

---

[12] Ballard 43, 59ᵛ–60ʳ, sent to Ballard in a letter dated 23 November 1738. The memoir (59ʳ–60ᵛ), written throughout in the third person, is only 67 lines long. It is reproduced, not totally accurately, in M. Reynolds, *The Learned Lady in England 1650–1760* (Boston and New York, 1920), pp. 170–1.

As early as 1684, when he was still Dean of Worcester, Hickes preached a sermon before the Lord Mayor of London and the powerful business interest of the city on the subject of alms giving. It is his familiar contention that instituted charity is an obligation on and a safeguard of the interests of the established order. But among the new schemes he proposes are colleges ('much like unto those in the Universities, for the Education of young Men') for the education of women; and among the advantages such colleges would serve, he numbers national security and religious orthodoxy, the reassertion of Church of England values:

> Such Colleges might be so ordered, as to become security to your Daughters against all the hazards to which they are exposed at private Schools, and likewise a security to the Government, that the Daughters of the Land should be bred up according to the Religion now established in it, to the unconceivable advantage of the Publick, in rooting out *Enthusiasme*, with her Daughters *Schsime*[sic], both which are upheld by nothing among us so much, as by the Women, who are so silly and deceiveable for want of Ingenious, and Orthodox Education, and not for want of Parts. Methinks the Rich and Honourable Ladies of the Church of *England*, the *Elect Ladies* of her Apostolical Communion should be Zealous to begin, and carry on such a work, as this; which upon more accounts, than I have mentioned, would make the Daughters of *Israel* be glad, and the Daughters of *Judah* and *Jerusalem* rejoyce.[13]

Later, in 1707, Hickes was to publish as a single volume revised versions of two free translations from the French on the subject of women's education – *Instructions for the Education of a Daughter* by François Salignac de la Mothe-Fénélon and *Instructions for the Conduct of Young Ladies of the Highest Rank*, 'written by Monsieur *de la Chetardy,* a Gentleman of the *French* Court'. The work went into a second edition the following year. In his seventeen-page dedication of the tracts to the Duchess of Ormond, Hickes again refers to the low regard in which the Anglican establishment and its priesthood are presently held and points to the useful lessons which can be learned from the two tracts: 'I believe, *Madam,* that as there never was a better Book of Instructions of both sorts, so there never was an Age in *England*, wherein there was more need of them in an *English Book*'.[14] Fénélon, though a bishop in the Church of Rome, is, Hickes asserts, an advocate of a reformed and rational Christianity. In confirmation of this, Hickes points to his recommendation that young ladies should be taught Latin so that they might understand the Church offices.[15] Though de la Chetardy and Fénélon concentrate on the moral, spiritual, and domestic education of women, Hickes's address to the Duchess of Ormond and the emphasis of both tracts serve to show how fundamental

---

[13] G. Hickes, *A Sermon Preached at the Church of St Bridget, on Easter-Tuesday, being the first of April, 1684 . . . upon the subject of alms-giving* (London, 1684), pp. 26–7.

[14] *Instructions for the Education of a Daughter, by the Author of Telemachus. To which is added, a small tract of Instructions for the Conduct of Young Ladies of the Highest Rank. With suitable devotions annexed, done into English and revised by G. Hickes* (London, 1707), pp. A^v–A2^r.

[15] *Ibid.* p. A4^v and pp. 244–5.

to the well-being and orthodox renewal of Christian society as a whole is the education of women and how important it is for this reason to rectify certain inequalities of opportunity between the sexes:

> Thus you have the Employments of Women, which are hardly less important to the Publick than those of Men ... To which you may add, that Virtue is no less the Business of this, than of the other Sex; but laying aside the Good or Ill, which they might do to the Publick, still they are the one half of Mankind redeemed by the Blood of *Jesus Christ*, and designed to Eternal Life.
>
> Lastly, we must consider, besides the Good which Women do when they are well brought up; the Evil they cause in the World, when they want that Education which inspires them with Virtue. It is certain, that the bad Education of Women doth generally more Mischief than that of Men ...
>
> What intrigues occur to us in History? what subversion of Laws and Manners? what bloody Wars? what Novelties in Religion? what Revolutions in State have been caused by the Irregularities of Women! Thus we have seen the necessity of a right Education of Daughters; the *Means* of it we are now to enquire after.[16]

As Hickes's disciple,[17] Elstob both exemplified and extended in her own scholarship the female-empowering implications of his Anglican orthodoxy. Her Christian piety is clearly implicated in her Old English studies and in Hickes's promotion of them, as he makes plain in a letter of 23 December 1712 to Arthur Charlett, Master of University College, Oxford, informing him of Elstob's mission there to arrange publication of her edition of Ælfric's *Catholic Homilies*. He writes: 'I suppose you may have seen Mrs Elstob, sister to Mr Elstob, formerly fellow of your Coll., and the MSS. she hath brought to be printed at your presse . . . the publication of the MSS. she hath brought (the most correct I ever saw or read) will be of great advantage to the church of England ag[ains]t the Papists; for the honour of our predecessours the English Saxon Clergy, especially of the Episcopal order, and the credit of our country . . .'[18] That the preservation and continuance of an uncorrupted *English* Christianity is bound up with the educational opportunities of women and the public exercise of female authority is the foundation of all Elstob's researches. Elstob's edition of Ælfric's homilies in part fulfilled Hickes's own

---

[16] *Ibid.* pp. 6–7.

[17] It seems to have been Nichols (*Literary Anecdotes*, IV, 139–40) who first decided to account for Elizabeth's proficiency as a Saxonist with the explanation that George Hickes was her maternal grandfather. There is no evidence that this was their relationship. Nichols may have been misled by the ambiguous wording of a letter from Elstob in the Ballard papers in which she describes several of her early drawings now sent to George Ballard. (See Ballard 43, 42ᵛ.)

[18] Oxford, Bodleian Library, Ballard 12, 129ʳ. See, too, Elstob's early letter to Ralph Thoresby, 10 October 1709: 'Having nothing else to do, I have some thoughts of publishing a set of Saxon homilies, if I can get encouragement, which I believe will be very useful; the doctrine for the most part being very orthodox; and where any errors have crept in, it may not be amiss to give some account of them'. (*Letters of Eminent Men, Addressed to Ralph Thoresby, FRS, now first published from the originals*, 2 vols (London, 1832) II, 198–9.

polemical design for such a work.[19] For both, as for other early scholars since the time of Queen Elizabeth, Old English studies were legitimated by a politico-religious conviction that in the records of the Saxon past lay the true origin and best defence of the latterly Reformed Church of England. For Hickes, this was fighting talk, religious orthodoxy being linked in his mind, as in the minds of many, with the inalienable rights of kings. A fervent supporter of the deposed Stuart monarchy, from 1690 to 1699 he suffered the hardships and dangers of a political refugee, deprived of ecclesiastical office and in hiding.[20] For Elstob, the Saxon origin of the Anglican establishment was the basis of an equivalent political conviction – a matrilineal conception of history. She quotes Pope Gregory's letter of thanks to Queen Berhta for the conversion of the English and notes the spiritual influence of her daughter Edelburga. 'I might give many more Instances of this kind', she continues; but '[i]t were endless to repeat all the Instances of illustrious Women that might be enumerated, as contributing to the advancement of Religion, in their Several Ages.'[21]

In his postscript to Fénélon's *Instructions for the Education of a Daughter,* the unnamed translator suggests specific books which a young lady might profitably read. Among these are the *Discourses* of 'Mademoiselle Scudery', and two anonymous works – *A Serious Proposal to the Ladies for the Advancement of their truest and greatest Interest* (in two parts, 1694 and 1697) and *The Christian Religion, as profess'd by a Daughter of the Church of England* (1705).[22] Only a year later, in 1708, Elstob published anonymously, but with a dedication addressed to her aunt, 'Mrs Elstob, at Canterbury', a translation of Madeleine de Scudéry's *An Essay upon Glory*. The justificatory epigraph tagged to her title-page is drawn from the same recommendation appended to Fénélon's tract and is only the first of Elstob's public references to Hickes to authorize her interest in women's learning. Dedications and appeals to him throughout her published works confirm his originating influence over all her productions.[23]

It is highly likely that Elstob was already acquainted with the two anonymous works mentioned as suitable for female reading, both by the philosopher and feminist Mary Astell. We learn, from the Ballard correspondence, that Elstob and

---

[19] See the 'Dedication' to volume one of Hickes's *Sermons*, and the account, given by Ballard, of his intention to publish a collection of Saxon homilies as an aid to sound doctrine in the Church of England, and further comments on Elstob's suitability to succeed him, in Pegge, 'An Historical Account of . . . the Textus Roffensis . . .', pp. 24–5.

[20] For Hickes's political persecution, see Douglas, *English Scholars*, pp. 77–97.

[21] *An English-Saxon Homily*, p. lix.

[22] *Instructions for the Education of a Daughter,* pp. 292–7.

[23] See, in particular, her appeal to Hickes in the 'Preface' to *An English-Saxon Homily*, pp. vi–vii, as one who recommended its publication and 'hath ever since persevered to encourage' her Old English studies and her plan to extend Saxon scholarship to women. In this, she argues, Hickes is comparable to the early Church Fathers, including Gregory himself (p. viii). Subsequently Elstob used as an epigraph to the title-page of the *Rudiments of Grammar* (1715) a few lines written to her by Hickes on women's superior authority in language studies, and she addressed its long and polemical preface to him.

Astell were known to each other and were friends. Both were northerners from a similar social rank and background, natives of Newcastle-upon-Tyne, and for a time they may even have lived near each other in Chelsea.[24] Among the many women subscribers to the 1709 *English-Saxon Homily on . . . St Gregory* are the names of several of the Astell circle, though oddly not Astell herself;[25] while echoes of Astell's feminist tracts of the 1690s mix interestingly with the corroborative testimony of Hickes in Elstob's long Preface.[26] Through the convergence of the Saxonist and the feminist in Elstob's work, a significant strand in Astell's own thinking can be recontextualized. Like Hickes, she was a royalist, an adherent of the Stuart monarchy, and a High Anglican.[27] In particular, Astell's suggestion (in *A Serious Proposal to the Ladies*) for the establishment of an all-female college, a Protestant convent for the intellectual advancement and mutual support of women, chimes closely with Hickes's proposal of ten years earlier. If anything, Astell's proposal is less ambitious than Hickes's; but like Hickes, she envisages such a college as strengthening orthodox religion as it extends women's educational opportunities.[28] 1709, the year which saw the appearance of the *Homily*, also saw Steele's series of satirical attacks in *The Tatler* on Astell as 'Madonella', the foundress of a monastery for women. *Tatler* No. 63 (3 September 1709) introduces Elstob as one of the female professors in the new establishment, where she is described as having written 'two of the choicest Saxon novels' highly popular at Queen Emma's Court.[29] Clearly, in the public imagination at this time, Saxon studies, Anglicanism, and feminism represented a recognizable combination of interests.

Less obviously but no less powerfully enabling of Elstob's peculiar Saxon feminism is the example of Ælfric himself. Her Old English scholarship centres on

---

[24] See Ballard 43, 31ʳ, a letter of 24 December 1736, from which it is clear that Ballard has begun to question Elstob about Mary Astell. Elstob remarks how pleased she has been that Ballard was 'so merry at my relation of Mrs Astell and her Pigeon'. For the possible proximity of Elstob and Astell in Chelsea, see R. Perry, *The Celebrated Mary Astell: an early English feminist* (Chicago and London, 1986), p. 289.

[25] Women subscribers include Lady Elizabeth Hastings and Lady Catharine Jones, both friends of Astell. However, a letter from Astell to her friend Lady Ann Coventry (June or July 1714) reveals Astell subscribing to Elstob's projected edition of Ælfric's homilies in Lady Ann's name. (Perry, p. 366)

[26] Cf., for example, [M. Astell], *A Serious Proposal to the Ladies, for the Advancement of their true and greatest interest. By a lover of her sex* (London, 1694), pp. 79–83; and *An English-Saxon Homily*, p. ii. Both passages address the contemporary Anglican-feminist interest in the equality and comparable intelligence of the male and female soul as an argument in favour of women's learning.

[27] Hickes's admiration of Astell's work is quoted in G. Ballard, *Memoirs of Several Ladies of Great Britain who have been celebrated for their writings or skill in the learned languages, arts, and sciences* (1752), ed. R. Perry (Detroit, 1985), p. 386.

[28] See *A Serious Proposal to the Ladies*, pp. 73–8.

[29] See *The Tatler*, ed. D.F. Bond, 3 vols (Oxford, 1987) I, 440, where Steele, as Tobiah Greenhat, embellishes an attack begun in No. 32 (I, 236). While Swift and Addison were long assumed to be collaborators in the 'Madonella' satires, it is now argued (I, 236 and 434) that there is no evidence for this.

him, and it is possible to argue good reasons for this. As one of the few named Saxon authors known to early scholars, Ælfric was also unusually connected with a recognizable corpus of texts. For Elstob and her fellow Saxonists he was the prime authority for and commentator on the orthodoxy and independence of a pure Saxon Church. Importantly, too, he was a 'political' linguist, a champion of learning in the vernacular and himself an elegant prose stylist, for whom the dissemination of texts in English was linked to the preservation of orthodox views. As early as 1567, in a modest volume entitled *A Testimonie of Antiquitie*, Matthew Parker had presented Ælfric as the expounder of sound English doctrine in religion and the advocate of 'plaine interpretation' in learning.[30] Finally, it might be argued, there was that personal connection so valued by Elstob in justifying her endeavours. For her, Ælfric represented the early glory of the Church and of native English scholarship as they were established in Canterbury, and she, brought up by an uncle and aunt within its Cathedral precincts, was Ælfric's heir and interpreter in a new age.[31] In Canterbury, as she points out in her translation of *An Essay upon Glory*, Elstob laid the foundations for her future linguistic accomplishments and discovered the support of a female world of learning.[32] Later, the scholarly encouragement of Hickes and the feminist example of Astell combine to produce a strange hybrid – a polemical Anglican-feminist interpreter of Ælfric. Further, its subject-matter, its often idiosyncratic editorial embedding, and even the details of its typographic presentation, suggest that Elstob's first Saxon publication – Ælfric's St Gregory homily – was no randomly chosen apprentice text but one which heralded and precisely served her polemical designs.

Thomas Hearne's theory of texts is at the service of a masculinist reading of history. More particularly, it is informed by that abiding Saxon status anxiety which has at different times manifested different symptoms. He knew little or no Old English, and most of his acquaintance with Saxon history was gleaned from Latin translations: William Somner's Latin-Anglo-Saxon Dictionary of 1659 and Hickes's immense *Linguarum Veterum Septentrionalium Thesaurus* (1703–5) were prescriptive models and indispensable tools for the early eighteenth-century Saxon scholar. Their method of elucidation was narrowly comparative, with Latin vocabulary and grammar providing the uncongenial paradigms for the expounding of Old English usage. Partly a matter of academic politics – of establishing respectable credentials for Saxon studies – this classical contextualization reinforced the remoteness of Old English from the vernacular tradition and aimed to divest it of

---

[30] [M. Parker], *A Testimonie of Antiquitie, shewing the auncient fayth in the Church of England touching the sacrament of the body and bloude of the Lord here publikely preached, and also receaved in the Saxons tyme, above 600 yeares agoe* (London, [1567]), preface.

[31] Elstob, along with her contemporary scholars, was confident in identifying Ælfric the homilist as Ælfric Archbishop of Canterbury.

[32] [E. Elstob], *An Essay upon Glory. Written originally in French by the celebrated Mademoiselle de Scudery. Done into English by a person of the same sex* (London, 1708), pp. A2^{r-v}, from the dedication 'To Mrs Elstob, at Canterbury'; and pp. a–a2, a letter appended 'To Mrs Mary Randolph, at Canterbury'.

its barbarous antecedents. The message was clear, with Latin grammar determining the cultural reproduction of value within the vernacular as linguistic correctness and as the Saxon past's claim to rationality.

It was the good work of dignifying Saxon studies which Elstob proposed to undo by suggesting that Old English was not an esoteric system of hieroglyphics reserved for a long-dead manuscript tradition but rather a vital link in her own female linguistic history. She considered herself to be, she wrote in one of her earliest letters to Ballard, 'the first Woman that has Studied that Language since it was spoke'; she supported her claim with the gift of a transcript of Psalm 100, together with a specimen of a runic inscription.[33] For Elstob, a living rope of language links the English of Saxon and eighteenth-century England, and it is women, by virtue of their educational and linguistic suppression by classically-trained men, who can render the connections articulate. What women share, in their linguistic experience, with Old English is inarticulacy through history. The point is driven home by Elstob's preoccupied return to the gendering of language: Saxon, she insists, in her Preface to the *English-Saxon Homily*, is our 'Mother tongue'; and her defence of its inherent respectability is grounded in her own rights as a woman to scholarly participation. '[B]y publishing somewhat in Saxon, I wou'd invite the Ladies to be acquainted with the Language of their Predecessors, and the Original of their Mother Tongue.'[34] The impertinence of the linked linguistic and gender claims does not go unrecognized. For Elstob they represent a route to liberation, or as she herself suggests, driving deep the analogy with her carefully chosen text on St Gregory, a historic opportunity for conversion – for social transformation, that is. The inference to be drawn from her attempts to integrate Saxon studies with a vernacular tradition of inquiry is that the recognition of Saxon's full status within the academic mainstream will create a change of cultural consciousness and a resignification of Britain's history, in women's favour.

In line with this conviction, Elstob's text of the St Gregory homily is embedded in a framework whose preoccupations determine the limits on the interpretation of that text. While this is the case with all editorial practice (the meaning of every text being in part constituted by, emerging from, and changing with its *con*text), however much individual editors might plead the non-intervention or 'truthfulness' to the 'integrity' of the text of their particular method, it is emphatically the case with Elstob's chosen work. Here text is harnessed to context as part of a special editorial intention and to enforce a particular reading experience.

Elstob's editorial procedure is grounded in an understanding of conversion as a mutually informing cultural and textual process – the present appropriating the past, the past illuminating the present – which turns editing into a larger exercise in recovery than the merely bibliographical. In remodelling, as the informing method of her edition, the subject matter of her chosen homily – St Gregory's mission to convert the English – she demonstrates the convertible characteristics of various

---

[33] Ballard 43, 5ᵛ, a letter of 29 August 1735.
[34] *An English-Saxon Homily*, p. vii.

historical phenomena: of the Saxon and the Reformed English Church; of the Old and Modern English Language; and, most significantly, of male and female authority. Her edition is, finally, an experiment in self-authorization. The comparative exercise is conducted with assiduous attention to detail, Elstob letting no opportunity, however small, slip by. The famous story of St Gregory's zeal in 'buying up *English* Slaves, and disposing of them in Monasteries, to be train'd up in the Christian Faith for the future Service of their Country' is made to yield a specific and topical recommendation to those whose business is engaged in the sugar plantations of the eighteenth century and who, in consequence, 'have doubtless a Power of turning many Souls to God, and of rescuing them from that Slavery, under which they are held by the Prince of Darkness'.[35]

But the weight of Elstob's propagandist argument in her sixty-page Preface to the homily is directed towards one of the major topics of contemporary church-political controversy – the Roman establishment, through Gregory and Augustine's mission, of the Saxon Church and what this might imply for the purity of the later Anglican foundation.[36] In maintaining the identity of the Saxon and the Reformed Church with an uncorrupted Roman Church under Gregory, Elstob not only disposes of the counter arguments for a native British establishment, but she discovers in Augustine's mission to England the origin of a series of transferences of authority. Through Augustine under Gregory, the English Church, it appears, can lay claim to the original purity of the Roman, and Ælfric in Canterbury can be seen as continuing their apostolic work, while, by right of linguistic inheritance, Ælfric's authority eventually becomes Elstob's own.

'What is this Saxon? what has she to do with this barbarous antiquated Stuff? so useless, so altogether out of the way?'[37] With these linked linguistic and gender questions, Elstob pre-empts and rebukes the anticipated opposition to her edition, countering that, if the past were rightly scrutinized, then women, with their provincial perspectives and their homelier horizons, would be discovered to have the greater claim to be its interpreters. Not founding an aesthetics of the past on the elevated concept of the classical, women fill the informational vacuum with data drawn from a historically truer, because a native and progressive, source of expectations. Just as, for Elstob, the Saxon Church could be seen as inheriting and handing down to the Anglican the early purity of a subsequently corrupted Roman authority, so she insists on a comparable transference of linguistic authority from Latin to the vernacular, and from male to female:

> I fear, if things were rightly consider'd [wrote Elstob], that the charge of Barbarity would rather fall upon those who, while they fancy themselves adorn'd with the Embellishments of foreign Learning, are ignorant, even to

[35] *Ibid.* pp. xi–xiii.
[36] *Ibid.* pp. xiii–lv. For a survey of the Elstobs' religious views and how they colour their scholarship, see M. Murphy, 'The Elstobs: Scholars of Old English and Anglican Apologists', *Durham University Journal* 58 (1966), 131–8.
[37] *An English-Saxon Homily*, p. vi.

barbarity, of the Faith, Religion, the Laws and Customs, and Language of their Ancestors. I assure you, these are Considerations which have afforded me no small Encouragement in the Prosecution of these Studies.
. . .

Having accidentally met with a Specimen of K. *Alfred's* Version of *Orosius* into *Saxon* . . . I was very desirous to understand it, and having gain'd the Alphabet, I found it so easy, and in it so much of the grounds of our present Language, and of a more particular Agreement with some Words which I had heard when very young in the North, as drew me in to be more inquisitive after Books written in that Language.[38]

Elstob's argument here becomes specifically feminist, as the organization of the Preface in fact suggests: the account of the Saxon Church is no more than a long interpolation within a framing defence of women's rights to learning and to Christian authority. Now women's characteristic educational impoverishment, together with their atavistic adherence to the more primitive language of youth, the 'northern tongue' – which is both the homely vernacular (as opposed to the classical languages of the educated male) and the dialect around Newcastle-upon-Tyne, where Elstob spent her earliest years – is used to justify the most revolutionary departure in editing the homily. She explains in her Preface:

But, to come to the Homily upon St *Gregory*. When I had read it over, and transcribed it, I made no long Dispute of it, whether or no I shou'd make it *English* . . . This, I confess, I have not done with any great Elegance, according to the Genius of our present Idiom; having chosen rather to use such *English* as wou'd be both intelligible, and best express the *Saxon*; that, as near as possible, both the *Saxon* and the *English* might be discerned to be of the same Kindred and Affinity: and the Reader be more readily enabled, and encouraged to know the one by the other; which End I imagine would not be so well answer'd, by a Translation more polite and elaborate.[39]

Elstob's method is Ælfrician in its commitment to 'plaine interpretation'; her purpose is clear: to do away with Latin as the intelligible medium of exchange between Old and Modern English; and, by revealing the two stages of English to be capable of mutual explanation, to extend the readership of Old English, the Northern 'Mother Tongue' and the culturally suppressed language. That this wider readership is envisaged as female is attested to by the unusual and exclusive authority granted to women in the Preface to the *English-Saxon Homily* and by further remarks in Elstob's second Saxon publication, the *Rudiments of Grammar* of 1715. This Grammar, a Preface informs us, originated in the request from a young woman who proposed studying Old English with Elstob. Subsequently, it was written out of consideration for 'the Pleasure I my self had reaped from the

---

[38] *Ibid.* pp. vi–vii.
[39] *Ibid.* pp. viii–ix.

Knowledge I have gained from this Original of our Mother Tongue, and that others of my own Sex, might be capable of the same Satisfaction: I resolv'd to give them the Rudiments of that Language in an English Dress.'[40]

As she hoped, Elstob's example was eloquent to other women. Of the 280 subscribers whose names were appended to the *English-Saxon Homily*, almost half were female. Among them was Mrs Mary Thynne, a friend of the poet Anne Finch, Countess of Winchelsea; she later wrote: 'I am determin'd to be on a par with this Mrs Elstob, if the Expence of an Hour or two's Morning Study will enable me to conquer the Difficulties of the Saxon Tongue.'[41] Mrs Thynne suggests an irresistible picture of fashionable female heads bent diligently over their texts and grammars, united in a determination to become mutually conversable through the Anglo-Saxon language. However unlikely it now seems, for a short time Elstob may even have been responsible for making Saxon studies the latest craze among ladies who made a fashion of scholarship.

It was Hickes's opinion that Elstob's transcriptions were the most correct he 'ever saw or read'.[42] In the case of the St Gregory homily, Elstob describes her editorial procedure in establishing her text as follows:

> but to return to the Homily on St *Gregory*. It is printed from a Transcript I had made of it from one made by Dr *Hopkins*, I believe, out of the *Cottonian* Book, *Vitellius* D.17. because there I read it, Enȝliscere þeode. whereas, in all the other Copies, it is Enȝliscre þeode . . . The Transcript of this Homily I compared with that antient Parchment Book of Homilies in the *Bodleian* Library amongst *Junius's* Books *NE.F.4* being the second of those Volumes that had formerly belong'd to the *Hattonian* Library, an account of which we have in that most elaborate Catalogue of *Saxon* Manuscripts by Mr *Wanley*, which makes the second Volume of Dr *Hickes's Thesaurus* p. 43. I had access to this Book, by the singular Courtesy of Dr *Hudson* . . .[43]

In view of the subsequent fire in the Cotton Library, about which she herself inquired so anxiously of Ballard,[44] Elstob's reading of the now damaged version of the homily in the Cotton manuscript should be extremely valuable. But Malcolm Godden argues, from his collation of all the extant manuscripts of the St Gregory homily, that the transcript Elstob believed to be from Cotton Vitellius D.xvii (now a British Library holding), and used as her copytext, is in fact merely a further transcript of Oxford, Bodleian Library, Hatton 114, the source of her variant

---

[40] E. Elstob, *The Rudiments of Grammar for the English-Saxon Tongue, first given in English: with an apology for the study of northern antiquities* (London, 1715), p. ii.

[41] Cited in M.E. Green, 'Elizabeth Elstob: "The Saxon Nymph" (1683–1756)', *Female Scholars: a Tradition of Learned Women Before 1800,* ed. J.R. Brink (Montreal, 1980), pp. 137–60, at 146, n. 28.

[42] Ballard 12, 129[r].

[43] *An English-Saxon Homily,* pp. lvi–lvii.

[44] Ballard 43, 9[r], a letter of 16 November 1735, in which Elstob records her thanks for a report of the books and manuscripts lost in 'the late dismal Fire.'

readings. This being the case, then, the variants which she prints in her textual apparatus and the passion for correctness so admired by Hickes ironically reveal only discrepancies in her two transcripts.[45] The judgement of another twentieth-century editor of Ælfric on the general accuracy of Elstob's manuscript edition of the complete Saxon homilies might be allowed in her defence;[46] so, too, might the difficulties attending the female scholar at that time, reliant on the courtesy and competence of her male colleagues and, often, having to take on trust the accuracy and provenance of their information and their transcripts.

After the sixty pages of the Preface, itself the most extensive section of the whole, the homily and its parallel modern English translation take up the next forty-four pages, with variant readings and annotations filling up the bottom of each page or competing for status with the privileged space of the text. Notes are full and draw miscellaneously on the standard historical, theological, and philological authorities in the best editions of the day: Whelock's edition of Bede's *Ecclesiastical History* (1643), Gibson's edition of the *Anglo-Saxon Chronicle* (1692), Somner's Latin-Anglo-Saxon Dictionary, Hickes's *Thesaurus*, Wanley's Historical-Critical Catalogue (1705) to it, etc. Difficult words and phrases are glossed, and helpful reference is made to eighteenth-century survivals of Saxon terms. On page 12, for example, the Old English phrase *Wae la wa*, translated 'Alas! alas!' is glossed by the following remark: 'Well a way is in common use to this day in the North, to express their Grief, or Surprize'. Throughout the edition, the page is the unit of sense, with the comparative reading of Old and Modern English and of text and context encouraged. Separated from the Saxon and English versions of the homily is a Latin translation in eleven pages, the work of William Elstob, after which comes a forty-nine page appendix of annotated epistles of St Gregory intended to illuminate points in the homily. Finally comes the list of subscribers. The whole is an impressive imaginative recovery of a short sermon occupying no more than nine pages in its modern EETS edition.[47]

In Elstob's edition, formatting reveals the conversance and equivalence of the two stages of English. Each page is divided down the centre, with Old English in the left column and the Modern English translation in the right. We know that Elstob took more care than was usual even at that time in watching the work through the press,[48] and significance can be attached not only to the careful choice of a modern translation which demonstrates, through syntax and lexis, its Old

---

[45] See M. Godden, 'Old English', *Editing Medieval Texts English, French, and Latin Written in England*, ed. A.G. Rigg (New York and London, 1977), pp. 9–33, at 21 and n. 34.

[46] The judgement is that of Peter Clemoes, cited in Collins, 'The Elstobs and the End of the Saxon Revival', p. 115.

[47] *Ælfric's Catholic Homilies: the Second Series,* ed. M. Godden, EETS ss 5 (London, 1979), pp. 72–80. This is, of course, text only as yet.

[48] See, for example, Elstob's letter of 22 March 1709, to Ralph Thoresby, on the ornamental borders and letters for the *Homily. (Letters of Eminent Men* II, 147–8.) Matthew Parker may have been Elstob's model for her translation into English and its arrangement. His *Testimonie of Antiquitie* (1567) has text and English translation side by side, and his 1574 edition of King Alfred's Preface to the *Cura Pastoralis* has an interlinear English translation as well as a

English roots but to the close alignment of equivalent words in terms of their graphic display. In Elstob's translation, for example, *he hlod mid þurstigum breoste þa fleowendan lare þe he eft æfter fyrste mid hunig swetre þrohte þæslice bealcode* becomes 'He suck'd in with a thirsty Desire the flowing Learning, which he often, after some time, with a Throat sweeter than Honey, and with an agreeable Eloquence poured out'[49] (fig. 5).

The Latin translation (and with it exclusive male authority?) is relegated here to the status of a self-communing appendix. Before Elstob it was the essential quaranto of a text's respectability, and, just as importantly, the key to its meaning. By denying Latin its intermediary function, Elstob effectively democratizes the editing and reading of Old English. Her brother's (the professional scholar's) subordinate role in the edition and the actual placing of the Latin translation make the point effectively. It is Latin, it is suggested, which forms the barrier to the understanding of Old English, and not the inherent obscurity of Old English itself. With the aid of a comparative Roman-Saxon alphabet and a sensitively derived translation, the historical continuity of the English language, Elstob believes, will become apparent, and Old English will be made accessible to a wider audience. It is not recorded, though it should be, that the specifically female experience of educational neglect eventually becomes, through Elstob's editorial formula and later through her prescription for an English-Saxon grammar, an important influence on the subsequent agenda for Old English scholarship as the tracing of a self-accountable Germanic linguistic tradition.

Elstob extends her dialogue with the past in a series of full and personalized annotations to the homily. A note on King Ella, ruler of the province of Deira in the southern part of Northumbria, elicits sixty-nine lines of place-name evidence in support of her theory that her own Northern name of Elstob is derived from that of this first king of the Deiri:

> *Ella* being so great himself, and his Son after him so glorious, it is natural to imagine, that either the Father would desire to leave some Marks of his Conquests and planting there, or his Son do somewhat to perpetuate the Memory of his Father. Hence it is in all probability there are at this day some Towns that bear an affinity with the Name in those Parts, which come within the extent of those Kings Dominions; as *Ellecroft, Ellington, Elton, Elswic, Eslaby*, probably for *Ellasby, &c.* And since the Holy Father thought it not inconsistent with the Gravity of so great a Prelate to play upon the word *Ella*, and to give us an opportunity of alluding to the same Name, I will beg leave to insert one Allusion more, which I heard some time ago made to it in the Name *Elstob*, or *Ellestobb*, as I find it written, *an.*1345. This in all likelihood at first was

following Latin translation. I am grateful to Dr D.G. Scragg for drawing my attention to this possible connection.
[49] *An English-Saxon Homily*, pp. 5–6.

ʃpa þe cpæbon. pop po-
nulbe æþelbopen :· Ac
he openpcah hiʒ æþel-
bopenyʃʃ mib halʒum
þeapum ʒ mib ʒ-bum pe-
opcum ʒeʒlenbe :· Lpe-
ʒopiuʃ iʃ ʒneciʃc nama
ʃe ʃpeʒð on lebenum
ʒeneopþe Viʒilanciuʃ.
þæc iʃ on Engliʃce pa-
colpe :· Þe pæp ʃpyðe
pacol on ʒobeʃ bebobum
þa þa he ʃylp hepi-
ʒenblice leopobe. ʒ he
pacollice ymb maneʒpa
þeoba þeappa hoʒobe. ʒ

have faid, in refpect of
the World, nobly defcend-
ed: But he adorn'd, and
exceeded his high Birth,
with a holy Converfation
and good Works. *Gregory*
is a *Greek* Name, which fig-
nifies in the *Latin* Tongue
Vigilantius, that is in *Englifh,* *Watchful :* He was
very diligent in God's Com-
mandments, while he him-
felf lived moft devoutly,and
he was earneftly concerned
for promoting the Advan-
tage of many Nations, and

1   2   3   4   5   6
Pater, avos, proavos, abavos, atavos, tritavos.

Atavus eft quintus pater, the fifth Father, as *Tanaquil. Fab.* obferves in
his Notes on the firft *Ode* in *Horace.* This Mr. *Somner* did not take
notice of, explaining the Word by *Tritavus,* which would be the
ʃixta pæbep. The whole *Latin* Series is critically difcufs'd in the
Etymol. of *J. Ger. Voff.* under the Word *Avus.*

f Gpnʃbeiʘ.

g It is the fame alfo with *Vigilius.* And *Gofcelin,* in his. *Hift. Minor. cap.* 2. fpeaking of St. *Gregory,* calls him *Gregorius fecundum fuum
Nomen pervigil. Vid. Angl. Sacr. Part. II. pag.* 56. And *Paulus Diaconus,* who firft writ the Life of St. *Gregory,* and is follow'd by all the
after Writers on that Subject, obferves, that *ex Græco eloquio in noftra
lingua* [which is the *Latin*] *vigilator, feu vigilans fonat.*

h Pacolpe, *Wakeler;* of this kind we may reckon our *Wake,
Wakelin,* or *Wacelyn, Wakevil, Wakefield,* &c.

heom liʃeʃ pæʒ ʒeʃpu-
celobe :· Þe pæʃ ʃnam
cilbhabe on bochcum
lapum ʒecyð. ʒ he on
þæpe lape ʃpa ʒeʒæli-
ʒlice þeah þ on eal-
pe Romana byʃiʒ næʃ
nan hiʃ ʒelica ʒeþuhc :·
Þe ʒecneolæhce æʃcep
piʃpa lapeopa ʒebyʃnun-
ʒa. ʒ næʃ popʒycel ac
ʒeʃaʃcnobe hiʃ lape
on ʃæʃc-hapelum ʒe-
mynbe. he hlob mib
þupʃciʒum bneopce þa
ʃleopenban lape þe he
eʃc æʃcep pyʃpce mib
huniʒ ʃpecpe þnohce

made known unto them the
way of Life. He was from
his Childhood inftructed in
the knowledge of Books, and
he fo profperoufly fucceeded
in his Studies, that in all the
City of *Rome* there was none
efteemed to be like him.
He was moft diligent in following the Example of his
Teachers, and not forget-
ful, but fixed his Learning
in a retentive Memory. He
fuck'd in with a thirftyDe-
fire the flowing Learning,
which he often, after fome
time,with a 'Throat fweeter
than Honey, and with an

i *With a Throat, i.e.* Voice or Tongue. This is the very Character
which *Cicero,* the great Roman Orator, gives of *Neftor,* the wifeft of
the *Grecians;* of whom he fays, *Ex ejus lingua melle dulcior fluebat
oratio. De feneclute, cap.* 9. But he tells us *Homer* had faid it before
him; and you'll find he did, *Iliad.* 1. v. 249.

Τᾶ κỳ ἀπὸ γλώσης μέλι[θ]Ꝋ γλυκίων ῥέεν αὐδή.

——*Whofe Tongue pour'd forth a Flood
Of more than Honey fweet Difcourfe.*   *Chapman's* Tranfl.

This, it feems, was the received Character of St. *Gregory's* Eloquence,
as appears from *Gofcelin* of *Canterb.* who in his *Hift. Min. c.* 22. ftyles
him *Mellifum Papa Gregorium, Angl. Sacr. Part. II. p.* 65. And no
doubt this Author took the Notion from *Paulus Diaconus,* in the very
words which are tranflated in this *Homily,* and which are thus in *Latin : Hauriebatque fitibundo doctrinæ fluenta pectore, quæ poft congruenti
tempore mellito gutture eructatet.* See his Life of St. *Greg.* in the *Bened.
Edit. p.* 1. c. 2.

Fig. 5.   Pages 4 and 5 of Elstob's edition of the *English-Saxon Homily on . . . St. Gregory* showing the conversance of Old English and the Modern English translation

written *Ellanstowe. Ellastowe. Ellstowe.* signifying some Palace of King *Ella*, or some Town built in memory of him.

The name Ella itself we learn is not without meaning, it being 'customary with the Northern, as well as other Nations, to take Names which had somewhat of good Importance'. Elstob, to her obvious satisfaction, traces its origin from *Ellen* (variously *Eliun, Ellan, Ellean*), 'by which is understood Courage, Greatness of Soul, Study, Labour, Diligence, Virtue, &c'. And she calls on Hickes's scholarship to confirm her conclusion '[t]hat *Ella* had a most generous Signification, intimating all kinds of Virtue, but chiefly those of the Mind'. The effect of this ideal portrait of a virtuous, hard-working intelligence (more appropriate to the description of an eighteenth-century female scholar than an early Saxon warrior?) is not lost in the final summing up:

> And that which may yet further excuse the tediousness of the Allusion, may be this; that as the Holy *Gregory's* Affection to the Subjects of King *Ella* was the Occasion of bringing Christianity to all the *Saxons*; so it hath fallen out by Providence, to one not only born within the Circuit of those Dominions, but nearly approaching to his Name, to shew some sort of Gratitude, in restoring to the *English* this Memorial of their Apostle and Benefactor at so great a distance of time.[50]

Only two pages later, the attempt to capture the exact nuances of the Old English term *fædera* provides the ostensible excuse for an appropriately digressive fifty-three line footnote on the modern word *gossip*. Here again Elstob displays her normal practice of combining the scholarly, the homely, and the personal. Refusing conventional demarcations between kinds and areas of knowledge, she questions the usefulness of the official Latin gloss and provides instead an environment in which the Saxon past can speak to the eighteenth-century present:

> The Word fædera, Mr *Somner* in his Glossary explains by *Patruus*, that is, an Uncle by the Father's side, a Father's Brother: But it is probable, that the *Saxons* had besides that, another Meaning of the Word: For it does not appear from History, that there was any such relation between *Mauricius* and *Gregory*. One would rather imagine, that it was sometimes used to signifie what is exprest by the *Latin* Word *Compater*, a reciprocal Term between the Father of the Child, and those that stand Godfathers to it. This manner of speaking is well enough known at this Day in the North of *England* by the Word *Gossip*, from another *Saxon* Word God-sibbe, *Cognatus, Lustricus, Sponsor,* a *Gossip*, a Cosin before God; one that in Baptism stands forth in the Infant's behalf, and undertaking for it, makes its Peace with God, as Mr *Somner* interprets it. Which may yet be better understood by these and the like Phrases, which are still used in the North. My *Gossip Thomas* – stood Godfather to my Child: *Harry* and I are *Gossips*, for I stood Godfather to his Child . . .[51]

[50] *Ibid.* pp. 15–17.
[51] *Ibid.* pp. 19–20.

As if to emphasize her woman's right (as gossip and scholar) to parse correctly the Northern 'Mother Tongue', Elstob's youthful portrait, taken from her own drawing, gazes out from the enclosing curves of the initial 'G' of 'Gregory', the first word of the English translation of the homily[52] (fig. 6). The effect of the six-lines deep illuminated letter is to render the 'G' primarily a frame for Elstob's face, and to suggest the reasonable substitution of the woman's converting power for that of the holy bishop. Other decorated borders and letters, like the 'I' which opens the dedicatory epistle to Queen Anne, and the extravagantly ornamented tailpiece to the title-page, anticipate and legitimate pictorially the self-insertive purposes of the editor. This is a handsomely embellished octavo which, Elstob told Thoresby, she 'would willingly have . . . as beautiful as possible'.[53] The initial 'I' of the epistle (fig. 7) bisects an all-female representation of historical process: on the left Helena, distinguishable by the cross she holds, turns to a figure who may be Queen Berhta, while on the right, Queen Elizabeth, with crown and high collar, stands behind Queen Anne, who in turning to face Helena, Berhta, and the past, must look towards and beyond the figure of a young woman, dressed in the fashion of the early eighteenth century and bearing a resemblance to the more detailed portrait of Elstob herself in the letter 'G'. The tailpiece on the title-page (fig. 8) shows the warrior King Ella and spread out behind him his northern province of Deira, represented by the sites of Ellanstowe (from which the editor derives Elstob) and Foxesden (Foxden) clearly marked and both associated with the eighteenth-century family of Elstob. The extended note in the text on King Ella eventually explains Deira as Elstob's own birthplace and Elstob herself as the warrior-king's modern counterpart.

Later, the punches and matrices of the new fount of Saxon type which she had made to print her 1715 Grammar extend Elstob's interest in the typographical presentation of texts and form a significant element in her identification and invocation of a specifically female reading audience. The Elstob Saxon type, as it is still known, was copied and cut in imitation of the letters of Saxon manuscript originals and according to Elstob's own specifications. As Edward Rowe Mores records, in his *Dissertation Upon English Typographical Founders and Founderies* (1778), the Elstob type 'approaches nearly to the *old Saxon*'. In avoiding the modern elegances of Roman and Italian faces, the Elstob type conforms more closely to Mores's preference for the realistic representation of early northern literatures, stripping the Saxon language of 'masquerade' and revealing the 'native tongue'.[54] As part of the extended communication of texts, typography demands

---

[52] E.R. Mores, *A Dissertation Upon English Typographical Founders and Founderies* (1778), ed. H. Carter and C. Ricks (Oxford, 1961), pp. 28–9 gives fuller information: 'but if any one desires to see [Elstob] as she was when she was the favourite of *Dr Hudson* and the *Oxonians* they may view her pourtraiture in the initial G of *The English-Saxon homily on the birth-day of St Gregory*. the countenance of *St Greg.* in the *Saxon* G is taken from *Mr Thwaites*, and both were engraved by *Gribelin*, though *Mich. Burghers* was at that time engraver to *The Univ.*'

[53] *Letters of Eminent Men* II, 148.

[54] Mores, *A Dissertation Upon English Typographical Founders*, pp. 27–9.

NATALE

S. GREGORII *Papæ.*

˙ON THE
BIRTH-DAY
of St. Gregory.

Reȝoniuɼ
ɼe halȝa
Papa En-
ȝliɼcene
þeoðe Ᾱ-
poɼtol on

REGORY
theHoly
Father ,
theApo-
ſtle of
the *Eng-*

þiɼum anðɼeanðan ðæȝe *liſh* Nation, on this preſent
æɼteɼ mæniȝɼealðum ȝe- Day, after manifold La-

˙ Which was the day of his Death, the *Obit,* or *Feſtival,* or *Com-memoration,* or *Birth-day* of the *Saints,* being uſually celebrated yearly on the day whereon they died ; the Church being then aſſur'd of the Bleſſedneſs of the Saint, or that he had a new Birth or Tranſlation from the Church Militant to the Church Triumphant : By ſuch Com-memorations the Church was thought to communicate with the holy Combatant, Confeſſor, or Martyr of Chriſt. That this was agreeable to antient Practice is evident from the account we have of the *Martyrdem of St. Ignatius.* See the Right Reverend the Lord Biſhop of *Lincoln* Dr. *Wake's* Tranſl. page 229. According to which Primitive Cuſtom the *Saxon* Church alſo obſerved the Commemoration of the Obits of her Saints : as more particularly with a juſt Gratitude ſhe here does

B   that

Fig. 6. Elstob's personalized initial 'G' on the opening page of her edition and translation of the *English-Saxon Homily on . . . St. Gregory*

TO THE
QUEEN.

Madam,

T might feem too great a Prefump-tion to approach Your Royal Pre-fence in fo un-ufual a manner, to addrefs Your Majest in a Language fo out-

A 2 dated

Fig. 7. The initial 'I' from the dedicatory epistle to Queen Anne which begins the edition and translation of the *English-Saxon Homily on . . . St. Gregory*

A N

Englifh-Saxon Homily

ON THE

BIRTH-DAY

OF

St. GREGORY,

Anciently ufed in the

Englifh-Saxon Church,

Giving an Account of the

Converfion of the *ENGLISH*

FROM

PAGANISM to CHRISTIANITY.

Tranflated into Modern *Englifh*, with NOTES, *&c.*

By ELIZ. ELSTOB.

LONDON:

Printed by *W. Bowyer,* MDCCIX.

Fig. 8.   The lavish title-page of Elstob's edition of the *English-Saxon Homily on . . . St. Gregory*

234

the recognition of cultural difference and equivalence in history. The Elstob fount, like Elstob's own famous skill in the accurate reproduction of the characteristics of old manuscripts,[55] signals a vigorous alliance between textual and gender politics in the linked search for scholarly authority for women and for the 'native tongue'.

Her anomalous position as a female scholar seems to have provided Elstob with a keen understanding of biblio-politics – that, as Jerome McGann and others have argued, a book is meaning-constitutive, not simply in the delivered message of its contents but in every dimension of its material existence.[56] The physical appearance of Elstob's edition of the St Gregory homily forms part of the complex structure for its critical analysis. Hers is a consciously personalized editing space, which forces the reader to consider how the interpretation of the text relates to the conditions of its reproduction, not only in terms of the scholarly and non-scholarly apparatus for its recovery, but also through the typographical boundaries set for its reconstitution in the present. Different editorial methods engender different reading experiences. In working to make articulate to the early eighteenth century the cultural and historical determinants of her Old English text, Elstob demonstrated, quite self-consciously, the complex cultural pressures of her editing present. Neither of the homily's historical explanations – Elstob's conception of its original context or the conditions for its eighteenth-century reproduction – is extrinsic to the text itself. Declaring the partisan allegiances of her edition, Elstob locates the text within a field of political, sexual, and typographical relations which, for the life of the edition, become part of its meaning. An extreme case, Elstob's openly engaged method may yet have something to teach the modern editor who fondly envisages a detached textual authority and an ideal edition cleared of the 'corrupting' social and cultural influences on its production and reproduction.

POSTSCRIPT

The early decades of the nineteenth century saw a brief revival of interest in Elstob's work, as part of the upturn in Old English studies generally. Joseph Bosworth's *Grammar* of 1823 contains extracts from the St Gregory homily, with a note on Elstob's edition, and extracts from Ælfric's homily on the Creation as edited by Elstob. Bosworth acknowledges: 'The above is taken from some printed but unpublished folio sheets in the British Museum. They are the first sheets of work begun by Mrs Elstob: for reasons now unknown, the press was stopped'. (J. Bosworth, *The Elements of Anglo-Saxon Grammar* (London, 1823), p. 272.) In a long introduction to his work, Bosworth explained the appeal of Saxon studies to women as arising from 'the liberal spirit of our Gothic ancestors' towards the

---

[55] See Nichols, *Literary Andecdotes* IV, 140; and Collins, 'The Elstobs and the End of the Saxon Revival', p. 112.

[56] J.J. McGann, *A Critique of Modern Textual Criticism* (Chicago and London, 1983).

female sex, and he numbers Elstob among those women scholars to have studied Old English with success (pp. xxxiii–xxxiv).

Elstob's edition and translation of the St Gregory homily were reissued, but with some significant alterations, in 1839. The circumstances of the reissue are described as follows:

> The appearance, within the last few years, of several important works in Anglo-Saxon literature, and recently of the Rev. Dr Bosworth's extensive and valuable dictionary, has given a new impulse to the study of that language. The consequent increased demand for Anglo-Saxon books, will doubtless be an inducement to our more learned Saxonists, to commit to the press many manuscripts as yet inedited. This, however, must be a work of time, and, in order to answer the immediate exigency, it has been thought that a correct reprint of some few of the shorter Anglo-Saxon works formerly published, would be useful. With this view, Mrs Elstob's Saxon Homily has been selected, on account of the general accuracy of the text, the interesting nature of the subject, and the fact of the original edition having become scarce. (*An Anglo-Saxon Homily on St Gregory's Day, with an English Translation by Elizabeth Elstob. A new edition: with a preface, containing some account of Mrs Elstob* (London, 1839), pp. xvi–xvii.)

The sixteen-page Preface describing Elstob's life and work is signed with the initials J.S.C. (J.S.C. can be identified as J.S. Cardale, who edited King Alfred's Boethius in 1829.) Elstob's own substantial Preface is considerably reduced, to approximately one fifth its original length. What are most obviously omitted from the framework are the dedicatory epistle to Queen Anne and the Anglican-political controversy, both of which are necessary to the contextualization of the feminist argument. The general lay-out of the 1709 edition is retained in the body of the text, with Old English on the left-hand page and a facing modern translation on the right, notes appearing at the foot of the page. William Elstob's Latin version is retained, as is Elstob's appendix of relevant epistles of St Gregory. But the annotations have been effectively pruned and many rooted out altogether. Elstob's note on King Ella, for example, is considerably reduced, with the omission of all personal information on the derivation of the name of Elstob. Similarly, her linguistic speculations on 'godfather' and 'gossip', and her tracing of connections between Old English and the English 'of the north' are all omitted. Where the 1709 edition gloried in lavish engravings and borders and meaningfully decorated initials, this new edition is a soberer work, its embellishment confined to five simply patterned initials. The overall effect, of which the notes are most representative, is to diminish Elstob's historical and personal engagement with her material – to render the editor's presence less substantial and the edition duller.

A further edition of the St Gregory homily appeared in 1839 which, though not a reissue of Elstob's edition, takes hers as its starting point. (See *Principia Saxonica: or an Introduction to Anglo-Saxon Reading, comprising Ælfric's Homily on the Birthday of St Gregory; with a preliminary essay on the utility of Anglo-*

Saxon, ed. L. Langley (London, 1839).) A short Preface pays tribute to Elstob as one by whom this homily 'was rescued from oblivion and given to the world' (p. vi), and explains in what ways the present editor has departed from her more learned model. Instead of a translation, he includes 'a copious Glossary', and annotation is confined to the philological rather than the historical and theological. After the text, which appears to be based on Elstob's, there is a list of 'Various readings of the Junian MS of the Homily in the Bodleian Library'. This thin volume is designed, writes its editor, to be an introductory reader, and 'that novelty in Saxon Literature, – a cheap book' (p. vii). Economy was not part of Elstob's lavish project.

THE FIRST TWO EDITIONS OF *BEOWULF*:
THORKELIN'S (1815) AND KEMBLE'S (1833)

J.R. Hall

THE Thorkelin transcripts have rightly overshadowed Thorkelin's edition of 1815, the first edition of *Beowulf*. By Kevin S. Kiernan's count, the two transcripts restore or help to restore 1,970 letters lost from London, British Library, Cotton Vitellius A. xv before 1845, the year the manuscript was rebound under Frederic Madden's direction and further losses arrested.[1] In contrast, Thorkelin's edition of 1815, published more than a quarter of a century after the execution of the transcripts and derived from them, is not useful for restoring lost text.[2] Thorkelin's edition is nonetheless important in its own way. The Thorkelin transcripts had limited influence outside Denmark – and in Denmark influence on only Erasmus Rask and N.F.S. Grundtvig – until they were used by Julius Zupitza in his facsimile edition of *Beowulf* in 1882.[3] Indeed, the transcripts were not generally accessible to

This essay is for Kevin S. Kiernan.

[1] On the rebinding of the manuscript, see K.S. Kiernan, *Beowulf and the Beowulf Manuscript* (New Brunswick, 1981), p. 69; on the number of lost letters restored by the transcripts, see Kiernan, *The Thorkelin Transcripts of Beowulf*, Anglistica 25 (Copenhagen, 1986), p. 144. I am pleased to dedicate this essay to Professor Kiernan, whose first book (to say the least) raised the *Beowulf* manuscript to a new level of attention and whose second book has immensely enriched our understanding of Thorkelin's work at the British Museum and of the Thorkelin transcripts. As David N. Dumville has remarked, 'no one has yet been able to demonstrate a detailed knowledge, comparable to Kiernan's, of the manuscript and its physical history'. Dumville goes on to call *Beowulf and the Beowulf Manuscript* 'an admirable book which must be acknowledged as marking a turning point in the study of *Beowulf*, however much one may disagree with its thesis or with parts of its argumentation': 'Beowulf come lately: Some Notes on the Palaeography of the Nowell Codex', *Archiv für das Studium der neueren Sprachen und Literaturen* 225 (1988), 49–63, at 49 (text and n. 5).

[2] Grímur Jónsson Thorkelin, *De Danorum Rebus Gestis Secul. III & IV: Poëma danicum dialecto anglosaxonica* (Copenhagen, 1815).

[3] On Rask's and Grundtvig's use of the transcripts as early as 1816, see below at note 29. Benjamin Thorpe knew of the transcripts from having studied under Rask, having translated Rask's Anglo-Saxon grammar in 1830, and having read Grundtvig's 1820 Danish translation of *Beowulf* (in which the transcripts prominently figure), and expressly mentions them in a note he entered in his copy of Thorkelin's edition on 5 June 1830. For the note see T. Westphalen, *Beowulf 3150–55: Textkritik und Editionsgeschichte* (Munich, 1967), p. 113. Yet Thorpe does not so much as mention the transcripts in his edition of *Beowulf* (Oxford, 1855); and Kemble – despite his friendship with Thorpe and with Jacob and Wilhelm Grimm, each of whom knew of the transcripts (n. 29 below), and despite his various references to Grundtvig's translation – reveals no knowledge of the transcripts in print. What brought the transcripts belated attention was Grundtvig's repeated reference to them in his edition, *Beowulfes Beorh eller Bjovulfs-*

scholars until 1951, when Kemp Malone published them in facsimile.[4] Thorkelin's edition, however, made an impact soon after its appearance in the early nineteenth century. After reviewing some background on the edition and noting Sharon Turner's work with the *Beowulf* manuscript, I would like to consider Thorkelin's edition as an edition and its influence on subsequent students of the poem. Then I shall take up John M. Kemble's edition, published in 1833.

As Kiernan has shown, when Thorkelin came to England in 1786, he did not come with the idea of editing *Beowulf*; rather, *Beowulf* was a text Thorkelin discovered in the course of surveying manuscripts concerned with Danish antiquities.[5] In time Thorkelin came to realize the importance of the poem for his purposes. After discovering the poem in October 1786, Thorkelin in 1787 commissioned a copyist, whom Kiernan convincingly identifies as James Matthews, Accomptant to the Trust of the British Museum, to make a transcript of the poem, now known as Thorkelin A. Apparently two years later, during the last six months of 1789, Thorkelin made his own copy, now known as Thorkelin B. When he returned to Copenhagen in the spring of 1791 to assume the post of Danish National Archivist, Thorkelin brought with him the two transcripts, plus the idea of publishing an edition of the poem – a work more rare, as he later put it, than a white raven ('res hæc albo rarior corvo', edition, p. vii).

Drapen (Copenhagen, 1861). In his edition of 1863 (Paderborn) Moritz Heyne cited the transcripts via Grundtvig but seemed only dimly aware of their importance. (For making Heyne's first edition available to me, I am grateful to Professor Daniel Donoghue, Harvard University.) In C.W.M. Grein's edition of 1867 (Cassel and Göttingen) and Heyne's of 1868, however, the transcripts play a larger part, although, again, each scholar is content to cite them from Grundtvig's edition. (Even so, copies of Grundtvig's edition were rare in Germany at least fifteen years after its publication; see E. Kölbing, 'Zur Beóvulf-handschrift', *Archiv für das Studium der neueren Sprachen und Literaturen* 56 [1876], 91–2.) The first editor after Thorkelin and Grundtvig to have examined the transcripts in person appears to have been Julius Zupitza, who arranged to have the Royal Library at Copenhagen send them to the British Museum in 1880, where he was able to use them side by side with the manuscript for his edition, *Beowulf: Autotypes of the Unique Cotton ms. Vitellius A.xv in the British Museum, with a Transliteration and Notes*, EETS 77 (London, 1882). A second edition, with new photographs of the manuscript, was edited by Norman Davis, EETS 245 (London, 1959).

4   *The Thorkelin Transcripts of Beowulf in Facsimile*, ed. K. Malone, EEMF 1 (Copenhagen, 1951).
5   Most of the information in this paragraph comes from Kiernan, *Thorkelin Transcripts*, pp. 1–41. For the date of Thorkelin B as 1789, rather than 1787, see Kiernan, 'Madden, Thorkelin, and MS Vitellius/Vespasian A XV', *The Library*, 6th ser., 8 (1986), 131–2. Kiernan's dating, along with some of his other findings, has been challenged by J. Gerritsen, 'The Thorkelin Transcripts of *Beowulf*: A Codicological Description, with Notes on their Genesis and History', *The Library*, 6th ser., 13 (1991), 15–18. Gerritsen argues that by February 1787 Thorkelin seems to have enjoyed a privileged status in the British Museum allowing him to work in the Department of Manuscripts itself. 'Any manuscript seen by Thorkelin in the Department will not have appeared in the Reading Room register' (p. 18); hence the negative evidence of the Reading Room Register cited by Kiernan in dating Thorkelin B is hardly conclusive. Gerritsen may be correct. His argument would be more convincing, however, if he could explain why Thorkelin's name continues to appear in the Reading Room Register beyond February 1787 (Kiernan, *Thorkelin Transcripts*, pp. 18–20, 25–28), when he may have worked with presumably greater convenience in the Department of Manuscripts. Gerritsen, p. 15, n. 27, considers Kiernan's identification of the Thorkelin A copyist as James Matthews 'reasonable' but 'not proven'.

The edition did not appear until 1815. A decade earlier another scholar had independently discovered the poem. In the fourth volume of his monumental *History of the Anglo-Saxons* (1805), Sharon Turner calls attention to *Beowulf*, translates nearly 180 lines, and excerpts another 41 lines in Old English – committing more than two dozen errors of transcription.[6] Two years later in his second edition Turner increased the number of lines translated to some 330 but gave the same excerpts of the poem itself, correcting three earlier letter-errors but introducing a new letter-error as well.[7] To my knowledge, Turner's early work on Beowulf exerted influence upon only John J. Conybeare, who, in 1809, called for a complete edition of Turner's recently discovered 'Saxon Romance'[8] and who, in his posthumously published *Illustrations of Anglo-Saxon Poetry* (1826) discloses that he 'made for his own use a faithful transcript of the part analysed by Mr. Turner'.[9]

But 1807, the year of Turner's second edition of his *History*, was important for another reason. It was then that, as Thorkelin observes with grief in the preface to his 1815 edition, the British bombardment of Copenhagen destroyed all his work on the poem, nearly ready for the press, together with his entire literary collection, gathered over more than 30 years (pp. xv–xvi). Every reader of Thorkelin's preface will grieve with Thorkelin. 'But it is only fair to remark', T.A. Birrell notes, 'that Thorkelin's marriage to a rich widow, and his directorship of a brewery, hindered his Anglo-Saxon studies far more than the shells of Admiral Lord Nelson'.[10] In any

---

6 *The History of the Manners, Landed Property, Government, Laws, Poetry, Literature, Religion, and Language of the Anglo-Saxons*, vol. 4 of *The History of the Anglo-Saxons* (London, 1805), pp. 398–408, 414–16. Turner first referred in print to the poem in 1803; see E.G. Stanley, 'Sharon Turner's First Published Reference to "Beowulf" ', *N&Q* n.s. 22 (1975), 2–3. According to the British Museum's Reading Room Register, Turner frequently consulted the *Beowulf* manuscript between August 1800 and September 1803. See E.H. Harvey Wood, 'Letters to an Antiquary: The Literary Correspondence of G.J. Thorkelin (1752–1829)', (unpubl. D.Phil. Thesis, University of Edinburgh, 1972), p. 80, n. 109; and Kiernan, 'Madden', p. 131. (I am grateful to Dr Harvey Wood for permission to cite her thesis.) Turner reveals no knowledge that Thorkelin had worked with the manuscript a dozen years earlier than he, and Thorkelin shows none that Turner had published on *Beowulf* a decade before *De Danorum Rebus Gestis* appeared. (Cf. Thorkelin, p. xi, n. 5, where he cites Turner's third volume – which contains no reference to *Beowulf* – and erroneously gives the date as 1808 [for 1801?].)

7 *The History of the Anglo-Saxons* (London, 1807), II, 294–303, 329–30. Turner corrects his earlier *Ofter* to *Ofer* (MS *ofer*), 200a; and his earlier *thareedon* to *thancedon* (MS *þan/cedon*), 227b. But he gives *fyr pit* for his earlier more accurate *fyr pyt* (MS *fyr wyt* [with *wynn*]), 232b.

8 J.J. Conybeare, *The Romance of Octavian* (Oxford, 1809), p. 49. Also calling for an edition of 'a curious unpublished Poem [*Beowulf*] among the Cotton Manuscripts in the British Museum' is the anonymous reviewer of the fourth volume of Turner's *History* in *British Critic* 26 (1805), 387.

9 *Illustrations of Anglo-Saxon Poetry*, ed. W.D. Conybeare (London, 1826), p. 31. The context shows that John Conybeare made his transcription 'some years' before the appearance of Thorkelin's edition in 1815, presumably before or during 1809–12, when Conybeare held Oxford's Professorship of Anglo-Saxon; see *Illustrations*, pp. (iii)–(iv).

10 T.A. Birrell, 'The Society of Antiquaries and the Taste for Old English 1705–1840', *Neophilologus* 50 (1966), 112. (Assuredly Nelson's shells did little to hinder Thorkelin's Old English studies. Nelson fought at Copenhagen in April 1801, but his death in October 1805 effectively precluded his presence – other than, perhaps, in spirit – at the bombardment in September 1807.)

case, encouraged by his patron, Johan Bülow, Thorkelin began anew, his edition appearing eight years later.

Thorkelin entitled his edition (to translate from the Latin) 'A Danish Poem in Anglo-Saxon Dialect on Exploits of the Danes of the Third and Fourth Centuries'. As the title indicates, he believed the poem to have been composed originally in Danish: indeed Thorkelin says that on his return to Denmark from England he brought with him an epic that had been absent from its *patria* for more than a thousand years (p. ix). He does not know when the poem was translated into Old English but speculates it might have been undertaken by King Alfred, who liked to turn foreign literature into his own tongue (pp. x–xi). Further – and here Thorkelin inaugurates the parlour game so beloved of later Germanic scholars – the explicit Christian references seem to have crept in (*irrepsisset*) during the Alfredian recension (p. xiii). Thorkelin identifies Beowulf as an historical figure who died in battle in 340 (p. ix).[11] The poet was an eyewitness to the events he describes and, to be sure, attended Beowulf's funeral (p. ix).[12]

Thorkelin also addresses important textual matters. The manuscript, he tells us, is a unique parchment quarto, with the poem occupying 69 folios, and is preserved in the Cotton Library of the British Museum as 'Vitell. A. IX' (p. xvi).[13] The text, he goes on to say, has suffered losses both because of the great age of the manuscript – which, on the advice of Thomas Astle, he dates to the early tenth century – and because of the damage it sustained from fire and water when the

According to Kiernan, *Thorkelin Transcripts*, p. 122, 'as late as 20 January 1807' Thorkelin reported to his patron 'he had arranged only half of the poem in verse, and had translated only a quarter of it'. In view of all the work Thorkelin had to do before completing his edition, it is difficult to take at face value the statement in his preface, p. xv, that he had the edition nearly ready for the press when (in September) all his work was destroyed.

[11] Thorkelin implies that Beowulf is the same person as Boe or Bous (son of Odin), as described by Saxo Grammaticus – an identification rejected out of hand by John Conybeare, *Illustrations*, p. 33. See further John Earle, *The Deeds of Beowulf: An English Epic of the Eighth Century Done into Modern Prose* (Oxford, 1892), p. xvii.

[12] In the only English review of Thorkelin's edition, published in the *Monthly Review* 81 (1816), 516–23, William Taylor also found the historical sense of the narrative so compelling as to suggest that the author was an intimate of Beowulf's – Wiglaf (p. 522). Taylor's understanding of the poem itself is as wildly wonderful as Thorkelin's. According to Taylor, for example, during the course of his life Beowulf sees mermaids, takes the body of Grendel aboard ship, and builds a hall in Norfolk, where he later slays himself atop his funeral pyre. (Forty-five years later, without knowing Taylor's review, Daniel H. Haigh advanced an equally appealing geographical scheme: Beowulf sailed from Suffolk, 'Hygelac's territory', to Hart in county Durham – none other than Heorot – and there did some of his doughty deeds. See Haigh's *The Anglo-Saxon Sagas: An Examination of Their Value as Aids to History* [London, 1861], pp. 20–28 and *passim*.)

[13] Kiernan, 'Madden', p. 127, characterizes 'A. IX' as 'a late, wild guess by Thorkelin, since we know that he failed to record the number "XV" on the title-pages of his transcripts'. (Cf. Thorkelin's Cotton Notebook, where he accurately lists the manuscript number: Kiernan, *Thorkelin Transcripts*, p. 7.) The misnomer lingered, appearing again in a report on a prospective edition of *Beowulf* discussed at a meeting of the London Society of Antiquaries; see the *Gentleman's Magazine* 101 (1831), 254. Similarly, in his edition of 1861, p. xvi, Grundtvig mis-cites the manuscript as 'Vitellius A. X'. In *Illustrations*, p. 30, John Conybeare refers to it simply as 'Cot. Vitellius A'.

Cotton Library burned in 1731 (p. xvii). Of the text, Thorkelin says, he made a faithful transcript – nowhere does Thorkelin mention Thorkelin A – and that piety forbade his changing anything ('vetuit religio, aliqvid mutare', p. xviii). Nonetheless he has felt obliged to arrange in verse-form the material that in the manuscript is copied in continuous lines across the page and to alter the often capricious morpheme-division of the scribe (pp. xviii–xix). In his translation, Thorkelin says, he has aimed at rendering the poem word for word and begs the reader's indulgence for inaccuracies, as the text is very difficult (p. xix).

Thorkelin prints the text down the page in half-lines, begins each half-line with a capital, and capitalizes proper names – conventions he borrowed from George Hickes's *Thesaurus*.[14] Thorkelin also expands abbreviations without note, preserves the section-numbers of the poem (but does not number the lines of verse or supply folio-numbers), attempts to preserve manuscript pointing, and uses dots in a general way to indicate textual losses. Thorkelin's literal translation is on the same page as the Old English text and forms a second vertical column, making comparison easy.[15] In accord with the times, he furnishes no glossary but does give three appendices: an index of subjects (often with explanatory notes) in which a reader interested in, for example, 'Amor patriæ', is directed to p. 197 of the poetic text (pp. 237–56); an index of proper names, with notes (pp. 257–68); and an index of poetic synonyms arranged by category (e.g., *Bellum*), with frequent reference to Danish and Icelandic cognates (pp. 269–99). At the book's end Thorkelin includes 'Addenda et corrigenda' (pp. [301–4]).[16]

For 175 years Thorkelin's edition has been ridiculed – with, admittedly, good reason. But here I would like to pause to stress the intelligence with which Thorkelin conceived of his task. First, he undertook the expense of having a skilled copyist (although one completely inexperienced in Old English) make a transcript of the text. Apparently finding the transcript imperfect, Thorkelin assumed the arduous task ('improbo . . . labore', p. xvii) of copying the poem for himself. Second, in his preface he dates – not wisely but not whimsically either – the historical setting of the poem and the time of the poem's composition,[17] suggests

---

14 On p. vii Thorkelin cites Hickes 'in suo Thesauro antiqvitatum septentrionalium Tom. I. p. 218' (Oxford, 1703–5), and refers to Hickes again on pp. x, xiv, and xv. In each case the reference should be, rather, to Wanley's catalogue in Hickes's *Thesaurus*, II, 218 – a fact Thorkelin once knew, as in his Cotton Notebook with reference to Cotton Vitellius A. xv he writes, 'See Wanlej in Hickes' (Kiernan, *Thorkelin Transcripts*, p. 7). What Thorkelin really got from Hickes is the manner of printing verse.

15 Thorkelin may have borrowed the parallel-column format of printing the OE text and Latin translation from Hickes, who uses it for his edition of *Durham* (*Thesaurus*, I, 178–9).

16 John Conybeare, *Illustrations*, p. 140, characterizes Thorkelin's list of *corrigenda* as 'for the most part, more incorrect than even his text'. This in itself is incorrect. In his *corrigenda* Thorkelin makes more than 60 accurate letter-corrections to his text of *Beowulf*, introducing only a handful of new errors.

17 Thorkelin's third/fourth century date for the poem's setting is by no means the worst guess on record. W.D. Conybeare, *Illustrations*, pp. 281–6, places the setting at 150–200 A.D.; and Taylor, pp. 519–23, puts it in the tenth or early twelfth century.

how an originally Danish work came to be translated into Old English, introduces the question of pagan and Christian elements, cites a consultation he had with Thomas Astle (perhaps the best palaeographer in England then) on the date of the manuscript,[18] refers to the loss of text in the manuscript from the Cotton fire, discusses the margin-to-margin appearance of the poem in the manuscript as well as the scribe's unsystematic morpheme-division, prints the text clearly and on the best model then available (the verse in Hickes's *Thesaurus*), supplies a convenient parallel translation – by far the most extensive translation of Old English verse published to that time – and provides three useful appendices. Thorkelin's *conception* of what an editor should say and do seems to me much superior to that of Francis Junius, who in 1655 published another famous *editio princeps* – the first edition of the so-called Cædmon poems – supplying the text virtually alone and that printed as prose.[19]

Where, then, did Thorkelin go astray? He went repeatedly astray in morpheme-division and in the metrical division of half-verses;[20] he went wildly astray in his translation, believing, for example, that Scyld Scefing's ship-funeral was a voyage undertaken by Beowulf and his companions;[21] and he went repeatedly and wildly astray in the accuracy of his text. Kemble remarks in his 1833 edition of *Beowulf*: '. . . not five lines of Thorkelin's edition can be found in succession, in which some gross fault either in the transcript [i.e., in the edited text] or the translation, does not betray the editor's utter ignorance of the Anglo-Saxon language'.[22] Kemble's criticism is somewhat self-serving but not too wide of the mark. My collation of

---

[18] Astle wrote, to great acclaim, *The Origin and Progress of Writing* (London, 1784; 2nd edn, 1803), which contains discussion of Anglo-Saxon script and plates from Old English manuscripts (some of which he owned). *Beowulf* is not mentioned. After first agreeing with Astle on a tenth-century date for the manuscript, John Conybeare came to ascribe it to the eleventh century: cf. *Illustrations*, pp. 30, 32, 157. Also favouring the eleventh century is Thorpe in his edition, p. xi.

[19] F. Junius, *Cædmonis Monachi Paraphrasis Poetica Genesios ac præcipuarum Sacræ paginæ Historiarum, abhinc annos M.LXX* (Amsterdam, 1655). In *Die Beowulf-Handschrift* (Leipzig, 1919), pp. 58–59, 61, Max Förster notes that Junius was familiar with Cotton Vitellius A. xv, as he transcribed from it *Judith* and the Old English version of Augustine's *Soliloquies*. Junius must have at least looked at *Beowulf* a good eighty years before the Cotton fire.

[20] John Conybeare in his published collation of Thorkelin's text with the manuscript, *Illustrations*, pp. 137–55, corrects many of Thorkelin's errors in morpheme-division. Conybeare's published collation is (as he says) selective. His original collation, as recorded in 1817 in his copy of Thorkelin, is more comprehensive in all ways (including the repair of many false metrical divisions); see W.F. Bolton, 'The Conybeare Copy of Thorkelin', *ES* 55 (1974), 97–107. I am much indebted to Professor Bolton, who owns the Conybeare Thorkelin, for permission to examine the book.

[21] On Thorkelin's many misunderstandings of the narrative – including a failure to recognize 39 proper names – see F. Cooley, 'Early Danish Criticism of *Beowulf*', *English Literary History* 7 (1940), 48–51. On Thorkelin's promotion of some common nouns to proper names, see Kiernan, *Thorkelin Transcripts*, p. 123.

[22] *The Anglo-Saxon Poems of Beowulf, The Travellers Song and The Battle of Finnes-burh* (London, 1833), pp. xxix–xxx. Kemble's assessment is fairly typical of comments on Thorkelin's accuracy.

Thorkelin's text with the text of *Beowulf* as it stands in the Zupitza-Davis facsimile (i.e., apart from letters for which we depend on Thorkelin A or B) reveals about 1,900 letter-errors, an average of one every 1.7 long lines.[23]

Two main factors account for the inaccuracy of Thorkelin's edited text. First, it is based on Thorkelin A and B: A has well more than a thousand letter-errors; B, well more than 1,500.[24] Many of the errors were simply carried over into the edited text. But Thorkelin's edited text has hundreds and hundreds of errors even where the transcripts accurately reflect the manuscript. And this brings me to the second factor: Thorkelin himself. No later than at age 37 Thorkelin made a transcript, Thorkelin B, with (as I have said) more than 1,500 letter-errors; little wonder that some 20–25 years later, with the manuscript not at hand, Thorkelin should produce an even more inaccurate edited text. Simply put, he was not a meticulous scholar, and his knowledge of Old English was too slim to alert him to textual folly. He should, of course, have returned to the British Museum to check his edited text against the manuscript. But the journey might have taken as long as two weeks,[25] his health (to judge by what Malone calls Thorkelin's 'shaky hand')[26] was probably not robust, and he probably had little idea his text was so faulty. At the very least, however, Thorkelin should have placed in brackets or otherwise marked his deliberate emendations, including sixty-nine letters he inserted in his edited text corresponding to places where the reading was lost or damaged when he examined the manuscript in the late 1780s, letters with no basis in Thorkelin A or B. But he gives no such indication. Had the two Thorkelin transcripts not survived, we would now be debating whether some of these sixty-nine letters had manuscript authority.

---

[23] The figure 1,900 takes into account Thorkelin's list of *errata*, which reduced the letter-errors of his text by about three percent (n. 16 above). I count as errors letters misreported, abbreviations incorrectly expanded, letters omitted, and letters added without manuscript authority. (The total number of errors would be greater still had Thorkelin attempted, like Kemble, to distinguish between thorn and eth; instead, Thorkelin converted all eths to thorns. See below n. 42.) Several 'errors' (in addition to the 69 inserted letters mentioned below) are probably deliberate emendations; but there is little basis for deciding which, as Thorkelin does not mark his deliberate departures from the manuscript.

[24] My calculations, based on the lists of copying errors for A and B compiled folio by folio by Kiernan, *Thorkelin Transcripts*, pp. 47–95. My total for Thorkelin B does not include the many instances (exceeding 450) in which Thorkelin departs from the manuscript by not reproducing manuscript capitals or (much more frequently) by his introducing capitals for proper names. The instances are germane to Kiernan's argument that Thorkelin A gives a better, more literal record of the manuscript than does Thorkelin B (which Kiernan justly calls an 'edition-in-progress', p. 123) but are not letter-errors as I use the term. Further, as Kiernan stresses, many of the errors in either transcript were occasioned by ambiguous or damaged places in the manuscript.

[25] It took Thorkelin two weeks (20 July–3 August) to journey from Copenhagen to London in 1786: Kiernan, *Thorkelin Transcripts*, p. 36, n. 22 (cf. p. 38, n. 45). More than 40 years later it took Grundtvig about two weeks (3–16 May) to make the same trip in 1829: F. Rønning, 'N. F. S. Grundtvig og den oldengelske literatur', *Historisk månedsskrift for folkelig og kirkelig oplysning* 4 (1885), 349–50. With luck, however, the trip – as on Grundtvig's return to Copenhagen from London – might take only a week (Rønning, pp. 363–5).

[26] Malone, *Thorkelin Transcripts*, p. 22.

Thorkelin's edition had immediate impact. In Copenhagen N.F.S. Grundtvig, who had known since 1808 that Thorkelin was at work on an important Anglo-Saxon poem,[27] sharply attacked Thorkelin's understanding of the text shortly after its appearance.[28] Although Thorkelin answered in kind, the two men came to be reconciled. Through the offices of Erasmus Rask, who planned with Grundtvig to bring out a new edition of the poem, Grundtvig had brief access to the Thorkelin transcripts in 1816, using them to good effect in subsequent essays and in his Danish translation of *Beowulf* in 1820.[29] Meanwhile in England John Conybeare in 1817 made a collation of Thorkelin's edited text with the manuscript, an inaccurate and abbreviated version of which appeared in 1826 in Conybeare's *Illustrations* (n. 20 above), along with a lengthy précis of the narrative in prose and verse, several Old English passages, and textual notes (pp. 30–167). In 1824 a young friend of Conybeare's, Frederic Madden – his interest kindled by seeing Conybeare's page-proofs – made his own collation of Thorkelin's edited text with the manuscript, finding hundreds of errors Conybeare had missed.[30] Five years later Grundtvig showed up at the British Museum to make his own collation.[31] The next year, 1830, Benjamin Thorpe, a former student of Rask's, also journeyed from Copenhagen to London to collate Thorkelin's edited text.[32] Finally, in the summer of 1832 John M. Kemble transcribed the poem from the manuscript.[33] Many years passed before Thorpe (1855) and Grundtvig (1861) published their editions; Kemble had his out in 1833, the year after he transcribed the poem.

Who was this Kemble, who suddenly appeared on the scene and stole a march on older, more experienced scholars? He was born in 1807 into a family closely associated with the stage. After receiving an excellent early education, in 1826 he matriculated at Trinity College, Cambridge. In the summer of 1829 he travelled and studied in Germany, becoming enamoured of German scholarship, especially the new philology. Back at Cambridge, he received his degree in 1830 and two

---

[27] N.F.S. Grundtvig, *Nordens Mytologi* (Copenhagen, 1808), p. 130. I am grateful to Ms Helen Maclean, University of Manchester, whose translation of the passage has given me a precise sense of Grundtvig's statement.

[28] Cooley, 'Early Danish Criticism', pp. 54–61.

[29] On Grundtvig's hurried use of the transcripts in 1816, see his *Bjowulfs Drape: Et Gothisk Helte-Digt fra forrige Aar-Tusinde af Angel-Saxisk paa Danske Riim* (Copenhagen, 1820), p. xxxiii; and *Beowulfes Beorh*, p. xix. On Grundtvig's use of the transcripts elsewhere and Rask's use of them, see Cooley, 'Early Danish Criticism', pp. 62–6. Jacob and Wilhelm Grimm knew of the transcripts from Grundtvig's references to them in his 1820 translation. Jacob alludes to the transcripts in his review of *Bjowulfs Drape* in *Göttingische gelehrte Anzeigen* (2 January 1823), 4, and Wilhelm uses them implicitly via Grundtvig in the passages he quotes from *Beowulf* in *Die Deutsche Heldensage* (Göttingen, 1829), pp. 14–17.

[30] Madden's copy of Thorkelin's edition is held by the Houghton Library, Harvard University, where I happened upon it in June 1984.

[31] Grundtvig, *Beowulfes Beorh*, pp. xvii, xx; and Rønning, pp. 341–54.

[32] Westphalen, *Beowulf 3150–55*, pp. 109–24.

[33] The date of Kemble's transcription is considered below. I am now writing a book on the work of Conybeare, Madden, Grundtvig, Thorpe, and Kemble on the *Beowulf* manuscript.

years later undertook studying philology in great earnest, especially the work of Jacob Grimm.[34] After writing Grimm a fan letter on or about 30 June 1832 and receiving an encouraging reply, Kemble wrote him again in late September, saying that he had transcribed *Beowulf* from the manuscript for Grimm but that his friends had persuaded him to publish the poem himself. After discussing *Beowulf* in letters to Grimm for some time, Kemble sent Grimm a copy of his edition on 8 January 1834, remarking, '. . . I hasten to present you with a copy of Bëówulf: he has at last made his appearance, and I trust one that will be found creditable to the editor no less than the printer & publisher'.[35]

Kemble's *Beowulf* was creditable to its 26-year-old editor. In his preface he cites many medieval and modern Scandinavian sources to argue that the main events in the first part of the poem occurred in the mid-fifth century (pp. vi-xx, passim) – about sixty-five to seventy years too early, according to our present knowledge, but a century closer than Thorkelin's dating and on much better grounds.[36] Identifying the Geats with the Angles, Kemble maintains that Beowulf was an Angle hero living in Jutland or Sleswic (Schleswig),[37] the story of whose adventures was brought to England during the Anglo-Saxon migration at about 495 (pp. xv–xx). Because of its Christian allusions, Kemble concedes *Beowulf* as we have it must have been composed later than 597. He contends, however, that 'the numerous blunders both in sense and versification', the archaic forms, and the cursory historical allusions show that the original version of the poem was composed on the continent (p. xxi). Thus does Kemble, like Thorkelin, strive to place the time of the poem's composition back to a romantic age of pagan antiquity, favouring, however, an Anglian rather than a Danish origin.

---

[34] Biographical data are from R.A. Wiley, *Anglo-Saxon Kemble: The Life and Works of John Mitchell Kemble 1807–1857, Philologist, Historian, Archaeologist*, Anglo-Saxon Studies in Archaeology and History 1.9 (Oxford, 1979), pp. 174–207.

[35] *John Mitchell Kemble and Jakob Grimm: A Correspondence 1832–1852*, ed. and trans. R.A. Wiley (Leiden, 1971), pp. 19–21 (letter of 30 June 1832), 23–31 (letter of September 1832), 47–50 (letter of 8 January 1834). In *Anglo-Saxon Kemble*, pp. 190, 204, Wiley cites evidence that Kemble had the idea of editing *Beowulf* as early as February 1832 and that he was actively working on it in mid-summer of that year. Kemble had a great advantage over other would-be *Beowulf* editors: his residence, at 79 Great Russell St., was 'adjacent to the British Museum' (Wiley, *Correspondence*, p. 23, n. 1).

[36] Kemble repeated the dating in the preface to the first volume (text) of his second edition (London, 1835), pp. vi–xx, *passim*; but in the second volume (postscript, notes, translation, glossary), published in 1837, he declared his earlier dating 'null and void', it being almost impossible, he now thought, to disentangle history from myth (p. xliv). For Thorpe's ironic rejoinder, see his edition, pp. xvii–iii.

[37] Kemble was not the first to associate Beowulf with Schleswig; unbeknownst to him, the claim had been advanced years earlier by Nicolaus Outzen in his review of Thorkelin's edition in *Kieler Blätter* 3 (1816), 310–13. See Franklin D. Cooley, 'Contemporary Reaction to the Identification of Hygelac', *Philologica: The Malone Anniversary Studies*, ed. Thomas A. Kirby and Henry Bosley Woolf (Baltimore, 1949), pp. 269–70. (Today most scholars identify the Geats with the Götar of southern Sweden and consequently differ from Kemble's placing Beowulf's home in Jutland or Schleswig.) For other reviews of Thorkelin, see Andreas Haarder, 'The Seven Beowulf Reviewers: Latest or Last Identifications', *English Studies* 69 (1988), 289–92.

Unlike Thorkelin, Kemble in discussing Cotton Vitellius A. xv does not date the manuscript, does not note that the verse is written across the page like prose, and does not discuss morpheme-division. Kemble does, however, observe that the poem was copied by two different scribes (pp. xxii, 134) and does note – although without reference to the burning of the Cotton Library – that the edges of the folios are progressively deteriorating (p. xxvi). Kemble's contempt for Anglo-Saxon scribes is emphatic. Any one experienced in Anglo-Saxon manuscripts, he says, knows 'how hopelessly incorrect they in general are', with their repeated errors of grammar and orthography (pp. xxiii-iv).[38] In fact, Kemble asserts, a modern editor who really knows philology would be able to produce a text that would 'in all probability be much more like the original than the MS. copy, which, even in the earliest times, was made by an ignorant or indolent transcriber' (p. xxiv). Yet, says Kemble, 'no man is justified in withholding the original readings', and so he has given the text 'letter for letter' as in the manuscript (pp. xxiv–v).

Like Thorkelin, Kemble prints the text down the page in half-verses, capitalizes proper names, preserves manuscript pointing, and gives the section numbers of the poem. Otherwise the two edited texts are quite different. Kemble begins each line with a lower case letter (unless the first word is a proper name), introduces a hyphen between the elements of compounds and often between the immediate constituents of complex words, attempts to mark long vowels ('the first [such] attempt ever made in England', he later boasted),[39] preserves manuscript abbreviations, places all conjectural restorations of lost letters in parentheses (not always accurately),[40] records proposed emendations at page-bottom without introducing them into the text, numbers the half-lines consecutively at every tenth, and cites the manuscript folio-numbers in the margins. Although, unlike Thorkelin, Kemble supplies no parallel translation, he does furnish an abbreviated glossary (twenty-three words, fifteen pages) and a brief discussion of proper names (seven names, six pages).

Thorkelin's text and Kemble's differ in yet another way: in the first 500 long lines of *Beowulf* Thorkelin has nearly 300 letter-errors, while Kemble has twenty-one.[41] Obviously, Kemble's text is much more accurate than Thorkelin's. But Thorkelin's text seems nonetheless to have influenced Kemble's. Five of Kemble's

---

[38] In his second edition, vol. 2, n. to line 3853, Kemble remarks, 'The MS. of Beówulf is unhappily among the most corrupt of all the A. S. MSS. and corrupt they all are without exception'. Similarly, Thorpe in his edition, p. viii, refers to the 'numerous and . . . enormous and puerile . . . blunders of the copyist'. See also p. xi.

[39] 'Letter to M. Francisque Michel', F. Michel, *Bibliothèque anglo-saxaonne* (Paris, 1837), p. 22. I find it hard to reconcile Kemble's claim with Benjamin Thorpe's earlier attempt to mark long vowels in his edition, *Cædmon's Metrical Paraphrase of Parts of the Holy Scriptures, in Anglo-Saxon* (London, 1832), a work Kemble mentions in 'Letter' immediately before his own edition.

[40] Kemble's occasional inaccuracy in signalling conjectural restorations is noted by B. Kelly, 'The formative stages of *Beowulf* textual scholarship: part I', *ASE* 11 (1983), 254–5 (notes to lines 2063a, 2228a, 2363b). Even so, my preliminary finding is that Kemble saw more than 300 letters since lost from the manuscript.

[41] The figures reflect the corrections made by Thorkelin and Kemble in their lists of *corrigenda*. In

twenty-one departures from the manuscript are also found in Thorkelin, suggesting that Thorkelin's text played a part in Kemble's transcription.[42] Much more important is the influence Thorkelin's text evidently exerted on Kemble's restoration of letters gone from the manuscript when he studied it in 1832. Kemble says that 'in cases where portions of the text have perished' from the crumbling of the folio-edges, 'I have generally from conjecture (if conjecture it can be called, to restore letters to words whose form no scholar can doubt for a moment,) endeavoured to supply the deficiencies . . .' (p. xxvi). In fact, the great majority of Kemble's restored readings – for example, well over a hundred letters in his text of the first 500 long lines of *Beowulf* – agree with readings in Thorkelin's edition (most of them taken by Thorkelin from his two transcripts). Even if Kemble arrived at all the restorations he shares with Thorkelin independently of Thorkelin – which I am unable to believe – Kemble still should have acknowledged Thorkelin's edition.

But some of Kemble's restorations did, in fact, originate with him. According to Birte Kelly, thirty-two letters among Kemble's original restorations in his first edition have been accepted by all editors since 1950, and another thirteen letters have been accepted by most editors since then.[43] Further, again according to Kelly, among Kemble's outright emendations in his first edition all editors since 1950 have accepted twenty-six of the proposed letter-changes (including letters to be deleted from the manuscript).[44] Although Kemble's second edition of the text in 1835 was only a slight improvement on his first, his apparatus to the second edition – including a postscript to the preface, copious and learned explanatory notes, and a comprehensive glossary of 128 pages – published along with his translation in 1837, was as dramatic a contribution to understanding *Beowulf* as his first edition. 'Kemble's editions', says Chauncey B. Tinker, 'became at once the authoritative commentary on the text, and held this position until the appearance of Grein's *Bibliothek* (1857)'.[45]

Although Thorkelin had a sound idea of what an edition should be, his execution was unfortunate; his influence came not simply from publishing an unpublished priceless text but from publishing it so provokingly. Although Kemble had an

---

[42] his second edition Kemble eliminated eight of the twenty-one letter-errors in these lines (one in his text of 1835, seven in his *corrigenda* of 1837).

[42] Kemble agrees with Thorkelin in the following departures: -*þearfe* (MS *ðearfe*), 14b; -*wircean* (MS *wyrcean*), 20b; *þæt* (MS *þ*), 62a; *þa* (MS *ða*) 140b; *Ie*, with the query 'Ic?' (MS *Ie*), 240b. (In the last instance Thorkelin's reading is 'Ic', the same as Kemble's query; both Thorkelin and Kemble give capital 'I' in their texts for MS 'I'.) I do not count the readings at lines 14b, 62a, and 140b as errors in Thorkelin, who, unlike Kemble, did not attempt to distinguish thorn from eth or to preserve manuscript abbreviations.

[43] 'The formative stages', pp. 254–5, 257–8. My calculations.

[44] *Ibid.* pp. 260–2. My calculations.

[45] *The Translations of Beowulf: A Critical Bibliography* (New York, 1903), p. 37. Tinker's assessment is strictly true of the second edition alone, of which the translation and learned apparatus did serve as 'the authoritative commentary on the text' for many years. I have discussed the question in 'Kemble's Two Editions of *Beowulf*: A World of Difference', Twenty-sixth International Congress on Medieval Studies, Western Michigan University, 10 May 1991; for an abstract see the *OEN* 24.3 (1991), A-20.

unfortunate idea of the *Beowulf* manuscript – a contemptibly corrupt record made by blundering copyists, a record of a glorious, distant pagan past, the more distant and pagan, the more glorious – his execution was competent; his influence came from editing and understanding well the literal text of a witness whose testimony he disdained.

What Thorkelin and Kemble are to us, we will be to our successors in a century and a half: objects of curiosity. It is unlikely we will surpass the courage of Thorkelin, who – his work blasted from his grasp – persevered to complete an edition taken in hand many years earlier. It is unlikely as well we will surpass the pioneering intelligence of Kemble, who brought the editing of Anglo-Saxon verse into what we are pleased to call the modern era. We can, however, surpass Thorkelin and Kemble in conveying the testimony of manuscripts with more rigorous precision and greater sympathy for and understanding of the scribes and culture that produced them. Kemble once remarked arrogantly with regard to John Conybeare, 'man is frail, and so are Anglo-Saxon professors'.[46] Kemble had his own shortcomings, as did Thorkelin. Yet either scholar is a source of inspiration. If we mind our manuscripts, our successors may also find in us something more than frailty.

---

[46] 'Letter', p. 20.

EDITING THE ANGLO-SAXON LAWS:
FELIX LIEBERMANN AND BEYOND

Richard Dammery

IN 1568 John Day of Aldersgate printed the *editio princeps* of the Anglo-Saxon law-codes, using the same Old English type which he had cut under commission from Matthew Parker for *A Testimonie of Antiquitie*.[1] This edition of the laws, entitled *Archaionomia*, was published in the name of William Lambarde (1536–1601); however, as the preface (*epistola*) reveals, it was in effect a joint venture between Lambarde and his friend and mentor Laurence Nowell.[2] Not only did Nowell teach Lambarde many of the skills necessary for antiquarian research, but prior to his journey to France on 25 March 1567,[3] he also provided the young lawyer with transcripts of the law-codes, encouraging him to translate them and publish an edition. This was the beginning of a long editorial history; indeed no century has passed since the sixteenth without the production of a new edition of the Anglo-Saxon laws.

The process of defining a corpus of law-codes and relevant manuscripts was a gradual one, which culminated in the publication of Felix Liebermann's monumental, three volume *Die Gesetze der Angelsachsen*.[4] A review of this work, by the renowned legal historian Frederic William Maitland, praised it as capable of bearing comparison 'with the best work that has hitherto been done upon any historical materials of a similar kind', although Maitland could not resist a wry lament:[5]

---

[1] *A Testimonie of Antiquitie, shewing the auncient fayth in the Church of England*, ed. M. Parker (London, 1566 or 1567).

[2] *Archaionomia, sive de priscis Anglorum legibus libri, sermone Anglico, vetustate antiquissimo, aliquot ab hinc seculis conscripti, atque: nunc demum, magno iurisperitorum, & amantium antiquitatis omnium commodo, é tenebris in lucem vocati*, ed. W. Lambarde (London, 1568). Cf. R.M. Warnicke, *William Lambarde. Elizabethan Antiquary* (Chichester, 1973), pp. 23–35. On this generally, see my forthcoming facsimile of the *Archaionomia* (to be published in the series Early Studies in Germanic Philology).

[3] In the Lambarde family diary (London, Drapers' Company, MS H./Add. 27, p. 88), *s.a.* 25 March 1567, William wrote: 'Anno a nato saluatore 1567 in Galliam vehitur Laurentius Noelus, mei amantissimus'. Extracts from the diary were printed by Multon Lambarde, 'The Lambarde Diary', *Miscellanea Genealogica et Heraldica* 2 (1876), 99–114.

[4] *Die Gesetze der Angelsachsen*, ed. F. Liebermann, 3 vols (Halle, 1898–1916). The first complete volume of Liebermann's edition was published in 1903; it was also issued in separate fascicles, beginning in 1898.

[5] F.W. Maitland, 'The Laws of the Anglo-Saxons', *Quarterly Review* 200 (1904), 139–57, at p. 139.

If Englishmen cannot or will not do these things, they can at least rejoice that others can and will.

As a product of its time, Liebermann's edition is certainly remarkable. Not only does it provide extensive detail about both the language and legal content of the codes, but the texts, which are set out synoptically by manuscript, are extremely accurate. Having collated the relevant codices with Liebermann's texts of both *Alfred-Ine* and the entire corpus of Æthelred's codes, one may assert with some confidence that Liebermann's errors are few, and generally insignificant.[6] On this basis, one might assume that it is safe to rely on the texts as printed in the *Gesetze*; and, if one only uses the edition to study legal vocabulary, this is probably true. For other purposes, however, the same cannot be said.

There are three fundamental flaws in Liebermann's treatment of the manuscript sources: the first is his handling of the textual transmission; the second is his naming and classification of the law-codes; and the third is his division of the texts into chapters. These problems necessarily affect the utility of his edition, for the manuscripts form a corner-stone upon which any analysis of the laws themselves must be constructed.[7] Ultimately the problems with Liebermann's stemmata are the result of his analytical method, for he examined each of the codes individually, and failed to give due consideration to the groupings of codes within related manuscripts. As a result, many of his stemmata are unnecessarily convoluted; and when one examines the transmission of the codes, manuscript by manuscript, one finds that Liebermann's individual stemmata do not fit together.

In order to resolve some of the difficulties inherent in his approach, Liebermann was forced to imply the existence of lost manuscripts. In several of the stemmata he asserted, on the basis of inconclusive textual evidence, that William Lambarde had used lost manuscripts to prepare his texts in the *Archaionomia*, and he suggested that these formed the missing links between known codices. Evidence which has come to light since the publication of the *Gesetze* suggests that while lost manuscripts may have existed in the sixteenth century, they were certainly far fewer in number than Liebermann supposed. In 1934 Lord Howard de Walden gave the British Museum eight transcripts in Nowell's hand, including a copy of the badly burned Cotton Otho B.xi, a codex which contains in fragmentary form the second oldest extant version of *Alfred-Ine*, together with the codes known as *II As.* and *V As.*[8] This transcript, which bears annotations made by Lambarde, is most

---

6 The most common mistakes are mis-spellings and a failure to indicate the expansion of abbreviations; both these categories of error could have originated when the work was typeset. A more substantial error occurs in Liebermann's G-text of *VIII Æthelred* (*cap.* 5,1), where the words 'þær nan legerstow ne sy' were omitted after the word 'feldcyr'i'can' (see Liebermann, ed., *Gesetze*, I, p. 264).

7 On the manuscripts of Anglo-Saxon law generally, see Mary P. Richards, 'The Manuscript Contexts of the Old English Laws: Tradition and Innovation', in *Studies in Earlier Old English Prose. Sixteen Original Contributions*, ed. P.E. Szarmach (Albany, 1986), pp. 171–92.

8 The following abbreviations are used in references to particular law-codes: *Alf.* (Alfred); *Edw.* (Edward the Elder); *As.* (Æthelstan); *Edg.* (Edgar); *Atr.* (Æthelred the Unready); *Cnut* (Canute).

probably one of the sources provided to Lambarde by Nowell for the preparation of the *Archaionomia*, and it is valuable both for the important textual evidence which it contains, and also because it provides tangible proof of Lambarde's collaboration with Nowell. Since its discovery, several other transcripts used by Lambarde have also reappeared, although they vary considerably in importance.[9]

Felix Liebermann saw only one of these Nowell transcripts: Canterbury, Cathedral Library Lit. B.2 (which he called *So*). He did not, however, recognize its true provenance, and he mistakenly attributed it to William Somner (1606–1669) who had acquired it from the Lambarde library. To judge from the introduction to his *Gesetze*, Liebermann never used the other transcripts by Nowell at Canterbury (Lit. E.1 and E.2), which is surprising, given that they had been described in a published catalogue as early as 1911.[10] Had he seen these manuscripts, Liebermann might have recognized the true provenance of *So*, since all three transcripts are written in Nowell's characteristic Old English script, and both Lit. E.1 and E.2 bear Lambarde's *ex libris*.[11]

Yet, as it happened, within two decades of the appearance of the *Gesetze*, in which Liebermann had defined the corpus of manuscripts and set out in detailed stemmata the relationship between them, new textual evidence had come to light, throwing doubt upon his work. Even before the 'rediscovery' of the Nowell transcripts in 1934, Kenneth Sisam had suggested that several of the passages in the *editio princeps* for which there is no extant source occurred as a result of sixteenth-century translation into Old English from the twelfth-century Latin translation of the law-codes, *Quadripartitus*.[12] Liebermann did not accept Sisam's arguments, and he continued to assert steadfastly the existence of lost manuscripts known to Lambarde.[13] One can only regret that Liebermann did not have the opportunity to debate the matter in light of those transcripts given to the British Museum in

---

9   Professor C.T. Berkhout has identified another related Nowell transcript of *Alfred-Ine*: London, British Library, Henry Davis Collection, M30. There are also several relevant transcripts by Nowell in the United States. San Marino, CA, Huntington Library, HM 26341 is a transcript by Nowell (dated 1565) of the *Decreta Willelmi Bastardi*; and Los Angeles, University of California Research Library, MS 170/529 is a commonplace book written by Nowell, which contains a virtually complete transcript of the twelfth-century Latin translation of the laws, *Quadripartitus*.

10 C.E. Woodruff, ed., *A Catalogue of the Manuscript Books in the Library of Christ Church Canterbury* (Canterbury, 1911).

11 Canterbury, Cathedral Library Lit. E.2 is also marked with printer's ink (and thumb-prints) throughout. It is likely that John Day type-set the text of *I-II Cnut* in the *Archaionomia* from this transcript. On one of the final leaves of Lit. E.2 Lambarde wrote the inscription 'excusum 3 Septemb. 1568'.

12 K. Sisam, 'A review of *The Laws of the Earliest English Kings*', *MLR* 18 (1923), pp. 100–4, and K. Sisam, 'The Authenticity of Certain Texts in Lambarde's "*Archaionomia*" 1568', *MLR* 20 (1925), 253–69. See also, in this connection, R. Flower, 'Laurence Nowell and the Discovery of England in Tudor Times', *PBA* 21 (1935), 47–73, at p. 72, n. 16. On *Quadripartitus* generally, see F. Liebermann, ed., *Quadripartitus, ein Englisches Rechtsbuch von 1114* (Halle, 1892), and P. Wormald, '*Quadripartitus*', in *Law and Government in Medieval England and Normandy. Essays in Honour of Sir James Holt*, ed. G. Garnett (Cambridge, 1994).

13 F. Liebermann, 'Ist Lambardes Text der Gesetze Æthelstans neuzeitliche Fälschung?', *Beiblatt zur Anglia* 35 (1924), 214–19.

1934,[14] for, as Neil Ker observed, they suggest that the sources from which the *Archaionomia* was printed are not (as Liebermann thought) 'numerous and now largely missing', but 'few and extant'.[15] Furthermore, as a result of his 'stemmatische Überzüchtung',[16] Liebermann's manuscript sigla are clumsy and misleading, since they reflect his now discredited view of the relationship between the codices. In short, if one chooses to be guided by Liebermann's stemmata, one must exercise extreme caution.

The other two deficiencies in Liebermann's edition, namely the division of the law-codes into chapters and the naming and classification of the texts, are both derived from Reinhold Schmid's 1858 edition of the laws.[17] It is ironic that Liebermann, who was the first editor to examine the law-codes systematically in their manuscript contexts, should have chosen to follow Schmid in this respect, for although Schmid's second edition contains the earliest attempt by an editor to catalogue the Anglo-Saxon legal manuscripts, he never actually saw any of the codices in person.[18] The text of Schmid's first edition was taken from the 1721 edition of the laws by David Wilkins, and the text of his second edition was derived from Benjamin Thorpe's 1840 edition, published under the auspices of the Public Records Commission.[19] Schmid's description of the manuscripts, and hence his classification of the texts, was based largely on Humphrey Wanley's catalogue;[20] and Liebermann's classification (as already pointed out) was based on that of Schmid.

As a result, several of the texts in Liebermann's *Gesetze* are described inaccurately. The codes which Schmid called *II Edg.* and *III Edg.* are in fact one law (and Liebermann recognized this); the same is true of the codes *I* and *II Cnut*. Similarly, the so-called appendix to *II Atr.*, on vouching to warranty, bears no relation whatsoever to the treaty which precedes it, and may not even belong to the reign of that king. The code *VI As.* is not a royal law at all, but was issued in the name of the bishops and reeves of the 'peace-guild' at London. It is extant in only one manuscript, and four clauses at the end of the code seem to have no association with the London document in its original form.[21]

---

14 Felix Liebermann died after being hit by a car in Berlin on 7 October 1925.

15 N.R. Ker, *Catalogue of Manuscripts containing Anglo-Saxon* (Oxford, 1957), p. li. Cf. *Eine altenglische Übersetzung von Alcuins De Virtutibus et Vitiis, Kap. 20*, ed. R. Torkar, Texte und Untersuchungen zur Englischen Philologie 7 (München, 1981), p. 4.

16 Torkar, *Eine altenglische Übersetzung*, p. 124.

17 *Die Gesetze der Angelsachsen*, ed. R. Schmid, 2nd edn (Leipzig, 1858).

18 This fact was noted by H.D. Hazeltine, 'Felix Liebermann, 1851–1925', *PBA* 25 (1939), 1–44, at p. 13.

19 *Die Gesetze der Angelsachsen*, ed. R. Schmid (Leipzig, 1832); *Leges Anglo-Saxonicae Ecclesiasticae et Civiles*, ed. D. Wilkins (London, 1721); *Ancient Laws and Institutes of England*, ed. B. Thorpe, 2 vols (London, 1840).

20 H. Wanley, *Antiquæ Literaturæ Septentrionalis liber alter. seu Humphredi Wanleii Librorum Vett. Septentrionalium, qui in Angliæ Bibliothecis extant, nec non multorum Vett. Codd. Septentrionalium alibi extantium Catalogus Historico-Criticus, cum totius Thesauri Linguarum Septentrionalium sex Indicibus*, in *Linguarum Vetterum Septentrionalium Thesaurus Grammatico-Criticus et Archæologicus*, edited by G. Hickes, II (Oxford, 1705).

21 See S. Keynes, 'Royal Government and the written word in late Anglo-Saxon England', in *The*

The composite law-code *Alfred-Ine* poses a slightly different set of problems, which are again related to the question of classification of texts. This code traditionally has been divided into four component parts: a table of rubrics; an introduction consisting of translated excerpts from the Bible (particularly of Mosaic law from the Book of Exodus); a law-code in King Alfred's name; and a code which purports to have issued by King Ine (688–726) some two centuries earlier. There are good textual grounds for regarding the Ine appendix as something less than an integral part of Alfred's law-code as he conceived it, for it is clear that Alfred repeatedly borrowed from Ine's code when framing his own laws, amending his source as he thought fit. This is what the king claims to have done in the prologue to his code (Bib. Int. 49.9), where he states that he gathered into his own code ('ic þa heron gegaderode') those laws which seemed to him most just, and omitted the others ('and þa oðre forlet'). While this statement of method is usually regarded as implying that chapters were omitted from the Ine appendix as Alfred annexed it, in my opinion it is preferable to construe Alfred's prologue to his code literally, thereby explaining the contradictions between the Ine appendix and those chapters in Alfred's own law derived from the earlier work.

It is certainly beyond the scope of this paper to set out the complex arguments by which these conclusions may be justified, nor are they particularly pertinent in this context.[22] Conservative though it may be, the point to be made here is simply that tangible manuscript evidence must be preferred over mere editorial surmise. Since the presentation of an edition will influence a reader's interpretation of the text, it should not be used by the editor as a means to foist his interpretation upon others. In the context of *Alfred-Ine*, even if there is some internal basis for supposing that Ine's code is not an integral (or even original) part of Alfred's ordinance as he issued it, this alone is not sufficient justification for printing the code independently of Alfred's law, as most editors (except Milton Turk and Liebermann) have done. One must necessarily work within the confines of the material as it has been transmitted; and, as Turk put it in the introduction to his edition of 1893: 'Our code [*Alfred-Ine*] has suffered in the past from a too zealous separation into parts, and we prefer as far as possible to regard it as a whole, though gathered from different sources'.[23]

Knowing where to divide texts in vernacular English manuscripts is, of course, a common editorial difficulty. Fortunately most of the law-codes survive in more than one manuscript, and, in the case of those codices closely associated with

---

Uses of Literacy in Early Mediaeval Europe, edited by R. McKitterick (Cambridge, 1990), pp. 226–57, at pp. 239–40.

[22] *Alfred-Ine* achieves an artificial semblance of unity by virtue of a numbered table of rubrics with which the law-code begins. These rubrics were almost certainly composed by someone other than the author of Alfred's law, since a detailed comparison of the rubrics with the text reveals striking differences in vocabulary. For a more lengthy discussion of this, see my 'The Law-Code of King Alfred the Great' (unpubl. PhD dissertation, Cambridge Univ., 1990), pp. 181–212. On Alfred's use of Ine's Code, see *ibid.*, pp. 258–65.

[23] *The Legal Code of Ælfred the Great*, ed. M.H. Turk (Halle, 1893), p. 30.

Archbishop Wulfstan, the punctuation generally provides good evidence of how the author wished his texts to be construed.[24] Several of these manuscripts not only contain laws which are known to have been composed by Wulfstan, but they are also annotated in a hand which Neil Ker compellingly identified as that of the archbishop.[25] Some of these Wulfstanian annotations are punctuated using the same symbols as those employed in the main text, where the raised point (·), the *punctus eleuatus* (:) and the *punctus uersus* (;) all convey varying degrees of syntactic and rhetorical force. The pointing is often used rhetorically, dividing words and phrases into sense groups; the *punctus eleuatus* has a stronger rhetorical force, although it is also used syntactically (much as one might use a semi-colon today), and the *punctus uersus* always indicates a strong syntactic break, comparable with the modern full-stop. This manuscript punctuation has been largely neglected by editors; indeed Liebermann deliberately appears to have ignored it, dividing chapters not on the basis of manuscript evidence, but on purely subjective grounds. He also punctuated his texts in accordance with German (and not Old English) syntactic practice.[26]

Liebermann's treatment of the version of *VIII Atr.* contained in London, British Library, Cotton Nero A.i. offers a striking example of what can happen if one ignores manuscript punctuation altogether. This Nero manuscript is one of those closely associated with Wulfstan, and it bears annotations in what is probably the archbishop's own hand.[27] The only other version of *VIII Atr.* to survive is contained in Cambridge, Corpus Christi College 201, which also has connections with Wulfstan, and probably emanated from one of his two sees of York or Worcester.[28] The two versions of this code are in fairly close agreement up to clause 5.2, and from Liebermann's edition one might be forgiven for thinking that the Nero manuscript version of *VIII Atr.* ends after this clause, although this is not the case. In a note, Liebermann informed the reader that the last word of clause 5.2 (*mæðe*), and those immediately following, are 'kaum lesbar'; and if they were difficult to read when Liebermann used the manuscript, they are virtually impossible to decipher

---

[24] Wulfstan was Bishop of London (996–1002), Bishop of Worcester (1002–1016), and Archbishop of York (1002–1023).

[25] N.R. Ker, 'The handwriting of Archbishop Wulfstan', in *England before the Conquest. Studies in primary sources presented to Dorothy Whitelock*, edited by P. Clemoes and K. Hughes (Cambridge, 1971), pp. 315–32.

[26] For a discussion of the imposition of artificial systems of punctuation upon Old English texts, and of the problems created by ignoring manuscript punctuation, see B. Mitchell, 'The Dangers of Disguise: Old English Texts in Modern Punctuation', *RES* 31 (1980), 385–413. This essay is reproduced in Mitchell's selected papers, *On Old English* (Oxford, 1988), pp. 172–202, where he adds the following coda: 'To my regret, this paper seems to have sunk without a ripple in the ocean – or pond – of OE literary criticism.' Mitchell returned briefly to the question of punctuating Old English verse in an appendix to D. Donoghue and B. Mitchell, 'Parataxis and Hypotaxis: A Review of Some Terms Used for Old English Syntax', *Neuphilologische Mitteilungen* 93 (1992), 163–83.

[27] Ker, 'The handwriting of Archbishop Wulfstan', pp. 321–4.

[28] For a description of this manuscript, see Ker, *Catalogue*, no. 49, pp. 82–90.

now thanks to the dilute solution of sulphuric acid which was applied (at Liebermann's behest) to 'enhance' the readings.[29] Nowhere does Liebermann clearly indicate that a further nine lines of text occur in Cotton Nero A.i immediately after clause 5.2 – indeed he prints them in the *Gesetze* over two hundred pages later as an entirely separate tract which he called variously *Norðhymbra Cyricfrið* and *Norðhymbra Cyricgrið* (I shall use the latter form).

The first five chapters of *VIII Atr.* in both manuscripts pertain to church sanctuary (*cyricgrið*); indeed the version of *VIII Atr.* in the Nero manuscript is headed 'Be Cyricgriðe'. As the name suggests, the nine lines which Liebermann designated *Norðhymbra Cyricgrið* also concern sanctuary, referring specifically to churches in Northumbria including, most probably, the cathedral church of Saint Peter in York, Wulfstan's archiepiscopal see. If one examines the layout of this folio in the Nero manuscript (preferably using the British Library's video-spectral comparator to enhance the image using different types of light at varying intensities), one discovers that there is no textual justification for regarding *Norðhymbra Cyricgrið* as separate from *VIII Atr.* since the two are linked thematically, and the latter begins in the same way as preceding chapters with a shaded initial (a tironian *et* nota: see fig. 9, line 16). In this text the scribe frequently uses the tironian *et* nota (7) as more than a simple abbreviation for 'and'; indeed when enlarged it consistently indicates the beginning of a new chapter.[30] The scribe's methods are further clarified by the fact that such initials are always preceded by a *punctus uersus*. Furthermore, the scribe distinguished between clauses which introduce new subject-matter and those which merely elaborate on a previous chapter by shading in red the initials introducing new material. Shaded initials are not, however, used to mark the beginning of new texts. New texts in this part of the manuscript are always marked so that they are unmistakable. They invariably begin with a rubric, and, as Professor Loyn observed, the scribe generally employed 'heavy initials which intrude into the margin for the beginning of the law codes'.[31] Even from the facsimile, it is possible to ascertain with certainty that no such initial or rubric occurs on f. 96v.[32]

Thus, on both textual and contextual grounds, there is good reason to believe that *Norðhymbra Cyricgrið* forms part of a variant version of *VIII Atr.* This is important, for it provides further evidence of Wulfstan's penchant for redrafting the law-codes which he composed. The variant versions of this code are therefore comparable with the codes *V Atr.* and *VI Atr.*, which Schmid classified as two laws, but which in fact emanated from the same meeting of the *witan* at Enham in

---

[29] See Liebermann, ed., *Gesetze,* I, pp. 264 and 473.

[30] According to Professor Loyn, this scribe (S3) wrote ff. 70–96; see *A Wulfstan Manuscript containing Institutes, Laws and Homilies (British Museum Cotton Nero A.I)*, ed. H.R. Loyn, EEMF 17 (Copenhagen, 1971), p. 24.

[31] *Ibid.* p. 25.

[32] It is likely that this version of *VIII Atr.* is incomplete, and that several leaves are missing from the end of the quire. On this see Loyn, *Wulfstan Manuscript*, p. 23, and Ker, *Catalogue*, no. 164, p. 213.

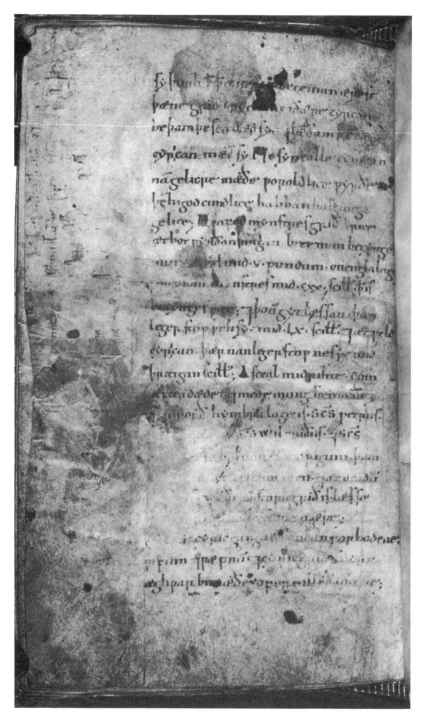

Fig. 9. *VIII Atr.* and the so-called *Norðhymbra Cyricgrið*

258

1008.[33] Kenneth Sisam, who discussed the relationship between these codes and the Latin paraphrase of *VI Atr.*, concluded that 'V Æthelred, in its original form, represents the laws approved for the English by the witan of 1008, whose chief draughtsman was Wulfstan', while the Latin and vernacular versions of *VI Atr.* are at different levels:[34]

> . . . promulgations of the same laws to clergymen by Wulfstan in his capacity as archbishop, with some explanations for their guidance, and some modifications of detail, not of policy, which he was authorized by the witan to make in his own province of York.

It is debatable whether Wulfstan was 'authorized' to issue these variant redactions, but, in any case, it appears that the Nero manuscript version of *VIII Atr.* provides further evidence of the above phenomenon described by Sisam. Thus, by analogy, Sisam's hypothesis about Wulfstan's methods of redaction is further substantiated.[35]

The other area in which Liebermann's *Gesetze* is particularly inadequate (indeed, on occasion, grossly misleading) is his division of clauses and their numeration; and once again these problems occur as a consequence of Liebermann's adherence to practices instituted by Schmid. Misdivision of clauses is a particularly common problem – in *Alfred-Ine* alone there are several instances where the numeration suggests a link between two pieces of law, although contextually they are clearly separate. For example, *Alf.* 9 prescribes the compensation payable for killing a pregnant woman, while the following clause, which Liebermann called *Alf.* 9.1, is about the proportion of fine (*wite*) to compensation. Although the clause numeration suggests that these two laws are related, the subject-matter is unambiguous, revealing that the latter is an entirely separate provision introducing new material. Neither *Alf.* 9.1, nor that which Schmid and Liebermann called *Alf.* 9.2, is related to the chapter about killing a pregnant woman (*Alf.* 9), although *Alf.* 9.2, which standardizes the fine payable for all types of theft except kidnapping, is certainly related to *Alf.* 9.1 (the more general stipulation about fines). Here the evidence of the manuscripts is unhelpful, for the only mark of punctuation used is the raised-point (and this is used sparingly), and the only initials are the 'G' of 'Gif mon' in *Alf.* 9 and 10.[36] The existence of rubrics relating to these two clauses suggests *prima facie* that Liebermann's numeration is correct; however, upon close examination, one discovers that the rubric list as a whole is less than adequate, for the rubrics generally fail to reflect the central concern of the laws which they

---

[33] See Liebermann, ed., *Gesetze*, III, p. 167; Cf. P. Wormald, 'Æthelred the Lawmaker', in *Ethelred the Unready. Papers from the Millenary Conference*, edited by D. Hill, BAR British series 59 (Oxford, 1978), pp. 47–80, at pp. 49–58.

[34] K. Sisam, *Studies in the History of Old English Literature* (Oxford, 1953), pp. 278–87, at. pp. 281–2.

[35] In his paper on Æthelred's laws, Patrick Wormald also endorsed Sisam's hypothesis: see 'Æthelred the Lawmaker', pp. 54–8.

[36] Liebermann, ed., *Gesetze*, I, p. 54.

purport to rubricate, and they often refer to sub-clauses while ignoring the main clause completely.[37] The division of the rubric list into 120 appears to be contrived (apparently for its symbolic value), and hence an editor cannot safely adopt the division when seeking to delineate the beginning of distinct chapters on the basis of manuscript evidence. When Liebermann came to write the third volume of his *Gesetze* (the 'Einleitung zu jedem Stück' and 'Erklärungen zu einzelnen Stellen'), he acknowledged the misleading nature of his numeration, and he pointed out that *Alf.* 9.1 and *Alf.* 9.2 are unrelated to *Alf.* 9.[38] From the reader's point of view, this is hardly satisfactory, since an irregular user of the *Gesetze* will rarely have the time, nor the tenacity, to search through all three volumes of Liebermann's gargantuan work, looking for relevant notes on a particular clause. In this instance, the problem is exacerbated by Liebermann's German translation, which fails to distinguish adequately between Old English *gield* meaning 'compensation' or 'money paid to a victim as recompense for a wrong' (*Alf.* 9) and Old English *wite* meaning 'fine' or 'money paid as a penalty' (*Alf.* 9.1). The former he translated into German as '[Wer]geld' (meaning '[man]price'), and the latter as 'Strafgeld' (meaning 'penalty-money').[39] In order to grasp the distinction between these two concepts, one requires a working knowledge of the difference between 'compensation' and 'fine' in Anglo-Saxon law; and to obtain the necessary enlightenment using the *Gesetze*, one is again forced to venture into the complex second and third volumes of the edition.

The central question, therefore, is how should an editor, coming to this material afresh, deal with the problem of clause division and numeration? There already exists a conventional method of describing the manuscripts, the law-codes, and the individual clauses contained therein; and to complicate matters, two of the most useful resources available to an editor of Old English material (the Toronto Concordance and Dictionary) adopt the numeration of Liebermann's *Gesetze*.[40] Furthermore, if an editor wishes to derive a base-text from the *Corpus of Old English in Machine-Readable Form*,[41] whether for editing purposes or to generate a specific concordance (perhaps as the basis of a glossary), one must either change all the numeration before doing so, or (like Liebermann) perpetuate Schmid's misleading interpretations. More significantly, if one changes the numeration one will immediately be out of step with all the other editions and secondary material published since 1858. The obvious solution, to re-number the clauses but cross-

---

[37] Cf. above, note 21.

[38] Liebermann, ed., *Gesetze*, III, p. 53. Although Liebermann was not particularly happy with Schmid's numeration, he maintained it for the sake of consistency with the secondary literature on the laws: 'Eine Änderung der Schmidschen Zählung hätte die Zitierung in der reichen Literatur unbrauchbar gemacht' (Liebermann, ed., *Gesetze*, III, p. 40).

[39] Liebermann, ed., *Gesetze*, I, p. 55.

[40] Antonette diPaulo Healey and Richard L. Venezky, eds, *A Microfiche Concordance to Old English*, Publications of the Dictionary of Old English 1 (Toronto, 1980) and Ashley Crandell Amos and Antonette diPaulo Healey *et. al.*, eds, *Dictionary of Old English* (Toronto, 1986–).

[41] On this, see Nancy Spiers and Lubo Cipin, 'The Catalogue Database of the Dictionary of Old English', *OEN* 25 (1991), 44–53.

reference to Liebermann's edition, is altogether too cumbersome, especially in an edition containing a glossary, where multiple clause references could be confusing to a reader. There is, it seems, no simple solution.

One of the perennial dilemmas facing any editor is the extent to which one should allow oneself to impose subjective judgement upon a text. One is forever seeking to maintain the precarious balance between innovation and showing a proper respect for the work of past generations, not least that of the author himself. The editorial history of the law-codes is a long and fascinating one, and there is no doubt that Felix Liebermann's edition represents one of the great editorial achievements of the nineteenth century in the field of medieval studies. Yet it would be wrong to call it 'definitive', nor should the editorial history of the laws be allowed to stop with Liebermann and his derivative successors. For although the Anglo-Saxon laws were first edited by William Lambarde in the sixteenth century, the study of England's pre-conquest legal history is still in its infancy. The material is intrinsically difficult, but its natural intractability is exacerbated by the presentation of the texts in the only reliable edition: that of Liebermann. As Maitland wrote of Liebermann's first volume in a review article:[42]

> It looks like the full score of an opera, and some time must be spent before we can master the manifold typographical devices which have been invented to save time and space. At first the editor seems to have a rooted objection to printing six consecutive words without a change of type; and the natural man sighs for the simplicity of a pianoforte arrangement.

The challenge facing scholars wishing to undertake fresh editions of this material is not to surpass Liebermann in erudition, although many of his conclusions are certainly dated and require substantial revision. Rather the primary objective must be to match his enviable accuracy, while presenting new texts and translations, for general use, in a more accessible form.[43]

---

[42] Maitland, 'The Laws of the Anglo-Saxons', p. 152.

[43] I should like to thank Simon Keynes, Michael Lapidge and Jürg Schwyter, of the Department of Anglo-Saxon, Norse and Celtic in the University of Cambridge, for their valuable comments upon an earlier draft of this paper.

HOW NOT TO EDIT GLOSSARIES

J.D. Pheifer

I

EVERY TEXT has its own problems for the would-be editor, but glossaries – lists of obscure or foreign words and phrases with their interpretations – present special difficulties with which editors trained in the techniques of nineteenth-century classical scholarship were ill-equipped to contend. Most medieval glossaries, including almost all the Anglo-Saxon ones, were compiled from other glossaries which belonged in turn to a tradition of commentary and lexicography that reached back into antiquity, so that the relationship of text and intertext is especially close and complex, and the tradition itself is an open one in which cross-fertilization took place regularly at every stage; moreover, words wrenched from their contexts are particularly vulnerable to corruption and more difficult to emend when corruption has taken place.

The lexicographical tradition began with the writings of Roman lexicographers such as Verrius Flaccus's *De verborum significatu*[1] (c. 10 BC), which reached the glossographers in Festus's early-second-century epitome.[2] and was progressively expanded by *glossae collectae*[3] extracted from the books read in schools, especially the Bible and the works of Vergil and Terence.[4] St Isidore of Seville (d. 636) is a key figure whose *Etymologies*[5] was a major source of Latin glossaries and thus provides a *terminus post quem*[6] for the medieval tradition, which began effectively with the Abstrusa/Abolita Glossary.[7]

---

[1] 'On the Meaning of Words'.

[2] Printed in *Glossaria latina* ('*GL*'), edd. W.M. Lindsay and others, 5 vols (Paris, 1926–31), IV, 93–467. Festus' text is fragmentary, but an epitome of it made by Paul the Deacon early in the ninth century supplies the bare bones of the rest. Cf. below, notes 18, 114, 120, 122, 129, 144.

[3] 'Collected glosses'. For the origin of the term see H. Bradshaw, 'Appendix containing an account of investigations among early Welsh, Breton, and Cornish manuscripts', *Collected Papers of Henry Bradshaw* (Cambridge, 1889), pp. 454–88, at 462.

[4] For examples see below, pp. 287, 293, 295–6, and notes 14, 18, 19, 20, 85, 102, 105, 114, 120, 129.

[5] *Isidori Hispalensis episcopi etymologiarum sive originum libri XX* ('*Etym.*'), ed. W.M. Lindsay, 2 vols (Oxford, 1910). See below, pp. 272, 279 and notes 18, 19, 51, 57, 58, 62, 75, 76, 85, 93, 94, 136.

[6] 'Limit after which' an era begins.

[7] Abbreviated 'Abstr.', 'Abol.' Printed in *Corpus glossariorum latinorum* ('*CGL*'), ed. G. Goetz, 7 vols (Leipzig, 1888–1923), IV, 3–198, and *GL* III. The entries quoted below are taken from *CGL*,

Abstrusa/Abolita, as its name implies, combines two alphabetical Latin glossaries that begin with the glosses *Abstrusa abscondita*[8] and *Abolita abstersa deleta*,[9] both arranged in *ab*-order (according to the first two letters of their headwords) in such a way that runs of Abolita glosses follow runs of Abstrusa glosses in each alphabetical sub-section.[10] It is important to note, however, that the older of the two Abstrusa/Abolita manuscripts, Vatican City, Biblioteca Apostolica Vaticana, lat. 3321, dates only from the mid eighth century,[11] at least half a century later than the two earliest manuscripts containing alphabetical Latin glossaries, St Gallen, Stiftsbibliothek 912[12] and Épinal, Bibliothèque Municipale 72(2),[13] of the end of the seventh or beginning of the eighth century, both of which contain entries that correspond to ones in Abstrusa and Abolita arranged in different order from Vatican 3321. St Gallen is an *ab*- (sometimes *abc*-) order glossary whose alphabetical sub-sections mingle Abstrusa and Abolita glosses with entries from other sources, e.g. its *Ab* sub-section:

201, 6   Abaso infirma domus : Abstr. AB7 *id.*
      7   Abest deest : Abol. AB24 *id.*
      8   Abit discedit : Abstr. AB9–10 Abiit discedit uel discessit (*v.l.* Abit discedit,
           Abiit discessit)
      10   Abemcat eradicat : Abstr. AV6 Auencat eradicat
      12   Abigat proicet minat : Abstr. AB33 Abigit minat uel expellit,
           50 Abicit proicet
      14   Abigeius qui tollerem aliena (*v.l.* tollit rem aut peculium alienum) : Abstr.
           AB17 Abigelus qui seducit seruum aū pecum alienum
      15   Abitudo abitus corporis uel uestitus : Abstr. AB43 Abitudo abitus corporis
           uel uestium
      29   Ab oris a finibus uel ab initiis : Abol. AB5 Ab oris a finibus *only*
      33   Aborrit dissonat discrepat : Abstr. AB28 Aborret discrepat
      37   Abusi male usi : Abstr. AB45 *id.*
      39   Abusitatiis minus instructus scientia : Abstr. AB14 Abusitatus . . . scientiam

which follows the spelling of the manuscripts, but the alphabetical section-numbers are taken from *GL*, which prints its two component glossaries separately in an edited text.

[8] 'Abstruse: hidden away'.
[9] 'Abolished: rubbed out, destroyed'.
[10] *CGL* prints the runs of Abolita glosses within square brackets. They can be distinguised from the Abstrusa glosses because the Abstrusa Glossary also survives independently.
[11] E.A. Lowe, *Codices latini antiquiores* ('*CLA*'), 11 vols and suppl. (Oxford, 1934–71), I, no. 15.
[12] *CLA* VII, nos. 967a; printed in *CGL* V, 337–401.
[13] *CLA* VI, no. 760; printed in *The Épinal Glossary, Latin and Old-English, of the Eighth Century* ed. H. Sweet, EETS os 79b (London, 1883), abbreviated 'Ép.'. For its date see now Malcolm Parkes in *The Épinal, Erfurt, Werden, and Corpus Glossaries*, edd. B. Bischoff, M. Budny, G. Harlow, M.B. Parkes and J.D. Pheifer, EEMF 22 (Copenhagen, 1988), pp. 15–16. Épinal glosses are cited below by their alphabetical section-numbers in A.K. Brown, 'The Épinal Glossary edited with Critical Commentary of the Vocabulary', 2 vols (unpubl. PhD dissertation, Stanford Univ., 1969), which are also used in EEMF 22. Between a quarter and a third are glossed wholly or partly in Old English.

40 Aboditur recusat : Abstr. AB12 Abutitur recusat aut contemnet uel aspernit, Abol. AB2 Abutitur contemnit

202, 3 Absono non simili sono : Abol. AB36 Absona . . . sono

4 Abdicat a re alienat : Abstr. AB2 Abdicat alienat uel respuit, Abol. AB1 Abdicat repudiat expellit aut alienat

5 Ablatum (*v.l.* Abditum) absconsum : Abstr. AB9 Abditum absconsum

8 Abluet emundat : Abbstr. AB27 Abluit mundat uel labat

9 Ablegatur condemnatur : Abstr. AB44 Ablegatus condemnatus

14 Abrogare lege tollere : Abstr. AB5 Abrogare legem tollere

15 Abstrusa abscondida : Abstr. AB1 Abstrusa abscondita

16 Abstemius subrius : Abstr. AB4 Abstemus sobrius

23 Abricum locus temperatiuus sine rigore : Abstr. AP4 Apricus locus temperatus sine vento[14]

Some pages of St Gallen 912 begin with a *littera nobilior*[15] whether or not it begins an alphabetical section, which suggests that it was copied from an exemplar written when this practice, common in the fourth and fifth centuries and occasional in the sixth and seventh, was still in use.[16] This argues the earliest possible date for the exemplar consistent with its use of Abstrusa and Abolita.

The most reasonable explanation of the different ordering of the glosses in

---

[14] St. Gallen 201, 6 'Infirmary (?): house of the sick'. See H.J. Thomson's note on Abstrusa AB7 (*GL* IV, 1). 7 'Is absent: is lacking'. 8 'Goes away: departs'. 10 'Weeds out: roots up'. Cf. Ép. A321 *aberuncat abstirpat* (below, p. 268). 12 'Went away: departed'. 13 'Drives off: casts out, drives (an animal) / drives (an animal), expells / casts out'. 14 'Cattle-thief: one who takes away another's property or wealth (in the form of cattle) / one who entices away another's slave or cattle' (*Dig.* XLVII. 14, 1 *abigeus*). 15 'Condition: state of one's body or clothing / or clothes' (Terence, *Eun.* 242). 29 'From the shores: from the borders or from the beginning' (Vergil, *Aen.* I. 1). 33 'Differs from: disagrees'. 37 'Abused: ill used'. 39 'Repeatedly abused: less trained in learning'. 40 'Abuses: accuses / accuses or disparages or spurns'. 202, 3 'Discordant: not a like sound'. 4 'Renounces: estranges from one's self, expels / estranges from ones's self or rejects / divorces, expels or estranges from one's self'. 5 'Removed / Put away: concealed'. 8 'washes off: cleans up / cleans or washes'. 9 'Banished: sentenced'. 14 'Repeal: annul a law'. 15 'Hidden away: concealed' (*Aen.* VI. 7). 16. 'Temperate: sober'. 17 'Departs from: is far away / is far away or ceases' (*Aen.* VII. 610; I. 192). 23 'Sunny spot: temperate region without severity / temperate region without wind'. (Unless otherwise indicated, titles of sources in this note and those that follow are taken from C.T. Lewis and C. Short, *A Latin Dictionary*, Oxford, 1879.)

[15] 'More distinguished letter', i.e. a capital.

[16] Cf. E.A. Lowe, 'Some facts about our oldest Latin manuscripts', *Classical Quarterly* 19 (1925), 197–208, at 202–5; 'More facts about our oldest Latin manuscripts', *Classical Quarterly* 22 (1928), at 56–7. *Litterae nobiliores* which do not begin an alphabetical section are shown in the photographs that accompany Lowe's nos. 968, 969 and 972 (second photograph); cf. St Gallen 203, 49, 216, 10, and 287, 47. Lowe's references to St Gallen 912 in 'More facts', pp. 46 and 56, do not affect the argument here, since St Gallen 912 is a palimpsest and he refers to one of the sub-texts, a fifth-century text of the Old Latin version of Jeremiah (*CLA*, no. 971), in which a *littera nobilior* begins every page; one can be seen in Lowe's photograph. The rough draft of the glossary which forms an intermediate text on pp. 271–8 (*CLA*, no. 972) may indicate that the alphabetical ordering of the main text, which differs from that of the other manuscript of the glossary, Milan, Biblioteca Ambrosiana, B. 31 sup. (*CGL* IV, xvi), was carried out in the same scriptorium.

Abstrusa/Abolita and St Gallen is that the compiler of the latter took them from a source in which they had not yet been reduced to *ab*-order. If that is the case, St Gallen is presumably a witness to the text of Abstrusa and Abolita at an earlier stage than that represented by Vatican 3321. The same applies to the Épinal Glossary, the bulk of whose alphabetical sections are arranged in *a*-order (according to the first letter only of their headwords) and contain sequences of Abstrusa and Abolita glosses mixed with other glosses,[17] some of which are also found in St Gallen, e.g. its *A* section:

A40   Aulea strel uel curtina ab aula : Abol. AU20 Aulea cortina regia,
           St Gallen 209, 37 Auleum et aulea straclum genus cortin regalis

A42   Acerra arca turis : Abstr. AC23 Acerra arca turaria, St Gallen 202,
           40 Acersa arcula toreania

A53   Assellum spolium : Abstr. AS10 Aslum spolium

A55   Aurifodina matçllum : St Gallen 209, 35 Aurifodina metallum

A56   Artefta genus uassis : Abstr. AR45 Arcepta genus uasis ut pigella

A57   Aquilium fuscum uel subnigrum : Abol. AQ1 Aquilum fuscum
           subnigrum, St Gallen 208, 26 Aquilum fuscum nigrum

A61   Aneatores tubicines : Abstr. AE25 *id.*, St Gallen 204, 13 Aenenitores
           tubicines

A62   Alogia conuiuium : Abstr. AL45 Alogia connubia, St Gallen 205,
           25 Alogia conuiuium grece

A63   Apodixis probatio uel exemplum : St Gallen 207, 13 Apodixin ostensio
           prouatio uel exemplum

A64   Archia initium : Abstr. AR46 Archia initium grece

A65   Apoliterium ubi ponuntur res labentium : Abstr. AP14 Apoliterium ubi
           reponuntur res labantio

A91   Adsaecula cliens : Abol. AD84 Adsaecula cliens uel susceptus

A92   Agasson minister officialis: St Gallen 204, 49 Agason minister officialis

A93   Amandat commendat : Abstr. AM2 Amendat effugiat aut longe mittit uel
           extra commendat

A94   Alluuies locus cenosus : Abol. AD69 Adlubies locus scenosus uel
           obscurum

A96   Ascenior inhonestum : St Gallen 208, 29 Ascemo inunestus

A99   Aedes aedificiam urbana : Abol. AE20 Aedes aedificia *only*

A108   Arepticius furiosus : St Gallen 202, 2 abrepticius furiosus

A109   Aria terra que aratur : Abstr. AR25 Arua terra *only*, St Gallen 207,
           39 Arua terra agrs et semenibus apta

A111   Ambulacrum spatium ambulandi : Abol. AM10 Amblacum spatium ad
           ambulandum

A112   Allux pollux in pede : St Gallen 205, 28 Alux pollex in pede

A113   Arcistis sagittaris : Abol. AR28 Arcistes sagittius

---

[17] W.M. Lindsay, *The Corpus, Épinal, Erfurt and Leyden Glossaries*, Publ. of the Philol. Soc. 8 (London, 1921), pp. 38–43. Glosses with wholly vernacular interpretations in Épinal are omitted.

A114   Amfariam pro ambabus partibus : Abstr. AM23 Ambigariae ex amrabus
           partibus

A115   Accape audi : Abol. AC13 Accipe audi

A118   Abacta inuiolata : St Gallen 201, 3 Abacta immolata

A122   Adstipulatus adiutus : St Gallen 203, 30 Astipulatus adiucntus

A122   Aestuca calor : St Gallen 203, 45 Aestus calor

A123   Ambrones deuoratores : Abol. AM6 *id.*

A124   Amfrite mare : Abol. AM14 Amfitrite mare

A125   Aplestia crapula : St Gallen 207, 11 Aplistia saturitas crapulat

A260   Actio puplica uenditi : St Gallen 209, 45 Autio puplica uinditio

A265   Affecta attenuata : Abol. AF6 Affecta addicta uel adtenuata

A299   Abnepus qui natus de pronepote : St Gallen 202, 12 Abnenepus qi
           nascitur de pronepote

A300   Accedeatur stomchatur : Abstr. AC39 Acidiatur stomachatur,
           St Gallen 202, 45 *id.*

A301   Adniue adiunge : Abol. AD56 Adhibe iunge

A302   Alligorit degustat : Abstr. AL23 Allegurrit degustat

A311   Asotus luxoriosus : Abstr. AS13 Asotus luxuriosus, St Gallen 208, 316 *id.*

A312   Ageatur hortatur : Abstr. AE2l6 Aegeator hornator, Abol. *post* AE6 Ageator
           hortator

A313   Agonantes explicantes : Abstr. AG14 Aginantes explicantes

A314   Acedia tedium : Abstr. AC5 Accidiam tedium animae, St Gallen 202,
           48 Acidia tędium animi

A315   Abaso infuna domus : Abstr. AB7 Abaso infirma domus, St Gallen 201,
           6 *id.*

A316   Acroceria ligator articulorum : Abstr. AC2 Acrocheria ligatura articulorum,
           St Gallen 203, 5 Acroceria ligatura articolorum

A317   Ambhibalus hircus bellosus : Abstr. AM19 Ambibalus birrus billosus,
           Abol. *post* AN22a Anfibulum birrum[18]

---

[18] Ép. A40 'Tapestries: bedspread or hanging, from "court" / regal hanging / Tapestry and tapestries: bedspread, species of regal hanging' (Vergil, *Aen.* I. 697; *Geo.* III. 25). Cf. Ép. A259
Auleum curtina ab aula. OE. *stræ(g)l* apparently translates *stragulum.* 42 'Incense-box: box for
incense' (*Aen.* V. 745). 53 'Asylum: spoil'. The glossator has confused ἄσυλον 'sanctuary' and
σῦλον (pl.) 'booty'. 55 'Gold-mine: mine' (*Dig.* III. 4, 1). 56 'Baking-tin: species of vessel /
species of vessel like a kettle' (Plautus, *Aul.* 400). 57. 'Dark-coloured: dusky or blackish / dusky,
blackish / dusky, black' (Festus 20, 7). 'Brass-players: trumpeters'. 62 'Luxurious feast: dinner-
party'. 63 'Demonstration: proof or example / showing, proof or example'. 64 'Beginning:
commencement'. The glossator or a scribe has confused ἀρχή 'beginning, rule' and the second
element of compounds such as μοναρχία 'monarchy'. 65 'Changing-room: where bathers'
things are put / where bathers' baggage is stored / where things are put, washing (*lavatio*)' (*Etym.*
XV. 2, 41 *Apodyterium ubi lavantium vestimenta* ('clothes') *ponuntur*). 91 'Follower: dependent
/ dependent or person taken under one's protection'. 92 'Equerry: magistrate's attendant'. 93
'Sends away: entrusts to / puts to flight (*effugat*) or sends far or sends abroad for protection'. See
Thomson's note on Abstrusa AM2 (*GL* IV. 9). 94 'Swamp: muddy place / muddy place or
obscurity'. 99 'House: building in the city' (Terence, *Phorm.* 753). 108 'Possessed: demented'.
109 'Tillage: land which is ploughed / land, fields (*agri*) and places (sc. *loca*) suitable for
sowing'. 111 'Gallery: area for walking / area to walk in' (Vulg. III Reg. 7: 2 *deambulacrum*).
112 'Big toe: thumb on the foot' (Festus 7, 21 *allus pollex pedis*). 113 'Archer: bowman' (Festus

The value of Épinal and St Gallen to potential editors can be judged from A42, 62, 65, 99 and 111.

In most alphabetical sections of Épinal the *a*-order glosses are followed by a substantial number of entries in *ab*-order which also contain Abstrusa, Abolita and St Gallen glosses in a different order from that of Abstrusa/Abolita or St Gallen, e.g. under *Ab*:

A321   Aberuncat abstirpat : St Gallen 201, 9 Aberunca abstirpat

A324   Abristit loNge est : Abstr. AB6 Absistit longe est uel desinit, St Gallen 202, 17 Absistit loge est *only*

A325   Abactus ab actu remotus : Abstr. AB3 Abactus ab acto remotus, St Gallen 201, 4 *id.*

A326   Abaro infirma domus : Abstr. AB7 Abaso infirma domus, St Gallen 201, 6 *id.*

A327   Abigelus qui tollit seruum aut pecus alienum : Abstr. AB17 Abigelus qui seducit seruum aū pecum alienum, St Gallen 201, 14 Abigeius qui tolle rem aliena

A328   Abcesit uocat : Abstr. AR31 Arcessit uocat

A329   Abolere neglegenter agere uel obliuisci : Abol. AB14 Abolere obliuisci neglegere

A330   Abstenus sobrius : Abstr. AB4 Abstemus sobrius, St Gallen 202, 16 Abstemius subrius

A331   Abusitatus minus instructus in scientia : Abstr. AB14 Abusitatus minus instructus scientia, St Gallen 201, 39 *id.*

A337   Abtet uos impleat uos : St Gallen 207, 4 Aptet impleat

A338   Abtemus abiungemus : St Gallen 207, 6 Aptamus adiungimus

A341   Abicies turba : St Gallen 202, 46 Acie turba

A342   Abacta inuolata : St Gallen 201, 3 Abacta immolata[19]

19, 10). 114 'Ambiguously: for both sides / on both sides'. 115 'Listen: hear'. 118 'Driven away: carried off' (*Aen.* VIII. 407 *inuolata*). 119 'Joined with in a stipulation: bound to' (Gaius, *Inst.* III. 112). 122 'Boiling: heat'. 123 'Gluttons: devourers' (Festus 15, 29). 124 'Amphitrite: sea' (Ovid, *Met.* I. 14). 125 'Insatiable greed (ἀπληστία)7): drunkenness / fullness, drunkenness'. 260 'Auction: public sale'. 265 'Weakened: reduced / reduced or diminished' (Festus 2, 21 *adfecta . . . adducta*). 299 'Great-great-grandson: one who (*qui*) is born of a great-grandson'. 300 'Becomes tired of: becomes annoyed with'. 301 'Unite with: join to / join' (*Aen.* VIII. 56 *adhibe . . . iunge*). 302 'Licks away / takes a taste of' (*Eun.* 235 *abligurrierat*). 311 'Profligate: extravagant'. 312 'Coxswain: encourager'. See Thomson's note on Abstrusa AE26 (*GL* IV. 6). 313 'Small dealers: those who settle things'. 314 'Sloth: weariness / weariness of soul / weariness of mind'. 315 'Infirmary (?): house of the sick'. 316 'Wrestling with hands (ἀχροχειρία): twisting knuckles'. 317 'Woolly both sides (ἀμθίμαλλος): shaggy cloak'. On the entry that follows Abolita AN22a see below, note 109.

[19] Ép. A321 'Weeds thoroughly: uproots'. 324 Departs from: is far away / is far away or ceases' (*Aen.* VII. 610; I. 192). 325 'Dismissed: removed from authority' (*Etym.* X. 20). 326 'Infirmary (?): house of the sick'. 327 'Cattle-thief: one who takes away another's property or wealth (in the form of cattle) / one who entices away another's slave or cattle / one who takes away another's property' (*Dig.* XLVII. 14, 1). 328 'Summon: call'. 329 'Efface; treat carelessly or forget / forget, neglect'. Cf. St Gallen 201, 26 *Abolere de memoria excludere* and *Aen.* 1. 720, IV. 497. 330 'Temperate: sober'. '331 'Repeatedly abused; less trained in learning'. 337. 'Fit you out;

If the compiler of Épinal had access to Abstrusa and Abolita in *a*-order, and also to an early *ab*-order glossary similar to but not identical with St Gallen, it is doubly important as a witness to the pre-history of Abstrusa/Abolita,[20] and wise editors will treat 'extract-glossaries'[21] like Épinal and St Gallen with the respect they deserve. But, alas, the history of modern glossology is for the most part a sad tale of their failure to do so.

II

Latin glossaries, both bilingual and all-Latin, were originally designed to teach Latin, but the bilingual ones have long been used inversely by students of the Germanic and Celtic languages to explain the glosses themselves. The first printed Old English dictionary, William Somner's *Dictionarium Saxonico-Latino-Anglicum* (1659), drew heavily on Latin-Old English glossaries, and early modern glossary users were only interested in vernacular interpretations. The first modern edition of an Anglo-Saxon glossary, F.J. Mone's text of the Épinal Glossary (1838),[22] gave only the Latin-Old English glosses, while the second, Friedrich Oehler's text of the Erfurt glossaries (1847),[23] omitted some all-Latin entries in Erfurt I and heavily abridged those in Erfurt II and III. The earliest modern editions of all-Latin glossaries were two texts of the Placidus Glosses and anonymous extracts from other glossaries in the Vatican Library published by the librarian, Angelo Mai, in the 1830s,[24] but the scientific study of glossaries in their own right

---

bring you to the full' (Heb. 13: 21). 338. 'Let us fit: let us join to'. 341 'Troop (*acie*): crowd' (*Aen.* XI. 498 *acie*). 342. 'Driven away: carried off' (*Aen.* VIII. 407).

[20] Another such witness is the fragmentary Arma Glossary (Leiden, Bibliotheek der Rijksuniversiteit, Bibl. Publ Lat. 67F, fols 119–28; printed in *GL* II, 1–22), which consists of *glossae collectae* from Vergil, Terence, Lucan, Prudentius and Abstrusa/Abolita in *a*-order.

[21] A term coined by W.M. Lindsay: 'This St. Gall Glossary (Sangall.) is of a type which prevailed from the Carolingian Revival of Learning, the extract glossary; for it offers us not Philox. [the Graeco-Latin Philoxenus Glossary (see below, note 29), another source of St Gallen] and Abstr.-Abol. fully transcribed, but merely selections from the pair. The compiler selects now an item from one, now an item from the other, and often blends his two authorities into a composite item or re-casts the words of the one to suit the words of the other' ('The Affatim Glossary and others', *Classical Quarterly* 11 (1917), 185–200, at 185).

[22] *Anzeiger für kunde der teutschen Vorzeit* 7 (1838), 134–53.

[23] *Neue Jahrbücher für Philologie*, Supplementband 13 (1847), 257–97, 325–87. The three Erfurt glossaries (Erfurt, Wissenschaftliche Bibliothek, Amplonianus 2° 42, 1ra–14va, 14va–34vc, 34vc–37vc) are printed (in reverse order) in *CGL* II, 563–84 and V, 259–401. Erfurt I ('Erf. 1'), printed in *CGL* V, 337–401, is an independent copy of the glossary in Épinal 72 which Goetz collates with it in his apparatus; it supplies the gaps in Épinal between C248 and F1 and from U116 to the end of the glossary. Amplonianus 42 was copied between 799 and 819 by a Cologne Cathedral scribe (Bischoff, EEMF 22, 18–19) from an Anglo-Saxon manuscript written about 750, to judge from the spelling of the Old English glosses (H.M. Chadwick, 'Studies in Old English', *Transactions of the Cambridge Philological Society* IV (1899), pp. 85–265, at 249).

[24] *Classici auctores e Vaticanis codicibus*, ed. A. Maius, 10 vols (Rome, 1828–38), III, 427–503, VI, 501–600, VIII, 1–632. For the Placidus Glosses see further below, note 79.

began with German scholars of the next generation and led to Gustav Loewe's *Prodromus corporis glossariorum latinorum*[25] (Leipzig, 1876), a systematic account of the Latin glossaries and their relationships, which set the guide-lines for subsequent research and is still useful today. The first two critical editions of Latin glossaries were Loewe's posthumous *Glossae nominum*[26] (Leipzig, 1884), a full text of the fragmentary third Erfurt glossary[27] and another fragment of the same glossary from Werden,[28] with full collations to demonstrate its affinity to the Graeco-Latin Cyrillus and Philoxenus glossaries,[29] and the American Minton Warren's edition of the St Gallen Glossary, which appeared in the same year and introduced the English-speaking world to Loewe's work.[30] Loewe's and Warren's editions made a promising start that was followed by the *Corpus glossariorum latinorum*[31] Loewe had projected. This monumental edition, which was edited by Loewe's pupil Georg Goetz in a series of volumes that appeared at intervals between 1888 and 1923, gives semi-diplomatic texts of the most important Latin and Graeco-Latin glossaries, including Abstrusa/Abolita, St Gallen and the three Erfurt glossaries, with a collation of Épinal,[32] and extracts from many others; there is no commentary, but vols VI and VII, the *Thesaurus glossarum emendatarum*,[33] are still an essential tool for editors of Latin glossaries.[34] Volume I, *De glossariorum latinorum origine et fatis*,[35] which was published last, brings Loewe's pioneer work up to date, with a supplement by Paul Wessner that takes account of publications by W.M. Lindsay and his pupils down to 1921.

Wallace Martin Lindsay, sometime Professor of Humanity in the University of

---

[25] 'Precursor to the Corpus of Latin Glossaries'.

[26] 'Glosses of Nouns'.

[27] *CGL* II, 563–84.

[28] Düsseldorf, Universitätsbibliothek, Fragm. K19: Z9/1; discovered in the Werden Pfarrhof by Ferdinand Deycks, who printed it in *Index lectionum auspiciis augustissimi et potentissimi regis Friderici Guilelmi IV. in academia theologica et philosophica Monasteriensi per menses hibernos A. MDCCCLIV–V. inde a die XV. mensis Octobris publice privatimque habendarum* (1854–5), 3–19. This fragment was deemed to be lost from Deycks's death in 1867 until it was identified by the late Professor Bischoff and reproduced with the other surviving fragments of the Werden Glossary (a cognate of Erfurt II and III) in EEMF 22. Its relationship with Erfurt III was demonstrated by Loewe in his *Prodromus*, pp. 126–7. Parkes believes that the manuscript to which these fragments belonged was written at Werden about the same time as Erfurt (EEMF 22, 22).

[29] London, British Library, Harley 5792, 1v–240v, and Paris, Bibliothèque Nationale, lat. 7651. The Cyrillus Glossary is printed in *CGL* II, 215–483, the Philoxenus Glossary in *CGL* II, 3–212 and *GL* II, 138–291.

[30] 'On Latin glossaries, with especial reference to the Codex Sangallensis 912', *Transactions of the American Philological Asssociation* 15 (1884), 124–228.

[31] 'Body of Latin Glossaries'. See above, note 7.

[32] See above, notes 7, 12, 13, and 23.

[33] 'Dictionary of Corrected Glosses'.

[34] 'Goetz in his Thesaurus Glossarum Emendatarum has provided an apparatus criticus for editing Latin glosses', as Lindsay rightly observed ('The St. Gall Glossary', *American Journal of Philology* 38 (1917), 349–69, at 349).

[35] 'On the Origin and History of Latin Glossaries'.

St Andrews, was one of the giants who walked the earth in that golden age of classical scholarhip; he came to the study of glossaries comparatively late by way of Latin and Celtic philology, but his memorable series of articles, published in classical journals from 1916 onwards, which he regarded as his war-work,[36] revolutionized glossology. This new-found interest led to publication on a larger scale after the War, first to his monograph on the Corpus, Épinal, Erfurt and Leiden glossaries[37] and his edition of the Corpus Glossary,[38] and then to *Glossaria latina*,[39] another multi-volume edition of Latin glossaries, including several in Goetz's collection, which he edited with his pupils.[40] *Glossaria latina* and Lindsay's edition of Corpus differ from Goetz's *Corpus glossariorum* and the earlier edition of Corpus by the Dutch scholar J.H. Hessels[41] in being critical editions which attempt to trace the glossaries' sources and in some cases to reconstruct, as far as possible, their hypothetical archetypes. Lindsay's great contribution to the study of the English glossaries was to place them in the context of the Latin glossographical tradition, to which they themselves are early and important witnesses, and to clarify their relationship with the *glossae collectae* of the Leiden Glossary (Leiden, Bibliotheek der Rijksuniversiteit, Voss. lat. Q. 69, 20ra–36ra), which had already been edited by Hessels in a diplomatic text with a full index of sources and parallels in Épinal/Erfurt I, Erfurt II and Corpus.[42] Since the Leiden *glossae collectae* and related collections are the best surviving witnesses to the 'new learning' brought to England by Archbishop Theodore and Abbot Hadrian after the Synod of Whitby, as Professor Lapidge has recently shown,[43] Lindsay's study placed Épinal, Erfurt and Corpus at the very centre of the first flowering of English scholarship, although he himself was not aware of it.[44]

---

[36] H.J. Rose, 'Wallace Martin Lindsay, 1858–1937' (*PBA* 23 (1937), 487–512, at 498. Rose prints Lindsay's own bibliography of his publications (*ibid.* pp. 507–12). Wessner also lists English publications on glossaries by Lindsay and his pupils from 1916 to 1921 (*CGL* I, 310–11).

[37] See above, note 17.

[38] *The Corpus Glossary*, ed. W.M. Lindsay (Cambridge, 1921) ('Cp.'). Strictly, this is an edition of the second glossary in Cambridge, Corpus Christi College 144 (4r–64v), which is preceded by a brief Bible-name glossary (1r–3v), headed *Interpretatio nominum ebraicorum et grecorum* ('Cp. Int.'). For the latter see below, note 41.

[39] 'Latin Glossaries'. See above, note 2.

[40] According to Lindsay's preface to *CL* V (p. 5) a further volume containing Épinal/Erfurt I and Erfurt II, edited by J.R. Mills, remained unpublished for financial reasons and was deposited with the editors of the *Medieval Latin Dictionary*. It cannot now be traced.

[41] *An Eighth-Century Latin-Anglo-Saxon Glossary preserved in the Library of Corpus Christi College, Cambridge*, ed. J.H. Hessels (Cambridge, 1906). Quotations below are taken from this edition and referred to by Hessels's alphabetical-section numbers, also used by Lindsay and EEMF 22. It includes the Bible-name glosses mentioned in note 38 (pp. 3–8), which are referred to below by the alphabetical section-numbers used in EEMF 22.

[42] *A Late Eighth-Century Latin-Anglo-Saxon Glossary preserved in the Library of the Leiden University*, ed. J.H. Hessels (Cambridge, 1890).

[43] M. Lapidge, 'The School of Theodore and Hadrian', *ASE* 15 (1986), 45–72, at 57–67.

[44] Cf. J.D. Pheifer, 'Early Anglo-Saxon glossaries and the school of Canterbury', *ASE* 16 (1987), 17–44, at 33–4, 41.

III

Sad to say, comparatively little new work has been done in this field since Lindsay's death more than fifty years ago, possibly because it was felt that he and Goetz between them had left little to be done, which is by no means true. Advances in palaeography have produced new evidence for dating and localizing early manuscripts, as Malcolm Parkes and Professor Bischoff have recently shown,[45] and Goetz's and Lindsay's editorial techniques have proved to be unsatisfactory in some respects. Goetz followed the old-fashioned practice of printing only extracts of less important glossaries with unfortunate results, as can be seen in the strange case of the Auxilius Glossary. There are two rival claimants to this ambiguous title, one a relatively short glossary in Vatican City, Biblioteca Apostolica Vaticana, lat. 1469, 223v–271v, and the other a much longer one in Monte Cassino, Archivio della Badia 90 (earlier 29), with virtually the same title and first entry. The latter was identified by the Vatican librarian, Cardinal Mai, who describes his visit to Monte Cassino, where 'several outstanding manuscripts',[46] among them Codex 29, 'a huge Latin dictionary by Auxilius the priest',[47] were shown to him by the librarian, Ottavio Frangipani,[48] Subsequently, in 1843, he published two of the Vatican 1469 Auxilius glosses in his *Glossarium novum latinitatis*:[49]

> Plaustrum, i. Auxilius in glossis mss. Plaustulum diminutivum est a plaustro [249ra]

> Pulicinus minus siccus est, ventrem procurat (Refertur, puto, ad herbam puliciariam). Auxilius in glossis mss. [248ra][50]

The identification was called into question in 1875, however, when the anonymous editors of the Monte Cassino catalogue quoted Mai's letter of December 1843, in which he says that the Monte Cassino 90 Auxilius glosses 'agree with the Vatican manuscript which bears the same title, almost all extracted from St Isidore',[51] and express their surprise:

---

45 See above, notes 13 and 23.

46 *non pauci insignes codices.*

47 *Auxilii presbyteri lexicon ingens latinitatis.*

48 *Scriptorum veterum nova collectio e Vaticanis codicibus* 'A New Collection of Old Authors from Vatican Manuscripts', ed. A. Maius, 10 vols (Rome, 1825–38), III.2, 163.

49 'New Latin Glossary' (*Spicilegium romanum* 'A Roman Gleaning', ed. A. Maius, 10 vols (Rome, 1839–44), IX.3).

50 (1) '*Plaustrum*, that is, Auxilius in his manuscript glossary: *plaustulum* is the diminutive of cart' (p. 52). (2) '*Pulicinus* is less dry, it takes care of the stomach (reference is made, I believe, to the herb flea-wort). Auxilius in his manuscript glossary' (p. 56).

51 *concordare cum Codice Vaticano eodem titulo inscripto, a S. Isidoro fere totum excerpto.* Cf. Mai's manuscript note below the title of the Vatican 1469 Auxilius Glossary (223vb): *Cuncta fere ex Isidoro A. Maius* 'Almost all from Isidore – A. Mai'.

But we marvel that the distinguished gentleman came to such a conclusion, since it is clear beyond a doubt that the beginning of the Vatican *Etymologies*, which is quoted from it in his *Roman Gleaning*, differs entirely from the Cassino one, and that nothing has been found in the latter that one might recognize as taken from Isidore. Perhaps Auxilius' *Etymologies* has not yet come to light.[52]

This should have set alarm bells ringing, but Goetz, although he cites the *Bibliotheca* entry in his introduction to *CGL* IV, still speaks of the 'riches of Auxilius the priest'[53] as a single entity, and his brief mention of Monte Cassino 90 in *CGL* I adds nothing new:[54] his promised treatment of the entries peculiar to Monte Cassino 90 never appeared. Lindsay fell into the same trap when he attempted 'to strip *Cass*.90 of its borrowed plumes' after Lowe redated it in the eleventh century,[55] assuming that Vatican 1469 was an older manuscript of the same glossary.[56]

In fact, the Monte Cassino cataloguers were nearer the truth when they denied that there was any connection between the two so-called Auxilius glossaries, as a brief collation will show:

---

[52] *Sed miramur, virum cl<arissimum> in talem ivisse sententiam cum extra dubitationem perspectum sit, initium* Ethimologicon *Vaticani, ab eo in suo* Spicilegio Romano *exhibitum, omnino a casinensi differe, et nihil in eo deprehendisse, quod ab Isidoro ablatum agnoscatur. Forte Auxilii* Etymologicon *lucem adhuc expectat* (Bibliotheca Casinensis, 5 vols (Monte Cassino, 1873–94), II, 324). The writer evidently refers to the long glosses on *Anima* and Adam printed below (pp. 274–5), but I have not located the Vatican gloss in Mai's *Spicilegium* or elsewhere in his volumnious publications.

[53] *copiae Auxilii presbyteri* (p. xviii).

[54] *CGL* IV, xviii–xix; I, 146.

[55] E.A. Lowe, *The Beneventan Script* ('*Script*') (Oxford, 1914), 2nd edn rev. V. Brown, Sussidi Eruditi 33 (Rome, 1980), I, 343, II, 64.

[56] 'The Festus Glosses in a Monte Cassino MS. (No. 90)', *Classical Review* 31 (1917), 130–2, at 130.

MONTE CASSINO 90[57]

Incipiunt Flosculi ethimolog\<or>um
breuiter ablati ab auxilio presbytero.
[p. 1]

ALFA ET Ω. quia nulla littera ante A.
Nulla post Ω. Ita et x̄p̄s primus quia
ante eum nichil est. et post eum nichil.
Nouissimus autem. quia iudicium
nouissimum ipse suscipiet.

NOTA augustinum. Adam nomen uero
illius per quattuor litteras sciebatur.
apud grecos. et alfa. delta. alfa. et my.;
Alfa. apud illos exprimitur unum. delta
quattuor. Alfa unum. my quadraginta.
Qui numeri simul coniuncti fiunt
quadraginta sex. Et infans. tot diebus
formatur in utero materno.; dominus
quidem similiter tot diebus formatus
est. Ideo iudęis dicebat. solui templum
hoc et in triduo excitabo illud. et iudęi
ęcontra. quadraginta et sex annis
edificatum est templum hoc. et tu tribus
diebus illud reedificas. Etiam et apud
grecos per has litteras. quattuor partes
mundi comprehendunt. Oriens.
Occidens. Meridies. et septentrio. quod
nos oriens illi dicunt anatolé. quod nos
occidens. illud dysis. quod nos
septentrionem illi arctos. quod nos
meridiem. illi mesembria. Quia iste
adam secatus per membra sua dilatus
est. per quattuor partes mundi. de
quibus psalmographus. in omnem

VATICAN CITY 1469[58]

In x̄p̄o nomine incipiunt flosculi ex
etymologiis breuiter ablati[s] ab auxilio
PRESBITERO. [223vab]

ALFA ET Ω. quia nulla littera ante a nulla
post o. ita et x̄p̄s. primus quia ante eum
nichil est. et post eum nihil. Nouissimus
autem. quia iudicium nouissimum ipse
suscipiet.

Angeli grece. nuntii qui etiam picti
uidentur pennas pro celeritate. [223vb]

Anima. a gentilibus dicta. quod quasi
uentus sit. Animos grece. uentus dicitur.
quod ore trahentes aerem uiuere
uideamur. sed falsum est. quia multo
prius gignitur anima. quam concipi aer
ore possit. hęc etiam in genitricis utero
uiuit. Sed hoc illi putauerunt. qui enim
incorpoream non potuerunt. Spiritum
idem esse euangelista confirmat dicens.
potestatem habeo ponendi animam
meam. et iterum summendi eam. Et
postmodum scripsit. inclinato capite
emisit spiritum. Anima dicta. quod
animet. idest uiuificet corpus. Spiritus
autem. uel quod spiret in corpore. Item
animum idem esse quod animam. sed
anima uita\<e> est. animus. consilii.
Unde et dicunt philosophi. etiam sine
animo uitam manere. Et sine mente
animam durare. unde et amentes. Nam
mentem uocari. ut sciat animam. ut

---

[57] 'Here begin little flowers of etymologies briefly extracted by Auxilius the priest'.

'Alpha and Omega: because no letter is before alpha and none after omega. So Christ is both first, because there is nothing before him and nothing after him. But he is indeed last because he will take upon him the Last Judgment' (*Glossa Ordinaria*, marginal gloss on Rev. 1: 8).

'Cf. Augustine: The name Adam was understood by its four letters in Greek: alpha, delta, alpha and mu. With the Greeks alpha stands for "one", delta "four", mu "forty". These numbers added up make forty-six. And an infant is formed for so

[58] 'Here begin in Christ's name little flowers of etymologies briefly extracted by Auxilius the priest'.

'Alpha and Omega: because no letter is before A and none after O. So Christ is both first, because there is nothing before him and nothing after him. But he is indeed last because he will take upon himself the Last Judgment' (*Glossa Ordinaria*, marginal gloss on Rev. 1: 8).

'Angels: in Greek "messengers" (*Etym.* VII. 5, 1), who are seen painted with wings (*cum pennis*) to signify swiftness'.

'Soul: so called by the gentiles because it is a wind as it were. Wind is called ἄνεμος in

terram exiuit sonus eorum. et in fines orbis terrę uerba eorum. Et illud. non sunt loquelle neque sermones quorum non audientur uoces eorum. Sciendum itaque est. quia non solum in adam aut in litteras eius nominis salus nostra signatur uerum etiam et in uerbis eius salus nostra est tinetur. quibus dicitur. Quam ob rem. Relinquet homo patrem et matrem. et adherebit uxori suę. et erunt duo in carnem unam. Reliquid namque patrem dei filius. quando uerbum caro factum est. Unde aptus semetipsum exinanauit formam serui accipiens. Et matrem idest synagogam. Cui dicebat ecce relinquetur uobis domus uestra deserta. Adhereuit uxori. etceterę scilicet ex gentibus. Erunt duo in carne una. quia ubi caput. illuc sequentur et membra. Relinquet homo patrem et matrem. Non quia filius reliquid patrem et recessit ab eo. sed quia non in ea forma apparuit hominibus. qua equalis est patri.

uelit. Mens autem uocata. quod emineat in anima. uel quod meminit. unde immemores. amentes. Quapropter non anima. sed quod excellet in anima. mens uocatur. tamquam in corpore caput. uel oculus. unde et ipse homo. secundum mentem imago dei dicitur. ita autem hęc omnia adiuncta sunt animę. ut una res sit. Pro efficientiis erunt causarum. diuersa sortita est nomina. nam et memoria. mens est. unde et immemores. amentes. Dum ergo uiuificat corpus. anima est. dum uult. animus est. dum scit. mens est. dum recolit. memoria. dum rectum iudicat. ratio. dum spirat. spiritus est. dum aliquod sentit. sensus dicitur. Nam modo animus. sensus nominatur. pro his quę sentit. unde et sententia nomen accepit. Anima est substantia incorporea. intellectualis. rationalis. habens immortalem originem. nihil tamen in natura sua mixtum concretumque terrenum. nihil

---

many days in its mother's womb; Our Lord, indeed, was likewise formed in so many days. So he said to the Jews,"Destroy this house and I shall raise it up in three days." And the Jews said in opposition, "This temple was built in forty-six years, and you will rebuild it in three days!" (Jn. 2: 19–20). And among the Greeks they also understand the four parts of the world by these letters: "East", "West", "South" and "North". What we call "East", they call ἀνατολή; what we call "West", they call δύσις; what we call "North", they call ἄρκτος, what we call "South", they call μεσεμβρία. For the foresaid Adam, having been cut to pieces, was spread abroad through his limbs, of which the psalm-writer says, "Their sound has gone out to all the earth, and their words to the ends of the earth"; and this, "Theirs are not speeches and words whose voices shall not be heard." (Ps. 18: 4–5). And so it must be understood. For not only in Adam or in the letters of his name is our salvation signified, but it is also signified in his words in whom (sc. *in quo*) our salvation is contained, in which it is said, "Wherefore a man shall leave father and mother and cleave to his wife, and they two shall be as one flesh"

Greek, because we seem to live by drawing in air with the mouth. But it is false, for the soul is born long before air can be taken in with the mouth; it also lives in the mother's womb. But those persons thought this because they could not think (*cogitare*) it incorporeal. The Evangelist confirms that spirit is the same thing when he said "I have power to lay down my life and take it up again" (Jn. 10: 18). And a little later he wrote "Bowing down his head he gave up his spirit" (Jn. 19: 30). Soul is so called because it animates, that is, because it makes the body live. But it is called "spirit" because it does indeed breathe in the body. Also, to be "soul" and "intellect" is the same thing, but soul pertains to life and intellect to understanding. And hence philosophers say that life remains even without intellect and soul continues without mind, whence also those "out of their minds". For (they say) to know is called "mind", to will is called "soul". Mind is so called because it is prominent in the soul, or because it remembers. Hence those who are out of their minds are "unmindful". Therefore not the soul but what is prominent in the soul is called "mind", just as the head or eye (is prominent) in the body. Hence man

Matrem reliquid. synagogam de qua
secatum carnem natus est inhaerendo
ecclesie et gentibus. Hęc cogitauit
apostolus dicens. mysterium hoc grande
est. Ego autem dico in x͞po et in
ecclesia. [pp. 1–2]

humidum flebileque uel igneum ex
quibus uiuimus. [223vb–224rb]

Aaron. sacerdos domini primum.
Aaron mons fortitudinis.

Aaron sacerdos domini primus. [227ra]

Canicula. stella est que essirius dicitur.
estiuis mensibus. In medio centro celi
est. et cum sol ardeat ascenderit.
coniuncat cum sole. duplicatur color
ipsius. et dissoluuntur corpora et
uaporantur. unde et ex ipsa stella dies
caniculare<s> dicitur. quando et
molestes purgationes. Stella canis

Canicula stella a cane. quod morbo
afficiant corpora. et propter flammę.
candorem. ut pre ceteris lucere uideatur.
hęc et sirion. [230vab]

(Gen. 2: 24). For truly the Son of God left
the Father when "the Word became flesh"
(Jn. 1: 14). Hence fittingly, "He emptied
himself, taking the form of a servant" (Phil.
2: 7). "And mother", that is, the synagogue,
to whom it was said, "Behold, your home
shall be left deserted" (Mt. 23: 38). "He
shall cleave to his wife", etc., that is to say,
of the gentiles. "They two shall be as one
flesh", because where the head is, there too
shall the limbs follow. "A man shall leave
father and mother", not because the Son left
the Father and departed from him, but because he did not appear to men in that form in
which he was equal to the Father. He left his
mother, the synogogue, of whom he was born
according to (*secundum*) the flesh, to cleave to
the church and the gentiles. The Apostle had
these things in mind when he said, "This is a
great mystery. But I speak in Christ and in
the church" (Eph. 5: 31–2)' (*Tractatus in
Ioannis euangelium* IX. 10, 12; *Enarrationes
in Psalmos* XCV. 15). The interpretations of
Jn. 2: 19–20 and Mt. 23: 38 are taken from
Tractates X. 10 and *Enarrationes* LXVIII. 2,
10, LXXXVIII. 2, 14, and CI. 2, 6 respectively; but Augustine interprets Ps. 18: 4–5
differently in *Enarrationes* XVIII. 2,5.

'Aaron: the first priest of the lord.
"Aaron" is "mountain of strength" (*Etym.*
VII. 6, 47)'.

'The Dog Star is a star which is called
Sirius. In the summer months it is in the very
centre of the sky, and it rises when the sun is
blazing. When it is joined (*coniuncta*) with
the sun, its heat (*calor*) is doubled and

himself is called "the image of God" (cf.
Gen. 1: 26) according to mind. But all these
things are joined to the soul in such a way
that it is one thing. For in respect to the effective powers of its causality it has received
various names. For mind is also memory,
whence those out of their minds are unmindful. Therefore when it gives life to the body it
is soul, when it wills it is intellect, when it
knows it is mind, when it remembers it is
memory, when it judges what is right it is
reason, when it breathes it is spirit, when it
feels something it is called "sense". For intellect is only named "sense" in relation to
the things that it feels. From this too "sentence" took its name. Soul is a bodiless, rational, intellectual substance which has an
immortal source, yet nothing earthly is mixed
and compounded in its nature, nothing moist
and tearful, or fiery, from the things we live
on' (*Etym.* XI. 1, 7–13).

'Aaron: the first priest of the Lord'.

'Dog Star: a star, from "dog" because it
affects (*afficiat*) bodies with disease, and because of the brightness of its flame, so that it
seems to shine more than the others. This star
is also called 'Sirion' (*Etym.* III. 71, 15).

uocatur eo quod habeat ante se longum
ignem ueluti flammam relucentem.
quem ammodum carnis linguam tracta
foris per estum nimium. Sęcałm
exemplum. Ideo canis stella dicitur.
quia eo tempore fugiat stella et
apparesciat. quo tempore canis linguam
foris portat longam ueluti per terram
trahentem. eo tempore uelociter se
super homines mittit. Tertium
exemplum. quia ista stella apparet eo
tempore. quo canis piscis marinus in
superiora maris mittit. attendens unde
possit apprehendere predam. [p. 53]

Margarita. multi separant a gemmis. et
    gemmas uolunt dicidi uersicoloris.
    margaritas uero. aluas uel gemmas in
    aegras. margaritas. et hoc margaritum.
    et hec margaris. que grecum est nays.
    [p. 146]

Margaritum. quod in conculis marinis
inueniatur. [250va]

Nauem. primum lidu fabricauerunt.
    petentesque incerta pelagi peruium
    mare humanis usibus. [p. 162]

Nauem quidam. quod querat rectorem
gnauum. ut illud. intellegens.
gubernacula possidebit. [253vb]

---

bodies are dissolved and vaporized. Hence
the Dog Days are called after this star, when
emetics too are hard to take (*molestae*). It is
called the Dog Star because it has before it a
long trail of fire, as it were a bright flame, the
way that the tongue of a dog (*canis*) is extended
through excessive heat. Second (*secundum*)
example: The star is called "the Dog" for this
reason, because the star shines (*fulgeat*) and
begins to appear at the time when a dog carries
a long tongue outside (its mouth), as it were
trailing over the earth. At that time it quickly
takes its place above men. Third example:
Because the aforesaid star appears at the
time that the sea-fish dog [shark] rises to the
upper part of the sea watching where it can
take its prey' (*Etym.* III, 71: 14).

'Pearl: many distinguish them from
precious stones and maintain that precious
stones of various colours are cut, but pearls
. . . or precious stones in sick bivalves
(*valvas*?). *Margaritas* (ὁ μαργαρτής) is also
neuter *margaritum* and feminine *margaris* (ἡ
μαργαρίς), which is a Greek word "ship"
(ναῦς)'. Cf. *Idiomata* ('Peculiarities' in de-
clension and/or gender), *CGL* II, 487–5, at
493,40 *Margarita* μαργαριτις (-ής).

'The Lydians first built the ship, and by

'Pearl, because it is found (*inveniatur*) in
marine shellfish (*Etym.* XVI. 10, 1).

'Ship, some say is so called (*perhibent dic-
tam eo*) because it requires a skilled steers-
man, whence also (*unde et*) this saying of
Solomon, "a wise man shall be in control of
the helm" (Prov. 1: 5)' (*Etym.* XIX. 1, 8
Navem . . . possidebit).

Pelicanus. auis ęgyptia est. ciconiis
corporis. granditate consimilis. quę
naturaliter acie semper affecta est.
quoniam sibi philosophi uolunt. tenso
intestino per uiscera. quicquid ęscarum
accipit. sine aliqua decoctione
transmutit. hinc fit. ut adipe proprio
nomine sarciatur. quia paruissima
ciborum suco reficitur. que non
gregatim ut cetere aues uolat. sed
delectationes solitaria consolatur. eorum
unum genus dicitur esse quod stagnis
inhabitat. aliud sicut dictum est. quod in
desertis locis secretisque uersatur.
[p. 183]

Pelicanus. a canopo. idest ęgypto. ubi
degit. [256rb]

Saterici. siue quod pleni sunt omni
facundia. siue a saturitate et copia. De
pluribus autem simul rebus loquuntur.
aut a satyri<s> nomen tractum. qui
inulta habent que per uinolentiam
dicuntur. [p. 214]

Saterici. siue quod pleni sint omni
facundia. siue a saturitate et copia. de
pluribus enim simul rebus loquuntur. aut
a satyri<s> nomen tractum. qui inulta
habent. quę per uinolentiam dicunt.
[26lvb]

---

seeking out the perils of the deep made
(*fecerunt*) the sea a thoroughfare for human
uses' (*Etym.* XIX. 1, 8 *Lydii . . . fecerunt*).

'The Pelican is an Egyptian bird (*Etym.*
XII. 7, 26 *Pelicanus avis Aegyptia*) very like
the storks in the size of its body. This bird is
always endowed by nature with keen sight
because, philosophers would have it, having
a stretched-out gut, whatever food it takes it
passes through the bowels without any diges-
tion. Hence it happens that it is restored on
its own account with fat, because it is re-
freshed very little with juice from its food.
This bird does not fly in flocks like other
birds but consoles itself with pleasures in
solitude. One of their kinds is said to dwell
in marshes, the other is that which likes in
solitary and remote places, as has been said'.
Verbatim in the Vatican 1469 Bede Glosses
(208vab), for which see below, p. 280–1.

'Pelican: from Canopus, that is, Egypt,
where it lives' (*Etym.* XII, 7, 26 *habitans . . .
nam Canopus Aegyptus dicitur*).

'Satirists: either because they are full of all
eloquence or from their fullness and abundance – for, indeed (*enim*), they talk about a
great many things at once –, or the name was
taken from the satyrs, who regard as licenced
what is said in a drunken state' (*Etym.* VIII.
7, 8).

'Satirists: either because they are full of all
eloquence, or because of their fullness and
abundance – for indeed they talk about a
great many things at once –, or the name was
taken from the satyrs, who regard as licenced
what is said in a drunken state' (*Etym.* VIII.
7, 8).

The distinctive elements in both glossaries are the long glosses, in Vatican 1469 mostly etymological and largely from Isidore like the gloss on *anima*, as Mai noted on the same page,[59] in Monte Cassino 90 inclined to mystical exegesis like the gloss on *Adam*, which was worked up from several passages in the works of Augustine.[60] In both glossaries these elements are interspersed with shorter entries, often drawn from Abstrusa/Abolita or related glossaries. Even when they both draw on the same passages in Isidore they sometimes differ, however, as in the glosses on *canicula*, *navem* and *pelicanus*. On the other hand, *Aaron sacerdos primus* and the whole of the glosses on *ALFA ET Ω* and *saterici* are identical. Goetz failed to see the problem of the two Auxilius glossaries because his acquaintance with Monte Cassino 90 was apparently limited to Loewe's extracts. He was therefore misled by the incipits, as Mai had been, and he in turn misled Lindsay, who clearly had no first-hand knowledge of Monte Cassino 90 either, so they both fell into the pit. But the Monte Cassino cataloguers only confuse the issue by suggesting that the real Auxilius Glossary still awaited discovery. The incipits of the two existing glossaries prove that some sort of connection exists between them, and in any case they share too many unusual entries to be wholly unrelated. Auxilius' *Flosculi* may actually have been quite brief, as his title says, like the *Liber de diversis rebus*, a seventh-century epitome of Isidore's *Etymologies* recently edited by Professor Lapidge,[61] which consists of 489 entries, including ones on *canicula* and *navis* that correspond to those in Vatican 1469 and Monte Cassino 90 respectively:

121 Lidi primum nauem fabricauerunt
429 Virius grece propter flammae candoremque et Canicula quod
     corpora morbo afficiat[62]

The use of such a collection of extracts would explain why the Isidore material in some glossaries is so scanty,[63] and *Flosculi* of similar dimensions could have formed the common nucleus of the Vatican and Monte Cassino Auxilius glossaries.

---

[59] See above, note 51.
[60] See above, note 57.
[61] 'About Various Things' (M. Lapidge, 'An Isidorian Epitome from Early Anglo-Saxon England', *Romanobarbarica* 10 (1988–9), 443–83, at 459ff.
[62] 'The Lydians first built a ship' (*Etym.* XIX 1, 8). 'Sirius in Greek because of the brightness (*candorem*; -*que* is untranslatable) of its flame and Canicula because it affects bodies with disease' (*Etym.* III. 71. 15 *Canis autem vocatur propter quod corpora morbo afficiat, vel propter flammae candorem, quod eiusmodi sit ut prae ceteris lucere videatur. Itaque quo magis eam cognoscerent, Sirion appellasse* 'It is called the Dog, then, because it affects bodies with disease, or on account of the brightness of its flame, because it is such that it seems to give more light than the others. And so, because they recognized it more readily, they called it Sirion (σείριον "bright" ').
[63] As I suggested many years ago apropos Épinal/Erfurt I (*Old English Glosses in the Épinal-Erfurt Glossary*, ed. J.D. Pheifer (Oxford, 1974), pp. liii–iv).

IV

Lindsay was right when he looked to Vatican 1469, which was written in 908, probably in central Italy, for the source of material it has in common with Monte Cassino 90 and the other Monte Cassino glossaries that Goetz associated with it, 217, 218 and 402,[64] all of which are written in the southern Italian beneventan script, probably in Monte Cassino itself,[65] although he did not fully appreciate the significance of this relationship. Vatican 1469 begins with the Asbestos Glossary (1ra–74va), which contains the entry that the manuscript is dated by, *Era domina uel capitulum Item era in calculi supputatione ponitur ut era. dccccviii.*[66] (23rb), and the otherwise identical entry in another copy of this glossary, Monte Cassino 218, has the date of the following year, *DCCCCVIIII.* (27rb);[67] the two copies are closely related and could have been taken from the same exemplar, which made the journey from Rome to Cassino in the interval. Other components of Vatican 1469, moreover, indicate its connections with the early English glossaries as well as the later Italian ones. (1) The Asbestos Glossary is followed by (2) Bible-name glosses and an assortment of didactic material including sections on weights and measures related to the *de ponderibus* glosses in Leiden XXXI-III[68] and also found in Monte Cassino 217 (79vb–80vb). The next item, (3) a short glossary, not in alphabetical order, beginning *Proaulum prima est porta ab oriente* (. . .),[69] which corresponds to the second glossary in Monte Cassino 402 (80vb–81vb), is followed by more didactic material, followed in turn by (4) *glossae collectae* on saints' lives and the apocryphal Book of Judith[70] (81vb–83va), (5) a copy of the Reichenau Bible glosses (82va–155va), also found in Fulda, Hessische Landesbibliothek Aa 2 (38r–117v) and many other manuscripts, including Monte Cassino 205,[71] (6) a set of *de canonibus* glosses (155va–161vb) also found in Fulda Aa 2 (136r–137v), and (7)

---

[64] 'Monte Cassino MS.', p. 130. Cf. 'St. Gall Glossary', pp. 355–7.

[65] Lowe, *Beneventan Script*, II, 76, 85.

[66] 'Era: a lady (*hera*) or a heading (*aera*); likewise an era (*aera*) is set in making a computation, as the era 908'. *Aera* in this sense is the bench-mark from which the reckoning is made.

[67] E.A. Lowe, *Scriptura Beneventana*, 2 vols (Oxford, 1929), I, plate xxxiii.

[68] Including 80ra *Argenteus idest pendingus* 'Silver coin: that is, pennies (*pendingas*)', for which see Lapidge, 'School of Theodore', pp. 61–2.

[69] ' "Fore-court" (προαύλιον) is the first gate to the east'. Cf. the Vatican 1469 Bede Glossary entry, 210rb *Proaulum porta prima est ab oriente*. The Monte Cassino 402 Proaulum Glosses are found on p. 164a.

[70] Printed by W.M. Lindsay, ' "Glossae collectae" in Vat. Lat. 1469. *CATONVM. NAVMACHIA.*', *Classical Quarterly* 15 (1921), 38–40, at 39. These glosses, which have not been found elsewhere, have affinities with Leiden and lead straight into the Vatican 1469 Bible Glosses, suggesting an Anglo-Saxon connection.

[71] Pp. 1–126. See *Die althochdeutschen Glossen*, edd. E. Steinmeyer and E. Sievers, 5 vols (Berlin, 1879–1922), V, 108–407, and Lapidge, 'School of Theodore', pp. 60 and 68–9. Steinmeyer lists 55 copies of these glosses (pp. 108–11), to which John J. Contreni adds sixteen more, including Monte Cassino 205 ('The biblical glosses of Haimo of Auxerre and John Scottus Eriugena', *Speculum* 51 (1976), pp. 411–34, at 418, note 36).

an expanded series of glosses on Bede, *De orthographia*, arranged alphabetically (162ra–223rb). Then comes (8) the Auxilius Glossary, followed by extracts from the Fathers and further didactic material (271vb–291vb), which conclude the manuscript.

Many of the Vatican 1469 *glossae collectae* are incorporated in Monte Cassino 90, for example 23 of the 31 glosses on Jerome's prologue to the Pentateuch (83va–84ra):[72]

	VATICAN 1469	MONTE CASSINO 90
1	PROLOGUS caput compositionis uel sequentis operis prephatio.	
2	et dicta prepahtio quasi prelocutio.	Proemium. idest initium dicendi. Sunt enim proemia principia librorum que ante cause narrationem ad instruendas audientium aures coaptantur. et dicitur. prephatio. quasi prelocutio. [p. 195]
3	Proimium est initium dicendi. Sunt enim proimia principia librorum quę ante causę narrationem ad instruendas audientium aures coaptantur.	
4	Pręsagium idest prescientia uel signum futurorum.	Presagium. signum quod antea dicitur. et postea uenit. uel diuinatio futurorum [p. 187]
5	Pręsagus prescius futurorum.	Presagus. prescius futurorum. [p. 187]
6	Pentateuchum quinque librorum.	Pentatheucus. quinque uolumina. [p. 184]
7	obtrectatorum idest detrahentium.	Obtrectans. resistens. maledicens detrahens. [p. 169]
8	Suggillationem idest suffocationem. [83vb]	
9	Suggilare est gula\<m\> stringere; suggillo uerbum actiuum et facit passiuum suggillor.	Sugillare stranguilare. accusare. subplantare subuertere. [p. 232]
10	Cudere idest condere.	
11	fedare sordidare.	Fedare. sordidare. [p. 99]
12	Asterisco idest stella ⁎	Asterisco. stella.
13	Obelo idest ueru uel uirga ÷	
14	Iugulat idest condempnat.	Iugulat. est condempnat. [p. 120]
15	Syntagma compositio.	Sintagma. compositio [p. 223]
16	Aeque similiter.	Aeque. similiter. uel iuste. [p. 12]
17	Apocriphorum dubiorum.	Apocriphorum. dubiorum. [p. 24]

---

[72] The Reichenau glosses on the prologue to the Pentateuch are printed in *Althochdeutschen Glossen* V, 135–7. The line-numbers in the references below are to Jerome's text in *Biblia sacra iuxta vulgatam versionem*, ed. R. Weber, 2 vols (Stuttgart, 1985), I, 3–4.

18 Hiberas idest nomen gentis, ispanas.   Hiberas. nomen gentis est. [p. 115]

19 Nenias uanitates uel mendatia, seu res superuacuę uel nouissima cantica quę mortuis dicuntur.

20 Autenticos auctoritate plenos uel antiquos.   Autenticis auctoritatae plenis. uel occultis uel antiquis.[73] [p. 33]

21 Dogma doctrina.   Dogma doctrina [p. 82]

22 Vatem prophetam uel sacerdotem.   Uates. diuini sacerdotes. prophetę. Vates a ui mentiis appellatus. Nam modo sacerdotem. modo prophetam. modo significat poeta<m> [p. 245]

23 Nisi forte putandus est tullius oeconomicum xenofontis et platonis pitagoram et demostenis pro thesifontem afflatus rhetorico in latinum interpretati sunt

24 Emulus inuidus.   Aemulus imitator uel inuidus [p. 12]

25 Charismata dona.   Charisma donum spirituale (. . .); Charismata dona spiritualia diuina gratia (. . .). Charisma autem dona. [p. 52]

26 Penę prope.   Pene. prope uel iuxta. [p. 184]

27 Liuore uulnere uel inuidia.   Libor quando per .b. scribitur. dicunt auctores significare; inuidiam uel odium. Cum uero per .u. dicitur significare uulnus[74] [p. 141]

28 Proethesi xenofontis proprium nomen auctoris.

29 Consulere interrogare.   Consululo. interrogo. uel est consilium quero [p. 67]

30 Vsurpata usu illicitę habita uel presumpta. [83vb–84ra]   Usurpare. usum inlicite habere. Usurpat. presumit. illicite agit. illicite utitur.[75] [p. 251]

---

[73] Corrected from *Autenticus . . . plenos uel occultos uel antiquos.*

[74] All except *Li* added in a later hand.

[75] Monte Cassino 90, 2–3. 'Proem: that is, the beginning of speaking, for proems are the commencements of books, which are composed to prepare the listeners' ears before narrating one's case, and it is called a preface in the sense of a preliminary address' (cf. *Etym.* VI. 8, 9). 4. 'Presage: a sign which is told beforehand and comes afterwards, or the divining of things to come' (Prol. 1 *praesagio*). 5. 'Presaging: foreknowing things to come'. 6. 'Pentateuch: five volumes' (Prol. 3 *Pentateuchum*). 7. 'Disparaging: opposing, slandering, detracting' (Prol. 4 *obtrectatorum*). 9. 'Beat black and blue: strangle, trip up, overthrow' (Prol. 5 *suggillationem*). 11. 'To foul: to dirty' (Prol. 7 *foedari*). 12. 'Asterix: star' (Prol. 9 *asterisco . . . id est stella*).

31 Subire excipere adire introire.[76] [84ra]

These correspondences clearly prove some connection between the Vatican 1469 Bible glosses and Monte Cassino 90, but it is also evident that the closeness of the relationship varies from entry to entry. Monte Cassino 90 lacks 1, 10, 13, 19, 23, 28 and 31, and has a different interpretation in 9. It alters the original form of the headword in 6, 7, 22, 25, 27, 29 and 30, but preserves it against Vatican 1469 in 20 after correction.[77] It combines with other explanations which sometimes do not fit the passage referred to in Vatican 1469 in 4, 7, 9, 16, 20, 22, 24, 25, 27, 29 and 30. Both glossaries give a wrong or misleading interpretation in 9 and 30. The glossing process is vividly revealed in 23, which does not appear in the manuscripts of the Reichenau glosses

14. ' "Cuts the throat of" is "condemns" ' (Prol. 10). 15. 'Arrangement: composition' (Prol. 16 σύνταγμα). 15 'Equally: likewise or equitably' (Prol. 19 *aeque*). 18. 'Iberian is the name of a people' (Prol. 20). 20. 'Authentic: full of authority or secret or ancient' (Prol. 20). 21. 'Dogma: teaching' (Prol 23). 22. 'God-like seers : priests, prophets. Seers are so called from their power of mind. For now it means a priest, now a prophet, now a poet' (Prol. 29 *vatem*). Cf. Horace, *Ars poetica* 400 *divinis vatibus*, *Etym.* VIII. 7, 3 *Vates a vi mentis appellatos Varro auctor est*. 24. 'Emulous: imitator or emulous' (Prol.39 *aemule*). 25. 'Grace: spiritual gift (. . .); Graces: spiritual gifts, divine favour (. . .). Grace, then, is a gift' (Prol. 41 *spiritualia charismata*). 26. 'Almost: nearly or next to' (Prol. 42 *paene*). 27. 'Bruise: when it is written with a "b" the authorities say that it means "envy" or "hatred", but when it is written with a "v" it is said to mean "wound" ' (Prol. 42 *liuore*). 29. 'I consult: I ask or seek advice' (Prol. 43–4 *interroga . . . consule*). 30. 'To have the use of: to make use of unlawfully. 'Has the use of: presume, treats unlawfully, uses unlawfully' (Prol. 45 *usurpata*).

[76] Vatican 1469: 1. 'Prologue: the first part of the composition or work that follows' (Prol., title). 2. 'and called a preface in the sense of a preliminary address'. Cf. *Etym.* VI. 8, 9. 3. 'Proem is the beginning of speaking, for proems are the commencements of books, which are designed to prepare the listeners' ears before narrating one's case'. Cf. *Etym., ibid.* 4. 'Presage is foreknowledge or a sign of the future' (Prol. 1 *praesagio*). 5. 'Presaging: foreknowing things to come'. 6. 'Pentateuch: of five books' (Prol. 3). 7. 'Of disparagers: that is, of detractors' (Prol. 4 *obtrectatorum*). 8. 'Beating black and blue: that is, choking' (Prol. 5 *suggilationem*). 9. 'To beat black and blue is to squeeze the throat; *suggillo* is the active verb and forms a passive *suggillor*'. 10. 'To forge is to build' (Prol. 5). 11. 'To foul is to dirty' (Prol. 7 *foedari*). 12–13 'Asterix: that is, star', 'Obelus: that is, spit or rod' (Prol. 9 *asterisco et obelo, id est stella et veru*). 14. 'Cuts the throat of: that is, condemns' (Prol. 10). 15. 'Arrangement: composition' (Prol. 16 σύνταγμα). 16.'Equally: likewise' (Prol. 19 *aeque*). 17. 'Hidden: that is, doubtful' (Prol. 19 *apocriforum*). 18. 'Iberian: that is, the name of a people, Spanish' (Prol. 20). 19. 'Wailing: nonsense or lies or useless things or the last songs which are uttered for the dead' (Prol. 20). 20. 'Authentic: full of authority or ancient' (Prol. 20 *authenticis*). 21. 'Dogma: teaching' (Prol. 23). 22. 'Seer: prophet or priest' (Prol 29). 23. 'Unless perhaps Cicero is to be represented as having translated (*transtulisse*) Xenophon's *Estate Manager* and Plato's *Protagoras* and Demosthenes' *In defence of Ctesiphon* inspired by the spirit of rhetoric' (Prol. 30–6 *nisi forte putandus est Tullius Oeconomicum Xenofontis et Platonis Protagoram et Demosthenis Pro Ctesifonte afflatus rethorico spiritu transtulisse . . . Illi interpretati sunt*). 24. 'Emulous: envious' (Prol. 39 *aemule*). 25. 'Graces: gifts' (Prol. 41). 26. 'Almost: nearly' (Prol. 42 *paene*). 27. 'Bruise: wound or envy' (Prol. 42). 28. 'Xenophon's *In Defence of Ctesiphon*: proper name of an author' (Prol. 31–2 *Xenofontis . . . Pro Ctesifonte*). Cf. Karlsruhe, Badische Landesbibliothek, Aug. 248.102 va *Pro tesifontę nomen est proprium Xenofonte proprium auctoris*, and see below, p. 284. 29. 'To consult: to ask' (Prol. 43–4 *interroga . . . consule*). 30. 'Been in use: made use of unlawfully or presumed' (Prol. 45 *usurpata*). 31. 'To undertake: to take up, approach, enter into' (Prol. 47 *subire*).

[77] See above, p. 282 and note 73.

collated by Steinmeyer. Here Vatican 1469 preserves a lump of the text from which a garbled phrase was extracted and interpreted (out of sequence) in 28.

Monte Cassino 90's entries, on the other hand, show how the compiler of an alphabetical glossary handled *glossae collectae*, and a survey of corresponding entries in the other Italian glossaries throws further light on both sides of the glossary-making process:

1　Abstr. PRO45 Prologus saequentis operis praefatio, Vatican 1468[78] 67ra
　　Prologus sequentis operis prophatium

2　St Gallen 269, 22 Praefatio praealogutio, Vatican 1469 Asbestos Glossary 50va
　　Prephatio prelocutio

4　Abstr. PRAE62 Presagium indicium futurorum uel signorum, St Gallen 268, 41
　　Presagium signum quod antea deus postea uenet, 269, 2 Presagium diuinatio
　　futurorum, Vatican 1469 Asbestos Glossary 50va Presagium signum quod antea
　　dicitur et postea uenit

5　Abstr. PRAE63 Presagus praescius futurorum, Vatican 1469 Asbestos Glossary,
　　50va *id.*

6　Vatican 1468 60rb Pentateuchum quinque librorum moysi

7　Vatican 1468 55vb obtrabatores detractores

9　Paris Placidus Glosses[79] 154, 36 Suggillare est guillam constringere quomodo
　　dicimus strangulare suggillo ueruum actiuum et facit passiuum sugillor,
　　Vatican 1468 79vb suggillare offucare stranguilare

11　Vatican 1468 28va Fedare inquinare cammanare sordidare

15　Ab Absens Glossary[80] 424, 28 Syntagma compositionem

16　Abstr. AE22 Aeque similiter, Vatican 1471 Terence Glosses[81] 6va *id.*

17　Vatican 1468 5vb Apocrifa occulta dubia fraudulenta[82]

19　Vatican 1469 Bible Glosses 138rb Nenias res superuacuas siue amentium proprie
　　autem nenias carmina funebria que mortuis dicuntur

20　Vatican 1468 7va Autentica antiqua auctoritas, autenticus auctoritate plenus

21　Abstr. DO4 Dogma doctrina, Vatican 1469 Asbestos Glossary, 20vb *id.*

---

[78] Vatican City, Biblioteca Apostolica Vaticana, lat. 1468 (Lowe, *Script*, II, 145), a glossary in *abc*-order (arranged according to the first three letters of its headwords), excerpted in *CGL* LV, 490–519. For its connection with Vatican 1469 and the Monte Cassino glossaries see Lindsay, 'Monte Cassino MS.', p. 130, and Goetz, *CGL* IV, xviii–ix, and I, 146.

[79] Paris, Bibliothèque Nationale, lat. nouv. acq. 1298, printed in *CGL* V, 104–58. The Placidus Glosses, which were used by Isidore himself, are one of the oldest Latin glossaries; they are a major component of the Vatican 1469 Bede Glosses (above, p. 281). See further W.M. Lindsay, 'The shorter glosses of Placidus', *Jnl. of Philol.* 34 (1916), 255–36, and, for the Paris manuscript, J.F. Mountford, 'The Paris "Placidus" ', *Bulletin Du Cange* 1 (1924), 31–49.

[80] Leiden 67F, 54r–62r; printed in *CGL* IV, 404–27.

[81] Vatican City, Biblioteca Ambrosiana Vaticana, lat. 1471, 6r–16r, excerpted in *CGL* V, 529–39. For their sequence see Goetz, *CGL* I, 147.

[82] *dubia* added in a later hand.

22 Vatican 1469 Asbestos Glossary 71rb Uates diuini sacerdotes prophete, Abstr.
    VA25 Vates prophetia aut poetas, Abol. VA7 Vates diuini, St Gallen 249,
    39 Vates diuini et prophete
24 St Gallen 232, 1 Emolus inuidus, Vatican 1469 Asbestos Glossary 22vb Emulus
    inuidus aduersarius, Vatican 1468 3ra Aemulus imitator inuidus persecutor[83]
25 St Gallen 214, 39–40 Carisma donum spirituale[m], Carismata dona spiritalia
    diuine gr<a>tie, Vatican 1469 Asbestos Glossary 13ra Charisma donum spiritale
    diuina gratia
26 Abstr. PE38 Pene prope uel iuxta, Vatican 1469 Asbestos Glossary 49va Pene
    prope iuxta
27 Abol. LI7 Liuor inuidia uel odium, Vatican 1468 45rb Libore uulnere
29 AA Glossary[84] C625 Confuere interrogare
30 Abstr. US5 Usurpat inlicite utitur, St Gallen 298, 5 Usurpat inlicite utitur
    praesumet, Vatican 1468 45rb Usurpat presumit illicite agit utitur
31 AA S1046 Subire excipere uel sustinere, Vatican 1468 78vb Subio excipio sustineo
    suscipio succedo, Abstr. SU15 Subit subcedit[85]

These correspondences show that the misinterpretation of *suggillare* goes back to the fifth-century Placidus Glosses, whose author was not unfairly described by Lindsay as *semidoctus*,[86] and, more generally, that the traffic between *glossae collectae* and alphabetical glossaries was not all one-way. The compilers of the Vatican 1469 Bible Glosses, which belong to the main stock of Bible-glosses that derive from the School of Canterbury,[87] took many of their interpretations from the

---

[83] *inuidus* added in a later hand.
[84] Printed in *GL* V, 159–388; it incorporates most of Asbestos (starred entries in *GL* V). For its connection with Vatican 1469 and Monte Cassino 90, see Lindsay, 'A Monte Cassino MS.', p 131.
[85] 1. 'Prologue: preface to the following work'. 2. 'Preface: a preliminary address' (*Etym.* VI. 8, 9). 4. 'Presage: indication of things to come or of signs / sign which is foretold (*antea dicitur*) and (sc. *et*) shall come after / the divining of things to come / sign . . . and comes after'. 5. 'Presaging: foreknowing of things to come'. 6. 'Pentateuch: of five books of Moses'. 7. 'Disparagers: detractors'. 9. 'To beat black and blue is to squeeze together the throat, to strangle, as we say; *suggillo* is the active verb and forms a passive *suggillor* / To beat black and blue: to suffocate, strangle'. 'To foul: to pollute, contaminate (*contaminare*), dirty'. 15. 'Arrangement: composition (σύνταγμα)'. 16. 'Equally: likewise' (Terence, *And.* 702). 17. 'Hidden: secret, doubtful, false'. 19. 'Wailing: things useless or appropriate to lunatics; properly, however, "wailings" are funeral songs which are uttered for the dead'. Cf. Jerome, *In Mattheum*, Pref. *nenias mortuis magis hereticis quam ecclesiasticis vivis canendas* 'laments to be sung for dead heretics rather than for living churchmen'. 20. 'Authentic: ancient authority', 'Authentic: full of authority'. 21. 'Dogma: teaching'. 22. 'God-like seers: priests and prophets / Seers: prophets or poets / Seers: god-like / Seers: god-like and prophets' (Horace, *A.P.* 400 *divinis vatibus*). 24. 'Emulous: envious / envious, antagonistic / imitator, envious, persecutor'. 25. 'Grace: spiritual gift / Graces: spiritual gifts, divine favours / Grace: spiritual gift, divine favour'. 26. 'Almost: nearly or next to / nearly, next to'. 27. 'Bruise: envy or hatred / wound'. 29. 'To consult (*consulere*): to ask'. 30. 'Has the use of: uses unlawfully / uses unlawflully, presumes / presumes, treat unlawfully, uses'. 31. 'To undertake: to take up or undergo / I undertake: I take up, undergo, undertake, begin, succeed to'.
[86] 'Half-educated'. Cf. W.M. Lindsay, 'The Abstrusa Glossary and the Liber Glossarum', *Classical Quarterly* 11 (1917), 119–31, at 119–20.
[87] Cf. Lapidge, 'School of Theodore', pp. 59–60.

already flourishing tradition of alphabetical glossography that produced Abstrusa/Abolita and its early progeny, and were drawn upon in turn by later-generation alphabetical glossaries such as Asbestos, Ab Absens, AA, Vatican 1468 and Monte Cassino 90. Meanwhile, the old stock put forth new shoots: Milan, Biblioteca Ambrosiana, M. 79 sup., which preserves the Canterbury Bible glosses in their fullest and earliest form, is an eleventh-century manuscript.[88] Sorting out these tangled relationships is a delicate task, and Occam's Razor, the tool that Lindsay recommends,[89] is too blunt an instrument for the job.

V

The relationship between Vatican 1469 and Monte Cassino 90 is therefore a question that should concern Anglo-Saxonists, and there is also a connection between these Italian glossaries and the early Anglo-Saxon alphabetical glossaries. Two of the Auxilius glosses quoted above, Monte Cassino 90 *Aaron mons fortitudinis* and Vatican 1469 *Canicula stella a cane*, have counterparts in the English tradition, the first in the Corpus *Interpretatio nominum*[90] and the second in Erfurt II, an *ab*-order glossary closely related to the *ab*-order sections of Épinal/Erfurt I,[91] and the Affatim Glossary, which is closely related to Erfurt II and probably of English provenance:[92]

> Cp. Int. A13 Aaron mons fortitudinis
> Erf.II C87 (274, 8) Canicula a cane, Affatim 492, 43 Canicula aut cane dicta[93]

More significantly, six of the Vatican 1469 glosses on Jerome's prologue to the Pentateuch have counterparts in Erfurt II, Corpus and Affatim:

3 Erf.II P375 Praemium initium dictionis
4 Cp. P586 Praesagium signum
12 Erf.II A605 Asteriscus stella, Affatim 473, 14 Asteriscum stella
18 Erf.II H93 Hiberi spani
19 Erf.II N38 Nenias res superuacuas uel species, Affatim 541, 8 Nenias res superuacuas

---

88 Lapidge, *ibid.*, pp. 59–60, 70.
89 'St. Gall Glossary', pp. 356–7.
90 See above, notes 38 and 41.
91 Erfurt II ('Erf.II') is referred to below by its alphabetical section numbers in EEMF 22. For its relationship with Épinal/Erfurt I see Lindsay, *Corpus, Épinal, Erfurt and Leyden*, pp. 44–80; Pheifer, 'Anglo-Saxon glossaries', pp. 29–37.
92 Leiden, Bibliotheek der Rijksuniversiteit, Bibl. Pub. Lat. 67F, 1r–54r; printed in *CGL* IV, 471–581. Its relationship with Erfurt II and the other early glossaries is discussed in the passages cited in the note above.
93 (1) 'Aaron: mountain of strength' (*Etym.* VII. 6, 47). Cf. the Vatican 1469 Bible-name gloss, 74vb *Aaron mons fortitudinis*. (2) 'Dog-Star: from "dog" / called after (a) "dog" '.

20 Erf.II A707 Auctenticum auctoritas, Affatim 473, 9 Autenticum actoritate plenum[94]

The glosses on *asterisco, Hiberas, nenias* and *autenticos* are only recorded in these two groups of glossaries, and there are many other links between the English and Italian glossaries,[95] which is not surprising since their histories are closely intertwined. Malcolm Parkes's dating of Epinal 72 c. 700[96] places the Épinal/Erfurt I Glossary in the age of Theodore and Hadrian, who apparently introduced the Latin glossographical tradition into England,[97] and the Vatican 1469 *de ponderibus, de canonibus* and Bible glosses, which belong to the Leiden family of glossaries described by Lapidge,[98] were presumably conveyed to Rome and from there to Cassino in the Carolingian period, when English missionaries and scholars in turn spread their native glossographical tradition about the Continent, as shown by the transmission of the Erfurt and Werden glossaries.[99]

The flag-ship of the English tradition is the Reichenau Bible Glosses, to which the Bible glosses in Vatican 1469 glosses belong, but many other glosses of Old English provenance also found their way into Italian glossaries, such as the interpretation added to *Nenias uanitates* in the Bible glosses of Cambridge, University Library Kk.4.6 (41ra–44vb), *carmina quę in tumbis id est in memoriis mortuorum scribuntur*, which was attached to a different *nenias* gloss in Monte Cassino 90.[100] Hence the Vatican and Monte Cassino glossaries are important to students of the early English glossaries and the Anglo-Saxon diaspora on the Continent, who need full and accurate editions with critical commentary of alphabetical glossaries like those in Vatican 1469 and Monte Cassino 90 for the same reasons that Lapidge forcibly put for editions of the Leiden-family *glossae collectae* in the conclusion of his seminal article:

> From the foregoing discussion it will be clear that much work lies ahead: we need reliable editions of the unprinted glossaries of the Leiden family and detailed source studies of the *lemmata* which they contain; these source studies

---

94 Vatican 1469: 3. 'Proem (*proemium*): beginning of speaking' (*Etym.* VI. 8, 9). 4. 'Presage: sign'. 12. 'Asterix: star'. 18. 'Iberians: Spaniards'. 19. 'Wailing: useless things or pretences / useless things'. Cf. Erf.II N44 *Nenias species*. 20. 'Authentic: authority / full of authority'.

95 Cf. W.M. Lindsay, 'The Affatim Glossary and others', *Classical Quarterly* 11 (1917), 193–4; Pheifer, 'Anglo-Saxon glossaries', pp. 33–4.

96 See above, note 13.

97 Cf. Pheifer, 'Anglo-Saxon glossaries', pp. 33–4.

98 See above, p. 271, and Lapidge, 'School of Theodore', pp. 53–72.

99 See above, notes 23 and 28.

100 Cambridge 41ra *NENIAS Vanitates Nenię sunt carmina quę in tumbis id est In memoriis mortuorum scribuntur Quę EPITAPHIA primum HIBERI inuenerunt*: Monte Cassino 90, p. 163 *Nenias finis uel ultimissimas fabulas uel epitaphia idest carmina quę In memoria mortuorum scribuntur* 'Wailing: nonsense. "Wailings" are poems which are carved on tombs, that is on the monuments of the dead; epitaphs, which the Iberians first devised / the end or last tales of all or epitaphs, that is poems which are carved on the monument of the dead'. The Cambridge Bible glosses are closely related to those in Leiden VII–XVII (cf. Hessels, *A Late Eighth-Century Anglo-Saxon Glossary*, p. xliii). This Cambridge gloss is also found in the Bible glosses attributed to Eriugena (Contreni, 'Bible glosses', p. 422).

in turn will entail new work on the transmission of Latin texts in early Angb-
Saxon England. The task is not small, but the direction is straightforward, and
we may proceed in the hope that some day soon we shall be in a position to
appreciate the high praise which Bede lavished on the teaching of Theodore
and Hadrian; and to understand the achievements of what was arguably the
most brilliant school of studies during the entire Angb-Saxon period.[101]

The extracts from the Vatican and Cassino glossaries in Goetz's volumes IV and V
are no use for such purposes and indeed misleading, for the extractors, in their
search for lexicographically significant entries, naturally avoided the duplications
by which relationships are established, and only rarely do exceptions like *CGL* V,
564, 52 *Cerinea nimpha aque*, from Monte Cassino 90, which also appears in St
Gallen and Erfurt II,[102] slip through their sieve.

The discrepancy between Goetz's impeccable texts of major glossaries and the
careless extracts he used for minor ones is also striking. Loewe's abbreviated
transcription of the Monte Cassino 90 *pelicanus* gloss, for example, which Goetz
prints in *CGL* V, 575, 13 *Pelicanus auis ęgyptiaca est ciconis corporis*, reads
ęgyptiaca and *ciconis* for *ęgyptia* and *ciconiis* and omits *granditate consimilis*.
There is a similar inconsistency between the admirable rigour with which Lindsay
insisted that more or less continuous sequences of entries, which he calls 'batches',
were the only sound basis for determining the literary sources of the Épinal/Erfurt
I Glossary,[103] and his laxity in dealing with material taken from other glossaries.
This is the more surprising because the complex nature of this material had long
been known. Loewe showed that most of the alphabetical sections in Épinal/Erfurt
I fall into two parts of unequal length, a longer one in *a*-order followed by a shorter
one in *ab*-order, and identified the source of the *ab*-order parts as a glossary
closely related to Erfurt II, in which the entries sometimes follow the same order,[104]
e.g. under *Ab*:

A337 Abtet uos impleat uos : Erf.II A1 *id.*
A338 Abtemus adiungemus : Erf.II A2 Abtemus adiungere
A339 Abigiata inuolata : Erf.II A5 Abeliata inuiolata
A340 Absedas aedificii latiores conculas : Erf.II A8
        Absidias aedificii lautiores conculas
A341 Abicies turba : Erf.II A11 *id.*
A342 Abacta inuolata : Erf.II A13 Abacta inuiolata
A343 Ab latere bnge : Erf.II A14 *id.*

---

[101] 'School of Theodore and Hadrian', pp. 66–7
[102] 'Cyrene: water-nymph' (*Geo.* IV. 321 *Cyrene*). Cf. St Gallen 216, 54 *Crine aqua nymfa*, Erf.II
C215 *Cęrere nimpha*. Wessner (*CGL* I, 324) noted the correspondence but misinterpreted its
significance: see Pheifer, 'Anglo-Saxon glossaries', pp. 32–3.
[103] *Corpus, Épinal, Erfurt and Leyden*, pp. 3–37.
[104] *Prodromus*, pp. 114–16. Cf. Pheifer, EEMF 22, pp. 55–6.

A344 Abtauit conparauit : Erf.II A15 *id.*[105]

Lindsay then identified separate batches of Abstrusa and Abolita glosses in *ab*-order in the sub-sections of Erfurt II, whose entries likewise sometimes keep their original sequence,[106] and what he termed 'Abstrusa-Abolita' batches in the *a*-order parts of Épinal/Erfurt I, in which entries with counterparts in Abstrusa and Abolita are mixed up with others not found in Abstrusa or Abolita but in related glossaries, like the St Gallen glosses in his *A*-section batches printed above, including a high proportion of entries with counterparts in Erfurt II and/or in the *ab*-order parts of Épinal/Erfurt I itself (marked '(2)' below),[107] as in his *R* batches:[108]

R41   Rati arbitrati : Abstr. RA13 *id.*, Affatim 560, 26 Rati arbitrati aut firmi accepti

R42   Rudentes funes uebrum : Abolita RU12 Rudentes funes uelarum, Erf.II R122
        Rudentes funes uebrum

R44   Rudus nouus : Abol. *post* RU14 *id.*,[109] Vatican 1471 Auxiliare Gbssary[110] 157va
        Rudis nouus

R52   Reduces incolumi : Erf.II R85 Reduces incobmes, Abstr. RE25 Reduces salvos
        uel inclumes reversos, Affatim 561, 21 Redocos sabs incobmes reuersus

R53   Rastros ligones id mettocas : Abavus[111] RA12 Rastros ligones *only*, Ép./Erf.I (2)
        R108 *id.*, Abstr. RA12 Rastri ligones, Affatim 560, 25 *id.*

R54   Rabula raucus : Erf.II R1 *id.*, Affatim 560, 22 Rapula raucus

R55   Repagula impedimenta : Abstr. RE61 impedimenta aditus introitus vel retinacula,
        Affatim 561, 56 Repacula uel impedimenta auditus introitus

R57   Rubeta rana : Juvenal Gbsses[112] 656, 28 <R>ubeta terrestris rana

---

[105] Ép./Erf.I A337. 'May he fit you out: may he bring you to the full' (Heb. 13: 21). 338. 'Let us fit: let us join to *(adiungemus)*'. 339. 'Taken away: carried off'. 340. 'Apses: wider hollows *(conchulas)* in a building'. 341. 'troop *(acies)*: crowd' *(Aen.* XI. 498 *acie)*. Cf. Ép./Erf.I A347a. *Acie turba.* 342. 'Driven away: carried off'. 343. 'At one's side: from afar' (Is. 60: 4 *de longe ... de latere).* 344. 'Fit out: prepare'.

[106] Cf. *Corpus, Épinal, Erfurt and Leyden,* pp. 53–75.

[107] Pp. 4–6. Cf. *Corpus, Épinal, Erfurt and Leyden,* pp. 37–43, at 38–9, and Pheifer, 'Anglo-Saxon glossaries', pp. 37–9.

[108] *Corpus, Épinal, Erfurt and Corpus,* p. 42 (omitting entries with vernacular interpretations only). All the entries in Lindsay's first batch (R39–44) are duplicated in his Orosius *R* batch *(ibid.,* pp. 23–31, at 30). This overlap may reflect the use of Abstrusa/Abolita and related glossaries to gloss Orosius, as they were used to gloss Jerome's preface in the Vatican 1469 Bible glosses (above, pp. 26–7): it does not invalidate Lindsay's batch principle, but it does show its limitations.

[109] Recorded in Goetz's apparatus *(CGL* IV. 165, 40) from Monte Cassino, Archivio della Badia 439, the later of the two Abstrusa/Abolita manuscripts (of the tenth century according to Lowe, *Script,* II, 85). Lindsay's text of Abolita in *GL* III omits this entry and also the entry that follows AN22a, although the latter does appear in Vatican 3321 *(CGL* IV, 18, 5).

[110] Vatican City, Biblioteca Apostolica Vaticana, lat. 1471, 157rb–vb; printed in *CGL* V, 546–7.

[111] The Abavus Glossary (Leiden 67F, 62r–104r); printed in *CGL* IV, 301–403, and *GL* II, 29–121. Cited by alphabetical section-numbers as in *GL.* For its connections with Abstrusa/Abolita and Erfurt II see Lindsay, 'Affatim Glossary', p. 199.

[112] Paris, Bibliothèque Nationale, lat. 7730; printed in *CGL* V, 652–6.

R59   Ringitur irascitur tractum a sono canum rir : Abavus Maior[113] 636, 49 Ringitur
       irascitur tractum de cancoris, Abstr. RI5 Ringitur irascitur aut indignatur,
       Erf.II R1O6 Ringitur irascitur indignabitur unde et ringentia[114]

Lindsay rightly divined that these batches 'might really belong to the AB-material,
i.e. to the "second portions" of EE', but failed to grasp the significance of their
a-order and their lack of Abstrusa or Abolita sequences like those in the sub-
sections of Erfurt II because he believed that 'items borrowed from extant glossaries can be referred to their source whether they preserve coherence in batches or
not'.[115] While the *ab*-order parts of Épinal/Erfurt I combine batches of Erfurt II
entries in its present order with glosses found in other Latin glossaries and presumably derive from an *ab*-order glossary that combined Erfurt II with other material
of the same type, Lindsay's so-called Abstrusa-Abolita batches consist of entries
presumably derived from a more primitive stage in the history of the Latin glossaries at which the material corresponding to Abstrusa, Abolita and other glossaries that was later incorporated in Erfurt II had not yet been reduced to *ab*-order.
Consequently, the relationship between the *ab*-order parts of Épinal/Erfurt I and its
a-order Abstrusa-Abolita batches can only be a collateral one.

VI

Because he did not distinguish between these two stages, Lindsay did not realize
the importance of Épinal/Erfurt I and Erfurt II as witnesses to the prehistory of the
central tradition of Latin glossography, and he made the same mistake on a larger
scale in his edition of Corpus. Parkes dates the Corpus manuscript in the second
quarter of the ninth century,[116] but the compiler of the glossary (who may have
worked considerably earlier) apparently still had access to the material used in the
composition of Épinal/Erfurt I, including the Erfurt II material still in *a*-order, as
well as to Épinal/Erfurt I in its present form. In his edition of Corpus, Lindsay
marked entries from the *a*-order parts of Épinal/Erfurt I with the siglum 'i' but
lumped together glosses from the *ab*-order parts of Épinal/Erfurt I (marked '(2)'

---

[113] The Abavus Maior Glossary, excerpted in *CGL* IV, 589–99, and V, 625–32. For its composition
see Goetz, *CGL* I, 135–8.

[114] Ép./Erf.I R41 'Reckoned: thought / thought or certain, accepted' (Festus 340, 23 *pro certo
firmo ponitur ratus et ratum*). Cf. Abol. RA6 *Ratum cartum uel infirmum*, Orosius, *Hist.* VI. 4,
4 *rati*. 42 'Ropes: sheets of sails' (*Aen.* III. 267, 682). Cf. Orosius, *Hist.* VI. 8, 13 *rudentes* 44
'Raw: new'. Cf. Orosius, *Hist.* VI. 15, 10 *rudi*, St Gallen 280, 41 *Rudem nouum*. 52 'Restored:
safe / saved or safe, returned / saved safe, returned' (*Aen.* I. 390, etc.). 53 'Rakes: hoes, that is,
mattocks'. 54 'Bullying speaker: hoarse' (Festus 354, 15 *rava vox rauca . . . unde etiam
causidicus pugnaciter loquens ravilla*). 55 'Bars: obstacles / obstacles to appproach, entrance,
or hindrances / Bars or hindrances to approach, entrance'. 57 'Toad: frog / land-frog' (Juvenal,
Sat. I. 70, VI. 659). 59 'Growls: gets angry, taken from the sound of dogs, "grrr" / gets angry or
indignant / gets angry, indignant, whence also growling' (Terence, *Phorm.* 341).

[115] *Corpus, Épinal, Erfurt and Leyden*, p. 37

[116] EEMF 22, 24–5.

below) with glosses from Erfurt II, Affatim and other Latin glossaries assumed by position to have come from the same source under the siglum 'ii',[117] for example the entries marked 'ii' in his *Ra*-subsection:

R1 Rapidus uelox : Abstr. RA6 *id.*, Abnuo[118] 556, 45 *id*, Erf.II R8 *id.*, Affatim 560, 18 Rapidus calumniatus rapidius aut uelox

R2 Ratum acceptum : Abstr. RA15 *id.*, Affatim 560, 29 Ratum acceptum aut firmum

R4 Racemus ramus modicus cum uvis : Abstr. RA1 Racemus modicus ramusculus cum uvis, Erf.II R10 Racemus modicus ramus cum uiuis

R5 Raptim uelociter : Affatim 560, 16 Raptim cursim uelociter

R6 Ratus arbitratus : St Gallen 217, 44 *id.*, Erf.II R6 Ratus arbitratus aestimauit,[119] Abstr. RA14 Ratus arbitratus uel firmus

R7 Raptamur trahemur : Affatim 560, 15 Raptamur trahimur

R8 Ratum certum : Abol. RA6 Ratum cartum uel infirmum, Erf.II R3 Ratum certum firmum uel aptum

R18 Rati arbitrati : Ép./Erf.I R41 *id.*, Abstr. RA13 *id.*, Affatim 560, 26 Rati arbitrati aut firmi accepti

R20 Rabula rauca : Ép./Erf.I R54 Rabula raucus, Erf.II R1 *id.*, Affatim 560, 22 Rapula raucus

R21 Ratus firmus : Ép./Erf.I (2) R103 Ratus firmus cuius contrarius inritus, Erf.II R11 *id.*, Abstr. RA14 Ratus arbitratus uel firmus, Affatim 560, 28 Ratus arbitratus aut firmus

R23 Rancet rancidum est : Abstr. RA7 *id.*, Ép./Erf.I (2) R104 *id.*, Erf.II R7 *id.*, Affatim 560, 23 *id.*

R24 Ramnus ramus spinae albae : Ép./Erf.I (2) R105 Ramnus ramus spinæ albae, Erf.II R2 Ramnus . . . albe

R25 Ramneta equi a romuli constituti : Ép./Erf.I (2) R106 Ramnete . . . constituti, Abavus Maior 636, 36 Ramneri a rumulo constituti

R26 Randum arbitrandum : St Gallen 277, 50, Ép./Erf.I (2) R107 Raidum arbitrandum

R27 Ramentum puluis qui radetur de aliqua specie : Abstr. RA4 *id.*, Ép./Erf.I R109 (2) *id.*, Affatim 560, 11 Ramentum . . . raditus de aliqua specie

R28 Ratis naues : St Gallen 277, 45 *id.*, Affatim 560, 32 Rates naues

R29 Rapax praedo : Abstr. RA9 *id.*, Affatim 560, 17 *id.*

R30 Rasile quod radi potest : Ép./Erf.I (2) R110 *id.*, Erf.II R9 *id.*[120]

---

[117] Cf. Brown, *Épinal Glossary*, pp. 17–19.

[118] The Abnuo Glossary is the third glossary in Monte Cassino, Archivio della Badia 402 (pp. 165a–181b); exerpted in *CGL* V. 548–59.

[119] Corrected from *aestimatus*.

[120] Cf. R1 'Rapid swift / false accuser (*calumniator*), wild (*rabidus*) or swift'. Cf. Affatim 560 20 *rapula rapidus rapiosus calumniatur* 'Bullying speaker (*rabula*): violent, raging (*rabiosus*), false accuser', 34 *Racula calumniatur* 'Bullying speaker: false accuser' (Abol. RA 7 *Rabola clamosus uel rauidus*, 12 *Ramosus* (sic) *calumniator*) and Festus 338, 21 *rabula . . . quasi rabiosus*. 2. 'Ratified: accepted / accepted or certain'. See on R8 below. 4. 'Bunch: little stem with grapes / little tiny stem with grapes'. 5. 'Hastily: swiftly / speedily, swiftly'. 6. 'Reckoned:

The sequence of entries beginning with R11 is an almost uninterrupted series of Épinal/Erfurt I *ab*-order glosses like the Épinal/Erfurt I *a*-order glosses marked 'i' that precede it, to which R18 and 20 (marked 'i, ii') really belong:[121]

R11   Radius hrisl : Ép./Erf.I R3 Radium hrisil
R12   Rabulus flitere in eobotum : Ép./Erf.I R8 Rabulus . . . ebhatis
R13   Ratiunculas partes rationis diminuti : Ép./Erf.I R29 Retiunculas rationis partes
           diminutiuae
R14   Rata perfecta : Ép./Erf.I R24 *id.*
R15   Ratinato ambaect : Ép./Erf.I R32 Ratinato ambect
R17   Rancor troh : Ép./Erf.I R48 Rancor throch uel inuidia uel odium
R18   Rati arbitrati : Ép./Erf.I R41 *id.*
R19   Rastros mettocas : Ép./Erf.I R53 Rastros ligones id mettocas
R20   Rabula rauca : Ép./Erf.I R54 *id.*[122]

Significantly, the glosses that correspond to the Épinal/Erfurt I *ab*-order entries in the second Corpus 'ii' series, R21, 23, 24, 25, 26 and 27, follow the same sequence as their Épinal/Erfurt I counterparts, like those that correspond to Épinal/Erfurt I *a*-order entries in the Corpus 'i' series, while the glosses that correspond to Erfurt II entries in the first Corpus 'ii' series, R1, 4, 6, 8, do not follow the same order as their counterparts in Erfurt II. This pattern is the normal one in Corpus, where entries corresponding to Épinal/Erfurt I generally follow the same order and entries corresponding to Erfurt II do not, although they do form some widely-spaced sequences like the Épinal/Erfurt I entries in the Corpus 'i' batches,[123] suggesting that the compiler of Corpus, unlike the compiler of the source from which the Épinal/Erfurt I *ab*-order entries were taken, did not use Erfurt II in its present form but an intermediate source in *a*-order like that of the Épinal/Erfurt I Abstrusa-Abolita batches, which also contain a high proportion of entries corresponding to

---

thought / thought, estimated / thought or sure'. 7. 'We are snatched: we are pulled' 8. 'Ratified: fixed, / fixed , sure / fixed, certain or fastened' (Festus 340, 23 *pro certo firmo ponitur ratus et ratum*). 18. 'Reckoned: thought / thought or certain, accepted'. 20. 'Bullying speaker: hoarse' (Festus 354, 15 *rava vox rauca . . . unde etiam causidicus pugnaciter loquens ravilla*). 21. 'Ratified: certain / certain, the contrary of which is "invalid" / thought or certain'. 23. 'Stinks: is stinking'. 24. 'Thorny shrub': branch of White-thorn (ῥάμνος λευχή)'. 25. Ramnetes: cavalry (*equites*) established by Romulus'. 26. 'To be reckoned: to be thought'. 27. 'Scrapings: dust which is scraped from some sort of thing'. 28. 'Raft: ships' / Rafts: ships' (*Aen.* I 43 *rates*). 29. 'Beast of prey: robber'. 30. 'Scrapable: that which can be scraped'.

[121] Lindsay presumably marked R18 and 20 'i, ii' because R20 appears in Erfurt II and both appear in Affatim. But their position in Corpus is surely decisive.

[122] Cf. R11 'Rod: shuttle'. 12. 'Bullying speaker: contender in lawsuits' (Festus 338, 21 *rabula dicitur in multis intentus negotiis*). 13. 'Petty little reasons: minute particles of reason' (Orosius, *Hist.* I. 10, 19). See above, note 108. 14. 'Ratified: completed' (I Macch. 8, 30). 15. 'Controller (*ratiocinator*): official' (*Dig.* XIV 4, 5). 17. 'Rancidness: rancid / rancid or envy or hatred'. 18. 'Reckoned: thought' (Orosius, *Hist.* VI. 4, 4). 19. 'Rakes: mattocks / hoes, that is, mattocks'. 20. 'Bullying speaker: hoarse' (Festus 354, 15 *rava vox rauca . . . unde etiam causidicus pugnaciter loquens ravilla*).

[123] Cf. Pheifer, *ibid.*, pp. 34–5, and EEMF 22, 53–4, 56–8.

Erfurt II and Affatim, including entries that correspond to Corpus R18 and 20.[124] Further speculation is risky, since the *a*-order Abstrusa-Abolita batches and *ab*-order sections of Épinal/Erfurt I and the Corpus 'ii' batches all consist of a similar mixture of entries corresponding to Abstrusa/Abolita and related glossaries on the one hand and to Erfurt II and Affatim on the other. It is clear in any case that, *pace* Lindsay, 'items borrowed from extant glossaries' cannot with any precision 'be referred to their source whether they preserve coherence in batches or not'.

Lindsay's reductionist approach to the sources of his Corpus 'ii' batches reflects his belief that the non-Abstrusa-Abolita entries in Épinal/Erfurt I and Corpus batches which are not flagrant 'intruders' could be attributed to 'full, original' texts of Abstrusa and Abolita of which the surviving copies of the combined Abstrusa/Abolita Glossary are a mere epitome.[125] In Corpus, for example, he labelled R20, which is found elsewhere only in Épinal/Erfurt I, Erfurt II and Affatim, '?"Abstr.-Abol." ', presumably because it belongs to an Abstrusa-Abolita batch in Épinal/Erfurt I,[126] and R25, found elsewhere only in the *ab*-order part of the Épinal/Erfurt I *R* section,' "Abstr."?', because he thought it once formed part of 'a long gloss (a Virgil gloss perhaps rather than a Festus gloss) on the three ancient Roman tribes', taken perhaps from 'Abstrusa major'.[127] The Vergil gloss that Lindsay had in mind, which he did not mention explicitly, was presumably the long scholion attributed to Servius on *Aeneid* V, 560 *Tres equitum numero turmae*,[128] mentioned in Goetz's *Thesaurus*, which begins with a reference to Livy's account of their origin:

> rem Romanae militiae suo inserit carmini. nam constat primo tres fuisse populii Romani: unam Titiensium a Tito Tatio, duce Sabinorum, iam amico post foedera: alteram Ramnetum a Romulo: tertiam Lucerum, quorum secundum Livium et nomen et causa in occulto sunt. (. . .)[129]

---

124 See above, p. 289. Cf. *Corpus, Épinal, Erfurt and Leyden*, pp. 38–9, and Pheifer, 'Anglo-Saxon Glossaries', p. 37.

125 See Lindsay's notes on individual entries in *The Corpus Glossary* (pp. 190–211), *passim*. He speaks of 'the full, original Abstrusa Glossary' in his note on Corpus E251–2 (p. 200) and calls Abolita 'an extract' in 'Abstrusa Glossary', p. 120.

126 Entries in his Épinal/Erfurt I Hermeneumata batches (*Corpus, Épinal, Erfurt and Leyden*, p. 17–20) not found in the Graeco-Latin Hermeneumata glossaries (*CGL* III) are similarly labelled 'Herm.' in Corpus.

127 'Affatim Glossary', pp. 197–8; cited in Lindsay's note (*Corpus Glossary*, p. 208).

128 'troops of horsemen, three in number'.

129 'He works the history of the Roman army into his poem. For it is certain that at first there were three (troops) of the Roman people: one that of the Titienses, named after Titus Tatius, the chief of the Sabines, now a friend after the treaty; another that of the Ramnetes,named after Romulus; a third that of the Luceres, both the name of which and the reason for it are shrouded in obscurity according to Livy' (*Servii grammatici qui feruntur in Vergilii carmina commentarii*, edd. G. Thilo and H. Hagen, 3 vols (Leipzig, 1887–1902), I, 634). There is no Festus gloss on *Ramnetes*, but cf. 503, 19 *Titiensis tribus a praenomine Tati regis appellata esse videtur* 'The tribe of the *Titienses* seems to have been called after the first name of King Tatius'. Varro also mentions the origin of the three tribes, but like Festus without reference to their military role: *Ager romanus primum divisus in partis tris, a quo tribus appellata Titiensium, Ramnum,*

An Abstrusa Maior that contained entries on this scale is hard to imagine. Surely it is more likely that the sources of the Épinal/Erfurt I Abstrusa-Abolita batches and *ab*-order sections included extracts from some lexicographer who quoted Festus on *rabula*[130] and the passage from Livy, which Épinal/Erfurt I echoes more closely than Servius did:

> Eodem tempore et centuriae tres equitum conscriptae sunt. Ramnenses ab Romulo, ab T. Tatio Titienses appellati: Lucerum nominis et originis causa incerta est.[131]

The trouble is that Lindsay believed Abstrusa and Abolita in their primitive form were huge *Ur-Glossare* compiled from *glossae collectae* and the other alphabetical Latin glossaries were parasitic growths which simply recycled Abstrusa-Abolita glosses *ad infinitum*: 'After some glossaries had been so compiled, subsequent compilers contented themselves with selecting material from these previous publications, and either adding no new marginalia-material of their own or adding very little.'[132] This may be true to some extent of Erfurt II and St Gallen, but it certainly does not apply to Epinal/Erfurt I or to Corpus, nor is Lindsay's concept of a 'full, original' Abstrusa or Abolita borne out by a comparison of Vatican 3321 with Monte Cassino, Archivio della Badia 439, the other manuscript of Abstrusa/Abolita, which does contain some entries not found in Vatican 3321 such as the entry that follows Abolita RU14,[133] but not on the scale that Lindsay's theory implies.

Fortunately, Lindsay and his pupil Thomson did not attempt to restore these hypothetical originals when they edited Abolita and Abstrusa in *Glossaria latina* III, but the baneful effects of the principle can be seen in the so-called Abba Glossary edited by Don Maurus Iguanez, the Monte Cassino librarian, and C.J. Fordyce in *Glossaria latina* V.[134] The real 'Abba Glossary' that begins *Abba pater* is the one in St Gallen 912, a manuscript that rivals Épinal 72 in antiquity. This Lindsay branded as an epitome[135] like Abstrusa and Abolita and supplanted by the

---

Lucerum: nominatae, ut ait Ennius, Titienses ab Tatio, Ramnenses ab Romulo, Luceres, ut ait Iunius, ab Lucumone 'The Roman Land was first divided into three parts, after which was called the tribe of the *Titienses*, of the *Ramnes*, of the *Luceres*. They were named, as Ennius says, *Titienses* after Tatius and *Ramnenses* after Romulus; *Luceres*, as Junius says, after Lucumo' (*De lingua latina* V. 55).

[130] See above, note 120.

[131] 'At the same time three "centuries" of cavalry were enrolled. The *Ramnenses* were called after Romulus, the *Titienses* after Titus Tatius; the reason for the name of the *Luceres* and for its origin is obscure' (*Ab urbe condita* I. 13, 8).

[132] W.M. Lindsay and H.J. Thomson, *Ancient Lore in Medieval Latin Glossaries*, St Andrews University Publications 13 (Oxford, 1921), p. vii. This passage was written after Lindsay's study of Épinal, Erfurt and Corpus, as shown by his reference to Corpus A22 immediately above it.

[133] See above, p. 289 and note 109.

[134] Pp. 15–143.

[135] *GL* V. 9–10.

Vatican 1469 and Monte Cassino 218 Asbestos Glossary, which, as its name implies, begins *A<s>beston lapis arcadię coloris ferrei* (. . .).[136] Asbestos incorporates the bulk of St Gallen's entries, though in different order;[137] the rest, with some omissions, are relegated to the end of the alphabetical sections in their edition. This is no way to treat an ancient glossary. St Gallen deserves a critical edition worthy to succeed Warren's, and Corpus needs one that brings out its relationship with Affatim and the other glossaries related to Abstrusa and Abolita. The question, however, remains: what, then, is the right way to edit glossaries? Lindsay himself suggested the answer when he observed that the *stemma codicum*[138] of a family of glossaries 'is not like the "stemma codicum" of a text of Virgil or Horace':

> Our glossaries were not full and conscientious transcriptions of the archetype and never pretended to be . They are extract glossaries. Each compiler selects, at his own caprice, some items of the mass that lies before him and passes over others. So no argument "ex silentio"[139] is possible. And the items selected are often re-cast at the compiler's caprice.[140]

It follows that each glossary is a text in its own right, and all its idiosyncracies, even of spelling and punctuation, should be accurately represented: even errors can be instructive, like the confusion between *rapidus* and *rabidus* in Affatim 560, 18.[141] If we are to trace relationships and transmission, there must be collations at the foot of the page, as in Loewe's *Glossae nominum*, a full commentary and indexes of headwords and Old English interpretations. If there are to be translations (which present their own special problems, as readers of the notes in this paper will be aware), let them be on facing pages, like those in the Loeb Library and some older Early English Text Society editions. But an editor's horizons should extend beyond the mechanics of his trade: evidence of their own history is not all that glossaries have to offer. Professor Lapidge's article on the Leyden family gives tantalizing examples of their wealth of information over a wide range of Anglo-

---

[136] 'Asbestos, a stone of Arcadia, of iron-grey colour' (Isidore, *Etym.* XVI. 4, 4 *Asbestos . . . ferrei coloris*). Lindsay was aware of this anomaly, as the exordium of his introduction shows: *Tuque, lector, accipe glossarium Asbestos ita paratum ut exeo glossarium Abba, Alienis glossis intra glossis inter cancellos quadratos incarcerais, evassisse videatur* 'Do you, reader, receive the Asbestos Glossary, so arranged, with foreign glosses enclosed in square brackets, that from it the Abba Glossary seems to emerge' (*CGL* V, 13).

[137] Vatican 1469 1vb *Abba syre, Graece pater, latine genitor* 'Abba in Syrian is πατήρ in Greek, "father" in Latin', the entry that corresponds to *Abba pater* 'Abba: father' in St Gallen, is A74 in the new 'Abba' (*CGL* V, 16). The Asbestos gloss does, however, begin the first glossary in Monte Cassino 217 and 402, which apparently offers a variant version (*CGL* IV. xviii–xix).

[138] 'Family tree of manuscripts'.

[139] 'From silence'.

[140] *Corpus, Épinal, Erfurt, and Leyden*, p. 52.

[141] See above, p. 291 and note 120.

Saxon life and learning,[142] some of which was inherited from antiquity. The Milan 79 gloss on Genesis 19: 3, for example, on which Archbishop Theodore commented,[143] incorporates one found in Abolita and Épinal/Erfurt I:

> 63rb Compulit illos oppido idest oppidum intrare. non est grecum. ut multi dicunt
> oppido quasi ualde. Quod negat theodorus esse aduerbium grecę : Abol. OP3
> Oppido ualde, Ép./Erf.I O1 *id*.[144]

The glossator presumably used a glossary (perhaps the one that supplied the Épinal/Erfurt I Abstrusa-Abolita batches) to interpret *oppido* in the same way that modern scholars use Hesychius and the Suda to interpret rare or difficult words in Greek poetry. Latin glossaries preserve occasional snippets of this Greek learning too. Ép./Erf.I T102 *toreum eduella / toreuma eduelli*,[145] records a meaning found elsewhere only in the correction of τόρνευμα in Euripides' *Heracles*, 978 δεινὸν τόρνευμα ποδός,[146] which appears in both manuscripts of the play. Latin lexicography offers less scope for such 'finds', since little early Latin poetry survives apart from Plautus and Terence, whose vocabulary is fully attested, and later poets avoided exotic vocabulary. The Bible glosses, however, preserve many readings from the Old Latin translations, one of which crops up in Lindsay's Épinal/Erf.I Bible batches,[147] the Vatican 1469 gloss on Acts 10: 30:

> 142vb Anudius quartana die. alia editio a quarta die usque in hanc horam : Ép./Erf.I
> A46 Anudus quartana die quarta.[148]

To do full justice to all aspects of glossography potential editors will therefore need their predecessors' classical and patristic learning coupled with a knowledge of Old English and the Anglo-Saxon missions on the continent.[149] This conclusion,

---

[142] 'School of Theodore', pp. 58–66.

[143] *Ibid.*, p. 59 and note 71.

[144] 'He pressed them strongly: that is, to enter the town. "Certainly", as it were, "strongly", is not a Greek word as many say. Theodore says it is not an adverb in Greek'. Cf. Festus 201, 9 *Oppido valde multum* 'Certainly: very strongly'.

[145] 'Drilling (τόρευμα): spinning round'.

[146] 'Dreadful spinning round on foot', referring to the deadly game of 'Round the Mulberry Bush' Heracles played with his son. Τόρευμα 'carving in relief' and τόρνευμα 'wood-turning' are also confused in St Gallen 293, 21 *Toregma tornatura*, Affatim 575, 25 *Toregina turnatura* and the marginal addition to Philoxenus *toreuma tornatura* (*CGL* II, 199, 22 app.).

[147] *Corpus, Épinal, Erfurt and Leyden*, pp. 32–5.

[148] 'It is now a period of four days: the other edition / from four days ago until this hour / fourth' (Acts 10: 30 *anudius quartana die usque in hanc horam*). Cf. Milan 79 116rb *Anudius quartana die. Alia editio a quarta die usque in hanc horam*. The Milan gloss belongs to the second series of Milan Bible glosses from Joshua onwards, which regularly cites the Old Latin text in this manner.

[149] Wilhelm Levison's *England and the Continent in the Eighth Century* (Oxford, 1940) is the indispensible guide, but much detail has been filled in since he wrote.

like Lapidge's, may seem wishful thinking, but the renewed interest in glossaries shown by the generous provision for them in the forthcoming *Sources of Anglo-Saxon Literary Culture* and by the first International Conference on Anglo-Saxon Glossography[150] are good omens for their future.

---

[150] Held in Brussels under the auspices of the Koninklijke Academie voor Wetenschappen, Letteren en Schone Kunsten van België, 8–9 September 1986. Its proceedings have been published in *Anglo-Saxon Glossography*, ed. R. Derolez (Brussels, 1992).

POSTSCRIPT
QUO VADIS, EDITIO?

D. G. Scragg

THE STUDY OF Old English is everywhere under threat. This is partly a result of the fact that, in English-speaking countries, the academic study of all foreign languages is in retreat, and few students now have the basic terminology for the study of language laid down two thousand years ago. Indeed in three decades, the ability to read Latin has shifted from being the *sine qua non* of undergraduates throughout the Humanities to an arcane discipline. Consequently, we have to rewrite the textbooks of Old English if knowledge of the language is to be passed on to a new generation. But this alone will not ensure the survival of the subject. All aspects of study of Anglo-Saxon have to be re-examined, including the most fundamental: how we present samples of the written language to readers.

Editorial principles for Old English were established in the nineteenth century and have been slightly refined in the twentieth, but there has been little in the way of theoretical textual criticism to place beside the practice.[1] In part, this book may remedy that. In part too it may encourage more experimentation. One of the most worrying aspects of the development of Old English studies in the second half of the twentieth century is that editors have become generally more conservative. It is true that there have been a very few senior voices raised against this conservatism, from Kenneth Sisam, whose 'The Authority of Old English Poetical Manuscripts'[2] should be read with care by anyone contemplating editing Old English verse or prose, to Michael Lapidge in his Toller lecture. But their views have not so far prevailed. One of the reasons for the conservatism is that many of the most influential editions of Old English texts have been published by the Early English Text Society, an organization set up specifically to serve the needs of the editors of

---

[1]   See Michael Lapidge's Toller Lecture, 'Textual Criticism and the Literature of Anglo-Saxon England', *Bulletin of the John Rylands University Library of Manchester 73* (1991), 17–45, and printed separately, and his essay in the present volume. Some editors, it is true, have offered a theoretical underpinning to their practice, but rarely within the confines of an edition is there room for full explanation of all the practices adopted. Also, even the most influential editors have sometimes departed from their stated intention, e.g. Fr. Klaeber, in his *Beowulf and the Fight at Finnsburg*, 3rd edn with supplements (Boston, 1950), states uniquivocally that he did not deem it proper 'to introduce a uniform, normalized orthography' (p. 274), yet he did normalize, e.g. *siex-* to *sex-* in line 2904.

[2]   First published as 'Notes on Old English Poetry' in *RES* 22 (1946), 257–68, but quoted here from the reprint in *Studies in the History of Old English Literature* (Oxford, 1953), pp. 29–44.

what was to become the *Oxford English Dictionary*. Lexicographers have special requirements of editors, in particular that they should prioritize manuscript forms, as Antonette diPaolo Healey makes clear in her essay above. But while it is right that editors should bear in mind these needs, they must also be aware that they are not writing exclusively for one client. Other contributors to this volume have stressed other editorial responsibilities, to the 'author' (Lapidge), to the text (O'Keeffe) and to the scribe (Doane), to the historian (Dumville) and to the student (Magennis). There is a distinct danger that dictionary makers will continue to direct editorial effort, partly because of the undoubted importance to Old English studies generally of the Dictionary of Old English, partly because Helmut Gneuss's *Guide to the Editing and Preparation of Texts*, which is again directed specifically towards the preparation of texts for lexicographers, is the only clear and systematic introduction to the subject available for graduate students and others contemplating editing. I hope that the essays in this book will stimulate the world of Anglo-Saxonists into a reconsideration of the rationale behind current editoral practice, and offer a new lead to take us into the twenty-first century, even if we decide that what we have been doing for the last 150 years is right for the next 150. Having myself produced editions of both prose and verse, I now feel able to make a number of suggestions, both about what of the old methodology should be retained and what we ought to rethink.

The most difficult question for an editor of Old English writings is how far to intervene in the text. Michael Lapidge argues above (p. 54), on the model of the editing of classical Latin, that 'it is the editor's principal duty to establish what the author wrote', whereas those who stress the difficulty of establishing an author in the medieval period, or those who are influenced by what is sometimes called the New Philology, will see their responsibility very differently. What must be recognized, however, is that editorial intervention is a continuum that stretches from interpretation of manuscript information (modernization of letter forms, expansion of abbreviations, word-division, verse and page layout, and the conventions of modern capitalization and punctuation) through to large-scale emendation. It is not only in the complex issue of emendation that we need to rethink our position. There is illogicality of practice all along the scale. To take an example from what might be seen as the simplest level of transference from manuscript to print, the representation of Anglo-Saxon characters by modern ones: despite the fact that some scribes regularly use þ in initial word or syllable positions and ð in medial and final ones, and likewise used different shapes of *s* in different positions (long *s* being reserved for initial positions by many scribes), editors invariably reflect scribal differences of þ/ð and ignore the different forms of *s*.[3] Similarly, most (although not quite all) Old English scribes wrote *cg* for the geminate *g* consonant

---

[3] Alexander R. Rumble, in his essay above, writes of 'the (from a palaeographer's point of view) unsustainable modern convention that the Anglo-Saxon letter *wynn* be replaced in print by a quite different letter'. Note also that yogh is normally represented by the modern *g* symbol in printing Old English.

(palatal and velar), probably because *g* was a difficult letter to ligature, but a few scribes wrote *gg*. Editors regularly print whichever they find in the manuscript, *cg* or *gg*.[4] Is there not an argument for regularizing *gg* in printed texts, if *cg* may be considered a mere 'scribal convention' like long *s* at the beginning of words? The retention of differentiation of *þ* and *ð* and of *cg* for *gg* in modern printed editions but not of other variant letter shapes is a convention which does not appear to have been thought through, and certainly not rigorously argued.

Editors must be allowed a degree of licence to intervene in the text since otherwise they have no function, and there must therefore be some measure of agreement about where that intervention should end. At the moment such agreement as exists has come about by precedent and practice rather than through careful consideration and consensus. If, for instance, an editor is allowed to insert marks of punctuation and spaces marking word-division, as well as altering the shapes of some letters (including blending different letter-shapes into one), why should not that same editor make changes to the sequence of letters? Here one must distinguish between different types of emendation, ranging from correction of spelling and grammar (usually seen as normalization) to correction of a perceived error of sense. Normalization has generally been avoided by later twentieth-century editors on the grounds that there is no obvious 'norm' in Old English to set a standard by.[5] But the question is not as simple as those who advocate conservatism would maintain. Take the instance of the early copy of King Alfred's translation of Gregory's *Regula pastoralis* in Oxford, Bodleian Library, Hatton 20. The principal scribe of this manuscript not only frequently simplified etymological double consonants within words (writing *monum* for *monnum*, for instance) but also across word boundaries (writing *eftome* for *eft to me*).[6] In what is still the standard edition of this work, Henry Sweet consciously presented a conservative text of the *Regula pastoralis* translation,[7] yet he felt obliged to insert a second *t* in *eftome*, just as he inserted spaces marking word division in that same sequence. If it is acceptable to alter MS *eftome* to *eft to me* to make the sequence more easily recognizable, why not normalize *monum* on the same grounds. My point is that some measure of normalization regularly occurs in printed editions, but most editors have neither justified what they themselves do, nor indicated where, in their view, such intervention should stop.

Editors face even more difficult choices in the normalization of grammar. Few

---

[4] Scribal confusion over the sequence *cg* is testified by inverted and blended forms *gc* and *cgg*. On *cg* as representing the geminating palatal and velar voiced stops, see A.Campbell, *Old English Grammar* (Oxford, 1959), §64.

[5] See Helmut Gneuss, above, p. 17, and note 13.

[6] I noted these and similar examples in D.G. Scragg, 'Initial *H* in Old English', *Anglia* 88 (1970), 165–96, at 171.

[7] *King Alfred's West-Saxon Version of Gregory's Pastoral Care*, ed. H. Sweet, EETS os 45 and 50 (London, 1871); note 'the main principle I have adopted in printing is to make the text as far as possible a facsimile of the original MSS., without introducing any theoretical emendations', Preface, p. viii.

editors of recent decades have been bold enough to advocate 'correcting' inflexions, since the grammar of eleventh-century English has yet to be written.[8] But mechanical errors frequently occur in grammar. Copyists lose their way in long sentences, especially those which contain lists of words and phrases,[9] and failure of subject-verb concord is widely recorded.[10] If the usual editorial conventions of capitalization, word-division and punctuation are made to assist the reader (and there seems to be general acceptance that they should be), is it not appropriate to normalize a scribe's -es/-as confusion or to regularize -eð/að?[11] This is all the more important in editions which students will use, for, as Sedgefield long ago pointed out to justify his own normalization of grammar, 'The study of Old English has hitherto been rendered unnecessarily confusing and difficult for beginners by the fact that whereas the early West Saxon dialect of King Alfred has been adopted as the standard for grammars, vocabularies and dictionaries, the actual texts employed in teaching have usually been printed practically as they occur in the MSS., representing no one dialect in a pure form. Thus the student has from the beginning had to reconcile the conflict of practice with precept.'[12]

Emendation on grounds of sense is perhaps the most difficult of all problems facing an editor.[13] Gneuss, in his *Guide to the Editing and Preparation of Texts,*

---

[8] Note that Campbell's *Grammar* has relatively little information on the eleventh-century. K. Brunner, *Altenglische Grammatik nach der Angelsächsischen Grammatik von Eduard Sievers,* 3rd ed. (Tübingen, 1965), has more but is still not comprehensive, e.g. it lists dative plural *heom* ('im 10. Jh. vereinzelt, vom 11. Jh. an häufig', p. 260), but not *hiom* about which the same might be said.

[9] Michael Lapidge, in 'Textual Criticism', p. 34, warns that 'an editor of medieval Latin texts must exercise extreme caution when emending to restore what would be "correct" Latin by classical standards'. The same may be true of Old English, in that we cannot be sure that native speakers always used what we – as non-native speakers – regard as correct grammar. The problem is made worse by the growing confusion of inflexional endings in late Old English. But it is often clear enough, at least in prose, that copyists have adulterated texts in the course of transmission, cf. *The Vercelli Homilies and Related Texts,* ed. D.G. Scragg, EETS 300 (London, 1992), homily XX, lines 83–5, where in a list of six nominative phrases there occurs the accusative *idelne.*

[10] Cf. B. Mitchell, *Old English Syntax* (Oxford, 1985), §20 and references. Many scholars fear that normalization disguises linguistic development (cf. Mitchell, §2) but it is at least arguable that the *text* is not the best place to highlight irregular grammar (See Tolkien's comment in note 17 below). Editors should rather draw attention to exceptional forms in their apparatus, preferably in a distinctly signalled section of the introduction. After all, virtually all the Old English that remains to us survives at second hand, not in authorial copy. A scribe *may* preserve for us evidence of his or her own or a predecessor's language, but he or she may just as likely be subject to one of errors that all copyists' flesh is heir to, from confusion of the sense to eye-skip.

[11] Klaeber normalized *reafeden,* line 1212, to *reafedon* yet left the potentially more ambiguous genitive singulars *Heaðo-Scilfingas,* line 63, and *yrfeweardas,* line 2453. Kenneth Sisam's comment (*Studies,* p.43) on the latter form makes my point most succinctly: '[it] is a nuisance to the reader'.

[12] *Selections from the Old English Bede,* ed. W.J. Sedgefield (Manchester, 1917), Preface.

[13] For a guide to the (limited) set of writings on editorial principles for Old English, see Lapidge, 'Textual Criticism', note 76. Readers wishing to consult the much fuller bibliography of writings on the subject by editors of Middle English should begin with the introduction to *Piers Plowman: the A Version,* ed. G. Kane (London, 1960), and *Piers Plowman: the B Version,* ed. G. Kane and E.T. Donaldson (London, 1975).

advocates avoiding emendation altogether 'unless there is an obvious mistake or omission in the manuscript'.[14] But this, as I shall show, is not a helpful guide to an inexperienced editor. It is also a diminution of the editor's role. All editors are likely to be faced with the possibility of emendation on grounds of sense in a range of instances, from an apparently simple one of lack of intelligibility in the base text which can be resolved by recourse to the reading of a variant manuscript, to one in which the editor feels uncertain about a base (or unique) text reading but has no evidence to support a change (in other words, one in which the emendation would be wholly conjectural). It is difficult to make rules in this area which would cover more than a limited number of obvious instances, but we should try. As W.W. Greg, the influential Shakespearian editor, has put it: 'If we can do nothing to help great critics in making brilliant emendations, we may at least hope to discover some rules that should prevent little critics from making foolish ones'.[15] Although I would not agree with Gneuss in forbidding conjectural emendation, I would suggest that it be attempted rarely and with caution. But even emendation based on the readings of variant manuscripts is not without its hazards. Accordingly, on the lines of Greg's rules, I offer a series of questions that editors need to ask themselves when confronted by a passage that makes no obvious sense.

Question 1: Is there a clearly identifiable mechanical error?

Any editor who fails to present the reader with a text cleansed of mechanical errors such as dittography or haplography is failing in his or her duty. Manuscript facsimile is cheap, and the reader is better served by a reproduction in which there has clearly been no intervention at all than by an edition which purports to offer conventional editorial assistance but which reproduces words (or parts of words) accidentally repeated across line or page boundaries.[16]

Most editors have followed the line taken by Klaeber who stated of his *Beowulf* edition that 'obvious mistakes have been corrected' (pp. 277–8). But one man's error is another's valuable linguistic evidence.[17] As we move from mechanical

---

[14] See above, p. 15.

[15] *Principles of Emendation in Shakespeare*, Annual Shakespeare Lecture of the British Academy 1928, p. 3.

[16] For examples of such dittography, see *The Vercelli Homilies*, homily II, line 59 *cealdan/cealdan* across a page boundary, and homily III, line 31 *sa/sacerd* across a line boundary. Haplography (homeoarchy) and homeoteleuton are also frequent mechanical errors, although they can be more difficult to spot. For an example, see *The Vercelli Homilies*, homily IV, line 164 *þæs ealdan* for *þæs ealwealdan*. For proof that editorial intervention is not automatic in such cases, see *The Dream of the Rood*, ed. M. Swanton (Manchester, 1970), line 17 *wealdes treow* (read *Wealdendes treow*), where the metre shows the manuscript text to be at fault.

[17] Cf. the notorious *wundini golde*, *Beowulf* 1382, which Klaeber (*Beowulf and the Fight at Finnsburg*, p. cx) called 'a mere scribal blunder', and which Wrenn wished to regard as 'a genuine MS. form which has remained as a kind of fossil through successive copying' (*Beowulf with the Finnesburg Fragment*, ed. C.L. Wrenn, London, 1953, p. 34), and which he earlier described as 'the only *certain* evidence for dating *Beowulf* before *circa* 750 on purely linguistic grounds' (*ibid*, p. 21, n. 2).

A rare comment by Tolkien on the role of the editor is worth quoting: 'It is futile to preserve

errors such as dittography and haplography to other sorts of miswriting, we become aware that textual criticism is an art, not a science. Nonetheless, we should always be conscious of a strong possibility of error in Old English writings. Sisam in the essay referred to above[18] pointed to the unreliability of poetic manuscripts. The study of Old English prose, especially of homiletic prose which frequently survives in multiple copies and which often is supported by knowledge of written sources, heavily underscores his point. Editors should therefore not be afraid to intervene, as long as they can justify their intervention:

Question 2: Can an adequate explanation be offered about how the text might have come to be corrupted by mechanical error during transmission?

Instances abound, and I quote one that has not, to my knowledge, been published. An anonymous homily printed by Bruno Assmann[19] has one sentence with an awkward phrase (here italicized):

> Ær ðam symbeldæge þæra eastrona . . . þa wiste se hælend, þæt seo tid com, þæt he of ðysum middanearde on heofonas to godfæder feran wolde, *þanon he næfre sona wæs þurh his þa ecan godcundnysse.*

> 'Before the Easter festival . . . the Saviour knew that the time was approaching when he would pass from this world to God the Father in heaven, from where he never at once was because of his eternal divinity.'   (Assmann, p. 152, lines 14–17)

Assmann chose Oxford, Bodleian Library, Bodley 340 as his base text for this homily. Cambridge, Corpus Christi College 198 and also (unknown to him) Cambridge, Corpus Christi College 162 have the same reading. The source of the first half of the sentence is scriptural (John 13, 1), but the suspect passage has no known source. However, two further copies of the homily which survive in twelfth-century manuscripts, London, BL, Cotton Faustina A.ix, and Cambridge, Corpus Christi College 302, have, as Assmann's variants show, not *sona* but *wena* in the last clause. On the surface, this looks like a late corruption, since *wena* 'hope' in the nominative case makes no sense grammatically or semantically. In fact, however, it offers a clue to the 'original' reading, which is surely *wana* (probably in its variant

---

forms which are supposed to have linguistic (dialect or period) significance: because the object of the edition is not linguistic, and we are concerned with the *identity* of the word only; no linguistic investigator should use any edited text for gathering statistics; while most of these forms preserved by editors are palaeographic in origin, or vitiated as linguistic evidence by suspicion of such an origin. Nearly all of the 'dialectal' forms preserved, for instance, in Klæber's *Beowulf* text, and classified and commented upon in his introduction, break down entirely under examination. The remainder can safely be relegated to the apparatus.' *The Old English 'Exodus': Text, Translation and Commentary by J.R.R. Tolkien*, ed. J. Turville-Petre (Oxford, 1981), p. 36.

[18] See note 2.

[19] *Angelsächsische Homilien und Heiligenleben*, ed. B. Assmann, Bibliothek der Angelsächsischen Prosa 3 (Kassel, 1889), homily XIII.

spelling *wona*), the sense of *þanon he næfre wona wæs* being 'from where he never was absent'. An editor is justified in merging spellings from two manuscript traditions (here *w-* from one and *-ona* from another) to arrive at a reading not actually recorded if such a change resolves a textual crux, in precisely the same way that he is justified in supplying text lost from a base manuscript.

In this case the editor's intervention is guided by the existence of multiple copies of the text, which offer different windows on the original reading, and emendation of the earliest surviving text in Bodley 340 (Assmann's base text) involves only the minimal change of *s* to *w*, two letter shapes (assuming insular *s* and wynn) which might easily be confused during transmission.[20] Here we may disregard questions of 'author' and 'redactor'. Because of misreading or miswriting of the word *wona*, one copyist deliberately or mistakenly wrote *sona* while another wrote *wena*. Neither change produced a sensible reading, and so neither should be regarded as worthy of preservation. But what if a copyist, faced with a text which he regarded (rightly or wrongly) as corrupt, made a change which did produce a sensible reading, even though *we* might suspect – or even know if we have access to a source – that it is not the original one? A useful pair of examples is provided by two versions of Vercelli homily I, one in the Vercelli Book (Vercelli, Biblioteca Capitolare CXVII) and the other in Bodley 340 again. (It should be stressed that, despite differences in the example cited here, the two are versions of the same Old English text, although Bodley has been fairly extensively altered in some places.[21] In this instance the homilist is following a Gospel reading (John 18,37) very closely:

> *Source* Ego in hoc natus sum, et ad hoc ueni in mundum ut testimonium perhibeam ueritati. Omnis qui est ex ueritate audit meam uocem.

> *Vercelli Book* 7 to þam ic wæs in woruld acenned 7 to þam cwom in middan-geard, þæt ic wolde soðe gewitnesse secgan. For þam ælc þara manna þe soð 7 riht gelyfeð, 7 ælc þara þe min word 7 min stefne gehyreð, se min bið.

> *Bodley 340* To ðan ic com hider on middaneard þæt ic wolde mancynne soð 7 riht cyðan. For ðan ælc þæra manna þe soð 7 riht lufað, ælc þæra min word 7 mine stemne gehyreð. (Scragg, pp. 26–7)

In the first sentence, Bodley omits the opening clause, and although both versions give the sense of its concluding clause, Vercelli is nearer the wording of the Latin, and Bodley has perhaps anticipated the *soð 7 riht* of the following sentence. Certainly the Bodley text has been rewritten. But even though comparison with the

---

[20] Another example involving a palaeographic explanation coupled with information drawn from the Latin source is in my *The Vercelli Homilies*. At homily XXII, line 59, MS *arisað* makes no sense, and does not accord with the source word *parcite*. Assumption that a copyist misread a loosely drawn *g* as a round *s* gives an archetype reading *arigað* which, although not to my knowledge recorded in Old English, is an acceptable spelling variant of a present tense plural form of *arian*, which is an appropriate translation of *parcere*.

[21] For a full discussion of the relationship of the two versions, see *The Vercelli Homilies*, pp. 1–5.

Latin may suggest strongly that Vercelli represents an earlier reading, an editor of Bodley would not be justified in emending. There is no clear evidence of accidental error here. Bodley represents what an Anglo-Saxon reviser of the text thought was meant, or what he wanted to say. In the second sentence there is an even greater departure from the Latin source, this time in the Vercelli text, where the introduction of an additional 7 has turned the *ælc . . . ælc* construction from a defining to a correlative one, and where someone has made sense of the whole by adding *se min bið*. Again, however, there is no clear evidence of mechanical error, only of rewriting. In both cases it might be argued that there is evidence of ignorance or misunderstanding of scripture on the part of Anglo-Saxon writers, but this is evidence which needs to be preserved. Hence I offer:

Question 3: Does the corrupt text suggest conscious adaptation on the part of a reviser?

In poetry, multiple copies rarely survive and comparison with a Latin source is hardly possible. But in verse, to add to suspicion of error aroused by difficulties of meaning, we have an extra check: metre. Two well-known examples are *Battle of Maldon* 183

Ælfnoð and Wulfmær begen lagon

which has no alliteration and where *begen* has probably dropped from the line above, and *Dream of the Rood* 9b:

Beheoldon þær engel dryhtnes ealle

where *ealle* alliterates as well as *engel*, where the verse is unusually long even for a hypermetric verse, and where the reference to the 'angel' is unclear. In the *Maldon* example, the line makes perfect sense, and although we may suspect the source of the replacement word, we cannot know which word it replaced.[22] The writing of *begen* was probably accidental, and the case therefore answers positively Question 2 rather more than Question 3. Nevertheless, what we see as faulty metre is of itself a dangerous guide to the existence of error (although faulty alliteration is safer than other sorts of disruption of metrical patterns), and in this case any emendation must be so wholly conjectural as to be unacceptable. The editor must ask:

Question 4: Is there any clear pointer to a better reading?

If the answer is no, then the text as transmitted must stand. The *Dream of the Rood* verse makes no reasonable sense, although many critics have tried to wrest an interpretation out of it. In this instance we have the brilliant emendation suggested by John Pope:[23]

---

[22] Lapidge, 'Textual Criticism', pp. 42–5, argues for emendation of this line.

[23] J.C. Pope, *The Rhythm of Beowulf* (New Haven, 1942), p. 101. The emendation depends primarily on seeing scribal confusion of *f* and the insular shape of *s*, as Pope made clear in his *Seven*

> Beheoldon þær engeldryhta feala,

a reading adopted in Dorothy Whitelock's revision of Sweet's *Anglo Saxon Reader*.[24] Since Pope offered a palaeographic explanation of how a scribe could have disturbed the text during transmission, a positive response may be given to Question 2 and the emendation is acceptable.

It is clear from the form of these questions that I advocate palaeography as the best answer to most textual questions. No editor can afford to be without a discriminating knowledge, not only of the habits of the scribe(s) of the manuscript(s) being edited, but of those of all possible antecedent manuscripts. I offer as a salutary lesson an example drawn from Vercelli homily XXII. For eighty years the Latin source of this homily has been accepted as Isidore of Seville's *Synonyma*.[25] Comparison of the Latin and Old English texts shows, however, that the homilist has been extremely selective, welding together sentences from quite distinct parts of Isidore's work to make a new and generally entirely consistent argument. A rare instance of failure of logical progression of the argument occurs in a passage in which Isidore discusses the power of fear of damnation, reproduced in a condensed form by the homilist, but confused at the last when the homilist switches inexplicably from fear to love.

> Nænig þing on þysse worulde þe gedo þinra synna sorhleasne, ac ðurhwunige on þinre heortan ege ⁊ fyrhtu. Þurh þone ege ðu gebetest þa synne. Þær lufu ne bið, þær bið ealles lifes tolysnesse.
>
> 'Do nothing in this world without care for your sins, and hold fear and dread in your heart. Through fear you will atone for the sins. Where there is not love, there will be dissolution of all life.' (Scragg, pp. 376–7, lines 171–4)

A simple answer to the confusion is to assume that a copyist of the Latin wrote *amor* instead of *timor*, or that the Old English translator read *amor* for *timor*. Misreading of *ti* for *a* (or vice versa) is a common error. In the Old English homily, the appearance of *lufu* where the Isidore ultimate source leads one to expect *ege* is not an error that an editor can contemplate correcting. Whoever first wrote *lufu* saw – or thought he saw – *amor* in the Latin source, and whatever nonsense it makes of the passage, the *lufu* reading must be retained.

No edition of an Old English text is complete without an apparatus, and the most important element of this is clear indication – preferable by a marker within the

---

Old English Poems (Indianapolis, 1966), p. 63. (Swanton's edition of *The Dream of the Rood* suggests the confusion might have been with long *s* (note to line 9), but insular *s* is closer to *f*. Pope does not specify the letter shape.) Pope was building on an editorial tradition that saw *engel dryhtnes* as a corruption of *engeldryht* 'company of angels', as Swanton's note shows. The religious context might have suggested an oblique form of *dryhten* rather than the heroic word *dryht* 'company' to a copyist. Pope reads the last word as *fela* but *feala* is a common variant.

[24] *Sweet's Anglo-Saxon Reader in Prose and Verse*, 15th ed., ed. D. Whitelock (Oxford, 1967).

[25] See *The Vercelli Homilies*, p. 366.

text – that the editor has intervened. In this context it is worth repeating what seems to me to be one of the most important warnings in Helmut Gneuss's *Guide to the Editing and Preparation of Texts* reprinted at the beginning of this book: that editions have to cater for the occasional reader 'who should not be expected to read through a lengthy introduction in order to be able to use the edition'.[26] In my opening address to the conference of which this book is a record, I called for the establishment of agreed conventions to be used in all Old English texts. The surviving corpus is relatively small, and it is shameful that there should be so little measure of agreement of practice between standard editions. But until this situation is remedied, perhaps a solution lies in editions having a running gloss of the conventions adopted at the foot of each double page spread.[27]

There are other features of the apparatus that I should like to see regularized. My own work with the Vercelli Homilies and many years using the Ælfric editions of Pope and latterly Godden[28] have convinced me that the EETS policy of citing only substantive variants from parallel manuscripts is wrong. It is a policy designed for Middle English texts, where often a large number of closely related manuscript versions of a text makes the citation of full variants cumbersome and unnecessary. But Old English texts rarely survive in large numbers of copies, and when they do, it is important that readers are able to see just how close the versions are. The citing of substantive variants leaves far too much room for editorial selection. On a somewhat wider question of what material should accompany an edition of a text, I assume that no editor would offer an Old English text without printing the nearest known version of a Latin source alongside it. The information offered by the source(s) should then feed into the glossary, with each Old English lemma showing which Latin word(s) have been translated. Furthermore, with the aid of a computer concordance, it is now relatively easy to include also a reverse glossary, Latin to Old English, so that a reader can see how Old English writers chose to translate specific Latin words.

---

[26] See above, p. 13.

[27] Editors should always mark letters or words for which there is no manuscript authority, preferably by square brackets, which is the convention used in EETS editions. In my view they ought also always to indicate in the text when they have omitted letters or words in the manuscript. EETS editions do not do this, the assumption being that the reader will pick up editorial intervention from the apparatus. But in Old English texts the need to excise what the scribe has written arises relatively infrequently. Italicization of a word (or remaining part of a word) would be a simple means of drawing the reader's attention to the apparatus. It is a typographical device which will hardly disturb enjoyment of the text for any reader not interested in such editorial niceties, and it need not conflict with the use of italics to signal expansion of manuscript abbreviations, since these are so regular and so limited in Old English.

[28] See *The Vercelli Homilies*, ed. Scragg; *Homilies of Ælfric: A Supplementary Collection*, ed. J.C. Pope, EETS 259–60 (London, 1967–8); and *Ælfric's Catholic Homilies: The Second Series*, ed. M.R. Godden, EETS ss 5 (London, 1979). Pope's apparatus omits only a limited number of common spelling variants. Roland Torkar's detailed critique of my edition of Vercelli homily III in 'Die Ohnmacht der Textkritik, am Beispiel der Ausgaben der dritten *Vercelli-Homilie*', *Anglo-Saxonica: Festschrift für Hans Schabram*, ed. K.R. Grinda and C-D. Wetzel (Munich, 1993), 225–50, shows the importance of textual variants. I accept many of his criticisms.

I conclude with the question of translation. Scholarship is advanced by experts writing books for each other, and criticizing each others' books. Consequently scholars have become wary of talking down, lest it should be thought that that is all they are capable of doing. Yet King Alfred warned us of the unfortunate consequences that followed when scholars concentrated too hard on the view *ðæt her ðy mara wisdom on londe wære ðy we ma geðeode cuðon* 'that there would be more wisdom in this land, the more languages we knew'. We should be readier to recognize that not all those who would – or should – have access to writings in Old English have the same understanding of the original that we as editors have, and we must therefore be more willing to offer translations for those not able to make sense of the texts for themselves, *as well as* a full apparatus and glossary for those who are able to check and refine our efforts. In order to edit in any sense, an editor must have a clear understanding of what the text means. Only in a facsimile or diplomatic edition is this not the case. As soon as an editor intervenes in the text, there is an element of editorial control which is directly dependent upon the apprehension of meaning.[29] It is appropriate therefore that such close involvement with a text should be transmitted to the reader, the editor's experience being passed on not just in his layout, punctuation and glossary but in a translation too. The informed reader has as much information in the context, the source if there is one, any variant readings, or knowledge of the same or related words elsewhere to judge the translation as he or she has to judge all other aspects of the edition. The less capable readers will be no more misinformed about the meaning of the text by a wrong translation than by wrong punctuation, an ill-judged emendation or a mistaken gloss. Indeed, perhaps the only editions of Old English which should not have translations appended in future are those intended for beginners.

Editors of texts from every period in all languages bear a heavy responsibility, one which increases in proportion to the age of the text and the difficulty of its transmission. Old English is so remote from us, and survives in such a random and partial form, that its editors must constantly ask themselves what they are doing and why. Before the 1990 Manchester conference, little collective thought had been given to the subject for some time, although since then the Toronto conference of 1991 and sessions at Kalamazoo in 1992 and 1993[30] suggest that the subject is now more central to the agenda. It should stay there.

---

[29] Even the electronic hypertext edition (see the essay by Marilyn Deegan and Peter Robinson above) does not avoid this, since although it has the potential of a fuller apparatus than a conventional edition, ultimately it offers a text (or a series of texts) subject to individual scholarly decisions.

[30] For the Toronto proceedings, see *The Politics of Editing Medieval Texts*, ed. R. Frank (New York, 1992). The Kalamazoo sessions were organized by Sarah Keefer and Katherine O'Brien O'Keeffe (proceedings forthcoming).

INDEX